Making a Difference

LEXINGTON STUDIES IN POLITICAL COMMUNICATION

Series Editor: Robert E. Denton Jr., Virginia Tech

This series encourages focused work examining the role and function of communication in the realm of politics including campaigns and elections, media, and political institutions.

TITLES IN SERIES:

Making a Difference

A Comparative View of the Role of the Internet in Election Politics

EDITED BY STEPHEN WARD, DIANA OWEN, RICHARD DAVIS AND DAVID TARAS

LEXINGTON BOOKS

A division of
ROWMAN & LITTLEFIELD PUBLISHERS, INC.
Lanham • Boulder • New York • Toronto • Plymouth, UK

LEXINGTON BOOKS

A division of Rowman & Littlefield Publishers, Inc.
A wholly owned subsidiary of The Rowman & Littlefield Publishing Group, Inc.
4501 Forbes Boulevard, Suite 200
Lanham, MD 20706

Estover Road
Plymouth PL6 7PY
United Kingdom

British Library Cataloguing in Publication Information Available

Library of Congress Cataloging-in-Publication Data

Making a difference : a comparative view of the role of the Internet in election politics /
edited by Stephen Ward ... [et al.].
     p. cm. — (Lexington studies in political communication)
   Includes bibliographical references.
   ISBN-13: 978-0-7391-2100-9 (cloth : alk. paper)
   ISBN-10: 0-7391-2100-6 (cloth : alk. paper)
   ISBN-13: 978-0-7391-2101-6 (pbk. : alk. paper)
   ISBN-10: 0-7391-2101-4 (pbk. : alk. paper)
   1. Internet in political campaigns—Case studies. 2. Elections—Computer network
resources—Case studies. I. Ward, Stephen, 1965–
   JF1001.M19 2008
   324.7'3—dc22   2007041115

Printed in the United States of America

This book is dedicated to the memory of Timothy Cook.

Contents

Preface

David Taras

Communication scholar Vincent Mosco has described the Internet as a "transcendent spectacle" (Mosco, 2004). But even if we don't accept Mosco's majestic description, there is little doubt that the Internet has transformed many aspects of contemporary life. It has become integral to the way that we gather news and information, do business, connect with each other and express and entertainment ourselves. For the young especially it has become as one journalist put it, "pervasive, unavoidable and indispensable" (Friedman, 1999). It is simply part of a way of life. If we take mass media industries alone, the changes brought by the Internet have been dramatic even revolutionary. In a short period of time the new medium has shaken the music industry to its very foundations, jeopardized the long term viability of newspapers by taking away a sizable portion of advertising and younger readers, and digital video recorders which merge TV and the Internet threaten the current business model for the television industry.

What has made the Internet so central to our culture is that it is the place where all of the other media both meet and converge. Newspapers, video, archives, music, gaming, films, radio and the telephone are all available in some form on the Internet and have both shaped and been reshaped by their encounter with the new medium. Its power is most often attributable to the lightening speed with which messages can be routed from one destination to another, its relative cost-effectiveness and its global reach. Most extraordinary perhaps is its powerful decentralizing rhythm. Users can share or swap music, videos and photos, enter the blogosphere with its cornucopia of tracts, opinions and controversies or connect to web sites representing virtually every interest, hobby, organization or institution imaginable. We can now swim in an endless sea of choices unimaginable to previous generations.

Little is known, however, about the effects that the Internet is having in the political realm. This is partly because the Internet continues to evolve in new and dramatic ways so that the Internet of 2001 is not the Internet of today. It is also because political parties, interest groups and of course citizens are still learning, experimenting and innovating. New forces and trends, such as blogs, are continually undoing and replacing older formats so that the Internet remains at best a moving target.

On one level, we know that the Internet has become a central meeting place for political activity and that it has as mentioned above stretched the boundaries of political discourse to include a vast array of texts and choices. We also know that in some contexts political party and candidate web sites have become effective organizing instruments. They are used for intra-party or campaign communication, fundraising, assembling data bases and archives, attracting volunteers and reaching younger well educated voters—a valuable slice of the electorate. Some party sites are alive with activity and indeed with connectivity. Yet in other circumstances these web sites remain little more than electronic billboards—static, lifeless and ineffective.

Our goal in *Making a Difference* is to test the thesis that context matters in the application of new technologies. The key question is whether technology overrides and reshapes political systems or whether the make-up of a political system determines how new technologies will be used? By "context" we mean factors such as the nature of the party system, the rules governing the election process, the role played by conventional media during campaigns and even the level of access to the Internet.

To test this thesis, we chronicle and evaluate the interaction that has taken place in cyberspace among political parties, candidates and citizens during elections in various representative countries. In doing so we intend not only to describe and in a sense catalogue the history of party and candidate Internet use but to also examine the factors and contingencies that shape the nature of web campaigns in different national contexts. In describing the dynamic interaction between web sites and the political cultures in which they operate we are opening the door to the larger debate about how the use of technology can be both shaped by national circumstances and attitudes and is in turn shaped by them.

In order to accomplish this task, we commissioned over a dozen authors who are experts on Internet and politics to write national case studies. In these case studies, the authors were requested to answer a number of fundamental questions. We wanted them to describe the contours of the political system generally, review the history of party web sites and describe how they functioned during recent national elections. Our authors were to gather as much information as they could about party and candidate strategies and the level of citizen usage and engagement. They were to survey party and candidate web sites, the use of email, pin-to-pin relationships, blogs and other forms of Internet communication. In other words they were to provide the basic foundations needed for effective comparison and theory building.

Making a Difference has an expansive sweep. While most of the articles describe cyber-campaigning in established democracies such as the United Kingdom, Germany, the United States, Australia, Italy and Canada, newer democracies such as Singapore, Spain, Indonesia and Chile are also included in the collection. The book covers a variety of contexts; presidential and parliamentary systems, developed and developing countries, libertarian and government restricted media environments and societies with varying degrees of broadband access.

Making a Difference also focuses on countries that have very different methods for electing governments and political leaders. In the United States campaigns last for very long periods of time and massive fundraising machines provide the fuel on which campaigns are run. In other countries election campaigns are relatively brief, tight spending restrictions are in place and in some cases political parties and candidates receive public funding.

An examination of party and candidate web sites also provides a window on the extent to which political operatives in different countries learn from each other. On the surface at least the amount of cross-pollination seems extraordinary. Communications directors and web masters routinely borrow ideas and cull the latest innovations from political sites in other countries particularly the United States. In specific terms the use of the Internet by the Howard Dean campaign during his run for the American presidency in 2004 seems to have created an international echo. In the wake of the Dean campaign, the notion of e-campaigning, of using party and candidate web sites as aggressive instruments for mobilizing and communicating with voters, seems to have taken hold at least in some countries.

On another level there is the issue of the "Americanization." Some scholars believe that American methods, strategies and indeed American political consultants have had on an extraordinary influence on the nature of election politics across globe (Blumler and Gurevitch, 2001). The story is often one of both acceptance and resistance. But does this phenomenon extend to the Internet? Do American strategies and approaches to campaigns and Internet usage apply in political systems that vary so dramatically from the American model.

Making a Difference is intended to be a basic guide to the study of election web sites and their use across the globe. In doing so it will reveal much about the interaction between citizens and political parties, which is the very nexus and perhaps the critical test of whether the Internet is a force for real change or whether it merely reorders and reinforces previous relationships. Our intention in mapping this terrain, and in asking the key questions, is to provide at least some of the answers. By knowing where we have been, we will be better able to understand where we are going.

Introduction

Parties and Election Campaigning Online: A New Era?

Stephen Ward

It is now over a decade since Internet election campaigning first emerged. Initially, as with the arrival of other technologies in the nineteenth and twentieth centuries, there were high hopes that the Internet might help reshape democratic politics (Rheingold, 1995; Budge, 1996; Morris, 2000). In the case of election campaigns, it was argued that the Internet would increase pluralism, mobilize citizens and produce a new age of interactive electioneering (Rash, 1997; Corrado and Firestone, 1996; Selnow, 1998).

Yet, as time has passed, there has been an increasing sense of disappointment. There has been consistent criticism from web advocates that political parties are failing to exploit new information communication technologies (ICTs) and simply using them to replicate their existing practices. Nor did the Internet appear to be making a difference in terms of gathering votes. The Internet, it seemed, was doing little more than engaging the already engaged.

However, despite the prevalence of this "politics as usual" viewpoint, we need to remember that, arguably, parties have adapted more quickly to new media technologies than to any previous technological advance. In many liberal democracies websites/email have already become almost routine tools of electioneering, whilst the emergence of blogging and, recently, videoblogs has begun to influence the way campaigns are reported, if not the campaigns themselves. Furthermore, two relatively well-publicized examples of Internet campaigning, Roh Moo-Hyun's successful 2002 presidential bid in South Korea and Howard Dean's innovative, but ultimately failed, 2004 U.S. presidential bid, remind us that the Internet still has potential, in certain circumstances, to act as a significant mobilizing tool and produce important consequences for electoral competition.

This volume seeks to move away from all or nothing accounts of the influence of the Internet to assess its subtler role in parties' and candidates' election campaigns. In this introductory chapter we identify the key themes of the developing research agenda on election campaigning online, as well as providing a potential comparative framework for assessing what shapes web campaigns and produces the key drivers and barriers to online activity.

The Online Campaign Research Agenda: Professionalization, Pluralism and Participation

Three main questions have tended to dominate the study of virtual campaigning: Can online tools facilitate changes in the nature of campaigning, potentially producing a new campaign era? In terms of party competition, is it an arena that supports minor and fringe actors more than mainstream parties? Finally, can new ICTs help parties reach and mobilize new audiences, generate new resources and even help win votes?

Professionalization and Postmodern Campaigns: A New Era?

The arrival of new media technologies in the 1990s, including cable and satellite television, the Internet and, latterly, mobile phones, has led some scholars to argue that many liberal democracies are entering a new campaign era. Farrell and Webb (2000), for example, refer to the development of a third stage in campaign professionalization while Blumler and Kavanagh (1999) also talk of the third age of political communication. Norris (2000) uses the concept of postmodern electioneering, while Denver and Hands refer to the development of "postfordist" campaigns to denote a similar new epoch (2002). Technologies and the media environment, although not the only driver, are central to many of the changes they all describe. Farrell and Webb (2000, pp.104-106) note, in the context of European countries, several key developments: the emergence of permanent campaigning; the growth of campaign professionals; the rise of narrowcasting and the targeting of campaign messages to particular groups; and also the increasing use of feedback mechanisms from the electorate to shape and subtly reshape party messages and even policy. More specifically, the Internet and associated technologies have been seen as providing further components of this shift in a number of respects.

Permanency—Websites and email provide a permanent campaign presence 24 hours a day, 365 days a year. The speed of ICT communication means that parties can respond quickly to events to rebut opponents' claims directly, almost instantaneously.

Targeting—Computer technologies, databases and email enhance the ability of parties to gather data on the electorate, identify key swing voters (Bowers-Brown, 2003), and target their campaign messages to particular groups or even personalize communication to individuals. Even websites can provide targeted pages for particular demographic groups such as retired people or women. While parties and candidates in several countries have engaged in targeting, notably through attempts to attract young people online, they also remain cautious about fragmenting the party message and confusing voters. One former UK party campaign official summed up the parties' dilemma on personalization and targeting via websites:

> Most people have better things to do than obsess about politics like we do. A party's message will only reach the voter if it adopts a disciplined laser like focus. If someone is reading about a party's proposals for tax cuts in her newspaper, watching the announcement on the evening news and driving past posters advertising it on her way to work—what is she to make of the party's website talking about something else entirely because it has been personalized for her (Jackson, 2001, p.150).

Interactivity—Perhaps what has excited the most attention is the interactive elements of new technology. In theory, the extent to which the public can become engaged with, and involved in, the campaign can be increased through ICTs. Parties can now provide numerous opportunities via websites, blogs and email to draw in the public and engage them in dialogue. In practice, however, numerous studies have indicated that parties have been wary of interactivity, fearing that opening up websites will allow opponents to attack them and control of the campaign agenda will be lost. As Coleman (2001, p.681) suggests, "letting political opponents loose on online bulletin boards is a high risk strategy and political marketing is about winning votes not chatting with the enemy."

Decentralization—While the modern television era helped produce a rather uniform and top-down electoral campaign, the postmodern era raises the prospect of fragmentation and decentralization in campaigns. One intriguing question is whether, within party organizations, new ICTs increase or decrease levels of centralization. On the one hand, computer technologies provide a further potential for centralization since party headquarters, leadership and campaign and party bureaucracies are often best placed to use the technology available (Nixon and Johansson, 1999; Smith, 1998, 2000). More directly, new groups of campaign professionals dedicated to web technologies (web designers, e-pollsters, e-campaigns managers) are emerging again based at party headquarters. Moreover, the growth of centralized database technologies targeting voters in key con-stituencies could further empower national party headquarters to coordinate and direct campaigns that were once the preserve of the local party organization. Yet, alternatively, web tools also allow a degree of decentralization. New media campaigning might challenge centralization by providing candidates and local parties with a relatively low cost platform for disseminating messages (Norris, 2000). With multiple communication channels, it might be difficult for parties to monitor these new information flows, thus creating more opportunities for di-versity, localization and fragmenting national party campaigns.

Americanization—One of the initial debates surrounding the evolution of campaigning was how far the trends described above were American in charac-ter and whether such practices were being transferred globally, leading to elec-tion campaigns being standardized and homogenized (Negrine, 1996; Swanson and Mancini, 1996; Kavanagh, 1995). The Internet, at least in its formative pe-riod, was seen as being very much American-dominated and, therefore, some wondered whether the Internet might be a further tool for the Americanization of campaigning. Others, however, preferred to see the trends as either growing professionalization or globalization, rather than Americanization per se (Scam-mel, 2001), while most commentators were keen to reiterate the continuing rele-vance of national context in shaping election campaigns.

Party Competition: Enhanced Pluralism?

Much of the debate about party competition online stems from initial expec-tations that the Internet could help level the communication playing field for small and fringe actors, allowing them to challenge major parties more effec-tively (Corrado and Firestone, 1996; Rash, 1997; Selnow, 1998). At the very least, it was thought that the Internet might foster pluralism in allowing more voices to be heard than previously (Hill and Hughes, 1998; Bimber, 1998; Nor-ris, 2001, 2003). This assumption was based on four main factors:

The unmediated nature of the Internet—The arrival of the World Wide Web (WWW) meant that smaller parties could theoretically find it easier to present their arguments to a wider audience. The web is both a global and an unmedi-ated medium, so for smaller parties, commonly ignored by newspapers or televi-sion, it offered the opportunity to produce their own new media platform free from the whims of editors.

The lowering of professionalized campaign costs—Unlike television and modern highly packaged campaigns, few resources are required to run a rela-tively sophisticated cyberspace campaign. Although major party and presidential websites may cost millions of dollars to create and maintain, but at other levels anyone with a computer, relevant software, access to the Internet and minimal computing skills can produce a professionally-appearing website at low cost, and an email list for practically nothing. In theory, at least, parties do not need to hire expensive specialized staff. Thus Corrado and Firestone (1996, p.11) confidently predicted that

> because of their low cost, new technologies will open the electoral process to groups and candidates who have been traditionally been priced out of the mass political market ... digital communications could make financial resources less important in electoral politics since candidates will have access to mass audiences without having to conduct expensive advertising campaigns or spend tens of thousand of dollars on direct mail ... it is clearly the case that emerging technologies will benefit candidates who lack significant financial resources or broad based public support.

The ethos of the Internet—It is not simply resources that might encourage pluralism. The ideologies and culture of many of fringe parties seemingly fitted well with some of the more libertarian or anarchic practices of the early Internet. Certainly, many of the loudest advocates of the benefits of Internet campaigning have come from small extremist parties on the left or the right (Copsey, 2003).

The multiplier effect—Because websites have relatively low costs and high production values and because fringe parties/candidates can appear alongside their mainstream counterparts in cyberspace, some suggest that this creates a multiplier effect for small or fringe parties/candidates. In other words, a well designed website can make them appear larger and more professional than they are in reality and, in some cases, add to their legitimacy and credibility (Rash, 1997; Copsey, 2003; March, 2005).

Overall, therefore, it was suggested that the Internet was a different type of campaign arena where the content of campaigns was more equalized; there was a more level playing field in terms of the coverage of party campaigns; and, as a result, the campaigns themselves were likely to become more competitive, with the increased possibility of successful challenges to mainstream party and candidate organizations.

However, by the late 1990s skeptics were already suggesting that, far from producing a different and more democratic sphere, the Internet was undergoing a process of normalization. The major players, such as traditional political parties, resource-rich candidates, and traditional news organizations, were beginning to dominate cyberspace in the same way that they dominated other communication outlets (Resnick, 1999; Davis, 1999; Margolis and Resnick, 2000; Margolis *et al*, 1999; Kamarck, 2002). Normalizers countered the level playing field argument in three respects:

Resources still matter—While initially the Internet might lower the threshold for campaigning, increasingly, over time, financial and human resources were becoming important, as with other types of campaigning. Hence, new media campaigns were demanding more money and more skills to compete professionally. Running sophisticated, interactive, permanent campaigns requires increasingly professionalized full-time staff that minor parties or fringe candidates are likely to lack (Strandberg, 2006). Moreover, in the case of candidate based systems, the established resource advantages of incumbents would be increased through new media tools since incumbents could use websites and email to conduct a permanent campaign but also develop a more long term relational approach to voters (Jackson, 2004).

The traditional media are still crucial—Although access to the Internet has increased rapidly the importance of the traditional media remains crucial in two respects (Bimber and Davis, 2003, p.169), both of which benefit major rather than minor party players. Firstly, because the Internet is largely a push medium, party websites cannot attract voters who lack a pre-existing interest in politics or know nothing about a party in the first place. Voters have to actively choose to seek information online rather than receive it passively via television or radio. Consequently, to reach the crucial swing voters or to mobilize those with only a marginal interest in politics the mainstream media remain central. Secondly, the already powerful use their pre-existing dominance of the traditional media to shape competition online because they have the ability to drive more traffic to their sites. In short, normalizers argued that the new and old media were not separate domains but intertwined, such that one influences the other.

The commercialization of the Internet—Margolis and Resnick (2000), in particular, point towards a more general trend on the Internet, the increasing dominance of business and commerce as the central driving force of the WWW. The consequence of this, they argue, is that the online world increasingly resembles the offline world. Hence, political-related content represents only a tiny portion of the web and fringe political interests, parties, and candidates only a miniscule fraction of that small political content. In essence then, those on the fringe remain precisely that—on the fringe.

While such normalization arguments have held sway in empirical studies of Internet campaigning, recently more nuanced studies have reframed normalization (Bimber and Davis, 2003). In particular, several studies have tried to move on from the all or nothing debates that have tended to dominate coverage of the influence of the Internet. These studies have concluded that the Internet is unlikely to produce huge democratizing changes or shifts in party competition overnight, but the potential for change remains (Cunha et al, 2003: 88-89). Even if the Internet does not shift votes for smaller parties, it is allowing them to organize and campaign more effectively (Dalton and Wattenberg, 2000, p.281). It may also be the case that it is not just simply size or resources that matter here but party culture (see below). A number of studies have found that Green parties and the far right especially have benefited more than most from the Internet (Gibson and Ward, 2003; Voerman and Ward, 2000; Conway and Dornan, 2004). Far from having no effect, the Internet may be supplementing, reinforcing or even accelerating pre-existing trends in politics.

Participation: Mobilization and Reinforcement

In the context of elections, much interest has focused on whether ICTs can reverse the apparent downward trend in electoral turnout in many liberal democracies and reinvigorate the parties' role as participatory vehicles (Norris, 2003a, 2003b). The debate here has centered on mobilization versus reinforcement and widening and deepening arguments. The mobilization thesis suggests that parties could reach new voters via ICTs, notably younger voters, who are the most regular users of ICTs and have grown up with the Internet as part of their everyday lives. These are often the voters who are least likely to turn out in elections, are hard to reach via the traditional media and are the most skeptical of conventional party politics (Norris, 2001, pp.84-86; Tolbert and McNeal, 2003). The increased mobilization argument rests largely on five main factors (Ward *et al*, 2003a):

Efficiency and convenience—The Internet makes it perfectly possible to participate in an election campaign without leaving one's home and also access information at a time of one's choosing. In other words, the consumer, rather than the producer, makes the decision on when and how to participate. Hence, for the time-poor, housebound or elderly, use of Internet technologies provides a theoretically easier means to gather information and become involved on a more regular basis. Equally, from a party perspective, Internet and email potentially offer additional opportunities for more efficient recruitment and mobilization (Ward *et al*, 2003b). Websites can act as marketing devices, while email can help target sympathizers by sending more information or requests for donations and by allowing online volunteering or membership applications.

Increasing the number of channels through which to participate—The interactive elements of ICTs provide many more opportunities and channels to get involved. One can now present one's views directly to party organizations and politicians via email or online fora without having to go through an intermediary.

Increasing information generates participation—Far more information is now available and accessible in the public domain than in the past. Arguably, more exposure to political news and information creates further socialization and stimulates additional political activity (Bimber, 2001). The Internet with its capacity to carry large amounts of information about parties, candidates, issues and the campaign generally could generate a better-informed and more engaged electorate.

Creating virtual networks—One of the key benefits of ICTs is their ability to erode time and geographic boundaries. Hence, it becomes easier to communicate with large numbers of people over wide distances. Moreover, it also makes identifying other individuals with common political interests simpler and, in turn, fosters the ability to create links and networks online that would be almost impossible to sustain offline. Thus parties can now mobilize expatriate voters, for example, and link up isolated supporters in remote areas, keeping them in touch with campaigns (Toulouse and Gross, 1998).

Increasing the quality and depth of participation—The speed of communication, the level of information stored and the interactive and networking possibilities supported by new ICTs could help participants supplement and extend their range of participatory experiences, i.e. deepen and enhance the quality of participatory experiences.

While such positive views on the capabilities of Internet technology can still be found, increasingly, commentators have cast doubt on the ability of the Internet to increase or enhance participation in the electoral context. Critics argue that, at best, it simply supplements existing patterns of participation. At worst, it might actually reinforce or increase participation gaps (Norris, 2000, 2001).

Reinforcement arguments are based on two key themes. Firstly, there are digital divide problems—access to the technology is still restricted and those without access tend to be the very people who are already disengaged from the political process (Norris, 2001). Secondly, there are motivation problems—technology may provide the means but not necessarily the motive to participate in electoral politics. As we noted above, in order to visit electoral or party sites one needs to make an active decision to do so. If one lacks interest in politics, and elections specifically, then technology alone is unlikely to provide the stimulus. The likelihood is that those who visit party sites are going to be the already engaged and interested or sympathetic. In short, party sites preach to the converted (Norris, 2003b). Finally, some have even questioned the quality of online techniques for enhancing participation. They see ICT communication as a largely solitary push-button experience (Street, 1997; Barber et al, 1997; Nie and Ebring, 2000). The large amounts of information available online may simply lead the public to become overloaded and disengaged or select only a narrow range of online information sources, merely reinforcing their own prejudices (Davis and Owen, 1998; Sunstein, 2001).

The Shaping of Online Campaigning

One of the arguments running through all three areas above is the extent to which technology drives change. For example, how far are trends of adaptation to ICTs uniform across different countries? Or, alternatively, what effect do national and political contexts have on shaping the way parties use ICTs? In this section, we further develop and expand the explanatory framework sketched out by Ward et al (2003c, pp.240-241) concentrating on three levels of factors (systemic, organizational-institutional and sub-systemic/organizational), which potentially influence the nature of online campaigns:

Systemic Factors

One area that is important in web campaigning is the national context or campaigns environment. Here two types of drivers to online activity can be considered potentially important:

New and old media environments—One element that might shape responses to the new media in a political system is the relationship between parties and the traditional media, e.g. patterns of ownership, levels of censorship and ease of access (Norris, 2000). Historically, for example, some parties have traditionally controlled their own newspapers or even television channels. Ease of access to the old media, and favorable coverage in it, provide few incentives to use the new media actively. Clearly, levels and patterns of access to the Internet may also be expected to impact on parties' use of the Internet. In countries where the Internet has become a mass medium, more online activity and more sophisticated campaigns are to be found, but even where there are relatively low levels of access, parties will still seek to address those they see as key opinion formers, such as journalists and political activists, who are the most likely to have access to technology.

The political/social campaign environment—It is not merely the direct technological factors that impact on use of ICTs but also the main contours of the political system. Hence, the key components of a nation's constitutional-political system influence both the uptake and use of technology. For instance, it might be argued that presidential, candidate-centered, federal systems are more likely to be responsive to interactive online technologies than highly centralized polities because, as Gibson and Rommele (2005a, p.282) suggest,

> This more multi-tiered governing arrangement with a large number of independent actors, therefore, arguably provides a wider platform necessary for electoral innovation and experimentation—with the result that it promotes the faster take up of new campaign practices.

Similarly, Zittel (2003, p.40) argues that:

> Only presidential systems based upon single member plurality electoral systems and decentralized legislative institutions will encourage legislators to exploit the technological potential of the Internet.

Additionally, others have argued that one of the key factors in adopting a more experimental use of the Internet is the (in)stability of the democratic system and political-institutional set-up. March (2005) argues that in new democracies the Internet might play a greater role where the political system and political communication are less fixed:

> There is less a sense of parties preaching to the converted in societies where the Internet is still a novelty, when the electorate is more fluid and when catch-all

information provision is still seen as a good in itself ... There is less of a sense
of add-on and more an experiment when parties are themselves new and rapidly
evolving.

More directly, electoral law and regulation of the campaign environment clearly
influence the role of online campaigning. Tkach (2003) describes how the Japanese government attempted (successfully) to use existing campaign laws to apply limits to parties' use of the Internet in the run-up to elections. More infor-
mally, of course, political culture can impact on online activities. Newell (2001)
has noted the initial reluctance of Italian parties to raise money online following
the political-financial scandals of the early 1990s.

Organizational-Institutional Factors

Naturally, one area that could shape online campaigns is the role of parties
themselves. It is not unreasonable to suppose that different types of party (ideological and organizational) with differing goals might respond to ICTs in ways
that reflect their unique history, norms and administrative structures (Nixon and
Johansson, 1999; Lofgren and Smith, 2003; Rommele, 2003). In particular, three
sets of influences can be identified:

Resources—As we have already seen, much debate has ensued about the
importance of resources in online campaigns. While new ICTs might lower the
threshold for professionalized campaigning it is likely that resource levels, especially professionalized staffing and advanced web-based programs, make a difference in the sophistication of the online campaign and the attractiveness of the
online presence to the voter. Hence, if parties or candidates can afford to employ
specialist web staff, journalists to write website copy and staff to answer email
and moderate online discussion they are more likely to produce more sophisticated online campaigns.

Culture and goals—Although resources are often seen as the key to new
media activity, arguably, candidate or party culture and strategy could be more
important in shaping the use of technology. For example, parties or candidate
campaigns with participatory grassroots ethos are more than likely to make use
of the interactive elements of ICTs to encourage discussion and mobilization,
whereas vote maximizing and office seeking parties are most likely to adopt a
top-down informational approach to ICTs (Rommele, 2003, pp.13-14). One example from the United States was the Howard Dean presidential campaign in
2004, which emphasized its movement-like character and relied heavily on websites, blogs, and email to stimulate mass participation.

Target audience—The extent to which a party has a significant target audience online will also make a difference. Parties with a traditional working class
base, whose supporters are less likely to have access to the Internet, will generally maintain their traditional structures of organization and communication
since there will be less incentive to invest scarce resources in new media technologies.

Individual Level Factors

Although we are primarily interested in looking at national campaign trends in this volume, there are also good reasons to think that local level and even individual (candidate) factors might also produce different types of campaign activity online. In countries with strong constituency-candidate traditions we could expect to see uneven adaptation to the new media technologies. Moreover, an increasing body of revisionist literature in a number of countries over the past decade that has challenged the pre-conceived wisdom that local campaigns no longer matter. Revisionists have argued that local campaigning is still an important feature of elections despite the growth of central control (Denver and Hands, 2002; Ward, 2003). In terms of the local environment, therefore, two sets of factors might well play a role in developing an online campaign (Ward and Lusoli, 2005):

Constituency environment—Candidate campaigns tend to reflect the local nature of their constituency or electorate. For example, the closeness of the race (marginality) is generally seen as encouraging candidates to move online (Ward and Gibson, 2003; Gibson and Rommele, 2005b). Where all the votes count, candidates are likely to use all the communication methods available to them even if they think there may be only a minor benefit. Moreover, candidate campaigns will also reflect the technological profile of the constituency. Just as we might expect national levels of access to make a broad difference to online activity, so connectivity in local areas will also impact on the online campaigning sub-nationally. In middle class urban areas, with high levels of broadband access, we can expect candidates to respond to their environment by making extra use of new media tools.

Candidate profile—The individual traits of the candidate themselves also have an impact. In general, one would envisage younger candidates, who are socialized in Internet use, to be more active online. The gender of candidates has been seen as possibly important. Women candidates, some have argued, receive a more hostile media coverage, consequently, one might make the case for them being more interested in a new media environment where they retain more control over projecting their image (Carlson, 2007). By contrast, however, others have suggested that given that men are generally more active online this will be reflected in the prominence of male candidates online. The evidence seems inconclusive with some studies indicating that gender has little impact on the way technology is used (Greer and LaPointe, 2004, p.130; Gibson and McAllister, 2003). Obviously, candidates with background or interest in IT or media communication are also likely to be more prominent online.

Conclusion: Moving the Agenda Forward

Whilst the "politics as usual" approach has dominated the study of electioneering online, the research agenda is far from complete. In particular, the research has often been narrowly geographically concentrated and somewhat one dimensional in terms of both methodology and empirical focus. This edited collection attempts to fill some of these gaps by extending the research agenda in a number of ways.

Firstly, it extends the geographical focus of study since most of the research has hitherto been conducted in typical liberal democracies, particularly the United States and, to lesser extent, northern Europe. Here we include research from campaigns in countries such as Chile, Singapore and Indonesia, which, thus far, have been largely absent from discussions of online electioneering. Moreover, broadening the geographical scope of study also helps illuminate the salience of contextual and systemic factors in understanding the deployment of the Internet in campaigns. The concluding chapter also focuses on the comparative importance of systemic context in shaping the use of the Internet as a campaign tool.

Secondly, research has tended to be from a relatively top-down perspective, concentrating largely on national party campaigns and using web feature analysis as the primary methodological tool. Whilst this is understandable given that websites present the public face of e-campaigning and provide an accessible and relatively rich data source for researchers, many of the chapters here seek to supplement this approach. In some chapters (Netherlands, United Kingdom, Australia and Italy), the focus is extended to include campaign activity beyond the national level to include candidate and party leader e-campaigns.

Thirdly, the book also moves beyond the parties' execution of their online campaigns to look at their external impact. One missing element in many studies is the electorate's response to e-campaigning. Outside the United States, our knowledge of the impact of the political Internet has often been extremely limited, notably in terms of the way the electorate engages with online campaigns. In many countries, even basic data regarding use of Internet is scarce. Where possible, some chapters, including the United States, United Kingdom, Netherlands and Australia, provide data from a voter perspective.

Fourthly, whilst the focus of this volume is on party and candidate campaigning, the Internet has also allowed a proliferation of unofficial voices and activists to engage with, and challenge, the official campaign. A number of the chapters here (for example, Canada and Singapore), chart the emergence and role of the blogsphere as a challenge both to journalists and also to tightly controlled party campaigns.

Overall, we aim to provide a more rounded account of e-campaigning. The Internet may not, as yet, have revolutionized election campaigning and certainly those mistakenly looking for direct effects on electoral results have been disappointed. Yet, if we dismiss the importance of the Internet on this basis, it is likely we will underestimate the more subtle and indirect role that new media are having on the way campaigns are fought and even on the nature of politics itself.

Chapter One

Chile: Promoting the Personal Connection—The Internet and Presidential Election Campaigns

Taylor C. Boas

In an article on political marketing in Chile published in 2000, Genaro Arriagada, campaign manager for the center-left coalition in three of Chile's last five presidential elections,[1] suggested that the Internet would dominate the 2005 electoral campaign. While portraying the rise of online campaigning as part of the same process of evolution that gave rise to television-centric campaigns, Arriagada also suggested that use of this new medium would counteract some of the characteristics of mass-media campaigns that are often considered negative. In particular, he argued, the potential to present information online in greater quantity and depth might challenge the "soundbite culture" that has emerged with the rise of television, and the interactive nature of the Internet could strengthen the types of ties between candidates and grassroots supporters that have weakened with the decline of political parties, unions, and other traditional intermediary organizations.

In this chapter, I argue that while the Internet certainly has not yet risen to the status of dominating electoral campaigns in Chile, it is becoming an increasingly important medium for the second of the two uses highlighted by Arriagada—establishing new forms of linkage between politicians and the public. Several of the candidates in the 2005 presidential elections established blogs to allow for interactive communication with visitors to their websites, and a third of them made extensive use of the Web and email to recruit, organize, and mobilize a network of campaign volunteers. Using the Internet for these purposes is one of many ways in which candidates are seeking to compensate for the declining presence of parties in Chilean political life and electoral campaigns. With respect to the soundbite culture of the mass media, although the Internet does allow for the presentation of greater depth and detail than television, radio, or print media, soundbites have also found their way onto the Internet and are currently featured much more prominently on candidates' websites than government programs in all their complexity. While the rise of the Internet in Chilean politics is able to further an existing trend toward the promotion of direct personal ties between candidates and supporters, it does not appear capable of countering the trend toward soundbite-centric campaigns.

This chapter examines use of the Internet during presidential election campaigns in Chile, with emphasis on the country's most recent election, whose first round was held in December 2005 with a runoff in January 2006.[2] Data include content and feature analysis of the websites and email lists of the three principal presidential candidates, Michelle Bachelet, Joaquín Lavín, and Sebastián Piñera; interviews with webmasters and other members of the campaign communication team of both Bachelet and Lavín; and newspaper coverage of Internet use during prior campaigns. My analysis of the candidates' websites is based on copies that were archived at three different points during the 2005 electoral campaign: early October, and election day for both the first and second round (December 11 and January 15, respectively). Due to limited available data, this chapter does not examine the effects of Internet use on voting behavior or public opinion during the 2005 campaign. Campaign effects of any sort are difficult to assess without panel studies or experimental data (Boas, 2005), which have not yet become common during electoral campaigns in Chile, nor have even simple single-wave campaign surveys asked about Internet use.

In the following sections of this chapter, I first introduce the Chilean case, discussing the larger environment in which electoral campaigns—both on- and offline—take place. I then go on to examine use of the Internet by political parties and candidates prior to the most recent election. The bulk of the chapter, presented in the third section, consists of an analysis of the ways in which the three major contenders in the 2005 presidential election made use of the Web, email, and related technologies to communicate with the public, mobilize supporters, and seek out financing for their campaigns. In the conclusion, I return to Arriagada's predictions about the importance of the Internet in Chile, assessing what uses have been most significant in the 2005 campaign and which are likely to become even more prominent in the future.

The Campaign Environment

The Internet may be an increasingly global technology, but the way it is used within any country responds largely to national-level variables. First and foremost, it is essential to consider how many and what types of people have access to the Internet. Moreover, regardless of the state of Internet diffusion, its political impacts depend upon the ways in which it is used by political actors, so it is important to examine who these actors are and what constraints they are subject to. In this section I first examine Internet diffusion in Chile. I then discuss the relative strength and influence of the actors involved in online campaigning in Chile—candidates and parties—and also examine the campaign regulations and larger media environment in which they operate. In the course of this discussion, I also offer an overview of the 1999 and 2005 presidential election campaigns.

Diffusion of the Internet: Growing but Unequal Access

A quick glance at the state of Internet development in Chile suggests that the country is a good candidate for the medium to play an important role in politics. The percentage of the Chilean population that uses the Internet has consistently been the highest in Latin America, and a 2003 survey by the World Internet Project found that 34.8 percent of the population is online, comparable to the percentage using the Internet in the United States in 1999 (Fernández and Goldenberg, 2003). If we allow for some growth during the remaining two years, the percentage of Chileans using the Internet during the 2005 campaign was probably comparable to similar figures for the United States in 2000, when the Internet played an important, if hardly dominant, role (Bimber and Davis, 2003). The diffusion of the Internet in Chile compares favorably with that of several European countries examined in this volume: according to the same survey cited above, 36.4 percent of Spain's population and 31.2 percent of Italy's population were online as of 2003.

While use of the Internet is increasingly widespread in Chile, it remains most common among the middle and upper classes due to the country's rather high level of economic inequality. Following radical market-oriented economic reforms under the Pinochet dictatorship in the 1970s, income distribution remains highly skewed: Chile's Gini coefficient for 2001 was 57.1, versus a figure of 45 for the United States in 2004, and numbers in the 30s or below for most European countries. Moreover, while it is one of the wealthier nations in Latin America, Chile's GDP per capita of US$ 5,847 places it squarely in the category of a middle-income country, significantly poorer than Western Europe and North America. Given these statistics, it is unsurprising to find that use of the Internet in Chile is more concentrated among the wealthy than in other countries. There is a 60 percentage point spread between the proportion of Internet users among the richest quartile and the poorest quartile of Chileans; the corresponding figures for the United States and Canada are 39 and 34, respectively (Caron, 2005).

Electoral and Party Systems: Increasingly Personalized Politics

In the Latin American context, Chile is probably the country with the best-organized and most "European" political parties, which tend to have clearly identifiable positions on the ideological spectrum, though these positions have shifted over time. Moreover, Chile's party system exhibits a fairly high degree of stability, with many of its parties having their origins in the democratic regime that pre-dated the seventeen-year dictatorship of Augusto Pinochet (Scully, 1995). Major parties include the Socialist Party (PS), Christian Democratic Party (PDC), and Radical Social Democratic Party (PRSD), all with origins prior to the 1973 coup d'etat; National Renewal (RN) and the Party for Democracy (PPD), established in the late 1980s as reorganized versions of pre-1973 parties or political forces; and the Independent Democratic Union (UDI), formed in 1988 by a group of Pinochet's strongest supporters who split off from RN. In contrast to other Latin American countries (such as Peru), there are no examples in Chile of loosely organized "parties" cobbled together merely for the purpose of participating in an election, nor are there any of the more highly institutionalized parties that are nonetheless closely associated with a single individual, such as Brazil's Workers' Party. In Chile, parties choose candidates rather than potential candidates creating parties.

Despite the strength of parties in Chile, several institutional factors combine to make individual candidates the central actors in presidential election campaigns—and by extension, the most important political users of the Internet. First, and most obviously, Chile has a presidential rather than a parliamentary system of government, where the president is elected by majority vote and where a runoff is held if no candidate wins a majority in the first round. Presidentialism tends to subordinate parties to individual politicians, both in government and during electoral campaigns. Moreover, the Chilean president is particularly powerful vis-a-vis the country's legislature, and is generally considered the strongest president in Latin America in terms of control of the budget and legislative agenda (Aninat et al, 2006; Baldez and Carey, 1999; Siavelis, 2002). While the institutional strength of the presidency is more directly relevant to policy-making than to campaign dynamics, it does have the effect of focusing more attention on the presidential race than if the president were a weaker political actor.

The role of parties during presidential campaigns in Chile is also limited by the fact that in almost all presidential elections, the major candidates have been supported by coalitions. The two major coalitions in Chile initially organized around opposite sides of the 1988 plebiscite that ended Pinochet's military dictatorship and ushered in democratic elections the following year. The center-left governing coalition, the Concertación de Partidos por la Democracia (Coalition of Parties for Democracy), currently comprises the PS, PDC, PRSD and PPD; the right-wing opposition coalition, most recently known as the Alianza por Chile (Alliance for Chile), brings together UDI and RN. In part because presidential candidates are typically supported by more than one party, campaigns are run by teams that are organizationally independent of parties, often forming a national network of local and regional campaign headquarters that runs parallel to the structure of the political parties in the coalition. Campaign staff include members of the various parties supporting the candidate, but independents also occupy prominent positions, particularly in the national-level campaign leadership.

Finally, Chilean political parties have weak societal roots and an unpopular, elitist image among the electorate, meaning that candidates increasingly seek to distance themselves from a party image during campaigns and make direct, unmediated appeals to the electorate (Roberts, 2002; forthcoming). This trend was first felt most dramatically in the watershed election of 1999, pitting UDI's Joaquín Lavín, a former mayor of the wealthy Santiago suburb of Las Condes, against Socialist Ricardo Lagos, a former minister of education and of public works. While Lagos in many ways embodied the image of a traditional party politician, Lavín consistently criticized traditional politicians and characterized himself as a non-political technocrat who got things done. Rather than appealing to either party identification or emphasizing specific policy proposals, Lavín's campaign sought to communicate a direct, personal connection with various social groups—workers, youth, women, etc.—and an intimate understanding of their problems. In the December 1999 election, Lavín came second to Lagos by only 30,000 votes, by far the strongest showing for the right in recent Chilean history. Because neither candidate obtained a majority, a runoff was held in January 2000, which Lagos won with 51.3 percent of the vote.

If the 1999 campaign was the first prominent example of a Chilean presidential candidate seeking to ditch the image of a party politician and emphasize a direct connection with the people, the 2005 campaign furthered this trend. On the right, the two parties of the Alianza failed to agree on a single candidate or to let voters choose one in a primary election, so both UDI and RN fielded candidates—Joaquín Lavín for the former, and Sebastián Piñera, a wealthy businessman and former party leader, for the latter. Because each was supported by a single party rather than the coalition, it was harder for Piñera and Lavín to present themselves as supra-partisan candidates—though neither did they seek to emphasize their party affiliations. In 2005, however, the strongest example of a candidate seeking to privilege direct personal connections over party image was Michelle Bachelet, a Socialist and the candidate of the Concertación. A favorite in the polls for years before the election, Bachelet and her campaign team stressed that she had been chosen as a candidate by the people—via public opinion—rather than by the party machinery. Her campaign slogan "Estoy contigo" ("I am with you") epitomized the nature of her campaign appeals, which, like Lavín's strategy in 1999, emphasized closeness to and identification with the people and an intimate understanding of their problems.

In the weeks before the first-round vote, as Bachelet's overwhelming lead began to slip, she backed off from the "empathy campaign" to some extent, seeking to portray herself more as a capable stateswoman who would continue the policies of the popular incumbent government (President Lagos was enjoying over 70 percent approval ratings at the time). The latter strategy prevailed during the successful second-round campaign against Sebastián Piñera, whom she defeated with 53.5 percent of the vote. Despite the shift in strategy, however, Bachelet's campaign remained centered on her as a person. With the exception of emphasizing her endorsement by several prominent Christian Democratic politicians—done largely to prevent votes from slipping away to Piñera, who was also trying to appeal to the centrist Christian Democratic tradition—Bachelet's second-round campaign did not emphasize party image any more than her first-round campaign had.

Campaign Regulations: Uncertainty Regarding the Internet

In the context of an electoral campaign, the Internet is first and foremost a medium of communication, and secondly a medium for financial transactions. As with other forms of both campaign communication and financing, electoral laws can have an important bearing on how these processes occur. While electoral campaigns are more highly regulated in Chile than in most other Latin American countries, none of Chile's electoral regulations says anything specific about the Internet. This lack of clarity, combined with the relative newness of the Internet, has created an uncertainty that is reflected in some candidates' approaches toward the medium, particularly with respect to online fundraising.

In contrast to the massive and prolonged advertising blitz that characterizes electoral campaigns in the United States, the restrictions that Chile places on campaign advertising make its electoral environment similar to that of many European countries (Plasser with Plasser, 2002). Chile prohibits paid television advertising during campaigns, and candidates receive free blocks of time on broadcast television every day during the month before the election. Candidates are permitted to buy advertising space in other media, such as radio, newspapers, and billboards, though they are similarly restricted to the last month of the campaign. In practice, this restriction can largely be ignored, since campaign advertising is defined as a message asking for a vote, and anything simply introducing the candidate is allowed outside of the official time period. Because the law does not say that all advertising is subject to these restrictions, but rather separately enumerates restrictions for television, radio, newspapers, and outdoor advertising via flyers and the like, it is not clear whether the electoral advertising law applies to the Internet. None of the major candidates in the 2005 election included propaganda on their websites that directly urged a vote prior to the last month of the campaign, though this could be simply because they tend to transfer offline advertising campaigns to the web with little modification.

Aside from the restrictions on campaign advertising, the other major law with a bearing on Chilean electoral campaigns is the campaign finance and expenditure law passed in 2003 (Fuentes, 2004). This law places limits on the total amount of money that can be spent on campaigns, establishes a maximum for both individual and anonymous donations (currently about US$ 67,000 and US$ 670 respectively), and prohibits contributions from foreigners without the right to vote in Chile. However, the law does not distinguish between different forms of donation and has nothing specific to say about the Internet. While the law remains somewhat unclear, online campaign donations are now theoretically possible. In 2004, before the country's municipal elections, several politicians were negotiating to get Transbank, the Chilean credit card clearing company, to allow online campaign donations via the Internet. After initially backing out, Transbank agreed to set up the service, and several candidates took advantage (*La Segunda*, 29 July 2004; *El Mercurio*, 17 October 2004). In 2005, Transbank handled online donations to Michelle Bachelet's campaign, as discussed below.

The Media Environment

Finally, it is important to consider the broader media environment surrounding electoral campaigns in Chile, and what opportunities the Internet provides to candidates and parties that they cannot achieve elsewhere. While Chile's media system has historically been considered the most public service-oriented in Latin America—primarily because television stations were initially run by the government or universities, and private ownership was not allowed until the 1990s. Chilean television has become increasingly commercialized in recent years, and the state and university-based stations now operate essentially as private entities (Fuenzalida, 2002; Tironi and Sunkel, 2000). In this respect, they have become more similar to radio and print media, which have always been commercially-oriented and privately owned—in the case of newspapers, by a few wealthy and politically influential families. The major effect on electoral dynamics of this increasingly market-oriented media environment is the promotion of a soundbite culture in which candidates have little opportunity or incentive to explore issues in greater depth. Candidates on the left of the political spectrum, as well as some analysts, also frequently allege a conservative bias in press coverage of politics, though such bias is much less severe than in many other Latin American countries.

In the face of a media environment that is increasingly oriented toward soundbites, and may be somewhat biased in favor of right-wing candidates, the Internet offers candidates two principal opportunities: to circumvent the mass media, and to influence its coverage. By communicating directly with the public via the Internet, candidates can present information in much greater depth and detail than is possible via soundbites, and they can spin the coverage of their own campaign any way they choose. In contrast to television, radio, and print news, however, information on a candidate's website attracts a much smaller audience, typically those who are already interested in the campaign and in politics. In addition to providing an alternative to the mass media, the Internet offers yet another way to influence the coverage of the mass media. A campaign team already oriented toward producing soundbites and photo opportunities can distribute these to the press much more effectively using the Internet. Moreover, these sorts of soundbites, rather than more in-depth information, may form the bulk of what candidates put on their websites for direct consumption by the public.

While the Internet does offer Chilean candidates the opportunity for more substantive (and potentially more sympathetic) communication than do the local media, the free advertising space provided to candidates on broadcast television somewhat reduces the Internet's unique advantage in terms of depth, detail, and control of message. Because of their length (usually two-and-a-half to five minutes) and regularity (broadcast at same time every day, usually at noon and during prime time), free television broadcasts give Chilean candidates the opportunity to go into much more detail regarding their campaign proposals, and to cover a larger portion of their overall program, than do the thirty-second spots that are typical of countries with paid advertising. Moreover, the length and regularity of Chile's free television broadcasts means that rather than catching the average viewer unawares like commercial advertising, they tend to attract only those viewers who make a conscious decision to watch. In this sense, therefore, television advertising and the Internet both reach an audience that has greater interest in the campaign, though broadcast television is obviously accessible to a much wider segment of the population.

The greatest unique opportunity that the Internet provides to candidates in Chile is probably the potential for interactive communication with supporters and stimulating a sense of community among them, particularly in an era in which parties no longer play an important role in performing these functions. While television provides a direct candidate-to-citizen connection, no other medium approaches the level of reciprocity in communication that the Internet offers.

The Development of Online Campaigning in Chile: Candidates as Protagonists

With the rise of the web in the mid-1990s falling between electoral periods in Chile, political parties established an Internet presence before individual candidates, but the sophistication of their online offerings was soon outstripped by that of presidential campaign sites. Consistent with their status as well-organized entities that are not dependent upon any one individual, Chile's political parties have websites that represent the party as a collectivity rather than its most prominent politicians. In general, party websites do no active campaigning on behalf of their candidates beyond naming them and possibly providing links to their own personal sites. Because party websites do little more than introduce the party, its history, its ideology, and its major figures, they have not significantly advanced beyond brochure-ware status since they debuted in 1997 and 1998. Only individual candidates, mainly in presidential elections, have moved substantially beyond the information-dissemination capacity of the web to make use of its capacity for interactive communication, mobilization, or fundraising.

Several Chilean parties established a web presence in 1997 and 1998, but their efforts were oriented more toward presenting the party as an entity than promoting any of its candidates. UDI was online by the time of the 1997 legislative elections; its site offered a history of the party and featured documents and the text of speeches, along with a roster page that had photos and emails of senatorial and congressional candidates (*La Segunda*, 16 October 1997). By September 1998, the PS, RN, and PPD had also established websites. None of these sites, however, offered much information on presidential pre-candidates for the 1999 election. The Socialist Party site made no mention of Lagos, and the PPD site just said he was preparing for the primaries. UDI's site only mentioned Lavín's name when listing the members of the party's political commission, and it devoted much more emphasis and space (including photos and a biography) to the party's deceased founder, Jaime Guzmán. Only RN's site had any information on the campaign activities of its pre-candidate at the time, Sebastián Piñera (who later withdrew his candidacy in favor of Lavín). A newspaper article concluded that parties were "more concerned about the diffusion of their principals and ideas than about seizing the opportunity to campaign with their eyes toward 1999" (*La Segunda*, 25 September 1998).

In the intervening years, party websites have not advanced much with respect to active campaigning on behalf of their candidates. Among Chile's major political parties, only UDI, RN, PPD, and the Socialist Party had functioning websites when examined in early October 2005. Those belonging to the Christian Democrats and PRSD were unavailable during the week of analysis, though they were later re-established. The four functioning sites all presented party history, basic principles, and news, as well as links to the campaign sites of their presidential candidates. None, however, included links to the websites of any senatorial or congressional candidates, even though some of those candidates were among the parties' most important politicians. All four of the parties published lists of their legislative candidates in the 2005 election, though these lists were not necessarily prominent: the PPD's was in the form of a downloadable file that could be found only by following the "documents" link from the home page. The most information that any of the party sites offered about their candidates consisted of photos and basic information such as age and profession; several parties just listed the candidate's name and district. Ironically, Lavín's presidential campaign site offered more information on UDI's 2005 legislative candidates—addresses of campaign headquarters and names and phone numbers of campaign managers—than did the party's own site.

In a political system as candidate-centric and hyper-presidential as Chile's, it is not surprising that the major campaign-related use of the Internet has been by presidential candidates. During the 1999 presidential election campaign, all of the candidates had established websites several months prior to the vote (*La Segunda*, 10 September 1999). Because Internet penetration was quite limited in Chile at the time of the campaign, with only about 4 percent of the population

online in 1999 (World Bank, 2006), the information on candidates' websites was
not necessarily intended for mass consumption, at least directly. Alejandro
Miranda, the webmaster for Lavín's site in 1999, stated that the principal use of
the Internet was communicating with the press and ensuring that journalists
throughout the country had ready access to the soundbites and photos released
by the campaign team (author's interview, Santiago, 17 October 2005). Perhaps
for these reasons, the site had a strong multimedia component, allowing downloads of jingles, audio clips from interviews, and several television spots. Other
components included the candidate's biography, news from the campaign trail,
and announcements of upcoming events. An email list was used for communication with the press, but not with the general public, partly because people were
still reluctant to share personal email addresses at that time. While Lavín's site
encouraged visitors to email comments, concerns, and suggestions to the candidate, the webmaster said they received little correspondence.

Internet penetration may have been limited in Chile in 1999, but the Internet
was already an important sign of modernity, and having a website with certain
features could communicate important things about a candidate. In addition to
the standard features such as news, biography, and a schedule of upcoming
events, Lagos's site placed an emphasis on basic forms of interactivity such as
allowing visitors to submit questions that would be answered on the site and
providing chat rooms for discussions of particular topics relevant to the campaign. In a newspaper article, the campaign's webmaster described the site as
"creating an opportunity for public participation" (*El Mercurio,* 28 November
1999). The number of people actually participating online in this fashion in 1999
was undoubtedly minimal, but the number reading about the opportunity to do
so in Chile's major newspaper was certainly higher, and probably more important.

Internet Use in the 2005 Presidential Campaign

By the time of Chile's 2005 campaign, use of the Internet by presidential candidates had definitely gone beyond being something of a novelty that campaigns
did primarily to show they were modern or to communicate with the press. Candidates' websites had become important ways to connect with the public, though
certain uses of the Internet were much more prominent than others. In the following section, I discuss the ways in which the three major candidates in Chile's
2005 presidential election made use of the Internet for publishing basic campaign information, facilitating participation and feedback, corresponding with
the public, recruiting and mobilizing campaign volunteers, and soliciting online
contributions.

A New Way to Deliver Traditional Information

All of the sites of Chile's major presidential candidates for 2005 had in common certain features which are not particularly innovative or unique to the Internet, but for which the web is simply a convenient form of delivery. Each site, for instance, featured a news section with an extensive archive of press releases; Bachelet and Lavín both offered audio and video clips from campaign events as well. All of the sites included biographies of the candidate, along with photos highlighting both their personal and professional lives. Each site also had a separate photo archive with photos mainly from the campaign trail. Bachelet and Piñera's sites included endorsements from various individuals, mostly well-known figures but also some from the "guy on the street." All of the sites made available the candidate's detailed governmental program, as well as more digestible forms of policy proposals or policy priorities: Lavín's 50 Promises for Chile, "Michelle's Ideas," and details on a number of Piñera's pet projects. During the second-round campaign, both Bachelet's and Piñera's sites included goals for their first 100 or 120 days in office. While all of this material was potentially availably offline as well, the web provided a useful way of publishing it all in one place. As Camila Benado, a member of Michelle Bachelet's communication team, put it: "We don't have our own newspaper; what we do have is the Web page" (author's interview, Santiago, 26 September 2005).

As suggested by the placement of Lavín's television spots on the Internet in 1999, the web is a very convenient medium for delivering forms of advertising that were initially developed for other outlets, and this trend continued in 2005. Lavín put all fifteen of his distinct five-minute spots online, and Bachelet posted a selection of hers, as well as video clips of Christmas and New Year greetings. All candidates' sites also featured jingles that could be downloaded as audio clips. Bachelet and Lavín both included downloadable images of campaign flyers and official photographs and graphics that appeared on banners, signs, and billboards. One gets the sense, however, that some of this material was simply uploaded to the website without a lot of thought. Lavín's site, for instance, featured images of t-shirts, balloons, and hats bearing the campaign logo, without the capacity to buy them online or any information on other ways to obtain them.

Consistent with the trend toward candidates de-emphasizing party affiliations in their political appeals, none of the campaign websites included prominent mentions or symbols of the candidate's party. While each candidate's biography discussed his or her party affiliation and prior party activism, party logos or links to party websites were hard to find. Bachelet was the most extreme in this regard: there was no logo of the Socialist Party or the Concertación anywhere on the website, nor any link to the sites of either the party or the coalition. Piñera, supported only by a single party, had almost as little party emphasis as Bachelet: only a tiny logo on the home page, under the heading "sites of interest," linked to the RN site. Similarly, Lavín included a link to UDI's site only under a list of affiliated websites contained on a separate page. By the end of the first-round campaign, both Bachelet's and Lavín's sites had posted lists of the legislative candidates supported by the same party or alliance, but the emphasis tended to remain on the presidential candidate rather than the party. The link to this list from Bachelet's home page said "A Parliament for Bachelet."

Blogs and Internet Surveys: Genuine Participation and Propaganda in Disguise

While much of the informational material on candidates' websites in 2005 could also be found during the 1999 campaign, interactive features such as blogs definitely marked a new phenomenon. Both Piñera and Bachelet's websites included blogs, while Lavín's linked to a blog that was hosted by a third-party site.[3] Piñera's blog began each week with a post purportedly from the candidate, and entries during the final days of the first round generated upwards of eight hundred comments. Piñera, or someone writing in his name, even responded to some of the comments himself. Bachelet's blog never purported to be run by the candidate herself or even the campaign team, but rather by a group of supporters. This particular format was not as popular, as only Bachelet's own entries consistently generated more than a hundred comments. Both candidates' blogs constituted fairly open spaces for debate; they claimed to be edited only for inappropriate language, and one could certainly find harsh criticism of the candidate among the comments that were allowed to remain.

While Bachelet's and Piñera's blogs can be considered genuine spaces for online participation, other participatory features seemed to be largely campaign propaganda in disguise. Lavín's "Wings for your ideas," an online survey about policy priorities, was introduced in May 2005 with much fanfare, and the campaign claimed that over 8,400 responses were received in the first month (*El Mercurio*, 29 May 2005). The questions on this short survey, however, dealt with what are clearly non-exclusive choices among policy priorities and, for someone of Lavín's ideological orientation, non-controversial as well. For the question about how to fight crime, for instance, visitors were asked whether the most important policy measure should be "that criminals be convicted and serve out their sentences," "that repeat offenders receive harsher penalties," or "that there be more police officers on the streets." Absent from these choices, of course, was a more stereotypically left-wing policy option, such as spending money on crime prevention programs in poor neighborhoods. Lavín's webmasters claimed that the online survey was consulted when putting together the candidate's governmental program, but surely the campaign's own internal surveys asked about a wider range of policy preferences and were taken more seriously than the opinions of a self-selected sample of web users.

Bachelet's "Question of the Week," an Internet survey like Lavín's "Wings for your ideas," was often but not exclusively used for propaganda purposes. A typical case of propaganda-in-disguise occurred during the middle of August, when the website asked the following: "What is the effect of Michelle Bachelet's triumph in all the surveys, five months before the presidential election?" The list of possible responses included "it generates useful space for disseminating her ideas," "it establishes a new type of politician," "it invites people to keep working responsibly," and "it consolidates a more emotional political leadership." As Bachelet's campaign began to stagnate about a month before the December election, however, questions began to touch on issues that could provide useful feedback for the campaign team, not with respect to programmatic issues, but with respect to tactics. In late November, for instance, respondents were asked whether in the final weeks of the campaign it was most important to increase the number of campaign events outside of the capital, promote closeness to the people, appear on a variety of television programs, or give greater visibility to political parties. These were precisely the sort of tactical trade-offs that were being debated within the campaign team.

Email for Public Communication: More for Feedback than Campaign News

Given the ease and minimal expense with which campaigns can send mass email, one might think that a particularly important component of Internet strategy would be sending messages to people who signed up to receive information from the campaign. All of the principal candidates' sites prominently featured an email sign-up link on the home pages, but interestingly, email did not seem to be a major form of outgoing communication to the general public. I signed up for each of the candidates' public email lists at the beginning of September, but only from Piñera's campaign did I receive messages on an approximately weekly basis. Lavín's list sent out only one message during three and a half months, and Bachelet's list never sent any, even though I tried registering twice. Piñera's and Lavín's mailings simply contained news updates, no different from material that could already be found on the site. Webmasters for Bachelet's and Lavín's campaigns said they were wary of sending out email too often and overloading recipients, but had not considered asking during sign-up how often subscribers wanted to receive messages (author's interviews with Veronica Molina, Santiago, 3 October 2005, and Carolina Guzmán, Santiago, 5 October 2005).[4]

Although sending email to the general public was not as prevalent in the campaign as one might expect, soliciting emails from the public did seem to be an important use of the Internet for Chilean candidates. All of the sites invited comments and questions from visitors, either via a web form or directly via email. While none of the campaign staff interviewed for this project knew exactly how many messages were received, each claimed that all of the messages were answered; one staff member from the Bachelet campaign said that the candidate even answers some emails personally (author's interview with Camila Benado, Santiago, 26 September 2006). In a small country such as Chile, where most citizens do not yet think to contact a presidential campaign directly via email, responding to every message appears to be something that is currently manageable.

Volunteers and Mobilization: Organizing and Preaching to the Converted

One of the major potential uses of the Internet in electoral campaigns is recruiting and mobilizing volunteers; doing so is particularly important in an era in which the role of party militants has declined. All of the sites featured web forms allowing visitors to sign up as campaign volunteers. Neither Bachelet's or Piñera's site had much information on what a potential volunteer was committing to, however, and Bachelet's site even omitted the word "volunteer," merely encouraging visitors to "sign up, participate with us." In the final weeks of the campaign for both the first and second rounds, the websites for all three candidates shifted their focus from signing up general campaign volunteers to recruiting poll monitors, an important activity in Chile where votes are counted by hand at the polls after they close, and ballot uncertainties are challenged on the spot by volunteers from each of the campaigns.

While each of the major candidates' websites allowed potential volunteers to add their name to an online database, Lavín's campaign went well beyond the others in its use of the Internet for recruiting and mobilizing volunteers. Clicking on the link "sign up as a volunteer" from Lavín's official campaign site took visitors to a separate site, voluntariosporlavin.cl (Volunteers for Lavín), also managed by the campaign team. The Lavín volunteers' site is probably the only example in Chile's 2005 presidential campaign of targeting online information specifically toward supporters. In some ways, the Lavín volunteers' site functioned as a parallel home page, with photos, news, and information on voter registration. News on this site focused on volunteer activities, and was clearly designed to stir up excitement in addition to informing; an article would cover Lavín's campaign trip outside of Santiago, for instance, but would also talk about what volunteers did to support the effort. The Lavín volunteers' site seemed to be speaking to a community of shared ideals and a common project much more than any of the candidates' official portals.

In contrast to the Bachelet and Piñera sites, where signing up simply submitted information to a webmaster, signing up as a volunteer on the Lavín site immediately created an online account with access to a volunteer intranet. Based on the extent to which people were active as volunteers during the campaign, they would be granted access to additional areas of the internal site; this approach made it more difficult for "spies" from other campaigns to uncover sensitive or strategic information.[5] The basic default level of access to the volunteer intranet featured a list of local volunteer coordinators in various parts of the country, a discussion forum, and an "ask the coordinator" forum that functioned as a sort of frequently asked questions list.

Signing up as a volunteer on the Lavín website also involved subscribing to an email list, which, in contrast to the list for the general public, received heavier traffic (nineteen messages in the final two months of the campaign) and was used specifically for targeted communication that was *not* sent to the general public. Some of these messages sought to mobilize people to turn out as volunteers or to attend campaign events. Others sought to reinforce support for Lavín, hoping to prevent votes from slipping away toward Piñera, who had been gaining ground throughout the campaign. Reinforcing emails of this sort were notable for their content, since they portrayed Lavín as something he studiously avoided being seen as in public: a die-hard right-winger. While Lavín consistently sought to distance himself from the Pinochet regime he had once supported—during the campaign, he said that if he had known about Pinochet's human rights abuses he would have voted against him in the 1988 plebiscite—emails to the volunteers list implied Piñera was a traitor to the right for having voted against Pinochet in the same election and that Lavín was the only true right-wing candidate in the race.

When analyzed in early October, before the Lavín campaign reached its initial goal of one hundred thousand volunteers, the site was clearly oriented toward the task of additional recruiting. It emphasized several different ways that existing volunteers could bring in new ones, including going out on weekends to recruit in person or signing up like-minded people through university networks. In addition, the site specifically emphasized the ability to help in the recruiting effort without having to take part in an organized activity or even hitting the streets as a volunteer. Visitors to the website who clicked on the "Sign up 10 more" link were taken to a page that encouraged them to "be an active volunteer and assist in the triumph of Joaquín Lavín, participating in this campaign without leaving your house," simply by entering into a web form the names of friends, family, and colleagues who were interested in becoming volunteers. Carmen Mena, the webmaster of the Lavín volunteer site, said that this particular online recruiting effort had brought in five thousand new volunteers as of early October (author's interview, Santiago, 5 October 2005).

The emphasis on volunteer recruiting and coordination of the volunteer effort is the most unique aspect of Lavín's web presence, and Mena characterized the computerization of volunteer records as a key strategic tool for the campaign. "I don't know how effective the website as a whole is," she said, "but I do know that the greatest asset that this campaign team has, apart from the candidate of course, is that database" (author's interview, Santiago, 5 October 2005). The computer-managed network of volunteers, she stressed, allowed them to circumvent potentially complicating party structures in running a campaign on the ground. The Lavín campaign sought to transcend a party appeal, reaching people that would otherwise be reluctant to vote for UDI, and they also wanted have a network of dedicated Lavín volunteers that they could rely upon—people who were not faced with deciding whether to devote time to the presidential candidate or a local candidate from the same party.

Online Contributions: Tentative Steps in an Uncertain Realm

One of the major campaign-related uses of the Internet in the United States, online campaign contributions, was not particularly prevalent among Chilean candidates; only Bachelet's site provided this capacity. The first and most innovative way to give money electronically to the Bachelet campaign involved paying a nominal fee (between US$ 1.50 and 2.50) to download campaign-related ringtones and screen images for mobile phones. Supporters could also sign up to have campaign news to be sent to their mobile phones via SMS, also for a small fee per message. In both cases, a portion of this fee went to the phone company implementing the service, but the majority went to the campaign. María José Becerra, in charge of online donations to the Bachelet campaign, emphasized the democratizing effect of this form of campaign contribution, since access to mobile phones, and thus the potential to give small sums of money, is so widespread in Chile (author's interview, Santiago, 5 October 2005).

Bachelet's website also provided the capacity for potentially much larger donations to be made directly via the Internet using a credit card—a form of campaign contribution that appeared to allow for possible abuse. When first implemented, the online donation feature simply requested a name and email address and then allowed the user to enter credit card information and an amount to donate. The site did not appear to prevent users from donating in excess of either the anonymous limit or the overall personal donation limit, nor did it seem to have any way of preventing foreigners from making illegal donations.[6] By December, the online donation portion of the Bachelet website had been moved to a separate site, www.aportesparabachelet.cl, which included a new section explaining the various restrictions in the campaign financing law. Nonetheless, the actual donation mechanism still did not appear to have incorporated any of these legal restrictions.

Clearly, online campaign financing, at least as it is currently implemented, seems to fall into a gray area in the law. One Lavín staff member said that they had considered allowing online donations, but ultimately decided against it because of the legal uncertainty, and also because not many Chileans are yet accustomed to online financial transactions (author's interview with Nicole Walcovinski, Santiago, 19 December 2005). In the next presidential election in 2009, however, she expected that all the candidates would offer the capacity for online donations and that it would be a much more important way of raising money for the campaign.

Conclusion: Promoting the Personal Connection

While the Internet has become an increasingly important medium of campaign communication in Chile, it still has significant room to grow. Between its political debut in the mid-1990s and the 2005 election, the Internet went from an interesting novelty or symbol of modernity to something that candidates took much more seriously, but it still pales in comparison to the attention that campaign teams pay to press coverage or to advertising on radio and television. Arriagada, the campaign manager who originally suggested that the Internet would dominate the 2005 campaign, has more recently acknowledged that his earlier predictions were somewhat premature, that the Internet in 2005 was only slightly more relevant than in 1999, and that it might take six or seven more years for it to become a "very important" tool for campaign communication (author's interview, Santiago, 11 October 2005). The webmaster for Lavín's site in 1999 and for several UDI congressional candidates in 2005, similarly maintained that not much had changed in terms of the overall importance of Internet from 1999 to 2005, but that the Internet would be the "pillar" of the campaign in the next election in 2009 (author's interview, Santiago, 17 October 2005).

Predictions such as these may be somewhat hyperbolic; the Internet is hardly the pillar of electoral campaigns even in the United States, and it seems unlikely that the medium could achieve that status in Chile in just a few more years. Indeed, there may never be a quantum shift from one election to the next in which the Internet suddenly comes to occupy the central place in the campaign. What seems more likely is that as greater and greater numbers of people begin to use the Internet in Chile, campaigns should consider it an increasingly important medium of communication, devoting more resources and attention to it.

More significant from a comparative standpoint than the pace of the Internet's increasing "importance" (however measured) are the specific ways in which the Internet is used in Chilean electoral campaigns, how these differ from other forms of campaign communication, and how this matrix of uses is likely to evolve over time. With respect to Arriagada's prediction that the Internet would challenge the soundbite culture that has come to dominate mass media-oriented political campaigns in Chile, the Internet certainly has provided *opportunities* for greater depth in the presentation of ideas, and candidates have taken advantage of some of that depth, i.e. by putting their government programs online. But candidates do not really promote or seek to advertise this depth to the general public. As Lavín's former webmaster notes, candidates discussing a particular issue in press conferences, debates, or advertising are still not in the habit of pointing the public toward the greater detail that can be found on their websites (author's interview, Santiago, 17 October 2005). Moreover, candidates' websites do not necessarily feature this depth and detail on prominent display. Rather, the most prominent component of these websites is the massive quantity of the same type of soundbite-style information that is distributed via the mass media—the various press releases, photographs and audio and video clips that adorn the home page and are archived on each candidate's site.

With respect to Arriagada's prediction regarding the role of the Internet in strengthening ties between candidates and grassroots supporters, it is still too early to assess the significance of this impact. Nonetheless, efforts to facilitate direct personal connections with supporters are one of the major ways that Chil-

ean candidates currently use the Internet and one of the areas that has potential
for growth. During the 2005 campaign, efforts to build ties with the grassroots
were manifest in two major forms: the blogs that Piñera and Bachelet included
on their websites, and the volunteer network, including an email list and access
to the volunteer intranet, organized by the Lavín campaign. For their part, blogs
represented only an initial foray into what could potentially emerge as more
substantial interactivity between candidates and supporters in the future, as more
and more Chileans get access to the Internet. Creating direct, unmediated connections with voters is an increasingly important part of electoral campaigns in
Chile, and the Internet, with its interactive capacity is the only electronic medium that approximates the two-way exchange of a candidate visiting a local
market to chat with vendors or greeting individual citizens in a town square.

If interactive and participatory spaces such as blogs have the potential to
create new types of direct, unmediated ties between voters and candidates, use
of the Internet to manage and mobilize a network of volunteers approximates a
more traditional form of political intermediation, the party. While mobilizing
party militants was an important way to get volunteer labor for political campaigns in the past, mobilizing a large network of campaign-specific volunteers,
and organizing and recruiting many of them via the Internet, has become an important way to get volunteer labor in an era in which parties have declined. Although there are important distinctions between the more long-term, political
identity-based commitment implied by joining a party and the more short-term
and contingent commitment involved in volunteering for a campaign, there are
also important similarities. Unlike visiting a website, receiving an email, or
commenting on a blog entry, participating as a campaign volunteer is not purely
an online phenomenon; a volunteer network is an organizational structure facilitated by the use of the Internet but not wholly dependent upon it. Like joining a
political party, signing up for the Lavín volunteer network involved associating
with a community of like-minded individuals and taking part in a common project encouraging participation and broadening of the ranks. Use of the Internet to
facilitate the building of new forms of political community (both real-world and
virtual), may be an increasingly important component of political campaigns in
the future.

While the Internet has not yet become a dominant medium in Chilean politics, it is likely to continue to grow in importance during future elections, probably keeping pace with the growth in access among the population. There do not
seem to be any inherent features of the Chilean case limiting its growth, and
some characteristics of Chilean politics seem to encourage it. Building direct
personal connections with voters, fast becoming the most important form of
political appeal in Chile, is something for which the Internet is comparatively
well-suited. Other uses of the Internet that seem tentative at present, such as
online campaign contributions, may become more prevalent in the future as their
legal status is clarified and as e-commerce becomes more common among the
population in general. Finally, the future of hybrid online-offline forms of political organization and mobilization, such as a volunteer network managed and

partially recruited online, will be important to watch. Where use of the Internet is fully integrated into other components of the campaign—whether this means using email to encourage physical participation at a campaign event, or using a candidate's television appearance to encourage voters to visit his or her website—it is likely to have its greatest impact.

Notes

1. Arriagada was campaign manager for the No campaign in 1988 (a plebiscite that ended the rule of military dictator Augusto Pinochet), the 1993 campaign of Eduardo Frei, and the first round of the 1999 campaign of Ricardo Lagos.
2. Chile also held congressional elections in December 2005. Because of limited space, and because the presidential campaign saw much more extensive use of the Internet, I do not specifically examine congressional campaigns.
3. This third-party site, paisdigital.org, also hosted blogs for the other candidates; few of the entries received many comments. Because they were not actually run by the candidates' campaign teams, these third-party blogs are not considered here.
4. All of the websites also featured sign-up forms for a press email list, which received mailings much more frequently, but interested citizens were unlikely to stumble onto this list since the registration form called for specific press-related information.
5. At the invitation of Carmen Mena, the webmaster of the Lavín volunteers' site, I registered in order to access the internal portions of the site and receive the emails sent to the volunteers list, but I was not, to my knowledge, granted access to any internal information beyond the default level. The following observations are thus based on the information that any Chilean could access by signing up by entering their national ID number and a few other personal details into a web form.
6. The only way to be completely certain about which safeguards were or were not built into the Bachelet online donation mechanism would have been to attempt to make a large donation myself, which I was obviously unwilling to do.

Chapter Two

Australia: Potential Unfulfilled?
The 2004 Election Online

Rachel Gibson and Ian McAllister

When democratic governments started to adopt new information and communication technologies (ICTs), there were early signs that Australia was becoming a world leader (Dunleavy *et al*, 2003). There was a flurry of activity in the mid to late 1990s, with the Australian Labor Party (ALP) claiming a world first in party website production in 1994 (Gibson and Ward, 2002), the Australian Senate becoming the first legislative body to officially recognise online petitions (Magarey, 1999), and the launch of pioneering e-government and e-democracy agendas at the national and state level (Clift, 2002). But progress has slowed in recent years. Politicians and government officials have become more concerned with the symbolic value of wiring up government, and sought efficiency gains rather than new ways to promote citizen participation and genuine structural modernisation (Bishop and Anderson, 2004; Flew and Young, 2004).

Certainly if one considers elections and campaigning in Australia there are signs of a lull in the use of new ICTs since the early years of the new century. After an initial rush by parties to set up their virtual 'shop fronts' in time for the 1998 federal election, studies of state and national organisations (Gibson and Ward, 2002, 2003; Chen, 2001) and their elected representatives in parliament (Chen, 2002a, 2002b) in the lead-up to the 2001 election have consistently shown a lack of innovation and enthusiasm. Parties' websites have focused on providing information in a largely static format with limited avenues for genuine interactivity or mobilisation of volunteers, support and donations. Furthermore, although the parliamentary parties and many fringe parties had established national websites by the end of the 1990s, candidates were much slower to follow, with only a minority from any party establishing an independent web presence by 2001 (Gibson and McAllister, 2006).

This chapter asks whether the Federal Election of 2004 saw any significant shift among Australian parties and candidates in their uptake of Internet campaigning. Elections serve as catalysts for the development of new campaign practices in their own right, and the wider social and political context surrounding the 2004 election suggested an environment more conducive to e-campaigning than had previously been the case. By 2004, the ALP had been out of power for the best part of a decade and was primed to exploit all means to reach out to voters and re-establish itself as a viable governing party. From a technological perspective, levels of Internet and broadband access had risen significantly in Australia since the 2001 election providing voters with faster and cheaper access to the more innovative aspects of the online campaign such as flash graphics and animated video clips.[1] Finally, at the global level, the Howard Dean revolution in Internet campaigning had come and gone only a few months earlier in the United States, a phenomenon that could not fail to attract attention of campaign strategists around the world.

In order to examine whether the 2004 Federal Election heralded the 'arrival' of the Internet as a significant campaign tool in Australia, the chapter is divided into five sections. First, we present an overview of the Australian electoral context and political system more generally, as well as some political background to the 2004 election. In the second section, we examine the evolution of Internet campaigning and the role that the new ICTs have played in both elections and the articulation of voter interests more generally. The third section focuses on the 2004 election specifically, presenting evidence on the overall presence of parties and candidates online and the messages that were sent out over the web. The fourth section examines the audience for these sites, what other sites they visited online, and what effect—if any—their exposure to these sites may have had on their electoral behaviour. Finally, the concluding section draws together the findings to assess whether or not 2004 represented a progression for the Australian parties into the era of e-campaigning.

The Campaign Environment

The Australian political system that was established in 1901 was modeled on the Westminster Parliament, departing from this mainly by using a federal system and a directly elected upper house, the Senate. The lower House of Representatives initially consisted of seventy-five members elected from all states and territories for a three-year term (now expanded to 150 members). The Senate initially consisted of thirty-six members (now seventy-five) elected for a six-year term and was intended to protect the smaller states from the numerical dominance of the larger states in the House of Representatives. In the 1880s and 1890s, the salient political division was an urban-rural cleavage, with the rural areas opposing the economic policies of the rapidly industrializing cities. This regional conflict was gradually overtaken in the early years of federation by conflicts between industrial owners and workers, although rural interests have remained politically important.

In the first decade of the twentieth century, three parties dominated federal politics: the Labor Party, which was formed in 1901 from the various colonial Labor parties, and the Protectionists and Free Traders (Loveday, 1977; McMullin, 1995). In 1909, the Protectionists and the Free Traders settled their differences and combined to form the Liberal Party (later the United Australia Party, and later again re-adopting the Liberal Party title), thereby establishing the pattern of two-party competition that has been the basis of the Australian party system ever since. Despite the dominance of the owner-worker cleavage, reflected in Labor-Liberal party competition, the urban-rural division has remained politically salient through the Country (later National) Party. Since the 1920s, the National and Liberal parties have been in permanent coalition, except for two short periods in 1973-1974 and 1987.

More than any other established democracy, Australia has experimented with a variety of electoral systems, at both state and federal level, and also between upper and lower houses (Farrell and McAllister, 2005; Sawer, 2001).[2] At the national level, lower house elections have been based on the alternative vote since 1918, and for upper house elections, on the single transferable vote since 1949. But perhaps the most distinctive aspect of the electoral system is compulsory voting, so that not only are voters required by law to register to vote, they are also forced to attend at the polling place (though not necessarily to vote). This system was introduced in Commonwealth elections in 1924, and by 1941 had been extended to all of the states and territories. Although it is an offence not to vote without a valid reason, there is strong public support for the system, and relatively few non-voters are ever fined (Mackerras and McAllister, 1999). One significant consequence of compulsory voting is that during election campaigns, parties focus their activities on conversion rather than on mobilisation, since the latter is institutionally enforced.

Historically, compulsory voting is credited with maintaining the strong two-party system, itself predicated on high levels of partisanship among voters. Since voters are compelled to vote about once every eighteen months (at either a state or a federal election), it is hardly surprising that partisanship is relatively strong. However, over the past decade or so, minor parties have begun to make some modest inroads into the two-party system, while at the same time the strength of partisanship, if not the direction, has weakened. During the 1980s and 1990s, the main minor party was the Australian Democrats; although formed by a disaffected Liberal in 1977, it has largely attracted its support from ex-Labor voters and activists (Warhurst, 1997). In the late 1990s, Pauline Hanson's One Nation Party attracted considerable support, peaking at almost one quarter of the vote in the Queensland state election in June 1998, on a populist platform that combined opposition to Asian migrants and aborigines with support for gun ownership (Gibson *et al*, 2002). In the 2004 election the Greens became the largest minor party, with 7.8 percent of the first preference vote.

The declining support for parties is illustrated in Figure 2.1, which shows patterns of partisanship from 1967 until 2004 based on national surveys. The proportion of major party identifiers has declined from a high of 91 percent in 1987, to 77 percent in 2004, representing a decline of just under 1 percent at each election. At the same time, the number of those who consider themselves very strong partisans has declined by almost half, though almost all of the decline occurred between 1979 and 1987. At the same time, those who have no partisanship have increased from 8 percent in 1967, to 16 percent in the 2004 election. These trends are similar to, though not as dramatic as, those found in most of the other advanced democracies (Dalton *et al*, 2002).

Figure 2.1 Trends in Partisanship, 1967-2004

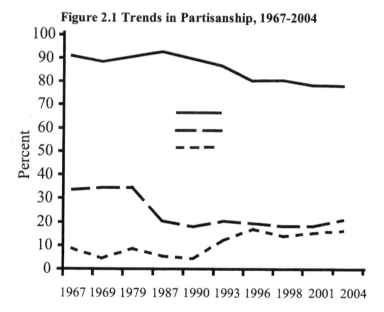

Sources: 1967-1979 Australian National Political Attitudes surveys and 1987-2004 Australian Election Study.

As party attachments have declined, this has also had consequences for the character of election campaigns. One trend has been an increasing proportion of voters who delay their decision until the campaign has commenced and, in the case of about one in ten voters, even until polling day itself (McAllister, 2002). In 1987, 27 percent of voters said that they decided on their vote during the campaign; in 1998 the same figure was 42 percent, although it declined to 32 percent in 2004. At the same time, the proportion of voters who say that they were interested in the election campaign, or who cared about who won, has also declined. For example, in 1993, 49 percent said that they had 'a good deal of interest' in the election; the same figure in 2004 was 30 percent. One indicator of this declining interest is numbers watching the leaders' debates. Televised debates began in 1984 and have been held regularly since 1990, when 56 percent of voters watched the debate; in 2004, just 35 percent said that they watched the debate.

Figure 2.2 Media Use During Election Campaigns, 1987-2004

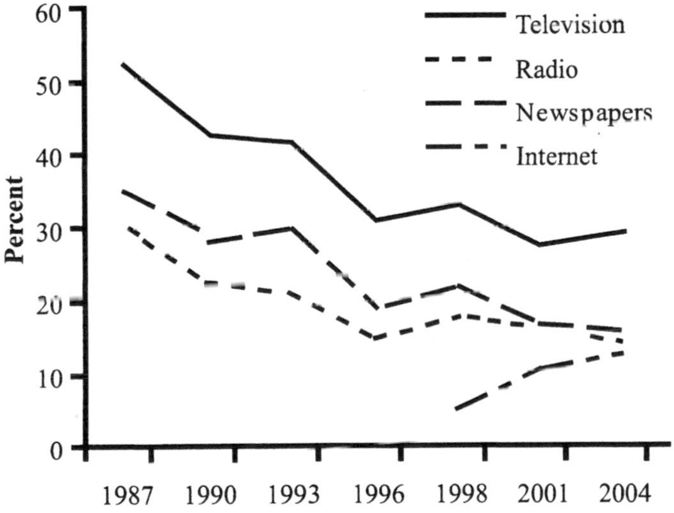

Sources: 1967-1979 Australian National Political Attitudes surveys and 1987-2004 Australian Election Study.

In line with declining interest in elections, those using the various media sources to follow the election campaign have declined consistently (Figure 2.2). In 1987 just over half of the electorate said that they regularly followed the election on television, but by 2004 the figure was just 28 percent, a major decline in a relatively short period of time. The use of newspapers and radio for election news has declined at a similar rate, albeit from a lower base. The only medium that is increasingly used for election information is the Internet; when the question was first asked in 1998, 4 percent of voters said that they had used it at least once for that purpose. By 2004, that had increased threefold, a substantial increase in just a six-year period.

Since 1932, the government and opposition parties receive free airtime on the government-funded free-to-air Australian Broadcasting Commission (ABC) on television and radio.[3] This consists of one hour of free airtime, composed of thirty minutes for the party's policy launch, and six slots of five minutes each to cover particular policies. There is no free airtime available on the free-to-air or pay-for-view commercial channels (Chaples, 1994). While parties must disclose donations of more than $1,500 (and individual candidates donations of more than $200), there is no cap on what can be donated, nor on what can be spent on political advertising during election campaigns. Since 1984, the parties have also received state funding, based on the votes won at the previous election. The amount is adjusted for inflation and a party must receive 4 percent of the vote in order to qualify. There are no restrictions on how state funds can be spent.

In the 2001 election, the two major parties together received $29.4m in state funding. However, their combined total income was $113.5m, the additional funds being made up of private and corporate donations (AES, 2005). Yet, the parties are estimated to have spent more than their total state funding on paid political advertising alone. Estimates vary (since there is no disclosure require-ment), but it seems that together they spent some $30m on media advertising, with the 2004 estimate being around $40m (Miskin and Grant, 2004). In line with the rules governing the traditional media, there are no restrictions on online political advertising, other than the general regulations that affect the online sector as a whole.

The Development of Internet Campaigning

The history of Internet use by parties in Australia, as in most countries, dates from the mid-1990s and the rise of the World Wide Web (WWW). Some inter-nal uses had been made of computing and digital technologies prior to this. Dur-ing the late 1980s the ALP developed *Electrac*—its electronic voter database compiled by constituency office staff and accessed by candidates to target swing voters. The Liberals' version—*Feedback*—emerged a few years later, becoming fully operational in 1996 (Van Onselen and Errington, 2004). These systems appear to have been essentially 'stand-alone' devices, located in an individual MP's or candidate's office, rather than operated as a networked and remotely accessible resource.

Starting with websites as a benchmark for parties' harnessing of Internet technologies, the ALP led the field, setting up a site in 1994. Most other parties soon followed suit, with the pace quickening in the lead-up to the 1998 election (Gibson and Ward, 2002). Although the parties saw the merits of being online, (or at least the potential for criticism in not having a web presence), individual candidates were less convinced about the need for a virtual identity. Using sites from 2001 that carried a listing of candidate pages, estimates run as low as twelve candidates online, a tiny proportion of the 1,324 candidates that officially stood for election.[4] Evidence supplied by the candidates themselves in the 2001 Australian Candidates Study (ACS), provides a healthier picture of online activity, however, with 37 percent of those responding to the survey reporting that they had maintained an independent personal campaign site.[5]

In terms of what the parties were actually doing with their sites, a study of the content of the national sites and the responses of party communication officials to surveys in 2000 indicated an information-centric approach with limited participatory initiatives, e.g. feedback forms, chatrooms, etc. (Gibson and Ward, 2002). Within these broad trends some interesting variation was observed. The One Nation Party proved to be among the most interactive of the parties, offering numerous channels for supporters to send their views to the leaders as well as a bulletin board for multi-way exchanges. While most parties did not take advantage of the resource mobilization potential of the web, the ALP and Greens bucked the trend, offering direct donation and membership sign-up facilities via their sites.

During the 2001 election there were few signs that the parties had recognized the power of the medium as a tool to convert voters. Most sites followed a formulaic pattern, migrating offline content to the online environment, offering media releases, policy statements and leader biographies along with a smattering of negative campaigning and a single organizational contact email address. The two major parties did provide sign-up facilities for e-bulletins but other than this made few efforts to exploit the immediacy and interactivity of the Internet. One notable exception was the ALP's political 'Big Brother' site, in which the audience was invited to vote out members of the government's front bench on a weekly basis. At the state level, efforts at web campaigning during 2001 proved even more patchy, with a study revealing that not all branches of the two major parties actually had active sites and among those that had, content was thin (Gibson and Ward, 2003). The Greens emerged as the best performer, showing a notably higher degree of interactivity and participatory initiatives, despite their minor party status.

Research conducted since 2001 has confirmed the perception of a minimalist Internet approach by parties, with their online materials being viewed as 'brochure-like' repositories for party documents and press releases and comparing poorly to the efforts made by pressure groups and protest networks (Edwards, 2005). From an internal perspective, while voter databases continued to be developed and enhanced by the major parties (particularly the Liberals), their maintenance and access appeared to remain the prerogative of local party offices. They were often used to support conventional forms of campaigning such as personal canvassing or direct mail, rather than online viral approaches using email (Van Onselen and Errington, 2004). A reluctance to engage in more active forms of online targeting was no doubt driven as much by the parties' concerns about annoying voters with unwanted spam as by any inherent fear of the new technology.

Beyond the organizational level, a study of the parties' elected representatives has shown high levels of personal usage of new ICTs in terms of web browsing and email. Survey data gathered in early 2002 reveal that just under 40 percent of all federal parliamentarians were browsing the web more than once a day and over 70 percent were using email with a similar level of frequency (Chen, 2002a). In terms of using it in their interactions with citizens, most saw new ICTs as a secondary channel for voter communication. Chen reports that less than half of state and federal parliamentarians had instituted a mechanism to log their email correspondence, a process that is long-established practice with offline constituent mail. There are, of course, exceptions to this general rule, a good example of the 'wired' politician being Victor Perton, the Victorian state Liberal MP who was an early adopter of the technology, setting up one of the first personal MP websites and using it as a discussion forum for registered users. A less positive example is the Victorian Liberal premier Jeff Kennett's ill-fated bid to retain his premiership in 1999. Lampooned for making his campaign more about personality and style than substance, his personal website *Jeff.com* became the focal point for this criticism, even spawning a series of spoof sites, the most famous of which, *jeffed.com*, was run by one of his former staff.

A range of other political organizations and groups have cultivated an active online presence. Particularly notable are the online discussion sites such as *Online Opinion*, *Political Lobby* and *Australian Politics*, which have proved to be lively spaces for a small but active number of voters to engage in meaningful debate (Chen, 2005). The 'insider' gossip site *crikey.com* enjoys a higher public profile, providing an alternative online news service constructed in part through anonymous tips collected via its website. Unions and community groups such as *Labor.net* and *Democracy Watch* also utilize the new media, presenting well-designed professional sites. In general, however, along with social advocacy groups, they have tended to adopt the 'flat' approach to content favored by the parties, with interactivity being limited largely to users downloading pdf documents or searching the site. More active sites include the aptly name *Activist Rights*, *Active*, and *community activist technology*, all of which view the Internet as a mobilizing tool in its own right, offering server space and lessons to those wanting to establish a websites, as well as direct downloading of software designed to help establish community groups online.[6]

The 2004 Federal Election

Given the relatively low profile the parties had adopted on the Internet leading up to the 2004 federal election, it was surprising to learn in July, only a few months before polling day, that the parties considered that the Internet would prove to be a 'significant' part of their campaigns. Observers in the media were clearly sceptical of such claims. Margot Kingston, a prominent commentator, journalist and blogger for the *Sydney Morning Herald* pointedly asking the readers of her web diary, "Have you ever seen anything from either major party trying to reach people through the Internet?"[7]

Such criticism notwithstanding, the environment for Internet campaigning had certainly improved since 2001, not least in terms of the growth in the potential audience. According to official government figures from August 2001, the proportion of those saying they had accessed the Internet in the week before the survey was 37 percent (Lloyd and Bill, 2001). The Australian Election Survey (AES) estimates of the electorate's access put the figure rather higher at 59 percent in November 2001.[8] By 2004 access had risen to 66 percent of the electorate, close to the figure of 63 percent produced by the Australian Bureau of Statistics in that year.[9] The numbers looking for election information, however, were much lower, and certainly not comparable to the majority of Internet users doing so in the U.S. presidential elections of the same year (Rainie *et al*, 2005). The AES data reveal that around 18 percent of Internet users were accessing election-related information online, with no more than around 5 percent viewing the parties and candidates' pages.

Research Questions, Data and Methodology

In this section we examine the 2004 online election in three particular respects:

- The extent to which the parties used new ICTs for campaign purposes at both the national and local level,
- The uses made by parties and candidates of the technology and, in particular, whether there were any new and innovative experimental applications trialled; and
- To what extent voters paid attention to the online campaign and whether it influenced their vote.

To address these questions, we present a range of data drawn from surveys and content analysis of party websites. We also utilise the Australian Candidate and Election Studies to profile individual use of the web and email. More specifically:

- To examine the extent of parties' use of the technology we provide a series of estimates of the use of the web by both national organisations and individual candidates, comparing the figures across parties and to those for 2001.
- The use that parties made of the Internet is examined through existing accounts of the content of national party sites as well more in-depth coding and analysis (conducted by the authors) of all candidate sites.
- The response of voters to the online campaign is characterised using AES data. In particular, we look at how interested they were overall in the online election and which sites were the most likely to be visited. We then examine the social background and political preferences of those visiting election related sites and ask how far they are likely to have been affected by what they saw.

Presence

A total of 1,421 candidates were nominated for the 2004 Federal Election, 330 for the Senate and 1,091 for the House of Representatives.[10] Of these, only a minority established a campaign website, although estimates of the actual number of candidates online varied. Table 2.1 provides an overview of the estimates from three major sources. The figures exhibit a considerable amount of variance, with the Australian Candidates Survey (ACS) figures revealing a much healthier picture of candidates' online presence than the other studies. The ACS puts the total proportion of candidates running sites at one third, while Ward *et al* (2004) estimate just over one in ten.[11] Chen (2005) does not produce an overall estimate across the parties but reports figures for individual parties by house; estimates for lower house candidates range from as low as zero for the Democrats to almost one in two of Liberals. Methodological differences in the studies' approach to data collection may explain much of this variation.[12] Despite these differences, however, all of the studies point to a stronger presence by the major parties compared to minor parties. Ward *et al* (2004) report the Nationals to be the most wired party, with 42 percent of its candidates online, the Liberals and Labor follow in second and third places, respectively. Similar rankings are found by Chen (2005) and also the ACS. One clear point of difference is the very high number of Green candidates online according to ACS estimates (see endnote 12).

Content Analysis

Most observers were largely unimpressed by the online efforts of the parties, particularly by the established parties. Reviewing the press's reaction to the parties' efforts, Miskin (2005) noted that two minor parties, the Greens and the Democrats, had the most innovative online campaigns. The Greens offered a campaign blog as well as daily opinion polls that allowed users to generate their own report of the cumulative responses. In a break with convention they also set up a separate website, *democracy4sale.org*, which gave users the opportunity to find out for themselves who was filling the parties coffers and by how much. The Democrats provided a flash movie, 'The Lie Detectors', to visitors entering the home page that could be emailed directly to others. The party also offered a highly tailored and personalized e-news service, with policy-specific options for voters to check when signing up to receive their updates. In addition, the leader, Andrew Bartlett, established a blog (the only parliamentary party leader to do so) that was regularly updated and appeared to be produced at his own keyboard rather than written by his staff.

The major parties, on the other hand, were seen as offering 'standard campaign brochures' (Jackman, 2004, p.6; Sinclair, 2004, p.10), and making very limited use of more specific e-campaign items. The Liberal Party offered some software downloads (backgrounds, screensavers, etc.) and their coalition partner the Nationals provided an interactive home loan calculator where voters could estimate how much higher their mortgage payments would be under a Labor government. Labor, for their part, offered a sign-up to RSS news feeds. Perhaps the most innovative use of the new technology by the major parties during the election came from a group of senior Liberal ministers who, on their own initiative, engaged Internet marketing companies to run a targeted email campaign directed at voters in their constituencies (Secombe, 2004).

A more in-depth study of site contents by Chen (2005, 2006) confirmed this picture of the smaller parties displaying more activity, although he took a less critical line toward the major parties' efforts, arguing that they ran 'sophisticated, attractive and relatively information-rich websites' (Chen, 2006, p.118). Interactive initiatives such as e-bulletin sign-up facilities, searchable candidate listings, online secure donation and joining facilities featured in most sites. While perhaps basic by U.S. standards, the consistency of the appearance of these sites did represent an improvement on 2001. Video and audio clips were also omnipresent, although most of these were embedded in the site rather than being made available for forwarding (the exception here being the Democrats' 'Lie Detector' video noted above). The adage of having too much of a good thing could be applied to the Nationals, however, who had the least user-friendly multi-media options—a campaign video taking up a huge twenty-two megabytes of bandwidth or almost half of the average monthly amount downloaded by individual subscribers (Chen, 2005, p.4).

The results of the more detailed analysis by Ward *et al* (2004) of the 110 individual candidate sites discovered in their search of the web are reported in Table 2.2. In terms of content, the main ingredients proved to be a biography and a contact email address, along with some pictures or images. Most candidates reported their stance on the main election issues along with news, both local and national. Below this baseline, however, the figures drop, both for traditional campaign activities and for more specific online activities. Concerning the former, facilities to sign up as a volunteer were offered on only one third of sites and donation and membership opportunities were even scarcer, with only one in six candidates providing this option. Surprisingly, speeches were also a relatively rare feature and online surveys were available in a minority of sites (15 percent) as were discussion boards and blogs (8 percent), sending links (5 percent) and material to distribute (4 percent).

In addition to these more standard features, Ward *et al* also examined sites for negative campaigning that they found to be a rarity; only 5 percent of candidates engaged in personal attacks of any kind toward their rivals. The use of satire and humor, while a growing phenomenon in online elections (Cornfield *et al*, 2003; Coleman and Hall, 2001), also proved rare among Australian candidates, with only 3 percent including some kind of humorous element on their websites. Overall, therefore, campaign websites were more akin to what has been described as cyber-brochures than with the heralded interactive online campaign.

Non-Party Players

Away from the parties, the election also saw a number of parody sites emerge, offering a lively diversion. Anti-Howard sites proved particularly prolific and popular, so much so that by the first week in September, a month before the election, some were registering a higher level of traffic than the Liberal Party's home page.[13] Mark Latham, the Labor leader, was also lampooned, with the delicately titled *marklathamsucks.com* providing some counter-balance to the attention lavished on the Prime Minister. In addition to the wide array of anti-party/anti-candidate sites, election-oriented material appeared from more established advocacy groups as well independent and mainstream media organizations and a growing number of bloggers. Many of these sites proved to be far more inventive than the parties in their adoption of viral techniques, promotion of genuine debate, and the use of multi-media formats to present their material (Chen, 2005; 2006).

Table 2.1 Candidates' Web Presence in the 2004 Federal Election

Party	Chamber	Estimate (percent)		
		Chen	**ACS**	**Ward & Lusoli**
Australian Labor Party	Senate	20	-	-
	House	30	-	23
	Total	-	42	-
Liberal Party	Senate	16	-	-
	House	44	-	28
	Total	-	43	-
Nationals	Senate	0	-	-
	House	33	-	42
	Total	-	64	-
Australian Democrats	Senate	17	-	-
	House	0	-	=
	Total	=	24	-
Australian Greens	Senate	0	-	-
	House	8	-	5
	Total		50	-
Other	Senate	-	-	-
	House	-	-	1
	Total		8	-
Total		-[a]	32[b]	16[c]

Notes

[a] No overall total provided.

[b] Figures based on self-reports from ALP, Liberal, National, Green, Democrat, One Nation, Family First, Citizens Electoral Coalition. Restricting figures to the first six parties (with parliamentary representation), the proportion online rises to 39 percent.

[c] Figures based on detection of an active campaign URL in House of Representatives' elections only.

Sources: 2005 Australian Candidate Study; Chen (2005); Ward, S. J., Lusoli, W. and R. K. Gibson. (2004). Unpublished data from ESRC E-Society Programme Award 'Parliamentary Representation in the Internet Age'. Award no. RES-335-25-0029.

Table 2.2 Features of Candidates' Websites

Campaign activity	Feature	%	Count
Baseline	Contact details	95	105
	Biography	92	101
	Images	97	107
Linkage	Link to national party	65	72
	Link to local party	38	42
	Links to other candidates	15	16
Campaign information	Issue positions / pledges	71	78
	Local news	64	70
	National news	63	69
	Voting information	43	47
	E-news on demand	15	17
Traditional	Volunteer	35	39
campaigning	Donate	17	19
	Join	15	16
	Speeches	13	14
	Diary / list of events	11	12
Online campaigning	Surveys / polls	15	17
	Discussion board	8	9
	Audio-video files	7	8
	Download material to distribute	4	4
	Send links from site	5	5
	Display software	2	2

Note: Percentages refer to proportion of total sites containing this feature. Counts are raw number of sites with the feature present. N = 110.

Internet Campaigning and the Electorate

While perhaps not breaking the mould, therefore, the parties were clearly making some strides to promote themselves and their programs online during the 2004 election, with the minor parliamentary parties proving the most adept. We turn now to the demand side of the campaign and the level of interest among the voters. We pose three basic questions: How many voters actually paid attention to the online campaign? Who were they? And most importantly, what effect did it have on their vote? The first question is easily addressed: since 1998, the AES has asked respondents if they followed the election on the Internet. Table 2.3 shows that following the election on the Internet has increased significantly, with the increase being broadly in line with increased Internet penetration across the population. In 1998, just 28 percent of voters had Internet access, and 5 percent of voters reported accessing election information at least once. By 2001, 59 percent were connected to the Internet, and 9 percent reported using it for election information. The 2005 election was the first election in which Internet use passed one in ten of all voters, in this case 12 percent. As we saw earlier in Table 2.2, the proportion accessing political information on the Internet in 2004 was almost on a par with those following the election on the radio.

Addressing the second and third questions (who these Internet voters are, and whether their exposure to election information on the Internet has affected their vote), is best examined in the form of two multivariate analyses. The first model predicts use of the Internet to access political information. The second model predicts the vote and adds Internet use as one of the independent variables. In terms of the explanatory variables, one set of explanations focuses on the demographic and socio-economic characteristics of voters, namely their gender, age, education and location. Despite the overall growth in the size of the Internet using population in Australia it remains the case that Internet usage is higher among younger, better educated professionals and white-collar workers (Willis and Tranter, 2006). In addition, we would expect them to be more likely to be located in urban areas, where broadband access is more easily available at a competitive price.

Table 2.3 Voters' Use of the Internet During Elections, 1998-2004
(Percent)

	1998		2001		2004	
	All	Internet access	All	Internet access	All	Internet access
Don't have Internet access	73	na	41	na	33	na
Have access, didn't use	23	84	50	86	55	82
Yes, once or twice	3	10	6	10	6	8
Yes, several occasions	1	3	2	1	3	5
Yes, many times	1	3	1	3	3	5
Total	100	100	100	100	100	100
(N)	(1,826)	(498)	(1,763)	(1,006)	(1,739)	(1,160)

Note: The question was: 'Did you make use of the Internet at all to get news or information about the 2004 federal election?' Sources: 1998-2004 AES.

Table 2.4 Use of the Internet for Election Information
(Ordinary Least Squares Regression Estimates)

	Used Internet to access election information	
	Partial	Standard
Socioeconomic Background		
Age	-.003*	-.067*
Gender (male)	.128**	.086**
Tertiary education	.097*	.052*
Urban resident	.031	.050
Patterns of Internet use		
Length of time used Internet	.023	.050
Frequency of Internet use	.115**	.200**
Election involvement		
Interested in election	.190**	.116**
Discussed politics with others	.213**	.121**
Care who won election	.023	.014
Media use		
Followed election in newspapers	.058	.068
Followed election on television	-.012	-.013
Followed election on radio	-.010	-.014
Constant	-.484	
Adjusted R-sq	.155	
(N)	(1,081)	

** p<.01, *p<.05, two-tailed.

Note: Ordinary least squares regression estimates showing partial (b) coefficient and standardized (beta) coefficients predicting use of the Internet for election information. Estimates are restricted to voters who had Internet access. Source: 2004 AES.

Certainly the evidence from rural or regional areas reported by the Australian Bureau of Statistics over time has indicated a significant geographic bias in Internet access (Curtin, 2001-2002).

A second set of explanations is associated with patterns of Internet use itself, namely the length of time that the voter had been using the Internet, and the frequency with which they use it. We would expect that the longer the time and the greater the frequency of use, the greater their skill in using the technology and the more likely they would be to use the Internet to access political information. We might also expect those who use the Internet to have greater interest in the election, and to use other means of accessing and disseminating political information. Here we include variables measuring whether or not the voter discussed politics with others, cared about who won, and the frequency with which they followed election news on the television, radio and in the newspapers.

The first model, predicting Internet use to access election information, is estimated using an ordinary least squares regression equation, since the dependent variable is nominal. The estimates in Table 2.4 show partial regression coefficients and standardized (beta) coefficients for each of the independent variables. The most important predictors are, not surprisingly, frequency of Internet use and election interest and involvement. Those who reported using the Internet frequently were significantly more likely to access the Internet for election information, as were those who were interested in the election and said that they discussed politics with others on a regular basis. Use of the traditional media during the election had no significant effect in determining whether or not the voter used the Internet. There are also consistent effects for the background variables, with males, younger voters and the university educated being more likely to use the new medium during the election. However, their overall impact is less than that for either patterns of Internet use or election involvement. Such a finding fits with other studies of online political participation in the United States and United Kingdom that have found traditional Socio-Economic Status (SES) resource models to be poor predictors once other variables tapping levels of Internet use or skills are taken into account (Krueger, 2002; Gibson *et al*, 2005a, Owen, 2005).

There are, then, distinct social, economic and behavioural groups that use the Internet. But does the use of the Internet for election information itself shape how people choose to vote, beyond these other factors? To make this estimate, Table 2.5 shows the results of a multivariate analysis among voters for the three main groupings, Labor, the Liberal-National coalition, and the Greens. Since the dependent variable has more than two categories, the appropriate technique is multinomial logistic regression. The results show parameter estimates and (parentheses) standard errors predicting three sets of contrasts in vote choice. Our most significant finding is the importance of Internet use in predicting the vote, in this case the contrast between the two major parties, Labor and the Liberal-National coalition.

Other things being equal, those who reported such Internet use were significantly more likely to vote Labor rather than for the Coalition. There is no similar effect for Internet use in the two other contrasts, between Labor and Green voters and Coalition and Green voters.

The results also show a variety of other patterns. In terms of other forms of media use, those who followed the election on television were more likely to be major party voters rather than Green voters; neither newspapers nor radio influenced the vote. Comparing following politics across the various media sources, the Internet was second only to television in political impact. Among other factors that were important in shaping the vote, Green voters were both younger and more likely to have a tertiary education than major party voters. Apart from Internet use, Labor and Coalition voters were distinguished only by Labor voters being more urban, discussing politics more frequently with others and by not caring who won the election—a reflection on their consistent trailing in the polls during the election campaign.

Table 2.5 Voting and Internet Use (Multinomial Logistic Regression Estimates)

	Labor/Green		Coalition/Green		Labor/Coalition	
	Est	(SE)	Est	(SE)	Est	(SE)
Socioeconomic Background						
Age	.025**	(.010)	.022**	(.009)	.003	(.006)
Gender (male)	.050	(.262)	.288	(.258)	-.239	(.166)
Tertiary education	-1.072**	(.264)	-1.248**	(.259)	.175	(.177)
Urban resident	.107	(.106)	-.034	(.104)	.141*	(.068)
Patterns of Internet use						
Length of time used Internet	-.073	(.104)	-.160	(.101)	.087	(.056)
Frequency of Internet use	-.060	(.111)	.026	(.109)	-.086	(.068)
Election involvement						
Interested in election	.038	(.346)	-.052	(.340)	.089	(.219)
Discussed politics with others	-.374	(.311)	-1.085**	(.309)	.710**	(.210)
Care who won election	-.378	(.302)	.707*	(.300)	-1.085**	(.195)
Media use						
Followed election in newspapers	-.154	(.182)	-.158	(.178)	.004	(.115)
Followed election on television	.617**	(.173)	.608**	(.171)	.009	(.116)
Followed election on radio	-.028	(.138)	-.206	(.136)	.177	(.092)
Used Internet for election info.	.092	(.155)	-.146	(.160)	.239*	(.118)
Constant	-.237		.724		-.962	
Nagelkerke R-sq			.176			
(N)			(813)			

** $p < .01$, *$p < .05$, two-tailed. Multinomial logistic regression showing parameter estimates and standard errors predicting three sets of contrasts between party voters. Source: 2004 AES.

How do we explain the significant effect of Internet use on the vote? We do not know from the survey what individual websites voters were accessing, so we have no way of taking into account exposure. However, three explanations are possible. First, the effect may simply be an artefact of some other, uncontrolled, factor. Since we have taken into account a wide range of other factors, it is not clear what that variable might be. Second, it could be that there was simply more pro-Labor information available on the web during the election and it proved more persuasive than the information with a pro-Coalition bias. In particular, if one compares the number of anti-Howard sites to those attacking Latham then it would appear that there was certainly more information that might appeal to the pro-ALP segment of the electorate than to Coalition supporters (Chen, 2005). Third, taking a broader view of the information that would have been available to voters over time it may be that an anti-incumbency effect is also at work here. At the time of the election the Coalition government had been in office since 1996—around the time when the web was first taking off—thus the cumulative amount of material critical of them online might be expected to be greater than that focused on Labor, particularly in relation to highly emotive and divisive topics such as Iraq and treatment of refugees and immigrants.

Conclusion

Given the 'pace-setting' role held by Australia at the turn of the twenty-first century in e-government and the overall technological readiness of its population, the idea presented at the start of this chapter that the federal election of 2004 might be a defining moment in the move toward online campaigning was perhaps not so far-fetched. As this review of the performance of the key players in that event has shown, however, the vital signs of the e-campaign among parties and candidates were on the whole rather faint. Certainly it does not appear that the country witnessed a Howard Dean-style breakthrough in terms of a candidate or party catapulting itself into public prominence through innovative uses of the new technologies. That said, some progress was made from the static approach favored in 2001, particularly among the smaller parties. Indeed, the results presented here challenge the idea that any normalization is taking place in online campaigning. While other countries may be seeing a divide opening up between the major and minor players in the quality of website production, Australia has retained a more egalitarian position on the matter. How far this balance is due to major parties' reticence, as opposed to minor parties' initiative, however, is clearly a question for future analysis. Once the major parties detect tangible returns on their investment in the new cybertools then we may see the competitive pressure on the less well-resourced organizations.

In light of the low-key approach taken by most political elites to the task of e-campaigning it is not surprising to discover the rather modest levels of interest among the Australian public in their online offerings. Nor is it surprising to find that most of those who do access election information online tend to be more politically interested, better educated and younger than the average citizen. However, it is also notable that, after factoring in all the usual political and socio-economic correlates, regular use of the Internet in itself appears to make people more likely to access election news, a finding that provides some support for the mobilizing influence of the Internet.

We are still left with a conundrum in understanding why Australian elections so far have remained relatively impervious to online campaigning. One possible explanation is that the distinctiveness of Australia's campaign environment, with its remote and vast constituencies and compulsory system of voting, discourages the widespread piloting of largely untried tools to communicate with voters. In addition, it could be that there is a stronger adherence among Australian politicians to the conventional face-to-face or 'door-stepping' style of campaigning, as it termed locally, than exists among their counterparts in other countries. Finally, while low levels of voter interest may be reflective of parties not building enticing sites, for parties to invest in any new mode of communication they also first need to perceive a popular demand for it. At present that does not appear to exist, at least not to the degree one sees in the United States, where Internet campaigning has come of age.

Notes

1. Figures from the Australian Competition and Consumer Commission (ACCC) in July 2001 estimated the number broadband customers to be only 122,800 (less than 1 percent of the adult population). By 2004-2005 this had increased exponentially, with Australian Bureau of Statistics (ABS) estimates reporting the number of households with broadband access to be just over one million (1.2 million). OECD statistics confirm the great leap forward with estimates of 0.8 broadband subscribers for every 100 inhabitants in 2001 rising to 7.7 by 2004. See OECD Broadband Statistics 2004 available at <http://www.oecd.org/document/60/0,2340,en_2825_495656_2496764_1_1_1_1,00.html#data2004>. Accessed on 19 June 2006. Democrats working on vBlogging, 17 August 2005.

2. As Goot (1985, p.179) puts it, "in no other liberal democracy, it seems safe to say, have the permutations and combinations of electoral reform been as great."

3. Free airtime is also available on the Special Broadcasting Service (SBS), which is also government funded.

4. Estimates are from australianpolitics.com, an information/archive site run by Mr. Malcolm Farnsworth, a school teacher from Victoria since 1996. Archived material on candidate sites available at <www.australianpolitics.com/elections/2001/websites.shtml>. Accessed on 25/04/06. For the total number of candidates nominated see Behind the Scenes: The 2001 Election Report Published by the Australian Electoral Commission, Canberra. 2002. Available at <http://www.aec.gov.au/_content/When/elections/2001/bts/04noms.pdf p.11>. Accessed 2 May 2006.

5. The ACS has been conducted in all federal elections since 1987 (except 1998) and is based on a self-completion, post-election mail questionnaire sent to all

candidates from the major parties as well as a selection of significant minor parties (i.e. with parliamentary representation, i.e. the ALP, Liberals, Nationals, Greens and One Nation). (Gibson *et al*, 2005a).

6. See <http://www.active.org.au/>.
7. Quoted in: Maley, J. 2004. "I surf and I vote", *Sydney Morning Herald*, 3 July, p.27.
8. The higher AES estimates can be explained by the fact that the question is not time-specific about when individuals used the Internet and simply asks if they have access to the Internet.
9. See ABS Report, 8146.0 House Use of Information Technology, Australia, 2004-05 Released 15 December 2005. Australian Bureau of Statistics, Canberra. Available at <http://www.abs.gov.au/Ausstats/abs@.nsf/0/acc2d18cc958bc7bca2568a9001393ae? OpenDocument>. Accessed 19 June 2006.
10. See Behind the Scenes: The 2001 Election Report p. 11 Published by the Australian Electoral Commission, Canberra (2002). Available at <http://results.aec.gov.au/12246/ pdf/BehindTheScenes.pdf>. Accessed 3 May 2006.
11. Ward, S. J, Lusoli, W. and R. K. Gibson. (2004). Unpublished data from a UK Economic and Social Research Council (ESRC) study 'Parliamentary Representation in the Internet Age'. Award No RES-335-25-0029. Available at www.i-pol.org.
12. ACS figures are based on self-reported data from the candidates and thus are susceptible to over-reporting. The estimates produced by Chen, and Ward *et al* were gathered by independent use of search engines and listings from party homepages—which can lead to under-reporting. The alternative methods of data collection also mean that the size of the population used to calculate the final reported figure differs significantly. Both Ward *et al* and Chen's calculations are based on the entire universe of candidates in the election, whereas the ACS relies on a much smaller sample (n =535) of candidates that chose to return the questionnaire. Even allowing for the differences in data collection and methods of calculation, however, it is clear that the ACS figures for Green candidates' sites are still far higher than those reported in the other studies. One possible explanation for this inflation may be that Green candidates viewed their well-developed individual pages on the party site as constituting their own campaign site, despite the questionnaire item referring specifically to a personally owned and operated election website.
13. "Crunching the numbers", *The Australian*, 23 September 2004, p.20.

Chapter Three

Singapore: Elections and the Internet—Online Activism and Offline Quiescence

Randolph Kluver

Singapore's relationship with the Internet and the potential impact of information technology for its political status quo have been the subject of numerous studies and international observation (Rodan, 1998; Kluver, 2005; Open Net Initiative, 2005). The contrast between the nation's obvious economic and diplomatic openness and the relatively closed political system illustrates the ambivalent relationship between technological sophistication and political openness that had been assumed just a few years ago (Becker and Slaton, 2000). Most previous analysis has demonstrated that the introduction of information technology has had little discernible impact on the way in which politics happens in Singapore, and has not significantly weakened the power held by the ruling party, the People's Action Party (PAP).

In an earlier study of the 2001 Singapore General Election, I examined the ways in which Singapore's political parties deployed information technologies, and particularly the extent to which the parties utilized their full technological potential to reach Singapore's voters (Kluver, 2004). At that time, the Internet was still something of a novelty in the political domain, although it had certainly become a major part of many Singaporeans' lives. Still, its political potential was such that the Parliament updated its elections laws to account for the various ways in which the technology might be deployed.

In the fall of 2005, another election was called, this time for the presidency. Given the unique nature of Singapore's political system (see below), however, out of the four candidates, only one, the incumbent S. R. Nathan, was declared eligible to stand in the election by the Presidential Election Commission, thus precipitating a walkover, with Nathan declared the president for another term as soon as he had submitted his declaration of candidacy. As a result, there was no official "campaign period," as there wasn't actually a campaign. During the brief period between the announcement of the election and Nomination Day, however, Singaporeans used the Internet as a mechanism for political discussion and debate that was quite novel, making the online political activity actually much more interesting than the actual offline election.

Four years is a short time in Singapore's political culture, but encompasses vast change in the use of technology in electoral campaigns. New technologies, including blogs, podcasts, and instant messaging systems have become much more popular, and many of these have political relevance and usage. The 2004 election cycle demonstrated the novel use of technology in campaigns in places such as South Korea and the United States. Moreover, Singapore's population has begun to use information technologies to comment more widely upon issues of public significance, making the Internet more politically important than it was in 2001. It is appropriate, therefore, to re-examine the way in which the Internet has become integrated into the political life of Singapore and, particularly, how the Internet was used during the 2005 Presidential Election.

This chapter, then, will examine how the Internet is deployed by the major political actors in Singapore, including its citizenry. I will first review recent findings regarding the impact of the Internet in Singapore, then turn to an analysis of new technological and political developments since the 2001 General Election. Finally, I will examine the ways in which the Internet was deployed during the 2005 Presidential Election, with a particular emphasis on the ways in which Singapore's citizens enacted the rituals of democracy online, even though there was no offline contest for the presidency. I will argue that the Internet has been utilized for political purposes far more effectively by traditionally non-politicized citizens than by the normal political players in Singapore—namely, the political parties. This case study provides an insight into the potential of the Internet to provide a context for political discussion, even in a non-competitive political environment.

The Campaign Environment

Political communication, no matter what its format, is greatly constrained within Singapore, and is regulated by a number of different legal provisions that, in many ways, guarantee the government "considerable influence over the operation of the mass media" (Kuo *et al*, 1993). As Kuo and his co-authors state, the relationship between the state and the media means that the media refrain from negative coverage of the state, in the name of development and state-building, and the state guarantees a near monopoly for the media outlets for information (1993, p.7).

There are a number of laws that actually constrain political communication in Singapore, including the Newspaper and Printing Presses Act, which mandates that any publication that would contain political information must obtain a license from the Media Development Authority (MDA, no date). Moreover, the Films Act prevents the production, distribution, or reproduction of "party political films," with a penalty of a fine up to S$ 100,000 (US$ 60,860) or jail for up to two years (Films Act, Chapter 107). This ban effectively eliminates of all visual political media, including television commercials. In 2005, a documentary about one of Singapore's opposition leaders was found to violate this Act, thus preventing the showing of the film at the Singapore International Film Festival. In response, political activists lodged a police report against the government-linked broadcaster Channel News Asia, complaining that the all-news channel violated the Films Act by showing pro-PAP documentaries (See, 2005).

Other laws are used to control media that might be critical of governmental policy. Foreign media, such as newspapers or magazines, are constrained by the ability of the government to limit or even ban the dissemination of media that the government determined have been interfering in the domestic politics of Singapore, which damages advertising and subscription revenues. One high profile example of this was when the government limited the distribution of *Time* magazine in 1986, when distribution was cut from seventeen thousand to just two thousand copies (Rodan, 2004, p.28). Another mechanism that is frequently used is the Public Entertainment Act, which prohibits the assembly of more than five persons in a public outdoor place without a permit from the police (Samydorai, 2005).

Finally, but perhaps most significantly, political actors are constrained by the application of libel laws. Opposition politicians and foreign media have both found that the libel laws can be an extremely effective way of silencing criticism (Ellis, 2002). Other mechanisms that are rarely used, but presumably remain open to the government include the Internal Security Act, which provides for indefinite arrest, and the Sedition Act, which seeks to limit any potential action that could harm the interests of the state.

All of these mechanisms mean that Singapore has kept a very tight lid on political discourse, in spite of the fact that there is presumably a tension between Singapore's semi-authoritarianism and its technological and social sophistication (Kuo *et al*, 1993; Rodan, 2004). What many analysts miss, though, is that Singapore's approach is not an unsophisticated and heavy-handed hammer to batter down criticism. The reality is far more complex, in that modernization seems to have actually given the government a better understanding of how to control critical media while still building an economically and culturally sophisticated country. As George (2005) argues, Singapore's handling of the press is both sophisticated and effective, a form of "calibrated coercion." George goes on to argue that the legal framework is only part of the overall dynamic, however, but the more important factor is the

> quality of political judgment that has maintained . . . a dynamic equilibrium that balances the political interests of the PAP government, the profit motives of publishers, the professional and pecuniary needs of journalists, and the public's demand for information and analysis (2005, p.14).

In fact, George argues that Lee Kuan Yew, Singapore's first prime minister, "recognized that he merely needed to tweak it's [the media's] incentive structure and install the right barriers" (2005, p.16).

The Singapore government's position when facing criticism of this tight control of the Internet remains consistent: that absolute freedom of speech is a Western concept that does not resonate with the Asian values of the city state, and is a luxury which Singapore's delicate political and racial balance cannot risk. Lee Kuan Yew, who remains active in politics, stated in 2001 that an open media presented a threat to the nation because it meant that the government might indeed lose its ability to put forth its own point of view in the cacophony of voices, and thus limit its ability to govern effectively (Kluver and Ang, 2004). The government remains concerned that unlimited political speech could present a real threat to racial and social harmony, and so has a right to limit potentially disruptive speech. Moreover, the government argues that the vehicles of mass political opinion in developed Western democracies, such as slogans, television commercials, and the like, actually weaken democracy by trivializing politics and discouraging critical thought. In an interview, current Prime Minister Lee Hsien Loong argued that the government was attempting to continue to provide greater political openness while maintaining "serious" politics:

> But at the same time you don't want your politics to become trivialized or glamorized. You want it to be a serious matter. People sit down and think about it, not just watch something and get excited (Strait Times, 2005, p.H4).

Indeed, a number of Western analysts, while not condoning the stance of Singapore's governments, have come to similar conclusions. Meyer and Hinchman, for example, argue that in the context of "media colonism," "political power tends to be embodied in the triangular recursive relation between the top political actors with media charisma, the media and permanent polling. Political deliberation and participation are losing relevance" (2002, p.117). Norris reviews the literature presuming a "media malaise hypothesis," or the argument that "public disenchantment with the political process is due, at least in part, to the process of political communications," and finds that it has become an "unquestioned orthodoxy" (2000, p.5), although she herself rejects the argument. My point is not to argue whether Singapore's government is correct or not, but merely to point out that there is serious academic thought that would make much the same argument, and that thus the government's perspective should be considered seriously.

The Development of Internet Campaigning

Given this context of political control over political communication, it is clear why Singapore is an interesting case study of the interaction between advanced telecommunications technologies and political development. The nation has an advanced technological infrastructure and a strong commitment from the government to increase the role of information technologies in the life of citizens. However, as a number of observers have noted, the actual impact of the Internet on the semi-authoritarian government has been quite limited (Banerjee and Yeo, 2003; Kluver, 2004; Kluver and Banerjee, 2005; Rodan, 1998).

In a number of other Asian nations, the Internet has proved to be a powerful tool for electoral campaigning, in at least three key ways: as a symbol of technological modernity, as an instrument of mobilization of party and candidate supporters, and as a tool of outreach for new voters. Moreover, in many Asian nations, utilizing information technology such as the Internet or SMS messages sends a sign of modernization. This symbolic power is significant even in nations where Internet diffusion is still low, such as the Philippines or Thailand, even though a web presence will not translate into many direct votes.

In Singapore, however, the Internet has had a remarkably muted impact on political campaigns. This is not for lack of trying, as civil society and opposition groupings have attempted to deploy the Internet to introduce a broad range of political reforms. In particular, civil society groups have used the Internet for purposes of mobilization and outreach, and believe to some extent that the Internet allows them to gain a greater reach, outside the normal controls of the media (Gomez, 2002; Lee, B., 2005). Moreover, as Soon (2004) has demonstrated, political entities use their web pages to form a sort of "community" of political and civic-oriented groupings in Singapore, by using hyperlinks to establish affinity.

To return to George (2005), he argues that the government's main tool in the battle for media control is not only the use of laws and regulations, but rather a strategic and shrewd use the equilibrium between the political interests of the PAP government, the profit motives of publishers, the professional and pecuniary needs of journalists, and the public's demand for information and analysis. New media technologies do indeed upset this delicate balance, as the Internet bypasses or makes irrelevant some of these concerns, thus negating their role in political information. In particular, the professional interests of journalists and the profit motives of publishers do not really feature in the new dynamic.

In the new media era, then, the government is left with only its harshest tools: specifically, legal measures to control information on the Internet. The question arises, then, to what extent does information technology change the political dynamics in the nation? Perhaps surprisingly, given the factors mentioned above, it seems very little. Several studies have identified several key factors that work to limit the ability of the Internet to have a marked impact on Singaporean politics. First of all, although the Internet does to some extent resist control, the government has enacted a system whereby Internet content is controlled through both fear of litigation and government scrutiny. A number of studies have examined the way in which the system of Internet regulation in Singapore diminishes the potential impact of the Internet, and it is important to summarize briefly those findings (Kluver and Ang, 2004; Kluver, 2005; Rodan, 1998).

Singapore's basic stance toward Internet censorship consists of what the Media Development Authority (MDA) calls a "light touch" approach, in that a symbolic list of one hundred sites is blocked, and self-regulation is encouraged within the Internet industry itself. In fact, a recent study by the Open Net Initiative based at Harvard University found that actual censorship within Singapore is "extremely minimal," as only eight sites from an extensive list were found to be blocked, and the blocked sites were primarily pornographic. Surprisingly perhaps, that study found that there was no blocking of politically sensitive sites, including Islamic extremist sites. It is important to note that the list of sites used by the ONI was a global list, rather than a Singapore specific list, which might have included a narrower range of specifically political sites. The authors of that study do, however, acknowledge that the government of Singapore is able to minimize the potential threat from the Internet by focusing on access controls (requiring registration of political websites) and legal pressure, including utilizing existing laws against defamation to create an atmosphere where political content is unlikely to be posted on the Internet (Open Net Initiative, 2005).

In fact, politically-oriented websites in Singapore are regulated by the government through a process of registration. Media Development Authority guidelines state specifically that "Content providers who engage in the propagation, promotion or discussion of political issues relating to Singapore on World Wide Web (www) through the Internet are required to be registered with MDA" (Registration of Internet Class Licensees, no date). The supposed objective of registering political websites is to ensure the accountability of those who run politically-oriented websites.

When a site has been gazetted as a "political website" by the MDA, then the owner of the site becomes legally liable for any content that might appear on the site, and can then be prosecuted for the posting of illegal content, or held financially accountable in cases of libel. This regulation led to the closure of one of the most well-known politically-oriented websites, Sintercom, in 2001 (Tan, 2001). Thus, there is a marked incentive for website owners to avoid political content, so as to avoid additional governmental scrutiny. One famous satirical website, talkingcock.com, has a disclaimer on its front page proclaiming that it is a humor site, emphatically denying that it is a "political website," even though most of the articles consist of political satire.

In 2001, just in time for the General Election, as part of a revision of the Parliamentary Elections Law (PEL), the laws governing Internet campaigning were amended to further define what was allowed. There was a positive benefit of this amendment, as it specifically allowed content such as political manifestos, announcements of campaign rallies, or recruiting, thus bringing some clarity to a previously murky set of rules. However, the amended PEL also spelled out a number of uses of technology that would be disallowed, such as online fundraising or the use of online polling (for a further discussion of these laws, see Kluver, 2005).

The application of laws that govern offline media to online content, such as laws on libel, is probably the most effective form of limiting political speech on the Internet. For example, just a few months before the August 2005 presidential campaign period, a Singaporean studying abroad posted content to his personal blog that was critical of the policies of a certain statutory board, and its CEO. The student was threatened with a lawsuit by the official, and forced to remove the comments and a promise to never post such material again. This case generated a significant amount of attention, particularly among Singaporean bloggers, many of whom had begun tentative explorations of the social and political potential of the blog.

A second significant factor that limits the ability of the Internet to achieve a significant political impact has to do with Singapore's own political culture, in which the citizenry has largely been "de-politicized" (Banerjee and Yeo, 2003), and in which citizens are hesitant to engage in political discussion. Moreover, Singapore's political culture stresses the formal aspects of politics, and the combination of an aggressive ruling party and restrictive regulations prevents citizens from engaging in political discussions online (Kluver, 2005).

This is reinforced by findings from surveys that show that, generally speaking, Singaporeans do not believe that the Internet will enable them to have greater political empowerment. Findings from the Singapore Internet Project showed that only about 14 percent of Singaporeans, both Internet users and nonusers, believed that the Internet would give citizens greater political power. Moreover, over half of the users were concerned about the impact of uncensored political content, and almost 64 percent felt that the government should take a role in regulating the Internet (Kuo *et al*, 2002). What all of these indicate is that there is some public apprehension about a "politicized" Internet, and support for government regulation.

A third significant factor limiting the impact of the Internet on Singapore's politics is perhaps a bit more mundane, but it is germane. Singapore's opposition parties, in fact, do not make good use of the information technology, and in spite of recognizing the potential, the offline organizational and political weaknesses of the opposition parties and civil society organizations translate into a seeming inability to use effectively new media technologies. In the 2001 General Election, for example, the ruling PAP made far better use of available technologies, and incorporated interactive features such as online forums to a far greater degree than did the opposition parties (Kluver, 2005).

In summary, then, the role of the Internet in Singapore's political processes has been limited. Governmental oversight and regulation, a depoliticized citizenry, and a weak opposition means that the Internet has played a marginal role up to this point in adding any significant new dimension to the election cycle. The next section of this chapter will examine the ways in which the Internet has been deployed, especially during the 2005 Presidential election.

The Internet in the 2005 Presidential Election

In the Republic of Singapore's Westminster-model parliamentary system, the office of the president serves as the symbolic head of state, and also has some constitutionally mandated duties, including watching over the nation's reserves. Regardless of this, there are a number of very stringent requirements for the presidency, the uppermost being a requirement that a candidate have extensive experience as either a senior civil servant or the CEO of a publicly listed company with a paid up capital of at least S$ 100 million (approximately US$ 60 million), or to have similar qualifications. The candidates are also expected to be Singaporeans, at least forty-five years old, and, significantly, not a member of a political party, including the ruling PAP. An individual's eligibility is decided upon by a three-person committee, the Presidential Election Committee (PEC), which evaluates applications for candidacy and then issues a certificate of eligibility to those candidates that it finds meet these tests.

What this means is that very few people can meet these criteria, as it is likely that no more than about six hundred people meet this test.[1] This test became instrumental in the 2005 election, as only four candidates put themselves forward as competitors during the pre-qualification period, and of the three newcomers, only one, Andrew Kuan, came anywhere close to meeting the criteria, although he had been neither in the civil service nor a CEO. In the end, the PEC determined that Kuan, in fact, did not have the qualifications to run, effectively short-circuiting the election.

Thus, on Nomination Day, the incumbent, S. R. Nathan, was easily returned to another six-year term without any electoral challenge. In fact, it was the second time out of three terms since the office came into being that there was no contest for the presidency (Peh and Rajan, 2005), thus prompting a significant online debate about how politics in Singapore was engineered. Although the government argued that it was better to have the "right candidate" than a competitive election, this argument seemed to be merely a rear-guard argument to deflect criticism, and many were angered at what they saw as the short-circuiting of the electoral process in Singapore. Thus, the 2005 election for president ended with a whimper, as no campaign was necessary. However, although there was no offline democratic exercise in the selection process, and traditional media were constrained by the existing set of controls to keep outright dissent to a minimum, the Internet became an important tool for Singaporeans to engage in the most significant political issue of the period in a way that did not exist in the offline forums.

By the time of the 2005 election season, a number of new information technologies had become integrated into the Singapore political Internet. Traditional activities, such as instant messaging and forums, continued to draw significant attention, but newer applications, such as blogging and podcasting, had also become well known. Generally speaking, the use of the Internet by parties and candidates had not progressed markedly beyond that of the 2001 General Election. In contrast, there had been a significant rise in the use of media such as blogs, or web logs, where citizens could post their thoughts on issues of significance. Here we examine how the traditional political entities, primarily the political parties, have attempted to update their own use of information technology, and how non-politicized Internet users, by deliberately obscuring the boundaries between the personal and political, have largely been able to avoid the scrutiny of the government. I will focus on party websites, as current restrictions prohibit individual candidate websites, although as I will show, it is possible for individual politicians to have non-partisan websites.

Singapore's political parties clearly do realize the value of harnessing information technology for political purposes, but this rarely translates into effective online action, except in the case of the ruling PAP. By 2005, the PAP and the Workers Party (WP) had both redesigned and updated their webpages to present a much more modern image. I have already argued that the PAP made more use of its website than any other political party in Singapore in the 2001 General Election, and this remains true at the time of writing. The redesigned website still primarily provides information about the party, and the key interactive feature, an online forum (actually hosted on the website of the party's youth wing, the Young PAP), does generate a significant amount of activity, including postings critical of the PAP itself.

By contrast, Singapore's opposition parties seem to have difficulty executing any strategy for web-based politics. Although the parties all articulate an expectation of using the Internet to get around the PAP's dominance of traditional media, they also tend to seem quite naïve in their approaches to technology, as illustrated by a number of mundane errors. The Singapore Democratic Party (SDP), for example, had to change its URL several years ago, as the original URL for the party was hijacked by a pornographic site, and later turned into a generic search engine.

In August of 2005, the SDP promised to roll out "Radio SDP," or a full Internet radio broadcast. The press release declared that this technology would enable them to bypass further the systems of control that the government and ruling party had placed on traditional media, and thus make them a more effective opposition party. The press release indicated that the party would fully utilize the new outlet, but without much sense of what was coming. What was then posted was a two-and-a-half-minute MP3 file of the party chief, Chee Soon Juan, in a short speech stating the party's core positions. A week later, a Chinese version of the same speech was released. The fact that the party got extensive coverage in all of Singapore's major media, including the *Straits Times*, Channel News Asia, Radio Singapore, etc.—the same outlets which the SDA declared were under the thumb of the government—served to undermine the party's claims, in that it drove significant traffic to the website.

However, although the SDP had promised a podcast, the site provided no mechanism for a podcast feed, or the ability to subscribe to the podcast. Thus, in order to access the file, a user would have to go to the site, find the file, download it to a hard drive, then either listen to the file at a desktop or load it to a portable device. The entire process would take about as long as the broadcast itself, if someone knew what they were doing. Moreover, in spite of announcements at the website announcing that there was international interest in syndicating the content, there seems to be little attempt to carry through. In addition to the introductory message, on 15 August 2005, the SDP provided at least one follow-up podcast, the same message in Chinese by Chee Soon Juan, the party's leader. Another posting later in August featured a telephone interview with a Bangkok-based advocate for civil disobedience. By the time of Election Day, however, the party had not used the podcast to discuss the election at all.

The SDP also promised a videoblog, or vblog, but as of early 2006, no content had appeared.[2] Ultimately, the tinkering with technology creates an appearance of amateurism, which is an impression that the opposition parties seem to carry with them in a number of other contexts.

Other opposition bodies also have failed adequately to deploy the available technology. The Chair of the National Solidarity Party (NSP), non-constituency MP Steve Chia, once declared that his constituency is the Internet, and he would be the "Internet MP," by using the technology to connect to the people (Lim, 2003). It is almost inexplicable, therefore, how the party allowed its domain name registration to lapse, after which it quickly turned into an anonymous search engine (Figure 3.1). Chia's fascination with technology later got him into serious political trouble when his wife reported to the police that she had found sexually-oriented digital photos of Chia and their maid on their home computer (Nadarajan, 2003). Regardless of this incident, the fact that Chia's party allowed the party's domain name to be taken over demonstrates that although the opposition says that it will utilize the Internet for serious politics, it seems a lower priority.

Perhaps the opposition party that has paid the most attention to the role of the Internet as a device for elections has been the Workers Party (WP) (www.wp.org.sg), which, like the PAP, maintains a website in each of the four official languages of Singapore. The WP positions itself as a leftist party, and identifies itself as a member of the social democratic movement. The WP had a fairly limited website during the 2001 election, but since that time it has been dramatically improved, with a better design and much more extensive content, including frequent updates and articles reprinted from the WP magazine, *The Hammer*. In addition, the party site has a number of interactive features, including email addresses for all party officials and office holders, a youth wing site, and separate sites for geographical electoral regions.

When the WP site is considered along with the presence of individually maintained websites by party members, it is clear that the party has made a major commitment to Internet-based campaigning. One party official, James Gomez, maintains an extensive website of his own, with a number of his speeches and writings. Interestingly, although Gomez is a member of the WP Central Committee, there is only one link to the WP webpage, and it would be possible to read entirely through the site and never spot the affiliation with the WP. Another party official, Goh Meng Seng, maintains a prominent blog, although he is careful to distinguish the views expressed on the blog from those of the WP, and has an explicit disclaimer on his blog. In spite of the fact that these officers keep some distance between their personal and political websites, however, it is quite clear that the personal sites are marked by support from the liberalizing political tendencies of the WP.

The other opposition parties, however, have much more limited websites. Although the Singapore People's Party (SPP) has redesigned its website and provided more content, and provided a number of new features, such as the ability to join the party, it still has a decidedly amateurish look, with many broken links. The Singapore Democratic Alliance, an umbrella gathering of a number of the different opposition parties, still doesn't have its own URL, but instead has one page on the SPP site. The PKMS, a Malay-based political party, still has a primitive website hosted on geocities.com.

In summary, Singapore's political parties have had different responses to the advent of information technology. Three parties have put up near professional quality websites, while some of the other parties seem to consider an Internet presence superfluous to their purposes. Among the active cyber-campaigners, the PAP still maintains the most extensive website, with the greatest amount of information. Unlike in the 2001 election, though, the WP has created a much more appealing website, and the SDP has also attempted to use new technological features to overcome the perceived media advantages of the PAP.

More important than the party sites, however, were individually driven web applications, such as blogs. For example, after the deadline for submission of candidate applications for the presidency, and prior to Nomination Day, the proposed candidate Andrew Kuan did in fact create a website which he attempted to use to introduce himself to Singaporeans (http://www.andrewkuan.com). The website had material in all four official languages, and primarily summarized Kuan's professional and political experience, as well as providing photographs of the candidate in activities such as eating, roller-blading, and meeting with other citizens. In line with the ban on "candidate" websites, the site actually did not mention his candidacy for the presidency, nor did it articulate any particular political vision. Moreover, the site contained no links to any other website that would indicate political affiliation. After the election, the only mention of the candidacy was a statement thanking all those who supported his candidacy.

Figure 3.1 Original National Solidarity Party URL (now used as search engine)

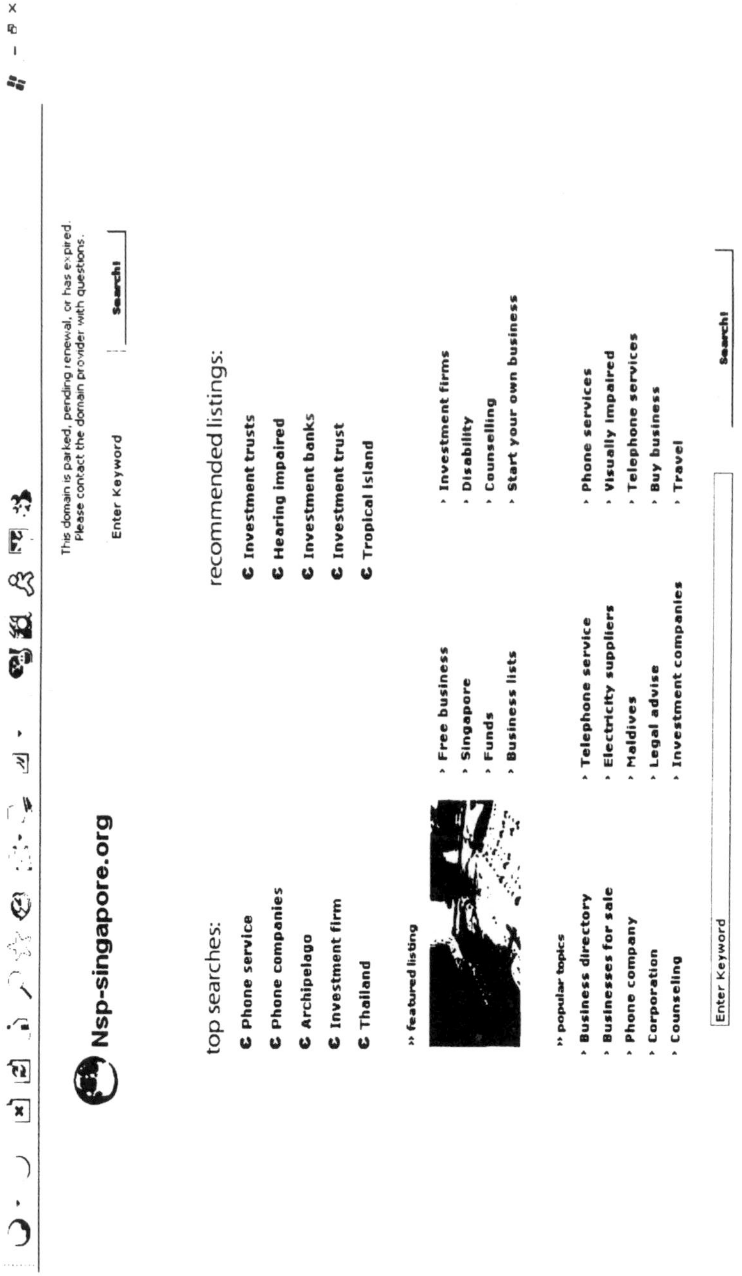

Kuan also added personal responses to criticisms that had been made of him in the press by former employers.

If Kuan's website didn't provide any ability to engage citizens, others did use the Internet to endorse his candidacy. Anonymous posters created a petition to support his candidacy at an online petition site (http://www.petitiononline.com/sg050817/), which garnered several hundred "signatures," although many of the signatures were not statements of support, but typical comments and banter, much of it unflattering to the candidate himself or his supporters. In addition, a number of forums, mailing lists, and bloggers supported Kuan's candidacy.

2005 also saw a marked rise in the role of blogs in Singaporean life and politics. The first blogs began around 1997 as typical websites, but around 2000, more Singaporeans began to blog, and in April of 2002, the *Straits Times*, Singapore's main newspaper, ran an article on blogs, the first in Singapore's media (blogtimeline.sg). After the Asian tsunami of 2004, the value of blogs as vehicles for commentary or information became evident, and one of the most important Singapore blogs started out as a resource of information about the tsunami. In June of 2005, a prominent personal blogger who had been known for her sexually-oriented blog, Sarong Party Girl, posted nude pictures of herself, generating a tremendous amount of publicity, and drawing large media coverage of the phenomenon of blogs.

In June of 2004, the government had obviously realized the growing importance of blogs and incorporated five bloggers to write about their experiences in chronicling the National Day Parade scheduled for August. One prominent member of parliament, Penny Low, started her own blog, and stated in an interview that the reason was to allow her to "better understand the psyche and dynamics of the younger generation."[3] Her blog is primarily personal in nature, chronicling her travels and other events, but avoiding explicitly political content (Low, no date).

The *Straits Times* between January and August of 2005 published over fifty-eight separate news articles that highlighted or commented upon the power of blogs, detailing their utility in education, politics, and personal interests, in addition to publishing excerpts from blogs, sometimes Singapore-based, but often based overseas. Media coverage suggested a certain skepticism of the intrinsic value of blogging, but a belief that the phenomenon would grow. Several popular bloggers were able to transfer their online presence into actual columns in local newspapers. For example, Benjamin Lee, whose blog is known widely as "Mr. Miyagi," was able to secure a regular column in the *Today* newspaper. In August of 2005, blogs had become so thoroughly integrated into Singaporean life that a General Paper question for a local A-level examination was "Blogging and podcasting have little worth beyond allowing the individual to indulge in narcissistic exhibitionism. Do you agree?" (Blog Timeline.sg, no date).

Two particular events, however, served more than any other to illustrate the political danger and opportunity presented by blogs. The first was the threat in

April 2005 to sue for libel a Singaporean blogger by an official of A*STAR, an official statutory board. This event, which came to be known as the "Caustic Soda affair" after the name of the blog, demonstrated that government officials did in fact pay attention to blog postings, and the laws that applied to other media would also be enforced in this context. The particulars of the case were not inherently political, but the postings did in fact question the policies and outcomes of a government body. What this case did, though, was to demonstrate that the government considered blogs as a medium that needed to be monitored. The blogger did, in fact, remove the blog and post an apology to the head of A*Star, but quickly set up a new blog.

The second event had its origins in a defamation lawsuit against the *Straits Times* by the head of one of Singapore's largest charities, the National Kidney Foundation (NKF). During the trial, information damaging to the NKF and its chairman came to light, which raised a number of questions about the financial status of the foundation and the salary of the CEO, and bloggers quickly began to post and comment upon this information. Eventually, an online petition calling for his dismissal generated over forty thousand signatures. The *Straits Times* ran an article attributing the credit to the bloggers, rather than its own news coverage: "Online forums were, after all, where much of the discussion gathered pace following the disclosures in court" (Jacob, 2005).

The significance of both of these events was that they illustrated the ways in which the Internet could, in fact, provide a relatively open forum for political discussion, in spite of government scrutiny, and how the government signaled its intention to continue to monitor the potential political impact of the Internet. In fact, the primary means of control, the law, depends upon fairly strict and well-understood definitions of what is "political." As the code of practice defines "political" as supporting a political party, what about websites that are not about parties at all, but do engage in political questions?

In fact, it is the ambiguity of what a blog is that has probably made it a device for greater civic debate to Singapore's politics. Here, I will give three examples of the ways in which this ambiguity has been exploited, all for the purposes of commenting upon politics in a way that is not overtly "political." In the first case, a blogger who identifies himself as "Mr Wang" recounted that he had received an email from a student asking if he had ever been contacted by the SBA and asked to register the blog as a political website. "My answer was no, the SBA has not contacted me. And I further added that if the SBA ever contacted me to register, I would immediately close down this blog. Then I would start a new blog. Under yet another user ID, of course. It's not like this is really anything new to me. Expressing an opinion in Singapore has always been a tricky affair" ("Mr Wang says so," 2005).

Another prominent blog that illustrates this tension well is the "Pilot and Jo Show," which describes itself as a "complete bang-up of a podcast featuring rants, raves and diatribes about life, love, pop culture and living in Singapore by two maladjusted individuals who have no business spouting their opinions to anyone, let alone a worldwide audience." In late August, the blog featured an interview with Chee Soon Juan, a well-known opposition figure, in a podcast entitled "Imagine." In an online discussion in the comments section of the posting, an anonymous poster raised the question of the legality of the action. The poster, who identified himself as a "Dr. Richard Lim," posted a somewhat friendly warning to the bloggers to remove the content, in order to avoid having to register as a political website. In the ensuing comments, other participants openly criticized Dr. Lim, and he himself responded in an increasingly stronger tone that the interview must be removed, with one posting saying "As a concerned citizen, I advise you to (1) register your website as a political website, (2) cease and desist distribution of all abovementioned and upcoming multimedia content, and (3) delete all unsanctioned comments and follow-ups by the public" (Pilot and Jo Show, 2005).

Finally, the blurring of the personal and political and the ambiguity of trying to regulate political speech is illustrated by a posting by a non-political blogger, "Jayce," who began a post on 6 September 2005 by stating how much she loved her country, and her government:

> About governments, they are darn effective.. from a nothing to something on the world map, that's not something everyone can do.. and look at the SARS period and see how we handled the whole situation?? everything was handled professionally and with such speed and efficiency . . . when the push comes to shove, we have the means to handle it. And that is really thanks to our government. So thank you PAP for doing such a great job (Jayce, 2005).

However, even in this idyllic situation, the author used her blog to question the political realities of the presidential election, based on her own experience:

> Talkin about the presidential election, I was watching the talkshow on channel u [A Chinese language channel] on friday and this guy brought up something which I found a very good idea.. that is, even if there is only one candidate running for presidency, we should still be allowed to vote . . . the voting results will show just how popular the candidate is, and how worthy we think he is . . . He's gonna be our president, we should have a say in deciding if he should stay there or not. Else why make voting complusory? If one does not want to hear our voices, why make voting a must? (Jayce, 2005)

This blog entry presents an interesting quandary in regulating these more expressive media. These political comments come in the middle of typical blog comments about new cars, psychological tests, teddy bears, new restaurants in Singapore, and dates with her boyfriend. The political suggestion is tentative, non-confrontational, but speaks directly to the heart of political legitimacy in the nation. Moreover, were the government to try to gazette the site as a "political site" in the midst of the clear context, it would ultimately have to prosecute Jayce's strong statement of approval for the PAP.

To return to the question of the value of the Internet during the election period, it is clear that the Internet served as the primary, if not the only, platform for the pro-election camp, by which I mean those Singaporeans who argued that regardless of Nathan's qualifications, a competitive election should have been held. In fact, online platforms began to influence the reporting in the mainstream press, if only by setting the agenda. In the Tan editorial noted above, for instance, the author argued that the "vicious diatribes" on the Internet are no substitute for actually engaging in the political process, and inadvertently called attention to the role of the Internet in allowing dissenting voices to occur: "They cannot snipe behind the anonymity of chat rooms and unaudited, online polls" and expect genuine candidates to emerge. Instead, they should have "harnessed the Internet to appeal to the conscience of well-qualified Singaporeans, use the scope of the Net to draw up shortlists and then cajole, beg, and try to win them over with sensible arguments as to why Mr. Nathan should have competition" (Tan, 2001).

All of these events illustrate the ways in which various Internet technologies were deployed during the election period, and the ways in which political leaders and the media perceived the role of the Internet within the political landscape of the nation, giving credence to many who felt that the Internet was finally ushering in the long-awaited political opening. More recent events, however, have illustrated the very tenuous relationship that the Internet has in Singapore's political scene, and that the government is resolved to keep tight control over politically significant discourse.

On 12 September 2005, two men in Singapore were charged under the Sedition Act for online comments that were deemed by the public prosecutor to be racist, and thus politically inflammatory. One of the men had posted the comments to his own blog, while the other made comments that were deemed insulting to Muslim Malays on a forum on a dog-lovers website. Several days later, another was charged for comments also made on a blog. The Sedition Act, which explicitly prohibits actions that "promote feelings of ill-will and hostility between different races or classes of the population of Singapore" (Sedition Act, 3.1), includes the uttering or publishing of any seditious words. Thus, the charges were brought against the two men on the grounds that racist speech is inherently threatening to Singapore's racial and religious harmony. Eventually, the two men charged were given short jail terms and fined.

It is appropriate, however, to examine the response within Singapore to the charges, and to speculate on what this means for the role of the Internet in Singapore. In particular, I will comment upon the responses to the events of firstly, the government, and secondly the blogging community in Singapore, which, as I have argued, is gaining momentum as a forum for public discussion.

The government's response to questions about the charges has stressed that racist speech is illegal in Singapore and, therefore, the police had no choice but to press charges and allow the public prosecutor to do their job. Regardless of whether online or offline, the speech is still illegal, and will be prosecuted to the extent allowable by law. In an interview after the charges, Prime Minister Lee Hsien Loong was asked about the government's response, and he replied:

Whether you do it on the Internet, whether you do it in the newspapers, whether you go and say it in public or even at the Speaker's Corner, it doesn't matter where you say it . . . if you publish such stuff, anywhere you go, we will act (Low, 2005, p.1.).

Prime Minister Lee's comments signal a determination that the Internet will not become an unregulated or unmoderated forum for political discourse, and the government will vigorously prosecute politically inflammatory speech.

Singapore's blogger community, meanwhile, had mixed reactions to the news. Some bloggers argued that the charges would have a significant chilling effect, but a number of other prominent bloggers, including many known for their advocacy of greater political space, argued that the charges were a positive development. One prominent blogger, Lee Kin Min, or "Mr Brown," was quoted by the *Straits Times* as saying that "Internet users have yet to realize they will be held accountable for their actions online—that lesson hasn't sunk in yet" (Chua and Luo, 2005, p.H4). Benjamin Lee, AKA Mr Miyagi, explained why the charges were brought under the Sedition Act, rather than the Maintenance of Religious Harmony Act, which seemed to many to be a more appropriate law (Laws of our land), and used his newspaper column to feature the diversity of blogger responses to the charges (Lee, B. 2005, p.26). Another blogger, the "virgin undergraduate," (2005) argued that:

from my point of view, those two (alleged) clowns deserved it, and the deterrent effect in punishing cyber racists may actually do some good in riding the blogosphere [of] morons . . . (Cartharsis).

While it is surprising to many Western observers that Singaporean bloggers didn't universally condemn the actions of the authorities, to many Singaporeans the actions of the police were entirely right and appropriate, and were even beneficial to online discussions.

Discussion of the Sedition Act and the offenses has continued in a number of other forums as well, including letters to the editor and a number of online forums. One prominent blogger even started a wiki to explore all the issues associated with the case (http://diodati.omniscientx.com/_wiki/BloggersChargedWithSedition). It is likely that these events did provoke a meaningful online discussion of the role of the law in Singapore and the appropriateness of these political charges. The tightly knit blogging community generated dozens of commentaries, with a significant number of comments, backtracks, and hyperlinks. For many Singaporeans who had never even heard of the Sedition Act, it was a tremendous opening for a discussion on what should and should not be regulated in online speech.

Conclusion

It is not a fast process, but the Internet is significantly broadening the scope of civic discussion in Singapore. Although the Internet has not yet provided a dynamic platform for election campaigns, its use during the 2005 presidential campaign season demonstrated its utility for engaging a broader public in issues of political and social significance, and it is likely that this will continue.

At this point, organized party efforts to utilize the Internet have been fairly insignificant, if only because of the overt political threat of a party website. But Singapore's Internet community is quickly capitalizing on a variety of new technologies to significantly broaden the stage of political discussion, and to extend political debate into a number of non-politicized forums. In many ways, this is a hopeful development, as one of the most significant complications to political communication in Singapore is its overt politicization. As political discussions move into non-politicized forums, it is likely that the stakes for participating in these discussions will fall, thereby bringing a greater number of Singaporeans into the discussion and demonstrating that political discussion can happen in a way that doesn't ultimately threaten the delicate social thread of the nation.

Notes

1. "A president for all." 2005. Editorial, *Straits Times* (Singapore). 18 August, p.22..
2. Democrats working on vBlogging, 17 August 2005.
3. "New kid on the blog." 2005. *Straits Times* (Singapore). Mind your body supplement, 14 September, p. 24.

Chapter Four

Indonesia: Electoral Politics and the Internet[1]

David T. Hill

In May 1998, Indonesia's second and longest-serving president, retired general Suharto, stepped aside in the face of sustained public demonstrations, and the world's fourth most populous nation emerged from more than three decades of authoritarianism. Suharto's overthrow came barely three years after subscriber Internet services arrived in Indonesia and only two years after public Internet cafes began fanning out across the archipelago, providing Internet access to those who could not afford personal computers. The Internet did not directly cause the fall of the dictator, for the mix of economic, social and political factors that catalysed the oppositional groundswell was much more complex—but 'neither the fall of Suharto nor its aftermath can be described or fully understood without reference to this new mode of communication' (Hill and Sen, 2005, p.16). Since Suharto's exit the Internet has continued to make a valuable, if less dramatic, contribution to the institutionalisation of democracy in Indonesia through its role in national elections, most strikingly in 1999 and, to a lesser extent, in 2004.

In a country where access to the Internet is the prerogative of only a tiny fraction of the population, this chapter suggests that it is not necessarily the socio-economic and geographic spread of the Internet within a society that determines the Internet's democratic impact. It can play a major moderating role, enhancing the transparency, and therefore credibility, of the democratic process. Such transparency alone may not guarantee a thriving democracy, but it is a vital prerequisite. In making this case, this chapter surveys Internet practices in relation to Indonesia's elections since the fall of Suharto. It discusses the use of the Internet by political parties for campaigning and organising, and by the state, the media and the public to monitor and assess the fairness of these elections.

In order to appreciate the role of the Internet, it is important to be aware of both Indonesia's turbulent post-independence history and the particular circumstances of the Internet's enmeshment within social and political practice there in recent years. It is to these two issues that we now turn.

The Campaign Environment

The equatorial archipelago of Indonesia covers more than seventeen thousand inhabited islands, home to dozens of separate ethnic and linguistic groups, comprising a total population of more than 220 million. After declaring independence from the Dutch in 1945 and fighting a four-year independence struggle, the young democracy postponed general elections until 1955, as coalition governments rose and fell with unsettling rapidity (Feith, 1962). Indonesia's first elections in 1955 were contested by a raft of fifty-two political parties, with twenty-eight gaining at least one parliamentary seat. The 1955 election was a chaotic but fundamentally fair representation of the popular will.

On 1 October 1965 half a dozen senior military officers were kidnapped and killed by a leftist faction of the armed forces in an attempted putsch, which opponents blamed on the Communist Party. Major-General Suharto launched a brutal pogrom against the Left that resulted in the deaths of up to one million and the incarceration without trial of at least another million accused of leftist sympathies. Suharto was appointed President by a pliant interim parliament. Employing a combination of terror and manipulation, backed by the military and buttressed by parasitic business groups, Suharto and his 'New Order' maintained a façade of democracy. In July 1971 the firm hand of the state was clearly visible in the country's second election (Ward, 1974; Suryadinata, 2002, pp.26-36). Ten political parties contested the poll, with Suharto's Golkar (*Golongan Karya*, Functional Groups) commanding an astonishing 62 percent of the vote. Suharto then forced all opposition parties into one of only two permitted amalgams: either the Muslim-oriented Development Unity Party (PPP, *Partai Persatuan Pembangunan*), or the secular nationalist Indonesian Democratic Party (PDI, *Partai Demokrasi Indonesia*). This ensured that these parties remained riven by factionalism and effectively emasculated.

One routine feature of the six New Order elections from 1971 to 1997 was the predictability. Pre-poll speculation focussed not on which party would win—for a victory for Golkar was assumed—but on what percentage victory the New Order would choose to declare (ranging from 62 percent in 1977 to 74 per-

Many opponents assumed that Golkar without Suharto would shrivel and die, cut off from the patronage that had sustained it. But with three decades of politicking behind it, the organisation managed to transform itself into a viable political party. It jettisoned Suharto and some of his cronies, recruited new leaders from its more liberal, reformist wing, and mobilised its nationwide infrastructure optimally to maximise its vote. The more reformist wing of the former PDI, re-cast after a schism into the PDI-P (Indonesian Democratic Party of Struggle) and headed by Megawati Sukarnoputri, daughter of Indonesia's first president, Sukarno, garnered the largest percentage of votes (33.7 percent) in 1999. Golkar managed a respectable second with 22.5 percent, ahead of four smaller Muslim parties, which collectively gained 32.4 percent, followed by a thin tail of forty-two other minor parties sharing the remaining 11.4 percent of the vote.[2] Despite gaining the highest primary vote, the PDI-P was out-manoeuvred in parliament when Abdurrahman Wahid was elected president after his Islamic National Awakening Party (PKB, *Partai Kebangkitan Bangsa*) stitched up a majority coalition. Wahid proved an erratic president, rapidly losing public and parties' support, eventually being replaced in August 2001 by Megawati (Suryadinata, 2002).

Twenty-four parties contested the 2004 elections, whose results showed support for all the major parties had fallen, but to varying degrees, with the PDI-P dropping most dramatically from 33.7 percent (1999) to 18.5 percent (2004). Golkar resumed its place as the largest vote getter though its 21.6 percent was lower than its 1999 result of 22.5 percent. Overall secular parties dominate. Islamic parties declined in number but gained in strength. In 1999, twenty Islamic parties garnered 37.4 percent of the vote while in 2004 seven Islamic parties achieved 39.4 percent.[3]

The Media Environment

The New Order had used a variety of mechanisms to control both media ownership and content. While the precise strategies varied depending on the medium, the effect was similar: to constrain the expression of anti-government criticism and to ensure a generally compliant media (albeit with occasional flourishes of 'openness' as inter-elite skirmishes opened cracks in the regime) (Hill, 1996; Sen and Hill, 2000). If they breeched unwritten taboos, newspapers were banned. Television licences were allocated only to members of the presidential family or Suharto cronies. Radio stations were limited in their broadcast range and had their content theoretically (though in practice, ineffectually) monitored by the powerful Department of Information. Non-government radio and television stations were not permitted to produce 'news' programs, instead having to relay the official 'news' bulletins from the government's national radio and TV networks.

cent in 1997). Critical to these ritual elections—and to Golkar's hold on parlia
ment—was control over the transmission of votes, away from public scrutiny.

> Using a sophisticated network of radios, satellites and computers, all hooked
> into a command centre at the military's Cilangkap headquarters in south
> Jakarta, technicians had election results pouring in from all over the country
> from the moment the polls closed (McBeth *et al*, 1999, pp.167-168).

Such dubious reporting mechanisms reinforced cynicism in a public that felt tha
'votes went into a "black hole" somewhere between the ballot box and the na
tional result announcements' (Stevensen and Albrectsen, 1999, Annex 1-2).

Parties and the Party System

To a large degree, all political parties in Indonesia still labour under the
shadow of the New Order, which undermined parties and subordinated formal
political expression to the central will of a military-dominated state. Even Golkar was, in some senses, disabled from birth. Golkar (or in its original formula-
tion, Sekber Golkar, the 'Joint Secretariat of Functional Groups') was established in 1964 not as a political party but rather as an umbrella entity for various
anti-communist organisations or 'functional groups' (Reeve, 1985). Under Suharto it was transformed into an electoral vehicle (technically, a non-party 'election participant'), remaining highly manipulated from above, lacking organic
roots into the electorate. The New Order had declared that the 'floating mass' of
rural people were not to be disturbed by party activities or interference except
for in a period of several weeks designated for 'campaigning' prior to each election. Golkar's status enabled it to skirt this prohibition—albeit feeding information downwards rather than soliciting input from below—throughout the year.

When Habibie inherited the presidency in May 1998 he bowed to demands
for reform and for an immediate, fair and open election. Three pivotal political
laws were passed by Parliament on 28 January 1999 to permit the free establishment of political parties, reform the election process, and reform the two
national representative bodies, the People's Representative Assembly (DPR,
Dewan Perwakilan Rakyat) and the People's Consultative Assembly (MPR,
Majelis Permusyawaratan Rakyat) (King, 2000). Within months, more than 180
fledgling political parties were established, with forty-eight meeting the
preconditions to participate in the Indonesia's first free and fair general elections
since 1955, namely an active organisation in one-third of Indonesia's twenty-
seven provinces and half of the districts within these provinces (King, 2000,
p.91). To organise elections that were truly fair and democratic within the very
brief preparatory time-frame provided for the administration of the 1999 polls
was a tremendous challenge for the reform movement, and one to which it rose,
collectively, with considerable distinction.

Since the fall of Suharto, however, the country has enjoyed one of the most liberal, diverse and spirited media environments in the region. Media ownership is virtually unregulated (although some limits on foreign ownership remain). Rather than state or military control, critical analysis of public figures by the media is now limited more by the punitive laws of libel (often narrowly interpreted by a sometimes intimidated judiciary), or by the simple threat of violence or thuggery to harass journalists or ransack media offices. To a large degree, those particular circumstances that inclined opposition groups to use the Internet for communication have waned. With a more open media, with less oppressive surveillance of most opposition organisations, encrypted electronic communication, which had proved so effective in evading state monitoring under Suharto, became unnecessary. Since 1998 the media has taken an intense interest in the elections, including coverage that was broad, generally balanced, and often in-depth. Included was the full range of material one would expect in any vibrant, liberal democracy—from the superficial and sensational, to the studied and insightful. Many news media websites included special election pages, usually hyper-linked to an Electoral Commission site, thereby providing far greater detail than was being published or broadcast by conventional media.

The Internet in Indonesia

President Suharto's 'developmentalist authoritarian' government recognised that the Internet could contribute to national economic development. A major proponent was B. J. Habibie, initially as Minister of Technology, later as Vice President and finally President (May 1998—October 1999). Habibie was an ambitious German-trained engineer, who enjoyed Suharto's blessing to establish a string of high-tech projects. Accordingly, he provided the political impetus for the local development of the Internet despite Indonesia's poor basic communication infrastructure. Even in mid-2000 the population of 210 million shared only 7.5 million telephone connections, three million of which were within the capital, Jakarta. Phone lines were a rare luxury in the countryside, with the ratio of public telephones to population falling to only about one-in-six phones per ten thousand people in some outer regions (P3TIE, 2002, viii). Even where such phone lines existed, connecting to an Internet Service Provider (ISP) usually involved a costly long-distance call to a nearby town, for a slow and unreliable connection, often less than 10 kbps (CastleAsia, 2002, p.22). Compounding this disadvantage, Indonesia has very low levels of personal computer ownership, with around one computer per one hundred inhabitants (ITU, 2002, p.2). The cheapest personal computer cost well over the median monthly earnings of the overwhelming majority of working Indonesians and, in 2001, exceeded the per capita Gross Regional Domestic Product in at least four of Indonesia's twenty-six provinces (*Warta Ekonomi*, 2001, p.81).

While statistics on Internet users are notoriously imprecise, the overall trajectory is clear. Prior to 1995 only a handful of university scientists were familiar with the Internet. By the end of that year there were an estimated fifteen thousand Internet users in Indonesia, serviced by five commercial ISPs and the initial university-based network, IPTEKnet. With the Asian financial crisis of 1997-1998 growth levelled at about eighty-five thousand subscribers, bouncing up to about two hundred and fifty thousand within months of the 1999 elections. At the start of the 2004 election year, Indonesia passed the million mark for Internet subscribers, with more than eleven million users (see Table 4.1).

Table 4.1 Indonesian Internet Growth: Subscribers and Users

Year	Subscribers	Users
1996	31,000	110,000
1997	75,000	384,000
1998	134,000	512,000
1999	256,000	1,000,000
2000	400,000	1,900,000
2001	581,000	4,200,000
2002	667,002	4,500,000
2003	865,706	8,080,534
2004	1,087,428	11,226,143
2005*	1,500,000	16,000,000

Source: Indonesian Association of Internet Service Providers (APJII)[4] * Estimated figures

It is salutary to remember however that, even with this burgeoning userbase, one million 'dial-up' subscribers still amounted to less than a paltry one half of one percentage (0.47 percent) of the population. Of course, subscription data underrepresents actual users, since corporate connections are invariably used by more than one staff member, and several household members share a single subscription. Estimates by the Indonesian Internet Service Providers Association (APJII) demonstrate that total user numbers grew at a much faster rate than subscribers, from a factor of 3.5 in 1996, to 10.3 in 2004, representing a much greater uptake of non-subscriber access modes over subscriptions. Internet users overall have increased markedly as a percentage of the Indonesian population: up from two percent in 2001 to about 4.9 percent in 2004.

Public Internet access was more common through commercial Internet cafes or educational institutions rather than home or office. It was the rapid expansion of the Internet café, known locally as a 'warnet' (from 'warung Internet', Internet kiosk or stall) that opened the medium to many who could not afford a phone or computer at home. By the time of the 1999 elections, the Internet was accessible to subscribers in more than a hundred cities and towns (Baskoro, 1998) with public access points in most provincial capitals. Estimates put the number of warnets distributed right throughout the archipelago by 2001 at between 1,500 and 2,500. This initial astronomical growth of 30 percent per annum was declining by 2004 as demand for public Internet access through commercial providers tapered (being met by a surge in access through schools and universities) (Hill and Sen, 2005). Nonetheless, reflecting greater access to telephone infrastructure, Jakarta hosts nearly 75 percent of the country's Internet subscribers and users. Through most of Indonesia, public Internet access is very rarely, if ever, found outside large provincial capitals.

Pivotally, the Internet was rapidly recognised by urban students and political activists in the Internet cafes, and members of the middle-class who had access through their homes or offices, as a powerful network of alternative political information, effectively beyond the control of the state. It quickly became the medium of this broad and ill-defined opposition. Such groups, developed a sophisticated range of electronic publications, often in the form of underground 'news agencies' (Hill and Sen, 2005). The Internet proved extremely useful in organising anti-Suharto demonstrations in the capital that were crucial to forcing Suharto's resignation, but its geographical limits rendered it far less suited to mobilising grassroots political activities and organisations throughout Indonesia's hinterland.

Election Campaigning Online

The arrival and dispersal of the Internet throughout Indonesia so close in time to fall of the authoritarian Suharto regime and rise of a new democracy meant that the most dramatic evidence of intersection between Internet and elections occurred in the first post-Suharto General (Legislative) Elections of 7 June 1999. While certain features remained in the 5 April 2004 General Elections and the inaugural presidential elections held over two rounds on 5 July and 20 September 2004, the role of the Internet was increasingly less dramatic and more open to criticism. For that reason this chapter will examine the 1999 poll before extending the analysis to the elections of 2004.

1999: Free and Fair Elections

While the 1999 elections were not conducted online, significantly this was first occasion when Indonesian voters were able to confirm the calculation of the poll statistics through an independent publicly accessible Internet site. They could track the calculations, from tens of thousands of individual polling stations, through all levels of government, to the final centralised national tally. As the first free election since 1955, its credibility and transparency relied primarily, though not exclusively, upon individual citizens' ability to monitor and judge the vote tabulation. Millions of citizens apparently did just that. In the largest event in Indonesian Internet history, at its height the volume of visitors to the election site took virtually all of Indonesia's available public Internet capacity.

By any measure the task of administering elections in a country like Indonesia is a gargantuan one, made even more challenging by the pace of legislative reform (Ananta *et al*, 2004; Antlöv and Cederroth, 2004; Benedanto, 1999; Blackburn, 1999). The 1999 General Election law governing the 7 June poll only came into effect on 1 February. With simultaneous elections for the national People's Representative Assembly (DPR), together with provincial and district parliaments, 413 million ballot papers had to be printed and distributed to 300,129 polling stations across the archipelago for 121 million eligible voters by a new and independent General Election Commission (KPU, *Komisi Pemilihan Umum*), which did not become operational until early March (Stevensen and Albrectsen, 1999, p.3).

While the government established relatively ineffectual election oversight committees (or Panwas) from national to sub-district level, domestic and international civil society organisations effectively mobilised hundreds of thousands of election monitors. Rudimentary election monitoring organisations had emerged during the New Order in Indonesia but in 1999 they developed national reach and impressive efficiency (NDI, 1999, pp.27-29). Several were based on university campuses. The largest, the Rectors' Forum (*Forum Rektor*), which mobilised about 220,000 volunteers, had 'the advantages of being part of "the establishment" [with] access to university resources and contacts and legitimacy in the eyes of the electoral authorities and other parts of the government' (Stevensen and Albrectsen, 1999, p.65 and p.70). The Forum had an impressive website to document and promote its activities. UNFREL (University Network for a Free and Fair Election) also mobilised nearly one hundred thousand volunteers through twenty-two branches, about half of which were linked by the Internet to the Jakarta HQ. It maintained a website, with a newsgroup, details of its monitoring activities, click-on email facility for criticisms and suggestions, and an online form so the public could report breeches of electoral regulations and procedures. Access to, and mastery of, the Internet enabled such groups to function more efficiently and effectively at a pivotal juncture in national politics. It was the 'biggest election-monitoring effort the world has ever seen' (Stevensen and Albrectson, 1999, p.64). Supporting such NGOs were international organisations, like the U.S.-based National Democratic Institute for International Affairs (NDI) and International Foundation for Election Systems (IFES), both active in Indonesia, alongside the United Nations Development Programme (UNDP) and agencies of sympathetic foreign governments, such as the United States, United Kingdom, Japan, Canada, Germany, and Australia. For the NDI, IFES and the UNDP, a website was an important communications tool.

For the KPU, haste was of the essence, with the Computerisation Working Group given only two months to develop a functioning network for results tabulation (Dharsono, D., personal interview with author, 29 November 2001). They decided to use a 'leased line' from the national banking system as the 'spine'. It was based on secure satellite links, was specifically devised for massive data collection and exchange, and had already been adapted to register applicants for the annual Muslim pilgrimage. Known as Siskohat (*Sistem Komputerisasi Haji Terpadu*, Integrated Pilgrimage Computerisation System), this adapted system did not require the KPU to buy substantial additional equipment, and could, instead, be leased for the several months required. Using trained bank staff to input the data meant only minimal additional instruction was necessary.

Only a small minority of the forty-eight contesting parties had websites, and most provided only static information, without interactivity. The National Mandate Party (PAN, *Partai Amanat Nasional*), with a strong appeal to middle-class university-educated voters, opened its campaign declaring it would 'establish democracy through the Internet' and quickly launched its website (www.amanat.org) in August 1998, barely one day after its formal establishment (Benedanto, 1999, p.58). By March 1999, as the campaign heated up, the party claimed around three thousand visitors per day. It gradually developed the site to include bilingual (Indonesian and English) pages, an open forum and an online donation facility. But, as was common with other party websites, the slow and broken transmission, and a string of programming glitches proved a turn-off for users. The website of the PDI-P (www.megawati.forpresident.com), was judged 'rather slow to access because of an excess of content', with journalists from Indonesia's most prestigious newsmagazine rating it 'still better than the PKB site (www.pkb.org) which for the previous few days has been stalled' (Pareanom et al, 1999). Golkar gave so little attention to its website that out-of-date information on its 1997 election campaign remained on the site until only months before the 1999 poll. Golkar did employ a public relations firm to supervise the development of a new Internet website (www.golkar.net) under the oversight of the party's central committee (DPP). Yet even during the most frenetic period of the election campaign and through the peak of polling, it attracted only about two hundred visitors daily.

At the other end of the political spectrum, the tiny Democratic People's Party (*Partai Rakyat Demokratik*, PRD), whose cadres had been forced underground by persecution under Suharto, used the Internet more actively than any party. Its sophisticated appreciation of the technology's potential was due partly to its origins in the radical student movement in the early 1990s, and partly because it relied heavily on Internet communication while underground. Since then the PRD had maintained a vibrant web presence. It bought computers for its regional offices and funded their Internet usage. Ultimately, being Internet savvy was not enough, since the PRD failed to win any seat, finishing fortieth out of forty-eight parties with only 0.07 percent of valid votes.

According to Internet analyst Onno Purbo, parties completely ignored the potential of emailing lists to generate two-way communication with sympathisers (Ahyani, 1999), and relied on established campaign methods, like mass public rallies, motorcades, and 'old' media (TV, radio and print) or public space advertising (banners, posters) to reach the overwhelming majority of voters who did not have access to Internet. The Internet was seen as peripheral to an electoral struggle over a 'mass' base.

However, the Internet was central to the KPU's vote tabulation. When the polling stations closed on election day, ballots were counted before authorised witnesses and election monitors, before being consolidated at village level and forward to sub-district level. When the ballots and the results sheets from these lower levels reached the district level all the figures (right down to individual polling stations) were entered into the KPU database. These statistics were then available virtually immediately at the central KPU server at their Jakarta headquarters, and backed up on other servers. After about an hour to pass through a series of security features, the statistics were accessible to the public. As the KPU Computerisation chief declared, 'If the community can see the official vote data right to the polling station level, they can reconcile their notes of the vote counting at the polling station where they cast their ballot with the data being broadcast by the KPU. If there is a discrepancy, they can lodge a protest by facsimile or phone or Internet' (*Kompas*, 1999). Thus the public could verify the accuracy of the data, allaying concerns about vote rigging or tampering. With full transcripts of all electoral legislation, regulation and forms, the KPU website (http://www.kpu.go.id/), which was set up with technical and financial support from the Japanese government, was in extraordinary high demand. For the fortnight following the poll, the daily hit-rate was around 860,000, with up to 30,548 megabytes of data accessed daily (*Kompas*, 1999).

There were numerous other sources of information originating from the KPU. Television, radio and print media carried regular updated statistics (with some television stations having an online link to the KPU's server). Yet no other media could match the range and depth of statistical information provided by the KPU website, which recorded the unfolding tally with unparalleled speed, precision and accuracy.

Cognisant of the crucial importance of accurate media coverage of the elections, the KPU established a Joint Operations and Media Centre (JOMC) at a central Jakarta hotel to provide statistics directly to the public and the media. Two separate but official routes for the transmission of results were thereby established. On the one hand the KPU's tally (dubbed 'formal and official') was aggregated manually from each polling station, through each administrative level up to the district, where it was entered into the banking computer system to become accessible via the KPU national database. Separately, results from the sub-district level were also faxed or phoned directly to the JOMC (NDI, 1999, p.30). The JOMC provided regular updates (termed 'informal and official') directly onto the Internet and to the national and international media. This rapid release of reliable data to the media and the public, separate from the KPU's official statistics, enhanced public confidence. The UNDP reported that 'provisional results produced by the JOMC one week after polling day were within 4 percent of the final results in accuracy' (Stevensen and Albrectsen, 1999, p.37).

Technologically the KPU data transmission ran smoothly, but the physical examination and counting of votes was a slow process at each administrative level. Asiaweek reported:

> Paradoxically, the main reason for the delay appeared to be the desire of hundreds of thousands of election volunteers—full of goodwill, if lacking in training and experience—to guarantee a free, fair and transparent poll (McCarthy, 1999, p.156).

The pace with which the computer links could register the data was out of kilter with the laboriousness of the ballot count. KPU Chair Rudini quipped to journalists, 'In the old days it was a lot easier because we knew the results beforehand' (McBeth et al., 1999, p.168). For the NDI, 'the greatest unknown for the post-election period is the willingness of the Indonesian people as a whole and the competing parties in particular to accept the results of the elections' (1999, p.iii). After considerable grandstanding by some defeated parties, the public accepted the official results as an accurate indication of the electorate's will. An IFES post-election study indicated 86 percent of the public regarded the count of votes to be honest and fair (IFES, 1999). Public confidence increased dramatically as a result of the 1999 elections, as demonstrated by pre- and post-poll surveys. In December 1998 only 36 percent of respondents were either 'completely' or 'somewhat' satisfied with the way previous elections were conducted, while the percentage soared to 88 percent when questioned two months after the June 1999 elections. Community responses generally indicated that Internet technologies were widely accepted as enhancing the transparency of the calculations. The KPU's computer verification team recommended, 'in order that the next election be conducted in an honest, secret, and fair manner, the calculation of votes would be better undertaken using a computer system located directly at each polling station, and with the voters able to enter the political party of their choice directly into such a computer system on providing their fingerprint identity details' (KPU, 1999, point 5.2).

If the 1999 election had demonstrated both the value and public acceptance of the Internet as part of the election process, the elections of 2004 generated a much more critical response. Expectations had been raised and the technology had difficulty meeting them. The magnitude of the polls in 2004 pushed the KPU's capacity—and its mastery of the technology—to its limits.

2004: The Year of Voting Frequently

More than 124 million voters took part in the April 2004 legislative elections, attending more than 580,000 polling stations in one of the world's most complex expressions of democracy. On this day, through four separate ballots, voters elected more than fifteen thousand representatives to four separate bodies: the national legislature (DPR); a newly constituted national council of regional representatives, rather like an 'upper house' (DPD); provincial assemblies; and either district or municipal councils. While problems were legion, international observers judged the process 'largely peaceful and despite the complexity of the balloting and counting process, no major administrative problems emerged' (NDI, 2004, p.1). Three months later, the first round of the presidential elections brought five competing pairs of candidates for president and vice-president to the electorate. When no single pair achieved an outright majority, the two front-runners returned to the voters in September, ending the most intensive period of electioneering in Indonesian history. Following the success of the 1999 polls, this was the only time that Indonesia has experienced the routine of two five-yearly democratic elections.

In preparation for 2004 a raft of new legislation was passed in 2002-2003 to revise the constitution, revise the laws on political parties and general elections (including changes to the composition of the KPU and the establishment of a new Council of Regional Representatives (DPD)) and introduce direct popular election of the president and vice-president; and to establish a new Constitutional Court with, among other responsibilities, authority to decide on disputes on election results. But while there had been these major revisions to the framework of Indonesian democracy, there was very little, if any, change to the parties' use of the Internet in campaigning.

The most visible and tumultuous form of electioneering in Indonesia was still mass outdoor rallies, that generated the most predictable volume of media—particularly television—coverage, given the visual spectacle. The NDI noted that

> many parties did undertake other, less visible but often more effective, forms of campaigning. The partial open-list system increased the salience of individual candidates in these elections, and some responded by attempting to connect with voters in new and creative ways. Village or neighbourhood dialogues (a sort of small-scale town hall meeting) and door-to-door canvassing—virtually nonexistent in Indonesia before this election—were used by many of the parties and their candidates and allowed for greater face-to-face contact with voters and some discussion of policy issues (NDI, 2004, p.10).

But while some parties, and particular high-profile leaders, did invest in Internet campaign sites, these remained insignificant in the totality of the campaign. Inducements of money, goods (such as T-shirts, rice, or other staple foods), bureaucratic patronage, or the construction of local facilities such as roads or street lighting proved a resilient legacy of the New Order, far outweighing any reliance upon 'new technologies' as a campaign tool.

It is not surprising that the Internet features so low on the horizon of political parties, given that only a handful of politicians had the requisite skills to access the Internet themselves. Even if an MP had an email address, it was usually only their secretary who accessed it. One Deputy Party Secretary General (with a masters degree in international marketing from a British University) admitted he only opened his email about once a month, 'because I find it very time consuming' (Hastuti, 2001). The portability and immediacy of the SMS and mobile phone were vastly preferred by politicians, despite greater expense. So, despite the growth in Internet usage in Indonesia, of the twenty-four parties that contested in 2004 election, fewer than half appear to have maintained official party websites.[5]

Of the official party sites, there were various common elements. Golkar, for example, provided information on the strategies and programs of the party, profiles of party figures and the organisational structure. It also posted recent news bulletins about the party and its candidates from various newspapers which were updated daily (Firmansyah et al, 2004, p.205). The PKS (*Partai Keadilan Sejahtera*, Justice and Prosperity Party) site provided similar profiles of party leaders and daily changing news reports, together with a list of contact details for both the national and regional offices of the party. The public could register themselves online as party sympathisers or actually join the party. Details were provided of the various stages involved in training, and information that would be provided if one registered in that manner (Firmansyah *et al.*, 2004, p.206). The PKB's official site innovatively included sheet music and downloadable MP3 audio files for the official party hymn and march, and a downloadable PowerPoint presentation outlining the official party 'yells' ('Long live the PKB!'), greetings (the Arabic blessing 'Assalamualaikum warahmatullahi wabarakatuh' or the Indonesian rendering 'Salam sejahtera untuk kita semua'), official catch-cries for mass rallies (such as 'Peace my country!') together with the preferred audience responses ('Awaken, my nation!').[6]

Some parties focussed sites around the name and high profile of their prime candidate. The former president and PKB leader Abdurrahman Wahid had a site dedicated to him at www.gusdur.net, in addition to the official PKB site. Similarly, Rachmatwati Sukarnoputri, who was sister of President Megawati Sukarnoputri, daughter of founding president Sukarno and leader of the Pioneer Party (Partai Pelopor), used www.rachmatwati.com rather than a party-specific site. Amien Rais, head of PAN, who enjoyed a high political profile as the chair of the national parliament (MPR), also had a personal site at www.m-amienrais.com. Such sites concentrated on the lives and achievements of these individuals (and in some instances provided an opportunity for visitors to pose questions electronically to them) rather than the political platforms of their parties.

One of the most active and user-friendly party sites was that of the minority Peace and Prosperity Party (PDS, *Partai Damai Sejahtera*).[7] It had an attractive layout in the party's signature purple, with a forum facility permitting members and visitors to post comments or suggestions on a wide variety of topics: political, legislative and religious (since the party was Christian). There were links to party policies and platforms, details of the party structure, and profiles and contact information for the various national office-bearers. Some local branches had their own linked sites providing local news and information on party activities. One click took potential donors to the website of a national bank to facilitate electronic funds transfer. Despite a small number of broken or inactive links, overall the site worked well—and speedily by comparison to most other Indonesian party sites. It gave the impression of an efficient party seeking to provide relevant policy and party platform information to the party faithful as well as the browsing public. The PDS was also praised by the National Democratic Institute for its 'village-to-village direct contact campaign in targeted areas', as a consequence of which, in the election it 'did better than expected despite a lack of campaign funds' (NDI, 2004, p.11).

As in 1999, election-monitoring organisations, with their four hundred thousand volunteers, were active on the Internet. The main domestic organisations included the University and NGO Network (known as *Jurdil Pemilu 2004*),[8] and the People's Voter Education Network (JPPR), associated with several large Muslim as well as interfaith and non-religious groups. Perhaps most skilled in its use of the Internet in electoral education was the Centre for Electoral Reform (CETRO), whose site provided a comprehensive range of educational, training and support materials for the organisation's six thousand monitors spread throughout the archipelago.[9] The CETRO site linked to a vast array of information about the election, including the timetable for the polls, legislation, latest election news, and voter education program and voting simulation exercises. The availability of Internet and email access for the volunteer monitors and the development and maintenance of effective websites by the national organisations was crucial for the smooth and effective management of the monitoring process.

On behalf of the monitoring organisations, Jurdil's LP3ES research agency was assisted by NDI to provide a nationwide 'parallel vote tabulation' (PVT) for the 2004 legislative elections. The NDI noted that 'for weeks following election day, the PVT projections were the only credible results available to election officials, party leaders and the public at large. Official results took a month to tabulate and certify, and unofficial results available through the national tabulations centre organised by the KPU were slow and sometimes misleading' (NDI, 2004, p.15).

The most politically significant use of the Internet and information technologies more generally in 2004 remained the KPU's vote calculation and results website. Replacing the Siskohat network, in 2004 the KPU contracted private industry to supply the data tabulation infrastructure. This included equipping the KPU's Data Centre and a back-up Data Recovery Centre, ensuring comprehensive network connections, and supplying and installing about eight thousand computer workstations into district and sub-district offices around the entire archipelago.[10] Bureaucratic and legal delays meant that the appointed tenderer was given only about two months to fulfil the contract, making it unlikely the system would run smoothly. About thirteen thousand data entry staff, primarily university students, teachers and other volunteers regarded as politically neutral, were to feed in the statistics at around 4,700 online districts. Locations without Internet access—some were even without electricity—had their data entered at the nearest online district office. From election day, encrypted data went to the KPU Data Centre, to be backed up in the Data Recovery Centre, and then made publicly accessible through the National Election Tabulation (TNP) centre, located at an international down-town Jakarta hotel, and online via the KPU's TNP website.

Vociferous criticism was directed at the effectiveness of the technology used in the tabulation of results. IT specialist academic Roy Suryo, for example, argued that the KPU had attempted to use vastly more sophisticated computing strategies than were necessary to achieve the required outcomes, and as a consequence the system proved 'more expensive, slower and less accurate' than alternatives. The IT infrastructure frustrated many. For example, election staff in the large provincial town of Solo complained that, for more than two days after the poll, staff were unable to transmit electronic data. The delay was partly due to having received incomplete, inaccurate, unauthorised or unwitnessed statistics sheets from booths, and partly because of the inadequate knowledge of data entry staff, who only received a single training session. The Data Entry Coordinator for Solo city complained that 'the modem connections are so slow as to make the IT calculation system slower than the manual method' (Rosyid, 2004). Some other sub-district committees, unable to connect to the network, did not bother entering electronic data and defaulted to manual counting and the submission of paper-based result forms.

There were complaints that figures on the TNP site remained unchanged for hours at a time. In one case, a candidate's name was omitted from the TNP list. More disconcerting for candidates generally and their political parties were occasional erratic fluctuations in the running totals provided through the TNP, which KPU staff claimed were due to errors in the calculations provided at data-entry points (Widyatmoko, 2004). Exasperated, at one point seventeen parties called on the KPU to cease releasing Internet results, and on television stations to stop providing these as 'running text' because of the danger of misleading electors and spreading confusion (*Kompas*, 2004). The protests were largely ignored.

APJII Secretary-General Heru Nugroho attempted to explain publicly the vast complexity of the election data that had to be processed, the limits of the technology, and the pivotal role of human agency in generating accurate outcomes. APJII used its good offices to try to bring the IT community together with the KPU and its critics, in workshops and other forums, to identify the systemic issues in the hope of resolving them. In Nugroho's independent judgement, however, 'with all its weaknesses, limitations and controversies, the information technology system which was used in counting votes in the 2004 legislative election has provided the community with adequate information on the election results' (Nugroho, 2004). Despite the numerous glitches, the official results were announced by the KPU exactly one month after the election, having examined 113.5 million valid and 11 million invalid votes (Ananta *et al.*, 2005: 19).

Despite ongoing disputes about the efficiency or technical suitability of the communications systems used by the KPU, clearly inadequate preparation time and training was a major impediment. Whatever the system's failings, the public overwhelmingly accepted the results, with one survey finding that 89 percent of respondents regarded the elections as very or somewhat well organised and 91 percent believed them completely or mostly fair and honest (IFES, 2005, p.42). No election in Indonesia's history has been subject to the level of public, administrative and judicial scrutiny applied in 2004. The KPU was subject to an unprecedented level of monitoring by the Election Supervisory Committee (Panwas), the Financial Inspection Board (BPK, *Badan Pemeriksa Keuangan*), the Anti-Corruption Commission (KPK, *Komisi Pemberantasan Korupsi*), as well as the Constitutional Court. There were numerous bruising and very public investigations, with several KPU members, including the chair, found guilty of corruption (such as taking kick-backs from companies awarded contracts by the KPU) and jailed for long periods. The corruption was, however, incidental to the election process and no KPU staff were accused of attempting to influence corruptly the outcome of the poll.[11]

What then did the application of Internet technologies bring to the 2004 elections? As we have seen, there was sustained criticism of the KPU for its inability to provide the public with a seamless flow of accurate and reliable results in a timely manner. Nonetheless, despite overall poor performance, the service did improve during the course of the election period as processes were refined and output became more reliable. Even the most vocal critic of the KPU's IT team, Roy Suryo, when reviewing the second round of presidential voting, wrote that 'Although the KPU's IT section experienced various problems, this time, objectively, we have to express our appreciation to the team in this second presidential election because it has demonstrated better performance than in the previous legislative and first presidential poll' (Notodiprojo, 2004). He acknowledged the KPU's provision of electronic data had enabled citizens to examine for themselves the recapitulation of poll data right down to their local polling stations, something not feasibly done using the official manual calculations. The loud demands for greater speed and efficiency in the tabulations of data may also be interpreted as a sign of increased public expectations of both the technology and the KPU.

Conclusion

The fundamental inequalities of computer illiteracy, poverty, and lack of public infrastructure through much of rural and regional Indonesia make widespread use of the Internet by the electorate unlikely for the foreseeable future. Parties vying for the popular vote do not commit scarce campaign resources to a medium whose reach is so marginal to the general community. There was no correlation between either visitor volume to, or quality of, party websites and the final percentage of votes won.[12] Yet, during the course of the 1999 and 2004 elections, the Internet has become an expected and accepted part of elections in Indonesia. Its value has been proven to the higher educated Indonesians living in major urban centres, who are using the Internet to seek information, and particularly to follow developments, such as result tabulations, at key points in the democratic process. Such social groups are driving reforms of the electoral system, demanding public accountability of government, and the Internet provides them with the sense of a direct line of communication into the government bureaucracy they seek to keep honest. It facilitates alliances and provides access to dynamic national and international networks—in the technological, organisational and political sense of the term.

The Internet's impact has been far greater than the specific numbers of Internet users, for it has exposed the election process to public view and scrutiny in a manner unparalleled by other technologies. Indonesia's most prominent proponent of public access Internet, Onno Purbo, on the eve of the 1999 poll, called on the 'community' to use the Internet to express their opinion rather than engage in demonstrations on the streets. One manifestation of this is the civil society groups that use the Internet to organise effective election monitoring across the country. The Internet has provided such groups with a mechanism to participate in, and feel part of, the grandest of democratic rituals.

While the complex tabulation process is highly dependent on human intervention, the capacity to cross-check changing figures, updating data, and precise cross-tabulations, against one's own experience of voting in a local polling station, provides a transparency that is reassuring, even given the glitches and errors that occasionally arise. The routine cycle of peaceful democratic elections may not be as dramatic or as spectacular for the media as the ousting of a president by mass street demonstrations. But in Indonesia, the use of the Internet to expose those election statistics to public scrutiny has been as important in engendering faith in Indonesia's future democracy as was its deployment by anti-Suharto forces in mobilising against authoritarianism.

Notes

1.   This chapter draws heavily on joint research undertaken with Krishna Sen and published as Hill and Sen (2005). However, while the insights included here are

the product of that collaboration, the limitations that remain are my responsibility.

2. The major Muslim parties and their vote shares were the PKB on 12.7 percent, PPP 10.7 percent, PAN 7.1 percent and PBB 1.9 percent. For details, see Suryadinata (2002, p.103).

3. I am including PKB and PAN as 'Islamic parties' because of the Muslim character of their supporters and their leadership, despite their explicit declaration as being 'Pancasila' (i.e. in this context, 'secular') parties. See Ananta, Arifin and Suryadinata (2005, p.21).

4. Various APJII statistics, most recently from http://www.apjii.or.id/ dokumentasi /statistik.php?lang=ind&PHPSESSID =3ed269d7c3a6609a95cf 6769 a95f4 a5a, sighted on 14 March 2006.

5. These were Golkar's partai-golkar.or.id (which was so painfully slow as to be unusable, and was replaced the following year with http://www.golkar.or.id), PKS's www.keadilan.or.id as well as www.pksejahtera.org, PDS's partaidamaisejahtera.com, Partai Merdeka's www.partaimerdeka.or.id; Partai Sarikat Indonesia (PSI) ran www.psi-online.or.id. Details of these and other election-related websites are provided in Firmansyah *et al.* (2004, pp.205-210).

6. http://kebangkitanbangsa.org, sighted 13 March 2006.

7. I visited the site at various times since mid-2004, though the following details are based on its contents on 10 March 2006.

8. Jurdil was a coalition of the NDI, the university Rector's Forum a leading social science research institute (LP3ES) and the Civil Society Alliance for Democracy (YAPPIKA).

9. www.cetro.or.id, sighted 9 March 2006.

10. The successful tenderer was a consortium led by PT Integrasi Teknologi, and including PT Pasifik Satelit Nusantara (PSN) (which provided satellite links to isolated regions) and PT Telkom (which provided the network connections for the majority of data-entry points, through a 'Virtual Private Network' for the KPU), and computer hardware company Hewlett Packard (KPU, 2004). See also Donny (2003). The KPU was criticised for letter the cost of IT provisions blow out from an initial Rp. 154 billion to about Rp. 225 billion (Pikiran Rakyat, 2005).

11. Gary Bell, Director of the Asian Law Institute, at the National University of Singapore (NUS) is currently conducting research into the operations of the Constitutional Court in relation to the 2004 elections. I thank him for insights given during his seminar on 7 March 2006 at the Asia Research Institute, NUS.

12. For example, while PAN claimed three thousand visitors per day, it won only 7 percent of the final vote, compared to Golkar's 22 percent of the vote, despite a paltry two hundred daily hits on its website.

Chapter Five

United States: Internet and Elections

Diana Owen and Richard Davis

Anticipating the following year's election, Michael Cornfield asserted in 2003: "For all campaigners, the year 2004 looms as the year 1 A.D" (Cornfield, 2004a: xv). Predictions of the Internet reshaping U.S. electoral politics in the 2004 campaign were rampant (Berke, 2003; Mack, 2003; Palser, 2003). Still, two political scientists cautioned that "any campaign that relies too heavily on the Internet to campaign had better start drafting a concession speech for election day" (Dulio and O'Brien, 2004: 191). These statements seem prescient, as Governor Howard Dean catapulted from obscurity to front-runner status in the Democratic primary seemingly on the basis of his skillful and innovative use of the Internet and then lost the nomination.

The Dean campaign did use the Internet in novel ways (Kerbel and Bloom, 2005; Kerbel, 2005; Hull, 2004). His campaign went online to find communities of activists sympathetic to the governor's issue positions, particularly on Iraq. In addition, the Dean campaign introduced the campaign blog and meet-up as campaign outreach technologies (Kerbel and Bloom, 2005; Williams *et al*, 2004). Although Howard Dean ultimately lost the Democratic nomination, the innovations in e-campaigning he pioneered in a presidential campaign were quickly duplicated by other candidates (Williams *et al*, 2004). In addition, the Internet became a significant fundraising tool for Dean as well as Democratic presidential nominee John Kerry (Kerbel, 2005). The Kerry campaign raised

$50 million following the senator's win in the March 2 primaries, including $1 million raised in seventeen hours over March 2 and 3 (Dickert, 2005).

In the United States, unlike many other systems, the candidate-centered focus of the electoral system dictates attention to the online efforts of individual candidate campaigns rather than the political parties. Although the two major political party organizations, the Republican National Committee and the Democratic National Committee, have engaged in online communications with voters, the real story of electoral communications in the United States revolves around candidates.

Over the past decade there has been a growth in candidates' use of Internet communication accompanied by an increase in the public's attention to election news online. Important questions remain about the effects of these developments. Has candidate transmission of an online message altered campaigns? Moreover, are there effects on voters? Are voters better informed? Are they more likely to become involved in voting, donating, or volunteering for candidates? Does online candidate campaign content affect vote decisions?

This chapter begins with a brief description of the American campaign environment followed by an overview of the evolution of the Internet's role in American elections. It then examines candidates' and voters' use of candidate campaign websites. We focus, in particular, on candidates' efforts to incorporate online tools that both reinforce voters' support of candidates and mobilize them into their websites. We employ data from two sources in our analysis: a content analysis of presidential candidate websites in 2004 and a survey designed to assess voter's engagement with these sites during the campaign.

Our evidence suggests that interactivity was the hallmark of the 2004 campaign online. Far more of the content of presidential candidates' websites was devoted to volunteer and voter mobilization than in previous campaigns. While visitors to candidate sites were more likely to engage the informational aspects of sites, they were favorably disposed toward the campaigns' online mobilization efforts. People who accessed the mobilization content of candidate websites were more inclined to be involved in the campaign offline. While it is difficult to determine the extent to which online mobilization efforts result in offline participation, it is clear that candidate websites and email alerts are designed to encourage electoral activation.

The Campaign Environment

U.S. presidential elections today involve a series of complex stages beginning with the nominating process. Candidates compete in state caucuses and primary elections for delegates who will represent them at the Democratic and Republican national nominating conventions where the party's presidential and vice presidential nominees are determined. More states currently use primaries, a direct election where voters choose among competing candidates, over caucuses, which are local meetings of activists. National party conventions are held the

summer before the presidential election. The general election for president officially begins after the party nominating conventions. Candidates traverse the
country stumping for votes until the presidential election on the first Tuesday in
November.

The presidential election process contributes to a campaign environment
that is dominated by mass media. The prevalence of primaries during the nomination phase compels candidates to broaden their appeal beyond party loyalists.
Candidates hire political consultants who devise sophisticated media strategies
that incorporate both free media, such as television and newspaper coverage,
and paid media, such as candidate advertising and Internet web sites. The
American mass media election is characterized by coverage that often privileges
style over substance. Horse-race journalism, featuring omnipresent polls speculating about who is ahead and behind in the campaign, abounds. Candidates re-
sort to attack strategies, especially through negative advertising, while reporters
focus on personalities to a greater extent than issues. Journalists and candidates
engage in a constant tug-of-war to maintain control of the campaign agenda,
with journalists frequently emerging with the upper hand.

The centrality of media in presidential elections has driven up the cost of
campaigns. In 2004, campaign-related financial activities by candidates and
conventions topped $1 billion, marking a 56 percent increase over the 2000
campaign. Attempts to legislate campaign finance by limiting donations to
campaigns by large givers has had the unintended consequence of promoting the
creation of political organizations operating outside of the official campaigns.
Independent expenditures on behalf of candidates by organizations and individuals not affiliated with a campaign was over $192 million (Federal Election
Commission, 2005). The lion's share of these expenditures went for media, especially television advertising.

The Development of Internet Campaigning in U.S. Elections

The Internet emerged at a time when candidates were becoming increasingly
frustrated by their portrayal in traditional news media. Politicians lamented their
inability to get a message across to voters, particularly via television news. In
the early 1990s, candidates began turning to non-traditional news sources such
as talk radio and television talk shows to reach voters (Owen and Davis, 1998).
When the Internet began to emerge as a mass medium, candidates were ready
for a medium that could disseminate information broadly but inexpensively and
without the intervention of journalists.

The Internet's electoral role in U.S. politics has a short, but intense history
beginning in 1992 when the Clinton campaign posted campaign information on
what was then a new public medium. Although limited to speeches and texts of
radio ads and crudely primitive compared to 2004, the Clinton site was the gene-
sis of online campaigning (Davis, 1999: 86-87).

The problem for candidates with that first foray into the Internet was the absence of an audience (Abernathy, 1992). One estimate placed the Internet audience at four million users at the end of 1991 (Cerf, 1992). The introduction of the World Wide Web in 1993 created a more user-friendly interface and made candidate websites more visually attractive to voters. The audience for the Net grew quickly during the mid to late 1990s. While an estimated eighteen million Americans were online in 1995, that figure had expanded to 164 million by the end of 2000 ("How Many Online," 2005). Use of the Net for campaign-related information also increased rapidly. According to the Pew Research Center, 22 percent of online users said they went online to read news about the 1996 election, a figure that had increased to 33 percent by the 2000 election and had reached 52 percent by 2004 (Pew Research Center, 1996; Pew Research Center, 2000; Dulio and O'Brien, 2004: 182; Pew Research Center, 2005b).

The Internet has acquired a growing niche as a news source, including campaign and election-related news. On Election Day 2000, CNN site traffic exceeded its previous record by 150 percent, and the site experienced technical difficulties as it was unable to handle the client load. (Donahue et al, 2000) Election 2004 set another record in site traffic, exceeding by over one-fifth the record set on September 11, 2001 ("CNN.com Election Night Traffic Eclipses Site's Record," 2004).

Candidate campaign interest grew accordingly. In 1996, online campaigning began to gain widespread notice and diverge from exclusively transmitting campaign literature. Republican presidential nominee Bob Dole's recitation of his website URL during speeches and television interviews was an important milestone for the Internet as an election information tool since it showed a candidate using a traditional media forum to advertise his Web presence (Davis, 1999: 85).

The late 1990s and the first years of the twenty-first century saw dramatic increases in candidate use of the Internet, reaching near saturation rates among major party candidates, at least in Senate and gubernatorial races (D'Alessio, 1997; Kamarck, 1999; Sadow and James, 1999). By 2000, 91 percent of major party candidates for the United States Senate had websites, up from 72 percent in 1998. Saturation was nearly achieved in gubernatorial races in 2000, as 95 percent of major party gubernatorial candidates had websites. Ironically, the only incumbent governor up for re-election in 2000 who did not have a website was Howard Dean (Kamarck, 2003: 86). In U.S. House races, 66 percent of candidates used the Web in 2000, up from only 35 percent in 1998. By 2002, the House figure had climbed to 73 percent. House races may continue to lag due to the lack of viable challengers in many House districts and even any major party challengers in a few (Kamarck, 1999: 86; Foot et al, 2003). Candidates in competitive races and open seat contests were much more likely than other candidates to use the Web for campaigning (Kamarck, 1999; Dulio et al, 1999; Kamarck, 2003; Gulati, 2003).

Early predictions of the Internet's electoral role suggested it would level the playing field between resource-rich and resource-poor candidates (Selnow,

1998; Corrado and Firestone, 1996). The assumption was that online campaigns would be inexpensive, especially compared to television advertising. Over time this assumption became increasingly flawed, as candidate websites became increasingly sophisticated and costly to maintain and update. The burden can be especially heavy on minor party candidates, who still lag behind major party candidates in Web use. One study of House candidates in 2002 found that only 40 percent of minor party candidates had a website. The gap between major and minor party candidate usage of the Internet remains large, although it is narrowing (Gulati, 2003).

Some scholars and political observers have gone so far as to suggest that the Internet would determine the outcome of elections. As early as 1994, one political activist predicted that "by 1996, we will begin to see some number of campaigns either won or lost because campaign operations either use or fail to use network communication and organization" (Powers, 1994). While this prediction obviously was premature, speculation remains that the influence of online campaigns, particularly on some audiences, will continue to increase.

Candidates Online

From the beginning, candidates used online communication much as they did traditional communication—to present themselves to the public. The initial brochure-like quality of candidate websites reflected this approach. In the early years, which voters were paying attention to the online campaign was not obvious. Increasingly, candidate campaigns have viewed websites as opportunities to perform two main functions: reinforce supporters and then mobilize them.

Reinforcement: Voters are disposed toward information that reinforces their preconceptions about candidates, parties, and issues, and to even engage in selective perception when confronted with opposing information (Tabor and Lodge, 1999; Mutz and Martin, 2001). Given the tendency of voters to be selective in information retrieval, use of Internet political messages for reinforcement would be similar to usage of other sources such as television or newspapers.

Reinforcement messages can be present in online campaign information. This includes news of what the candidate is saying on the campaign trail, positive news from established media sources, news of general campaign activities, news of what other activists are doing, etc. For instance, in 2000 the Bush campaign aimed at this kind of reinforcement through a home page feature called "Setting the Record Straight," which included frequently updated responses to criticisms of Bush's policy proposals and attacks on Al Gore's statements (Bimber and Davis, 2003: 49). Moreover, such messages are important since exposure to candidate sites does strengthen and reinforce voters' predispositions for some voters (Bimber and Davis, 2003: 131-137).

Mobilization: The most important form of mobilization ultimately is the vote. That effort to mobilize potential voters in support of the candidate begins with a distinct advantage: those who use the Internet for political information are more likely than others to vote (Tolbert and McNeal, 2003). But mobilization consists not only of voter turnout (which certainly is the crucial final function), but also mobilization to support activity during the course of the campaign. Beginning in the nineteenth century, supporters were expected to attend rallies and join in parades (McCormick, 1966: 349-50). As television became a more important campaign tool, especially for advertising, the role of the supporter became more passive. Supporters were asked more often to contribute funds, rather than their time.

Even with television as the primary voter communication mechanism, grassroots support still existed at the level of the city and county. Candidate organizations, often in alignment with local and state party organizations, used volunteers to staff phone banks and transport voters to the polls. However, party organizations that were expected to provide that grassroots support, always weak in American politics, became increasingly professionalized, top-down structures. Increasingly this trend moved beyond presidential politics to statewide races for offices such as governor or senator or even congressional races (Strachan, 2003: Shea, 2001; Medvic, 2001).

The Internet has provided a means for the supporter to play more than a spectator role in the campaign. Certain site features are useful to undecideds, but most of the messages on candidate home pages assume the visitor is ready to do more than search for a candidate. Links beckon visitors to join the email list to receive regular news, engage in online activities in support of the candidate, and donate to the campaign (Davis, 2004; Bimber and Davis, 2003: 47-67).

Financial donations still function as the most important contribution due to the costs of professional broadcast media-oriented campaigns. Online credit card donations offer campaigns quick and easy access to potential donors. In 1998, over 70 percent of sites of candidates in competitive races featured a donation solicitation. But the real impetus for online financial solicitations was the Federal Election Commission's decision in 1999 to allow candidates to solicit credit card donations online. Not surprisingly, larger amounts of money arrived in candidate coffers via the Internet than had before online credit card donations, and it came more quickly. Senator John McCain's campaign raised $1.4 million in three days following his surprise New Hampshire primary victory (Bimber and Davis, 2003: 38-39).

Volunteers can be recruited online to engage in both traditional and online volunteer activity. Often, mobilization messages are designed to assist the site visitor to recruit family and friends to support the campaign (Bimber and Davis, 2003: 54-59; Foot and Schneider, 2002). Online activity ranges from sending e-mails to friends to participating in online discussion communities and networks in behalf of the candidate.

Effects on the Audience

The object of online political communication, like messages through traditional means, is the audience. However, the audience for online electoral information is not the same as the general public or even Internet users generally. They tend to be male, affluent, conservative, and experienced Internet users. For the most part, they are also the already politically interested (Farnsworth and Owen, 2004; Dulio and O'Brien, 2004, Bimber and Davis, 2003).

Until recently, audiences were not using the Internet to replace other media. Instead, Internet use for political purposes was supplemental. Those who used the Internet for political information tended to be those who use other media for the same purpose (Jennings and Zeitner, 2003; Davis and Owen, 1998). There is evidence beginning in 2004 that online news and political information has become a main source for a substantial number of users. An analysis of survey data collected by the Pew Research Center in 2004 revealed that over 40 percent of respondents reported that they use traditional news sources less frequently as a consequence of going online more often. This finding was especially pronounced for younger audience members, as 50 percent of twenty-four to thirty year olds had cut down on their traditional media use in favor or online sources.[1] Further, a June 2005 Pew Research Center study reported that the Internet is now the main source of news for one fourth of all Americans, most of whom go online for news daily. While this trend is most evident for people under age thirty, 30 percent of respondents aged thirty to forty-nine consider the Internet to be their main news source (Pew Research Center, 2005a).

What do audiences go online for? They want to use online electoral information to make vote choices (Farnsworth and Owen, 2004: 425-26). People who participate in the campaign online also tend to hold established political predispositions in terms of candidates, issues, party, and ideology, and they use the Internet experience to reinforce those predispositions (Bimber and Davis, 2003).

Predictions have varied on whether the Internet would change citizens, particularly transforming them into interested participants. Some saw the Internet as a potentially powerful tool for reinvigorating civic involvement (Corrado and Firestone, 1996; Pavlik, 1996; Grossman, 1995). Others have countered that the Internet has produced a new digital divide between the politically interested and active and all others (Cornfield, 2004a; Norris, 2001; Margolis and Resnick, 2000; Norris, 2001; Davis, 1999).

The findings on whether the Internet increases levels of political participation are mixed. Bimber and Davis found that the audience for candidate websites tended to be the already politically interested (2003: 108-124). Bimber found little effect of online exposure on political participation or civic engagement (Bimber, 2001). And Jennings and Zeitner offered empirical support for the thesis that the Internet has exacerbated the divide between the politically interested and others (Jennings and Zeitner, 2003).

Other studies offer different results. Kaye and Johnson found Internet users reporting increased levels of political efficacy and participation after being on-line. Tolbert and McNeal concluded that Internet users who were exposed to online political news were more likely to vote (Johnson and Kaye, 2003; Tolbert and McNeal, 2003). According to Lupia and Philpot, political websites have the potential to affect voter interest and desire to participate in electoral politics if the site is perceived by the user as effective as an informational tool (Lupia and Philpot, 2002). A study of meet-ups in 2004 concluded that although the vast majority of participants had previously been involved in campaigns, the new recruitment method had mobilized new activists in the electoral process (Williams *et al*, 2004).

The 2004 Election

2004 seemed to be the year of campaign interactivity, as candidates found new ways, such as blogs, Web-linked email, and meet-ups, to seek to stimulate involvement in the campaign. But has mobilization become a more prominent online message than reinforcement and providing information?

Methodology: Content Analysis and Surveys

A content analysis of presidential candidate websites during the general election was conducted to determine the nature of online messages of reinforcement/providing information and mobilization. Content analysis is one of the best-known and most widely utilized methods of studying mass communication (Berger, 1991; Krippendorff, 1980; Carney, 1972; Holsti, 1969). In this study, the unit of analysis was the candidate Website.

By analyzing candidate online communication content, this study compares the presence of reinforcement information and voter mobilization messages in candidate-controlled Web content. Candidate websites were coded for components of the candidate's self-presentation. The emphasis of the coding was on the usage of links from the main page as gauges of the presence and prominence of candidate messages. The coding instrument examined the presence and placement of links related to reinforcement and mobilization.

Reinforcement information was defined as main page links to information about the candidate. These included candidate biographies, candidate issue positions, and campaign news. The candidate biography is one page dedicated to a brief description of the candidate's personal and professional background. The candidate issue position links typically connect to a section including one or more pages describing the candidate's stances on issues. Some candidate sites break down the issue section into separate issues (economy, education, foreign policy, etc.) accessible from the main page. The campaign news section typically includes press releases from the campaign and/or the text of media endorsements or other news coverage of the candidate.

Mobilization information was defined as main page links to information designed to facilitate voter involvement in the campaign. This involvement can take the form of communication with the campaign—joining a meet up or blog—or contribution to the campaign, such as making a financial donation, volunteering, attending a campaign event, or registering to vote.

The analysis centered on the presence of these particular messages. In other words, did such links appear on the site? It also included examination of their prominence on the site. This was measured by the number of times a link appeared on the main page, whether the link appeared at the top of the page, and whether the link was highlighted in contrast with surrounding text. In other words, was it bolded, italicized, or given a different color? The first measure was based on the assumption that the more emphasis the campaigns wanted to place on site visitors clicking through to retrieve certain information, the greater number of links they would place on the page to facilitate that objective. The second similarly assumed that campaigns desiring site visitors to use these links would place them in a prominent location on the main page, i.e. at the top of the page. The third was based on the assumption that highlighted text would stand out and draw the user's attention.

The coding was limited to the main page. The home page of a website is the main portal to the website. Since the main page is the first glimpse of the candidate's online presentation and the most visited page, it becomes the best gauge of the campaign's emphases in its online presentations. The question is whether that presentation is dominated by mobilization messages or reinforcement messages.

The sites coded were those of presidential candidates during the general election stage in 2004. Websites for George W. Bush and John Kerry were coded monthly over a period from May to November 2004. (The Nader site was coded from June to November.) The Bush and Kerry sites were coded seven times while the Nader site was coded six times. Three coders independently coded each of the sites. The composite reliability score for the three coders was .95. (Holsti, 1969: 137-138) There was unanimity among the coders on 63 percent of the 231 variables, while on another 31 percent there was two-thirds agreement. On another 6 percent of the variables there was no agreement. Pairwise comparison of the coders found that agreement ranged from a high of 88 percent between coders 1 and 2 and a low of 85 percent between coders 2 and 3.

In addition to the content analysis, we conducted a survey during the 2004 presidential election to examine the extent to which people who accessed candidate websites used them for reinforcement and mobilization. The study consisted of a three-wave panel survey, and was administered using the online survey tool, Surveymonkey.com. The first two waves of the study were conducted during the final month of the campaign; the first survey was in the field from October 7-18, and the second from October 21-30. The final wave was administered post-election, from November 9-20.

As our goal was to assess the extent to which voters respond to candidates' online reinforcement information and mobilization efforts, we sought subjects who would be more likely than the general population to engage the Internet campaign. A convenience sample consisting of individuals from all regions of the country was employed. We oversampled young people, especially students and young professionals. Subjects were recruited through universities and places of employment, including law firms and trade associations. The subjects ranged in age from eighteen to sixty-eight, with 37 percent aged eighteen to twenty (first-time voters), 21 percent aged twenty-one to twenty-four, 19 percent aged twenty-five to twenty-nine, and 18 percent aged thirty and older. The sample consisted of 43 percent males and 57 percent females.[2] Thus, the higher level of interest in the campaign and voter turnout by young women is reflected in their willingness to complete the three-wave study. By race, 84 percent of the sample was Caucasian, 6 percent Asian American/South Asian/Pacific Islander, 4 percent Hispanic, 3 percent Black, and 4 percent identified with more than one race. The survey respondents were more engaged in the 2004 presidential election than the general public. 80 percent reported that they were interested in the campaign, 55 percent stated that they were paying attention to the campaign in the media, and the vast majority turned out to vote.

Respondents were contacted through an email invitation, and received two follow-ups during each wave of the study. In an effort to decrease panel attrition, subjects who completed all three waves of the study received a $10 gift certificate to Amazon.com. 468 people completed the first wave of the study, and 355 participated in the second wave. A total of 322 participants completed all three surveys. The attrition rate between the first and second waves of the study was 26 percent, as 113 people dropped out. A total of thirty-three additional subjects were lost between the second and third wave.

Of the 302 subjects whose responses are analyzed here, 20 percent never accessed a candidate's website, 38 percent accessed a site at only one point in the study, and 42 percent accessed a site on two or more occasions. We characterize respondents who accessed a site in the period covered by only one of the waves as "infrequent visitors" to candidate websites, and those who accessed sites during both periods as "frequent visitors."

Results

Candidate Website Content

The content analysis reveals that interactive components such as sections for donating, volunteering, and meet-ups are present on presidential candidate websites almost as often as more passive elements such as biographies, press releases, and general campaign news. Table 5.1 shows that passive links were slightly more likely to be present than interactive links. While each campaign site included standard components of information retrieval, some failed to adopt interactive components. The Bush campaign did not use meet-ups. The Kerry campaign did, but stopped them by October. The Nader campaign never had a blog or an online activism kit. (Although counted as a blog, the Bush campaign blog lacked a comment capability that is frequent on many blogs and was present on the Kerry campaign blog.)

When interactive links were present, they were displayed more prominently than passive links (Table 5.2). They were far more likely to have multiple links on the main page, be featured with highlighted text such as bold or italicized font or color. And they more frequently appeared at the top of the page where site users would see them first. The only exception was text that was larger than surrounding text. Campaigns almost never used that technique to emphasize links. The Nader campaign had the least difference between passive and interactive, suggesting that they were running an old-style Internet campaign approach that more closely resembled the earlier online brochure.

Increasingly, interactivity is becoming a critical component of candidate websites. They nearly match the more passive features such as biographies and campaign news. When they do occur, candidates give emphasis to them in order to direct user attention to them.

These interactive messages—volunteer to help my campaign, donate money, post on my blog, etc.—suggest the movement of the use of the Internet towards utilizing a range of online capabilities, not just providing news and information about the candidate and the campaign. The candidate website may increasingly become a vehicle for political engagement more than mere political information delivery.

Table 5.1 Presence of Passive vs. Interactive Section Links on Candidate Websites. Percentage of sites with link from main page

	Passive Section Links	Interactive Section Links
Bush	100%	83%
Kerry	100%	76%
Nader	100%	53%
Other	100%	72%

**Table 5.2 Prominence of Passive vs. Interactive Section
Links on 2004 Presidential Candidate Websites.
Percentage of sites with prominence characteristic**

	Passive	Interactive
Multiple Links	48%	87%
Bush	31	100
Kerry	20	78
Nader	100	79
Larger Text	0%	3%
Highlighted Text	28%	58%
Bush	0	41
Kerry	23	69
Nader	54	70
Link at Top	39%	64%
Bush	20	49
Kerry	6	66
Nader	100	90

Audience Use of Campaign Websites

There was a marked increase in the number of people who visited campaign-related websites during the 2004 campaign compared to the 2000 election.
Republican candidate George W. Bush's site in 2004 received sixteen million
visitors, up from nine million in 2000. Twenty million people visited Democratic candidate John Kerry's site in 2004, compared to seven million who accessed Al Gore's site in 2000 (Cornfield, 2004b).

Parody sites, which poked fun at candidates on both sides of the aisle, were
a popular innovation in 2004, and attracted more young voters than did the candidate sites. (Cornfield, 2004b) Parody sites in the 2000 campaign tended to be
fairly standard text and picture-based presentations. In 2004, parody sites were
more technically sophisticated. The most frequently accessed parody sites included film, animation, and song. Jibjab.com's parody, "This Land," which depicts presidential candidates George W. Bush and John Kerry singing comical
lyrics to a Woodie Guthrie tune, was accessed by over ten million people in July
alone (see Figure 5.1). The progressive organization, Americans Coming Together (ACT), attracted visitors to its site (www.whitehousewest.com) with a

parody video featuring comic Will Ferrell imitating George W. Bush. The video was downloaded over one million times, and thirty thousand people clicked through to volunteer with or contribute to ACT (Cornfield, 2004b).

Figure 5.1 Opening Frame to Jibjab.com's "This Land" Parody

The survey respondents, as we anticipated, were more likely than the general population to visit campaign-related websites. In keeping with overall trends for voters generally, the respondents were more likely to visit a presidential candidate's website than a political party site. They focused most of their attention on major party presidential candidate sites. Further, parody sites were visited by more subjects than the official candidate sites. As Table 5.3 depicts, 68 percent of respondents visited a presidential candidate's website, with more people accessing the Kerry site than the Bush site. A small percentage clicked onto the sites of Ralph Nader and other independent candidates. Slightly more than one quarter of respondents accessed a local candidate's website, including those of candidates for sheriff, state legislator, or governor. 60 percent of participants visited a political party site. Parody sites, including jibjab.com and theonion.com, were visited by 70 percent of respondents. Many of these respondents were drawn to parody sites as a result of emails that were sent to them by friends and associates. A small percentage accessed parody sites to the exclusion of other campaign sites.

Survey respondents were asked whether they had engaged in a number of activities associated with candidate websites. Activities related to reinforcement consisting of subscribing to a candidate's email alerts and reading a candidate's web log. Recruitment/mobilization activities include using the site to contribute to, volunteer for, or help organize an event for a candidate, participating in an online discussion group about a candidate, contributing to a candidate's web log, taking part in an online chat on a candidate's website, and forwarding a link to a campaign-related site. Table 5.4 indicates the results for infrequent and frequent visitors to presidential campaign sites. The findings suggest that visitors to the sites were drawn more to the reinforcement aspects of candidate sites than the mobilization aspects. There was little difference in respondents' propensity to engage in activities related to reinforcement based on whether they were frequent or infrequent visitors. Over 50 percent in each category subscribed to a candidate's email alerts, and more than one-quarter read candidate blogs. There were significant differences in respondents' engagement in mobilization activities. Frequent visitors to candidate sites were more likely to take part in recruitment activities, such as contributing, volunteering, and organizing events than infrequent visitors. They were also more likely to take part in an online discussion group, contribute to a candidate's web log, and participate in an online chat, although very few respondents engaged in online chats via candidate sites. A high percentage in each group had forwarded a link from a political website, not necessarily a candidate site, to a friend or associate.

Table 5.3 Percentage of Survey Respondents Who Visited Campaign-Related Websites in 2004

Presidential Candidate Site	68%
Which candidate?	
Bush	47%
Kerry	61%
Nader	8%
Other	5%
Local Candidate Site	28%
Political Party Site	60%
Parody Site (e.g. Jibjab.com)	70%

The second wave of the survey contained a battery of questions that asked respondents to evaluate eleven elements of content for the Bush and Kerry websites. Content related to reinforcement includes information about the candidate's personal attributes, information about the candidate's issue positions, information contrasting the candidate with his opponent, candidate ads, and information about the campaign and voting. Recruitment/mobilization content consists of opportunities for visitors to get involved with the campaign, to keep informed about campaign events, to access campaign resources, such as bumper stickers and yard signs that can be used to campaign for the candidate, opportunities to communicate with others who hold similar beliefs, the ability to give feedback to the campaign, and the ability to make donations to the campaign. Each item was rated on a five-point scale, where one represents a poor evaluation and five means excellent. 103 survey respondents evaluated George W. Bush's website, and 110 respondents rated John Kerry's site.

Table 5.4 Percentage of Survey Respondents Who Engaged Reinforcement and Mobilization Aspects of Candidate's Websites

	Infrequent Visitors	Frequent Visitors
Reinforcement		
-Subscribe to email alerts	54%	52%
-Read candidate's blog	26%	29%
Recruitment/Mobilization		
-Recruitment activities*	7%	11%
-Discussion group*	11%	30%
-Contributed to web log*	5%	25%
-Taken part in online chat	0%	3%
-Forwarded link *	79%	84%

* χ^2 p≤.05

The mean scores for each indicator were computed, and t-tests performed to determine if there are significant differences between evaluations of the Bush and Kerry sites. As Table 5.5 indicates, the reinforcement items were rated, on average, between good and very good. John Kerry's site received slightly higher marks than George W. Bush's site, but the difference was only significant for providing information about the campaign and voting. For both candidates, the ability to view campaign ads on the site was the highest ranked type of reinforcement content. Both sites provided an archive of campaign ads that was regularly updated and easily accessible. New campaign ads were frequently previewed on the sites before they were shown on television. Campaign ads online served as a resource for journalists, as well.

Mobilization content generally was ranked more favorably by site visitors than reinforcement content with a few exceptions. Providing opportunities for getting involved with the campaign, keeping visitors informed about campaign events, and providing a mechanism for making donations to the campaign were given high marks. The ability to give feedback to the campaign received the lowest ranking of all items for both candidate websites, and was especially low for the Bush site. Evaluations of the Bush site were significantly lower than those of the Kerry site on all indicators.

Table 5.5 Respondents' Evaluations of Candidate Website
Content Mean Scores

	Bush	Kerry	t-test sign.
Reinforcement			
Information about candidate's personal attributes	3.55	3.68	n.s.
Information about candidate's issue positions	3.51	3.77	n..s.
Contrasting the candidate with his opponent	3.44	3.72	n.s.
Viewing the candidate's campaign ads	3.79	3.88	n.s.
Information about the campaign and voting	3.36	3.69	.05
Recruitment/Mobilization			
Opportunities for getting involved with campaign	3.91	4.23	.02
Keeping informed about campaign events	3.67	4.02	.01
Providing resources that could be used in campaign	3.43	3.86	.01
Providing opportunities to communicate with others	3.23	3.53	.01
Giving feedback to the campaign	3.00	3.41	.07
Making donations to the campaign	4.16	4.30	.00

Email alerts were a prominent part of both presidential candidates' online strategies. People who signed up for email alerts received messages from campaign managers, leaders of the candidate's party, and members of the candidate's family, such as the Bush daughters, Jenna and Barbara. During the final weeks of the election, campaigns increased the number of alerts sent to email list subscribers, especially those asking for donations. The 258 survey respondents who subscribed to candidates' email alerts were asked to evaluate them on a range of criteria. They were asked if they agreed, disagreed, or neither agreed nor disagreed with a series of ten statements. As Table 5.6 indicates, 57 percent of respondents believed that email alerts are a useful component of a candidate's campaign. However, far fewer respondents agreed that email alerts facilitated their ability to keep informed or become engaged in the campaign. 35 percent of survey participants felt that email alerts helped keep them informed, while 15 percent reported that they become more involved in the campaign because of the alerts. A small percentage, around 10 percent in each case, took part in a volunteer activity or contributed to the campaign because of email alerts. These figures should not be underestimated, as only a small percentage of Americans become involved in campaign activities. They invite speculation that email invitations to become active in campaigns may be stimulating increased participation, although that conclusion is beyond the reach of these data.

Table 5.6 Respondents' Evaluations of Candidate's Email Alerts
Percentage agreeing and disagreeing with each statement

	Agree	Disagree
-Email alerts were helpful in keeping me informed about the campaign	35%	17%
-I became more involved in the campaign because of the email alerts	15%	48%
-I took part in a volunteer activity with the campaign because of the email alerts	10%	78%
-I contributed money to the campaign because of the email alerts	11%	76%
-Email alerts are a useful component of a candidate's campaign	57%	13%
-I read email alerts regularly	29%	36%
-I deleted the email alerts before I read them	31%	43%
-I appreciated receiving email alerts from prominent politicians	45%	24%
-There were too many email alerts	49%	31%
-I was annoyed by the email alerts	31%	37%

Respondents also were asked whether they read the email messages. Less than 30 percent reported that they read the email alerts regularly, and 31 percent stated that they deleted the alerts before they read them. However, more people (36 percent) read the messages regularly and did not delete them before reading (43 percent). Finally, survey participants were asked to express their attitudes toward the email alerts. 45 percent reported that they appreciated receiving messages from prominent politicians. At the same time, respondents expressed some frustration with the alerts. Almost half of the respondents felt that candidates sent too many email alerts, while 31 percent disagreed. Nearly one-third of participants stated that they were annoyed by the email alerts. A small number of study participants (twenty-four) unsubscribed from a candidate's email alerts. Respondents reported that they felt overwhelmed by the number of messages they were receiving, that their inboxes were being flooded with the alerts, and that they did not find the messages useful or compelling.

The final issue we address is whether people who accessed political websites are more likely to take part in campaign activities offline than those who do not engage the Internet campaign. While it is impossible to establish a causal relationship between website use and campaign activity from our data, we can seek evidence of a correlation. The dependent variable, campaign activity, consists of a ten-point additive index constructed from a battery of questions asked of respondents during the third wave of the study. The items tapped if respondents had done any of the following: volunteered for a presidential candidate, volunteered for a political party, volunteered for a political organization (such as Moveon.org or Citizen Outreach), attended a campaign rally or speech, attended a campaign fundraiser or house party, wore a campaign button in support of a candidate or displayed a bumper sticker on a car or posted on sign, canvassed or distributed literature for a candidate, worked at a phone bank for a candidate, traveled to another state to work for a candidate, donated money to a candidate, or volunteered on election day for a candidate or political party. Only a small number of people had engaged in any single activity, with the exception of the 30 percent who reported wearing a campaign button or displaying a sign. Additive indexes for using candidate websites for reinforcement and mobilization also were constructed. The reinforcement item tapped whether the respondent subscribed to a candidate's email alerts or read a blog on a candidate's website. The mobilization item included whether the respondent had used the candidate's site for volunteer and recruitment activities, participated in a discussion group on a candidate's site, contributed to a candidate's blog, participated in an online chat on a candidate's site, and forwarded a link to a political site.

We performed an ordinary least squares regression analysis to establish if there is a relationship between survey respondents' use of political websites and offline campaign activity. The independent variables included accessing a candidate's website for reinforcement, accessing a candidate's site for mobilization, accessing a political party website (0=no; 1=yes), and accessing a campaign parody website (0=no; 1=yes). A control variable was entered for attention to the campaign, where a score of six corresponds to high interest and one to low interest.

As Table 5.7 indicates, using a candidate's site for mobilization is the strongest predictor of offline campaign activity. Accessing a political party website was the second highest predictor, followed by using a candidate site for reinforcement. These three website-related variables have higher coefficients than attention to the campaign. The parody site variable was the weakest predictor in the model.

Table 5.7 OLS Regression Analysis: Campaign Activity on Attention to the Campaign and Website Use

	B	Standard Error	beta	Sign.
Attention to Campaign	.351	.194	.101	.072
Candidate Site – Reinforcement	.324	.173	.102	.062
Candidate Site – Mobilization	.529	.131	.244	.000
Political Party Site	.490	.236	.121	.039
Parody Site	.344	.260	.075	.187
Constant	-1.342			.049

Adj. R^2 = .173   Sign. = .000
n = 301

Conclusion

The online presence of presidential candidates has evolved far beyond the bro-chure-ware of earlier websites. Increasingly sites are designed not merely to inform voters about the candidate, but to reinforce and, most importantly, to mobilize voters to take action in behalf of the campaign.

Our survey analysis provides some indication that candidate's mobilization efforts encourage people to take part in the campaign, especially among those who are oriented toward the online environment. While users mostly access presidential websites for reinforcement, especially to gain information about candidates, mobilization efforts are attracting voters. 11 percent of survey re-spondents reported that candidate's email alerts had caused them to become more involved in the campaign, with 10 percent stating that the alerts were re-sponsible for them taking part in a volunteer activity. Further, people who en-gaged with the mobilization elements of candidate websites were more likely to be active in the campaign offline than those who did not.

The candidates' online mobilization effort reinforces the conclusion that candidate campaigns in the United States perform many of the functions that parties carry out in other systems. Additionally, candidates have found a new vehicle for those functions. The Internet, like television, offers still another me-dium to bypass the weak party apparatus and reach voters directly. The status quo of a weak party organization vis-à-vis candidates remains intact as candi-dates discover still another tool to function autonomously.

Notes

1. Analysis performed by the authors of the Biennial Media Consumption Survey 2004 conducted by the Pew Research Center for the People and the Press, June, 2004.
2. Interestingly, the 2004 presidential election marked the largest gender gap in voter turnout ever recorded for eighteen to twenty-four year olds, as 50 percent of females cast a ballot compared to 44 percent of males (Lopez, Kirby, and Sagoff, 2005).

Chapter Six

Canada: Party Websites and Online Campaigning During the 2004 and 2006 Federal Elections

Tamara A. Small, David Taras and Dave Danchuk

Much has been written about the potential that the Internet has to create new global public spaces, spaces that transcend national borders and national communities. Much has also been written about the Internet's capacity for hyperfragmentation; every interest, every passion, every cause and every need seems to have found a place in cyberspace. Indeed, the acclaimed German author Gunter Grass has even written about the Internet's capacity to resurrect lost causes and reclaim and energize long-suppressed historical events and memories (Grass, 2003). Much less has been written, however, about how the Internet can become a vehicle for reinforcing national boundaries and national interactions. We will argue that party websites, at least in the Canadian context, are an example of how new information technologies can become a vehicle for national expression and cohesion.

Benjamin Barber (2004, p.33) has noted that a technology "generally reflects and mirrors the culture in which it evolves rather than guiding and directing it." Not surprisingly, the use of the Internet and indeed all other communications technologies in Canada is dictated, to a large degree, by the nature of the country itself. Canada straddles no fewer than six time zones, borders on three oceans and is so vast that single constituencies in the north are larger than all of Western Europe. The United Kingdom and Ireland together can fit neatly into the province of Saskatchewan, which is not one of Canada's larger provinces. This means that Canada is largely a country of regions, regions that, as Northrop Frye (1982, p.59) noted, are themselves "separations." In terms of human geography Canada might be described as an archipelago of city-states nestled along the American border. Although the country is constructed along an east-west axis, much of the economy flows along a north-south grid. Canada-U.S. trade is now close to $2 billion per day and Canada is the leading trading partner of close to forty American states. There is also the painful and nagging question of Quebec sovereignty. Canada came close to the precipice of national disintegration as a result of a Quebec referendum on sovereignty in 1995 and Quebec's future within the federation remains unresolved although support for the current federal government in Quebec is high.

Yet according to a number of commentators the very looseness of Canadian identity has become one of the country's major strengths. Canada is seen by some as a postmodern and post-national experiment that allows citizens to enjoy what Charles Taylor (1993) has called "deep diversity." Canadians have become comfortable with multiple identities and with different ways of being Canadian. There is also a strong consensus around the values that are found in the Canadian *Charter of Rights and Freedoms*, a consensus that cuts across and, some would contend overpowers regional and linguistic divides. In addition, the country's notable prosperity, fueled by exports to the United States and Asia, has created ever larger surpluses for the federal government and has helped dampen divisions and discontent.

Canada has always been an early adopter of new information technologies because of the need to reach across vast distances and because they have been seen as a nationalizing instrument. The first wireless experiments were funded by the Canadian government, Canada was the first country to use satellites for domestic television, the country has the second highest number of households with broadband capacity in the world and close to 70 percent of Canadians regularly used the Internet. Canadians are among the most digitally connected people on the planet.

Although Canadian elections are to a large extent a collection of regional contests, the Internet combined with other factors has brought a degree of centralization and unity to party campaigns that did not exist in the past. Indeed, the American politician Tip O'Neill's famous admonition that "all politics is local" is largely reversed when it comes to Canadian web campaigns. In addition, the Internet's much vaunted capacity to connect people across time and space, its speed, its cost-effectiveness and the degree to which it integrates other media (video, text, radio, telephone, etc), may mean more in the Canadian context than it does in those of other party systems.

Even though the Internet made its debut during the 1997 federal election, it should be noted that the Liberal Party had been an early adopter having established a site as part of the National Capital Free Net in 1993. The 2000 election, however, is generally considered to be the first Internet election. But in 2000 party websites seemed little more than electronic brochures or billboards. They were static, top-down and filled with only rudimentary information. One critic described early party websites as "drab pages that fail to take advantage of the medium's full potential" and that didn't take into account that a site "has to be flexible and interact with people" (Van Praet, 2000). Parties put up sites because it was fashionable and because everyone else seemed to have one but they still weren't sure how they could be used.

This chapter will mainly describe how the websites of each of the four main federal political parties were used during the 2004 federal election. We have also included a short addendum on party web strategies during the 2006 federal election, an election that took place after the sudden defeat of the Liberal government on a vote of non-confidence after only eighteen months in office. In our analysis of the 2004 election we describe the approach that each party took in organizing its web campaigns, how the web fitted into overall campaign strategies, the methods used by the parties to interact with their members, the general public and journalists, and how the parties used their websites to engage in new forms of campaigning. Our description is based on an analysis of websites as they appeared on each day of the 2004 federal election campaign and on interviews conducted with webmasters and senior campaign officials from all of the major parties.[1] Our reflections on the 2006 election are based on published reports, a review of websites and on some interviews. The main conclusion is that while the Internet and websites were mainly used to amplify traditional methods of campaigning, as adjuncts in effect to other aspects of the campaign, the old landscape is rapidly changing. There seem to be more and more instances in which what happens on the web can interact with and influence the course of the campaign. This was especially evident in 2006.

The Campaign Environment

Canadian web campaigns are largely conditioned by the rules imposed by Canadian election law and by the nature and positioning of the major political parties. Election laws present the most significant constraint. Canada has relatively short election campaigns. Due to Canada's parliamentary system, the party that is in power at the time that the election is called can decide the duration of the election campaign. Campaigns can last from a minimum of thirty-six to a maximum of fifty-six days. As soon as elections are called the existing party websites are transformed into campaign sites. They are well staffed, are updated virtually continuously and operate at almost a fever pitch. As soon as the campaign is over, however, the sites revert back to being little more than electronic brochures with few staff and little activity. This is a major difference from the United States where campaigning for party presidential nominations and indeed for valued Senate seats last for well over a year and hence campaign websites must operate at full speed for much longer.

The public financing (parties receive $1.75 (Cdn.) for each vote that they received in the previous election) of Canadian elections by the federal treasury and the sharp limits placed on how much parties and individual candidates can spend, has an enormous impact on the nature of web campaigns. Party websites do not have to become fund-raising engines to nearly same extent that they do in the United States. Indeed, the success of American campaign websites is often measured by how much money they have attracted. While fund-raising remains important in Canada, it is not the lifeblood or the measure of a web campaign's success.

An additional factor is that third parties or interest groups face tough spending restrictions; they are limited to $150,000 (Cdn.) for the entire election campaign. These severe restrictions mean that interest groups simply can't run ad campaigns of any consequence. While American campaigns involve a host of interest groups which sometimes coordinate their efforts with candidates and political parties and often act as their proxies, Canadian parties have the field largely to themselves. During the 2004 and 2006 elections, there were no Canadian equivalents of *Moveon.org* or *SwiftVets.com*.

Tight spending limits also apply to candidates at the riding level. They are limited to roughly $0.70 (Cdn) per voter or $60,000 to $80,000 (Cdn.) per riding depending on the population and geographic size of the constituency. In Canada's first past the post system, candidates for Parliament have little chance to control their own electoral destiny; they are carried to victory or go down to defeat based largely on how well or poorly the national or regional campaigns are being fought. As television and radio ads are mostly unaffordable, lawn signs and old fashioned "shoe leather" remain the principal means of campaigning. At the constituency level, websites tend to be rudimentary—little more than electronic lawn signs. Hence, national party sites are where the action is even for local candidates. In this respect, the Liberal website was typical. The party tracked the postal codes of visitors so that a picture of the local candidate would always appear on the top right-hand corner of the opening page. Visitors were then directed to the candidates' website.

In fact, in 2004 national party sites so dominated the electoral horizon that only 61 percent of local candidates had their own websites. This is up from only 30 percent during the 2000 federal election. There was much variance among the parties; 75 percent of New Democratic Party (NDP) candidates and close to 60 percent of Liberal and Conservative party candidates had a web presence. Remarkably, only six out of seventy-five Bloc Quebecois candidates had their own sites.

Party Web Strategies During the 2004 Election

The Liberal Party

Each of the four major political parties has its own history in cyberspace and each party positioned websites to carry out different objectives. The goal that they shared was in the words of one Conservative Party strategist "to turn the interest of the visitors into our interest" (confidential interview, October 2005). The Liberal Party, led at the time by Paul Martin, is generally considered to be the natural governing party. Going into the 2004 election they had been in power for thirty-three of the previous forty-five years and had governed since 1993. The 2004 election would be their fourth consecutive election victory, although they were only able to form a minority government. The key to the Liberal's supremacy was that they were the only party that could contend in each of Canada's regions. They are traditionally the party of the big cities (including seat-rich Toronto and Vancouver), win the lion's share of the women's vote, reach deeply into Canada's large immigrant communities, are the second party in Quebec and are the dominant force in Atlantic Canada.

During the 2004 election the party was shaken by two political storms: a scandal over the misappropriation of funds meant to boost federalist fortunes in Quebec and the breaking of a promise by the recently elected Liberal government in Ontario, Canada's largest and most populous province, not to raise taxes. Much of the campaign was devoted to trying to put the two firestorms out.

Preparation for the web campaign began soon after the Liberal Party leadership convention that elected Paul Martin in November 2003. By early March the layout was being finalized and members of the web team were meeting on a daily basis. Planners paid close attention to what was occurring in the American presidential race and to the websites of British and other European political parties. They also spoke to mostly American communications strategists and web designers to get their feedback. In the end the placement of icons and methods for "scooping" data were copied from what planners had seen on the Kerry, Bush, British Labour Party and MSN sites. They also took small tentative steps into the world of e-campaigning that Howard Dean had helped to pioneer. Users could send a page, a press release, or even a video clip to friends or to people that they knew.

Believing that the best defense was a bruising offense, their objective during the 2004 campaign was to keep their opponents constantly on the defensive, bloodied and off-balance from a hard-hitting negative campaign. The website was a main instrument in what became a no-holds-barred, brass-knuckle offensive. First, the Liberals erected a separate *Stephen Harper Says* website. The site was devoted to chronicling the positions and statements of Conservative party leader Stephen Harper—all of them cast in a negative light. The Conservatives responded by creating their own attack site—*TeamMartinSaid.ca*. The Tories

sought to caste a wider net by showcasing outrageous and contradictory statements made by Liberal cabinet members as well as by Martin himself.

Second, the Liberals' website featured a "reality checks" section with as
many as a dozen reality checks posted each day. The reality checks would lampoon, contradict and put a negative twist on statements that the opposition leaders were making on the campaign trail. In this regard, the communications team,
which was part of the larger Liberal war room operation, had a surveillance
function. It continually scanned the campaign horizon, including monitoring
other party sites, looking for convenient targets. Within days, and in the case of
the Conservative party just hours, after the launch of the Liberals' reality check
campaign the other parties responded with their own reality check offensives.
This soon became the political equivalent of missile warfare with web campaigns continually launching missiles at each other. The Conservatives alone
had fired off no less than eighty-one reality checks by the end of the campaign.

A third prong, and perhaps the most interesting one, was the BlackBerry
campaign. Almost all campaign personnel, and most crucially all of the reporters
who were covering the campaigns, carried BlackBerries, hand-held devices developed by Research in Motion, a Canadian company. BlackBerries, nicknamed
"CrackBerries" because of what some see as their addictive quality, are multimedia devices that provide Internet and email access in addition to being cell
phones. Reporters would be phoned or emailed while they were traveling on
opposition buses or planes and given the latest information from the Liberal
campaign. They were often directed to the party's website for the text of a particular statement or to a video or audio link that would support and verify what
the Liberals were saying. Armed with the latest information, reporters would put
opposition leaders' feet to the fire by asking them for their reactions to what the
Liberals were saying or were forced to rewrite their stories based on new developments. The goal was to alter the flow of the campaign and indeed of news
stories. But the "ping to ping" campaign had to be carried out with some sub-
tlety. Messages had to be kept "tight" and reporters could not be inundated with
too much information or pinged too often.

Other parties also had successes with the BlackBerry. One member of the
Conservative campaign team remembers watching TV and seeing his own
party's questions being asked of the Prime Minister. He remembers how good it
felt to "hit a home run" (confidential interview, October 2005). The Tories are
particularly proud of how "ping to ping" technology was used within their campaign. During the English-language leaders' debate, for instance, the party ran
several focus groups. They were able to record electronically when Stephen
Harper's arguments were making a positive or negative impact; and which lines
had "scored" and which had "tanked" (Johnson, 2005, pp.369-371). This information was then sent to the party's "talking heads" and "spin doctors" in real
time so that they would know which points to emphasize in their interviews with
reporters and in their on-air exchanges with their counterparts from the other
parties.

There were at least two instances during the campaign when websites may have proved decisive for the Liberals. In the second to last week before the election the Conservatives posted a press release on their website entitled "Paul Martin supports child pornography." Reacting quickly to a charge that was clearly outrageous, the Liberals were able to get the information to reporters who were on the Conservative buses before Conservative leader Stephen Harper even realized that the press release had been posted and before the Tories could soften their message. For the next few days, the Conservative leader was on the defensive—strangely refusing to apologize once the issue was in play.

Even more devastating was the controversial Randy White incident. As the last weekend of the election approached the Conservatives had a slim lead in the polls and appeared to be headed for a narrow victory (Marzolini, 2004). But on the Friday before the final weekend of the campaign the Liberals "discovered" a video of Conservative MP Randy White in which White attacked the legitimacy of the *Charter of Rights and Freedoms*, a document that has become the cornerstone of Canadian political nationality and loyalty. Within hours the Liberals had "blasted White's statement to all of the buses" and the video clip was displayed prominently on their website. Reporters who were reached by Black-Berry were invited to visit the party's website in order to watch the clip for themselves. The effect among voters was devastating. By Monday, the day of the election, the Conservatives' lead had evaporated and it was the Liberals who were on top once again.

Some scholars believe that elections are mainly determined by large economic and social forces and that what happens during campaigns has little overall effect on the outcome. The 2004 Canadian election provides eloquent testimony that the campaign itself can alter the result. In fact, the tide can turn with astonishing speed.

The Conservative Party

The Conservatives were in an entirely different situation. The party was the product of a very recent marriage between the Conservative party, whose strength was largely in Atlantic Canada, and the western-based Alliance party. The new party was also an amalgam, mostly uncomfortable, between Red Tories, who took socially progressive positions, and the more hard right and evangelical politics of the Alliance. The merger had not taken place until late in 2003 and the leadership race that anointed former Alliance chief Stephen Harper as leader had taken place in March 2004, only two months before the election call. Indeed, part of the Liberals' rationale for calling the election was to catch the new party unprepared.

The main objective in bringing the two parties together was to establish a national party that could have an appeal beyond the limited regional bases of the two former parties. The goal above all was to make the long awaited breakthrough into Ontario—the hinge on which Liberal power rested (the party won

100 out of 103 Ontario seats in the 2000 election). At the time the Conservative party had little if any following in Quebec.

With so little time to prepare, the Conservatives' website was rudimentary and passive. Party communications staff had looked at websites in the United Kingdom as well as Australia and New Zealand. They had also scoured close to twenty websites in the United States. They found that, as one operative put it, that they were able to learn more from "south of the border than from the rest of the world combined" (confidential interview, October, 2005). They did, however, copy the clickable map found on the Elections Canada site. By clicking on the map of Canada, visitors were able to locate their local candidates.

In the end, the Conservatives' website was little more than an elaborate brochure. It contained information on the leader's tour, party policies and the latest press releases and buttons for volunteers, campaign donations, etc. Each morning email messages would be sent to local candidates, campaign managers and key party insiders. These e-darts would consist of a daily greeting signed by campaign impresario Tom Flanagan, tour information and directives about the "message of the day."

But given the party's late start and the frantic nature of the campaign the website was not a particular priority. As one official who had some responsibility for overseeing the web campaign lamented, "We were always rushing off to do other things" (confidential interview, September 2005). One of those other things was a sophisticated and elaborate phone-based voter identification system inherited from the Alliance Party. In fact, the website was largely seen as an adjunct to the telephone campaign. The party's direct mail, sign location, volunteer prospecting and get out the vote campaigns were guided by a database collected over the years principally through phone canvassing but also through information "coupons" attached to party mailouts. This quite sophisticated voter ID system allowed the party to know where its volunteers were and to move surplus volunteers from one riding to another; sometimes to ridings in different provinces. But the essential goal was to cultivate and direct their base and ultimately to get their voters to the polls.

Interestingly enough, campaign officials were not particularly impressed by the type of e-campaigning that had been pioneered by Howard Dean's campaign in the United States. Some preliminary steps, however, towards e-campaigning were undertaken in 2004. Supporters could download wallpaper, the party sent emails to supporters asking them to visit the site and some videos could be sent virally.

The Tories' war room operation was probably typical of those of the other parties in terms of people and resources. A staff of three supervised communications operations, and there were four press officers who worked in staggered shifts. Regional desks were manned by a staff of four, with at least two of them on duty at any time. The largest contingent, a group of eight, monitored the media including the websites of the other parties and conducted opposition research. In addition, there were two webmasters. There was also a correspondence unit that, among its other duties, replied to emails.

The Bloc Quebecois

The Bloc Quebecois, a party devoted to Quebec sovereignty, had an entirely different outlook towards online campaigning. The Bloc did not integrate its website fully into the broader campaign strategy and saw the website mainly as a vehicle for reaching young people and young voters. Part of the reason for the low priority may have been that the party had a large lead in the polls in Quebec, was flush with money as a result of public financing and had a strong volunteer base because it could rely on its provincial brother, the Parti Quebecois, and on union support. It did not have to mount a particularly aggressive web campaign because most of its goals had been achieved by other means. Moreover, unlike the other parties it did not have to wage a cross-Canada campaign. The party ran candidates only in Quebec and the website was entirely in French.

The web campaign was essentially divided into two parts. One part was devoted to waging the political ground war. The site featured the daily pronouncements and activities of leader Gilles Duceppe and had side bars on its home page with patches on topics such as the sponsorship scandal, the Liberal government's supposed support for George Bush's plans for a missile shield over Canadian air space (the Martin government eventually decided not to participate), the future of the St. Lawrence River and the Prime Ministers' corporate record, including his use of tax loopholes while President of Canada Steamship Lines. The site was refreshed between one and four times a day based on decisions made on the campaign bus. Those who ran the website had little or no say over which materials were to be posted. Although the Bloc did not upload its election advertisements, there were some twenty-five videos available on its home page—the most of any party.

Most important perhaps was that the site acted as a gateway to a second site aimed entirely at young people. Here the objective was a long term one: to win young people over to the party, and to the cause of Quebec sovereignty, by appealing directly to them and making the site into a kind of political *Sesame Street*. The heart of the appeal to young people was "Les Capsules de George W. Net." These were black and white videos with cool music starring the character George W. Net, a young Quebecois. The character's comments were simple and funny and each video was extremely brief (approximately fifteen seconds). As part of its youth strategy the site was advertised on TV stations that had young audiences such as *Teletoon* and *Musique Plus* and on fifteen websites that had large followings among young people. While the success of the party's youth strategy is difficult to gauge, the site attracted 135 comments in its *Reagissez!* feedback section, not a particularly overwhelming response when compared to the 1,000+ comments on the main page of the Bloc site.

The development of the Bloc's site, however, was hampered by a more fundamental problem. While the party flies the flag of Quebec independence, there are times when political necessity demands that the flag be hidden from view.

During the 2004 election Quebec voters were intent on punishing the Liberals for corruption but were divided and ambivalent about Quebec independence. The Bloc strategy was to fuel the fires of anger and resentment towards the Martin government while downplaying the issue of sovereignty. This had repercussions for the web campaign. Although the Bloc webmasters were deeply impressed by Howard Dean's e-campaign, and liked its interactive nature and its emphasis on blogging, they were fearful that a more interactive site would bring a fistful of problems. A main concern was to ensure that the site did not become a forum for impassioned discussions about Quebec sovereignty. The party webmasters fashioned a not so subtle compromise. While comments were invited, visitors could only react to campaign news and once they had expressed their views they could not respond to what others had written. Moreover, comments had to be approved by the webmasters who in fact refused to publish many of them.

The Bloc was also discouraged by an event that had occurred early in the campaign. Visitors to the site were asked to answer a poll question about whether the new Liberal government led by Paul Martin was different from the previous Liberal government led by Jean Chretien. Webmasters were astonished to find that over six thousand respondents had clicked *No*, while only two hundred had voted *Yes*. They soon discovered that almost all of the *No* votes had come from a single IP address on Parliament Hill.

The New Democratic Party

For the left-leaning NDP the web campaign was primarily about mobilizing its base. The internal campaign of contacting and mobilizing party activists was seen as part and parcel of the external campaign of reaching uncommitted voters. The essential calculation was that grass roots party members would deliver the vote. A senior member of the NDP's campaign staff described the role played by the website in organizing the party's troops:

> If you are fast and efficient in getting a message up on the website on our emerging issue, then our people can take that and run with it and be our ambassadors on the ground. We know that we have thousands and thousands and thousands of people who can get out there and take that message. You've got to keep them motivated, keep them excited and a good website can help do that (confidential interview, October 2005).

The party found that many of its supporters visited the site to find out basic information such as who the candidate was in their riding. The site was the linchpin that connected supporters and potential supporters to the local campaigns.

The NDP had, like all of the other main parties, a password protected intranet or extranet (webmasters used both terms) site meant for internal communication among campaign workers. Communication on this site was almost entirely top-down. Key campaign officials would be informed about organizing techniques and receive campaign materials. In addition, a nightly newsletter, *E.NDP*, was sent out to every candidate, campaign manager, and party official describing the campaign events that were planned for the next day, the messages for the coming week and how to respond to attacks made by other parties. While the other major parties sent similar darts out to party loyalists and subscribers at the end of each day, the NDP saw this effort as being in keeping with its old socialist roots. The new technology was seen as helping to advance the much-touted ideal of bringing ordinary members into the fold of the campaign.

Planning for the web campaign began roughly two years before the 2004 election but day-to-day work really began in March 2003. Communications staff had monitored British and American websites and had been particularly impressed by the techniques in e-campaigning that media consultant Joe Trippi among others had developed for the Howard Dean campaign (Trippi, 2004). Indeed, the NDP was to mount the only real e-campaign of the election although these efforts did not begin until day 24 of the campaign, when the party made the following plea to supporters who visited the site:

> The NDP e-Campaign is Canada's first online election community that puts you in charge of your own personal campaign to raise money and bring new voters to support Today's NDP in this election. We want to put you in control, helping us to deliver the message about the NDP to as many Canadians as possible during the next few weeks of this election. Join the NDP e-Campaign today and we'll start you off running your own personal online campaign to collect pledges and rally support for the NDP. Using simple web and email tools, you can create and send messages to your friends, family and colleagues, inviting them to join you in supporting the NDP in the coming election.

Although the e-campaign had a late beginning, the party was enthusiastic about the results. Supporters were able to download wallpaper featuring leader Jack Layton and they could put an NDP.ca (or NPD.ca) banner on their websites. Most important, the party was able to galvanize an undisclosed number of activists into establishing their own fund-raising networks. According to one campaign official, the party was able to attract "dozens and dozens of people who never left their homes or offices and they raised thousands and thousands of dollars for the campaign" (confidential interview, October 2005).

The NDP considered the web campaign to be a surprising success. The site received 29 million hits, 410,000 visits, and raised roughly $200 (Cdn) an hour.

Like the other websites, the NDP site never slept. Continually refreshing a campaign site is a Herculean task in a country that stretches across so many time zones. When it is 9pm in Ottawa with party headquarters manned by only a skeleton crew, it is only 6pm in vote-rich British Columbia, with most people only beginning to catch up on the day's political events. Well before campaign staff arrive in the morning at headquarters in Ottawa, dawn will have broken in Newfoundland—a part of the country that is geographically closer to Ireland than it is to British Columbia. For campaign workers the wear and tear of fighting an around the clock battle was considerable.

One of the most popular and endearing attractions on the NDP site was a rap video starring former leader Ed Broadbent. The fifty-second video was originally produced for a segment of the CBC's comedy program *This Hour has 22 Minutes*. At sixty-eight years old, Broadbent was an unlikely rapper but the "Ed's back" video seems to take on a life of its own. At one point, it was downloaded almost as many times as the NDP platform (Chase and Galloway, 2004).

Centralization and Interactivity in the Web Campaign

Party websites in Canada serve as vehicles of centralization and national integration. Apart from the separatist Bloc Quebecois, party websites focus on national issues and connect party members to the national campaign. To begin with, all eyes are on the leaders' tours. Leaders are expected to display a kind of campaign machismo by traveling continually across huge distances, often making appearances in two or three provinces on a single day. The magic of the web is that it allows the public to experience the campaign trail. The sights and sounds of the campaign are now available at any time of the day and across all of the time zones. This is no small matter in a country where vast distances make it impossible for the great majority of Canadians personally to see or hear the party leaders or even prominent cabinet ministers.

Web campaigns mimic TV campaigns in as much as the main focus is on the party leaders. Indeed, websites can be thought of as part of the leaders' tours. One CBC correspondent described the sites as little more than a "cult of personality" with the leaders dominating almost every webpage (Guha, 2004). Event calendars, campaign diaries, photo galleries and news stories magnify the campaign tour and the activities and pronouncements of the party leaders. On the Conservative party site, for instance, there were no less than five pictures of Stephen Harper on the home page and two more on the splash page. These photos were regularly replaced by new photos from the campaign trail. The Liberal party site featured a slide show called the "Prime Minister's Tour." By clicking the link, a window would open featuring a number of campaign photos and descriptions. Without user prompting, the photos would automatically change. The feature was updated daily.

For party strategists the purpose of the leader's tour is to create what amounts to a larger than life campaign advertisement every day. Presumably the tour is choreographed so that the visuals symbolize and create a proper backdrop for the message of the day. Similarly quotable sound bites are prepared for each campaign stop. Strategists hope that the ad that they have just created is "hot" enough to make it onto the evening news. The difference, of course, between TV and party websites is that the online message can be more easily controlled. On TV, the party's message is often ignored, spun in a different direction, contradicted or held up to ridicule by the journalists who are reporting from the campaign bus or airplane. Websites give the party unmediated access to voters—a scarce commodity in politics. For this reason, it is hard to imagine party websites changing their look any time soon.

Another nationalizing effect is that visitors could download campaign commercials. Because of the regional nature of party competition in Canada election spots are often targeted at certain demographic groups in only certain cities or provinces where there are hotly contested races. For instance, in 2004 the NDP and the Liberals aired specialized ads that ran only in British Columbia and Quebec. These spots could not be seen by TV audiences elsewhere in the county. But visitors to party websites, however, were able to view the full flights of campaign spots. Sixteen TV commercials were made available on the Liberal and NDP sites, while ten could be downloaded from the Conservative site.

The great test for many observers about whether websites are effective tools is the extent to which they are truly interactive and connect citizens to political parties. Here the record was mixed. First, email was available on all four sites. But the only way that a user could send an inquiry or comment to any of the major parties was by using the feedback form supplied by the parties and submitting the information required to do so. A cynic might argue that the main objective for the parties was to be able to glean as much demographic information as possible in order to build their databases. Interestingly, the Liberals were the only party that made visitors aware of their privacy policy. They informed users about the ways in which they intended to treat the information that they had collected.

Although the majority of those interviewed for this study insisted that their parties replied to all of the emails that they received, and each of the major parties seemed to have employed a small army of people whose job it was to answer emails, we are skeptical about claims that the parties replied to all of the emails that that were sent. During the second week of the 2004 campaign, Tamara Small emailed all nine registered parties requesting information about their stances on the contentious issues of same-sex marriage. Only two of the parties—the Green party and the Canadian Action Party (both minor parties)—replied during the election. A month after the election, she received an email from the Conservatives signed by Stephen Harper. The note apologized for not responding earlier. The six other parties did not respond at all. Clarkson (2001, pp.47-49) found a similar response rate during the 2000 cyber-campaign.

Another device for receiving feedback from the public was the "discuss this item" links provided by the Liberals and the Bloc's *Reagissez!* link. Here the Bloc pushed the envelope further than the Liberals. The *Reagissez!* link was located at the conclusion of campaign stories on *blocquebecois.org*. By clicking on this link, a new browser window would open and allow visitors to type in a comment. The Bloc posted the comments on the site and allowed others to respond. But as noted earlier, the Bloc's webmasters tried to ensure that only "safe" topics were discussed. Nonetheless, the link proved to be extremely popular, with more than one thousand comments being posted.

The sites of the other major parties could be described as "closed shops." The reason was that the parties feared that online discussions could knock them off campaign message by raising controversial issues or bringing unwanted attention to the "crazies" that might invade or be planted in party chat rooms. Indeed, the Conservatives saw the possibility of such an invasion as a major drawback to e-campaigning. They had previously experienced problems with the unauthorized use of their logo and feared that even well-meaning party members could make "over the top" statements that could be embarrassing to the party.

The smaller parties had a lot less to fear and arguably much more to gain by interacting with the public. This is reflected in an invitation that appeared on *greenparty.ca*:

> The Green party does politics differently. We want to engage the public, our members and the opposition parties in a sincere debate about the future of Canada. Our definition of grassroots democracy includes bringing people—from all walks of life—together in discussion about the future.

Consequently, the Green party experimented with two interactive devices. First, there was a "Rank a Plank" link which allowed visitors to click on a "thumbs up" or "thumbs down" icon on any item in the party platform. According to the site, the party would re-open discussions on lower-ranked policy positions. Second, the party operated a discussion forum called *The Living Platform*. The Marijuana Party and the Communist Party of Canada had similar forums on their websites. Interestingly enough, despite the arrival of blogs as a popular form of Internet communication, blogs did not make an appearance on party websites in 2004.

Addendum: The 2006 Federal Election

On 29 November 2005, after only eighteen months in office, Paul Martin's Liberal government was defeated by a non-confidence vote in the House of Commons. An election was called for 23 January 2006, which meant that the campaign would take place during the harsh Canadian winter. Martin opted for a long eight-week campaign, calculating that the Conservatives would come unraveled under the strain of a longer campaign. There would, however, be a ten-day break between Christmas and New Year's day.

In most ways the 2006 cyber campaign was a replay of the 2004 campaign. Websites were mostly static and conservative except that they had become a bit more advanced in their uses of technology and that blogs had become both a centre piece and a weapon in the cyber war. Arguably, one could see the vague outlines of what might eventually become a new form of campaigning: the forming of alliances between parties and independent bloggers and greater attention to blogging by the mainstream media.

The Liberal Party website was revamped shortly after the 2004 election. Interestingly, on the opening page visitors were now asked "Please tell us a little about yourself." The party was well aware that it needed to build a database for its fund-raising, volunteer and get-out-the-vote efforts that was at least the equal of the Tories' and so data scooping had become a vital priority. While email messages were sent to subscribers, they were not targeted or customized in any way. In its critique of the 2006 web campaigns, a consulting firm, Hillwatch e-services, chastized all of the parties for failing to tailor their messages to key groups of voters. Their analysis contained the following warning:

> Ultimately, this indiscriminate approach to the use of email is dangerously close to being spam . . . Although email is one of the most effective tools available to online political campaigns, it can alienate as easily as it can engage. It would appear that Canadian political parties have discovered the tool, but not the instruction manual (Hillwatch, 2006).

The Liberal site also featured Martin speechwriter Scott Feschuk's "Now Bloggier" or "Stays crunchy in milk" BlackBerry Blog. Biting barbs against the opposition parties were leavened with irreverent and funny comments about the fruit platters on the campaign bus and the shampoo in hotel rooms. Feschuk was also able to lampoon a gaffe-prone senior member of his own campaign team, writing that public opinion was equally divided "about whether he is an 'idiot' or 'a complete idiot'" (Thompson, 2006). Feschuk later reported that he had received several thousand emails during the campaign.

But if 2006 was the year of the blog in Canadian politics, the Liberals would be its principal victim. Some of the wounds were self-inflicted while others were targeted assaults that did extensive damage. The most obvious self-inflicted wound occurred when Mike Klander, a vice-president of the Ontario wing of the party, posted photos showing NDP candidate Olivia Chow, the wife of party leader Jack Layton, and a chow chow dog under the caption "separated at birth." Although Klander quickly removed the posting in the face of a hail of media criticism, it remained in the cache on the Google search engine. More extensive searches led journalists to earlier postings in which Klander had written that Layton was an "asshole" and a "weasel," that Stephen Harper "creeps people out" and that his cowboy hat made him "look gay" (Bowman, 2006, pp.88-90). Klander was forced to resign.

Not long after the Klander incident, the Liberals' entire election program was leaked to the right wing *Western Standard* magazine, which posted it on its blog. The party's lavish and glitzy announcement ceremony was suddenly a lot less newsworthy.

A third blunder that occurred online was the posting on the Liberal website of a wildly inappropriate and offensive TV ad. The spot began by showing a sinister looking and out of focus picture of Stephen Harper. Then, against the backdrop of a militaristic drumbeat, a deep female voice gravely intones that, "Stephen Harper actually announced that he wants to increase military presence in our cities, Canadian cities, soldiers with guns, in our cities." The ad, which was never aired, was downloaded by CTV news before it could be taken down.

It was widely circulated within the blogsphere and became the subject of cruel commentary and jokes in the mainstream media. The absurd ad undermined the campaign by demonstrating that the Liberals were willing to level any charge, to go to any lengths, to remain in power.

The sharpest cuts, however, came from independent bloggers who were either allied with or deeply sympathetic to the Conservatives. The degree to which independent bloggers were tied to the party and had become an active part, a new tactical arm, of the campaign, remains unclear. What is not unclear is that a number of bloggers became adjuncts to the Tory campaign by reporting on Liberal wrongdoings. They allowed the party to extend its "eyes and ears" (Confidential interview, April 2006). Adding to their value was that some bloggers had the time and in some cases the technical knowledge that the campaign team did not have to investigate claims or delve into issues. Moreover, as independent bloggers, their tracks did not lead back to the official campaign.

Two examples of this new relationship are particularly revealing. The first is related to what many see as the pivotal moment of the campaign—the announcement by the Royal Canadian Mounted Police that it was investigating the Department of Finance because of leaks allegedly made prior to a government decision not to impose new taxes or restrictions on income trusts. For the Liberals the announcement was the political equivalent of a train wreck. Media coverage about the RCMP investigation dominated news reports for weeks and sidetracked the campaign. Coverage reinforced the perception that the party was rife with corruption and could no longer be trusted. Investigative work by bloggers into when stock trades had taken place played a role in keeping the story going. The Martin campaign would never recover.

Second, Tory bloggers investigated several prominent Liberal candidates, unearthing unsavoury details about their political connections. In one instance, Michael Geist, a law professor, chronicled on his blog the allegedly close association between the entertainment industry and MP Sam Bulte, a legislator who played a leading role in the re-writing of Canada's copyright laws. The story was picked up by the mainstream media and may have been a factor in Bulte's defeat (Bowman, 2006). The new symbiosis between blogs and mainstream reporting may also have played a role in ending the political career of Liberal house leader, Tony Valeri.

While blogging dominated the horizon, except for a few new wrinkles, the Conservative party's web campaign looked very much as it did in 2004. The party experimented mostly unsuccessfully with podcasting (podcasts were plagued by technical problems and they could not be downloaded), there was a youth site, and speeches and updates were made available in MP3 format (Thompson, 2006).

The Bloc Quebecois site was also pretty much a replay of the previous campaign except that it now featured *Le blogue de Gilles Duceppe* (11 entries were posted eliciting 521 comments) and the party again appealed to young voters, mainly through songs and music videos. Most of the tunes moved to the beat of the old sponsorship scandal. The party also produced customized Christmas cards that could be sent to friends and family members. The card campaign allowed the party to collect names and email addresses—the ammunition of future campaigns. Interestingly the Bloc's merciless and mocking attacks against the Liberals may have helped contribute to the rise of the Conservatives in Quebec. Even in the campaign's final days the Bloc seemed oblivious to the new reality. Stephen Harper's impressive knowledge of French, his view that Quebec was the heart of Canada and his seemingly genuine approach to Quebec's grievances were to lead to a long-awaited Tory breakthrough in Quebec.

The greatest disappointment, perhaps, was the NDP site. Not only was the site conventional and unremarkable but the party stepped back from most of the e-campaigning initiatives that it had undertaken in 2004. The only innovation was a debate night bingo contest that invited participants to check off a square on their bingo cards every time Paul Martin blurted out one of his predictable pat phrases.

There is little doubt that BlackBerrys, blogs and online reality checks have become an integral part of Canadian elections. In 2006, however, party websites and the online campaign played only a minor role. The old media dominated the new media in every way. One can argue, in fact, that the online campaign only became significant when its postings made it into or were certified and magnified by the mainstream media. Nonetheless, in 2006 this happened to a surprising degree. More specifically, a symbiosis between political parties, bloggers and mainstream reporting seems to have emerged. Some blogs become "hot" at various moments during election campaigns, creating enough buzz to attract attention from the mainstream media. The exact shape of these relationships is still somewhat murky. Although writing about the foreign policy realm, Daniel Drezmer and Henry Farrell (2004, pp.32-41) summarized the influence of blogs in this way:

> the blogosphere functions as a rare combination of distributed expertise, real-time collective response to breaking news, and public opinion barometer. What's more, a hierarchical structure has taken shape . . . A few elite bloggers have emerged as aggregators of information and analysis, enabling media commentators to extract meaningful analysis and rely on blogs to help them interpret and predict political developments.

The Tory victory, albeit in the form of a minority government, had little to do with online campaigning. Change was in the air and Canadians did not believe that the Liberals, after over a decade in power, had the resolve to renew themselves while still in office. The Conservatives were able to make two decisive breakthroughs: they won ten seats in francophone areas of Quebec with the prospect of winning many more in the next election and now dominate rural and, to some degree, suburban Ontario. It remains to be seen whether these breakthroughs represent long-term shifts.

Conclusion

Canadian party websites have come a long way since the 2000 election. Except for the Bloc Quebecois, Internet campaigns in 2004 and 2006 were well integrated into overall campaign strategies. Webmasters sat at the table alongside other key members of campaign teams and planning for web campaigns usually began many months before the elections were called. Although the strategies of each of the parties differed, websites were no longer the electronic version of lawn signs. They had become multi-media platforms that were used to organize campaign activities, get out campaign messages quickly and collect valuable data. They were also used in conjunction with other new technologies and media forms—telephone databases, BlackBerries, blogs, music videos, podcasting, etc. While all of the parties have taken small first steps into the world of e-campaigning, in 2004 the New Democrats went the furthest in demonstrating that the Internet could create a whirlpool of small private e-campaigns within a larger national campaign. They did not repeat this experiment during the 2006 election.

But any new technology must be adapted to and reflect national conditions and situations in order to succeed. This has certainly been true in the Canadian case. Canada's relatively short campaign season, its tight spending restrictions and the public financing of elections set much of the stage for party web campaigns. Moreover, there is a degree to which each of the parties saw the web campaign through the lens of its own needs and traditions. One can argue that the NDP and the Bloc used their websites to achieve long-range ideological goals—connecting with the grassroots in one case and introducing young Quebecois to the independence movement in the other. For the Conservatives, building their extensive database and refining their get-out-the-vote technology seemed to be the primary mission. For all of the parties, in both 2004 and 2006, raw and hard-hitting negative politics prevailed on the net just as in the rest of the campaign.

The big story of 2006 was the advent of election blogging. While official party blogs seemed to have little effect because they were a predictable part of a party's overall media strategy, the same cannot be said for so-called independent bloggers. But even the term independent blogger may be misleading. It is not clear at this point whether parties are coordinating their efforts with certain bloggers or whether eruptions in the blogosphere work to the advantage of some parties and not others at different moments during a campaign. Moreover, bloggers seem to have little impact unless their messages are ratified by coverage in the mainstream press.

What is perhaps most interesting about Canadian web campaigns is the degree to which they have had a nationalizing effect. Audiences are directed to the national campaign, TV and radio commercials that were once aimed only at regional and local audiences can now be seen and heard across the country, and websites are always open for business even as it is night in one part of the country and daybreak in another. In the case of the Bloc Quebecois, of course, their web presence was directed only to Quebec voters although they did receive large numbers of comments from English-speaking Canada and these were answered in English.

In terms of interactivity and responsiveness, all of the parties approached the net with a certain degree of wariness. They were not prepared to open their sites up to full-blown debate because they saw their sites as instruments of persuasion and election warfare rather than as instruments of democracy. Their objective was to package and control the party's message rather than debate uncomfortable issues or invite unreliable and potentially embarrassing "strangers" onto the site. There is no indication that website communication by the major parties will be anything but top-down for the foreseeable future. An important observer of Canadian politics, Bill Cross, wrote that

> parties are so central to our democratic life that if they are not participatory our politics cannot be participatory, if they are not inclusive our politics cannot be inclusive, and if they are not responsive then our politics cannot be responsive (2004, p.3).

If this is the standard, then Canadian political parties have very far to go.

Notes

1. The key books on the 2004 Canadian election are Pammett, J. and C. Dornan, eds., 2004. *The Canadian General Election of 2004,* Toronto: Dundurn; Clarkson, S. 2005. *The Big Red Machine,* Vancouver: University of British Columbia Press. The principal studies of Internet use during the 2004 election are: Small, T. 2004. *Canadian Political Parties and Candidates on the Net: A Case Study of the 2004 Cyber-Campaign,* Unpublished doctoral manuscript, Department of Political Studies, Queen's University, Kingston, Ontario; Small, T. 2004. "Parties@canada: The Internet and the 2004 Cyber-Campaign." In Pammett, J. and C. Dornan, eds., *The Canadian General Election of 2004,* Toronto: Dundurn Press, pp.203-234.

Chapter Seven

The United Kingdom: Parties and the 2005 Virtual Election Campaign— Not Quite Normal?

Stephen Ward, Rachel Gibson and Wainer Lusoli

By the time of the 2005 General Election, most UK parties had been running websites and using online campaign tools for a decade or more. This was the third general election campaign in which the Internet, World Wide Web (WWW) and email had played a role, but the first one where the majority of the UK electorate had access to them. The initial hype surrounding the democratizing potential of the Internet had subsided, but expectations were again raised that the net could play a crucial role in the election. Such expectations had been fostered by both technological and political developments. Since the 2001 General Election, broadband connections and also use of mobile phone technology had expanded rapidly. Politically, excitement had been stimulated by the high profile online campaigns developed in the 2004 U.S. presidential election, notably the Howard Dean phenomenon. Yet the 2005 online campaign barely registered with the media and much of the virtual election, at least superficially, appeared to mirror the election generally. In this chapter, therefore, we examine the parties' 2005 online campaigns and place them in the context of our earlier studies of the 1997 and 2001 elections (Ward and Gibson, 1998, 2003; Gibson *et al*, 2003a). We analyze how far party competition has become normalized on the web; whether new technologies are introducing new campaigning techniques and accelerating the existing professionalization of electioneering; and finally what sort of audience there is for online communication. Can the net attract the interest of parts of the electorate not reached by traditional communication routes or does it merely reinforce existing gaps in electoral participation?

The Campaign Environment

In order to understand the role and development of online electioneering in the United Kingdom, we first need to provide a brief overview of the campaign environment. Here we concentrate on two areas in particular: the broad systemic political environment and the regulatory campaign framework.

The Systemic Political Environment

The stereotypical picture of Britain at least until the 1970s was of a stable, two-party dominated political system (Webb, 2002), where the two main parties from left and right, Labour and Conservative, dominated the share of the vote and parliamentary representation and often rotated in government. Since the mid-1970s, however, the two main parties have faced significant challenges to their hegemony. From this point onwards, partisan dealignment, increasing electoral volatility and declining party memberships have seen attachments to these parties weaken and their combined share of the vote decline significantly (Crewe and Denver, 1985; Crewe and Thomson, 1999). During this period there has been a corresponding rise in support for third parties, such as the centrist/centre-left Liberal Democrats, the Greens, and, more recently, anti-EU parties like the United Kingdom Independence Party (UKIP) as well as the far-right British National Party (BNP). Moreover, the creation of devolved institutions with mixed electoral systems in Scotland and Wales in 1999 has further fragmented the party system, effectively creating different party systems there and more diversity at Scottish elections in particular (Dunleavy, 2005; Bennie, 2002). However, at the national (Westminster) level, change has been less obvious than these underlying trends would suggest. The main parties have been partially insulated from the full effects of volatility and dealignment. The peculiarities of the first past the post electoral system have minimized the impact of small parties with geographically dispersed support and tended to produce a 'winner takes all effect' in terms of seats. Whilst the Greens, BNP and UKIP have all scored notable successes at second order (local and EU) elections and although the Liberal Democrats gained their largest share of seats (sixty-two) at Westminster since 1923 at the 2005 election, Westminster remains dominated (in terms of seats) by the bigger players. Over the past twenty-five years, the system has produced eighteen years of Conservative government from 1979 to 1997 followed by two Labour landslide victories in the 1997 and 2001 elections, with record majorities in parliament.

One significant change over the past two elections has been the drop in turnout. Traditionally, electoral turnout at the national level has been between 70 and 80 percent. However, 2001 saw a steep decline, with just 59 percent of the electorate bothering to vote and this barely increased at the 2005 election (61 percent). Turnout has dropped amongst all groups, but young people especially are significantly less likely to vote, resulting in fears of a generational shift towards non-voting. Following the 2001 election, there was considerable debate about re-connecting people with the political system and trying to engage young people in the political process (Electoral Commission, 2002; Government Children and Young People's Unit, 2002; Howland and Bethall, 2002). One solution that came to the fore was the use of ICTs, both as a means of communication, especially with younger voters, but also as a means of boosting turnout via the introduction of e-voting. The government piloted e-voting schemes at local elections in 2002 and 2003 but enthusiasm waned somewhat as e-voting methods proved disappointing compared to traditional postal ballots as a way of promoting turnout (Norris, 2003a).

In terms of parties as campaign organizations (Farrell and Webb, 2000) the common picture has been one of the growth of electoral-professional parties where campaigns are driven centrally from party headquarters with an increasing focus on the party leaders. Certainly there has been increasing amount of professionalization in campaigning, with the growth of specialist staff and large amounts of money spent on advertising and promotion. Whilst, superficially, this would appear to spell the end for localized campaigning, especially with the decline of party activism, there is an increasing body of evidence suggesting that local campaigns still matter in the United Kingdom, despite the dominance of the national party label (Denver *et al*, 2004; Seyd and Whiteley, 2004; Fisher *et al*, 2005). The vagaries of the UK electoral system actually mean that the election is often won and lost in a relatively small number of marginal constituencies. Although parties have always concentrated their efforts, the focus on target seats and marginal constituencies has become ever more sophisticated and prominent, with the parties pouring resources into such seats (Fisher, 2005), partially at the expense of the bulk of their safer constituencies. To what extent this is truly localized campaigning is debatable, however, since much of the electioneering is driven top-down, but undoubtedly local issues, local campaigning and local candidates can make a crucial difference in marginal constituencies.

The Regulatory Environment: Finance and Media

The Representation of the People Act (RPA), last substantially amended by the Political Parties, Elections and Referendums Act (PPERA) 2000, is the central law applying to electoral competition. It focuses mainly on three things: campaign income, campaign expenditure and press/broadcast information. There is little dealing specifically with the online campaign. In relation to campaign income and expenditure, individual candidates can accept limited financial contributions, whilst political parties can raise and spend substantially more money. There is no cap to party donations, though contributions above £5,000 nationally and £1,000 locally have to be disclosed, and no anonymous contributions can be accepted over £200. Under PPERA there is a ceiling on the amount of expenditure that can be incurred in the year to election-day. The limit for 2005 was £30,000 per constituency contested equating to a grand total of around £19 million if a party contested all seats. For individual candidates, expenditure limits are just over £7,000. Not surprisingly, in terms of both income and expenditure, Labour and Conservative massively outstrip all other parties and whilst Liberal Democrat income has risen over the past decade they in no way compete on a level playing field with the big two (Fisher, 2005).

Regulation of the media is mixed, with newspapers having much greater freedom, and consequently reporting in a much more partisan way than broadcasters. The press can and does endorse candidates and parties. Indeed, the parties place considerable emphasis on gaining the backing of the national tabloid press. Labour managed to gain the support of the largest tabloid, *The Sun*, before the 1997 election and has maintained the support of the majority of newspapers at subsequent elections, although with significantly less enthusiastic backing by 2005 than previously. Parties are also free to target voters by buying advertising space in both national and regional papers. By contrast, broadcasters (both the BBC and commercial) have to be impartial at all times in relation to their reporting of the election and their election discussion programmes. Additionally, the major parties, defined as Labour, Conservative and Liberal Democrats—plus the Scottish National Party (SNP) in Scotland, Plaid Cymru (PC) in Wales and the Ulster Unionist Party (UUP), the Democratic Unionist Party (DUP), Sinn Fein (SF) and the Social and Democratic Labour Party (SDLP) in Northern Ireland— are also offered a series of broadcast slots during the election campaign.[1] These are carried on the BBC and a range of the main commercial broadcasters and must be shown at peak times. Some minor parties may also qualify for a single broadcast, depending on whether they are contesting more than one-sixth of the seats up for election.[2]

Very few regulations specifically affect online campaigning. One long-standing requirement that does is that incumbent MPs can no longer refer to themselves as MPs once an election has been called. Hence, campaign literature and now websites should not use the title 'MP'. Potentially, this is a disincentive for sitting MPs since it means they have to either create a new site or revamp their existing site to remove references to their MP status—a time-consuming exercise. We found in the 2001 campaign that a significant minority of MPs either failed to comply with the regulation or continued using their website seemingly oblivious to the requirement (Ward and Gibson, 2003). Following the 2001 election, there was debate about the need for additional regulation applicable to online campaigning. After a consultation exercise, the Electoral Commission produced a report (2003) that largely argued for maintaining the status quo. It argued that an overly regulatory approach at this early stage might restrict the use of ICTs and would not be beneficial to the electorate.

The Evolution of Net Campaigning in the United Kingdom: From Symbolic Politics to the Mainstream

Although much of the focus of this study is on web-based technologies, it is worth remembering that there is a longer history of parties adopting computer aided campaigning for things such as direct mail and telecanvessing (Swaddle, 1988; Wring and Horrocks, 2001). However, UK parties' use of the new communication technologies in the public domain is perhaps best traced through their adoption of websites. Beginning in 1994, there was a fairly rapid movement of parties to set up homepages (Gibson and Ward, 2000a). By 1997 virtually all parliamentary and larger non-parliamentary parties had sites (Ward and Gibson, 1998), although only a tiny minority (5 percent) of candidates/local parties bothered with a web presence. The content of the sites at this stage was fairly haphazard with most adopting the philosophy that 'more was indeed more' and loading up their pages with flashing icons, reams of text, and very few navigational aids (Auty and Nicholas, 1998). With only 7 percent of the UK public online at this point, it is not surprising that parties' efforts were largely experimental and symbolic. Indeed, the importance of web campaigning in this early period can be gauged by the fact that many of the sites were still controlled by amateur activists or officials from the IT wings of the party. Even the professionally run ones were not integrated into the parties' mainstream campaign organization. Labour's 1997 e-campaign, for example, was run out of the party's youth section (Ward and Gibson, 1998).

By the time we reported on the EU elections in 1999 (Gibson and Ward, 2000b), the mainstream parties had already begun to professionalize their web operations, often with specialist web design teams, the creation of e-campaign units or dedicated staff integrated within communications departments. At the local level, however, there was again less activity. Evidence reported by Ward and Gibson (2003) on the incidence of candidate and local party websites at the 2001 General Election revealed that only around one in four or five of the candidates from the three main parties were operating an election website. Those that did venture online remained wedded to the national party message rather than developing any localized e-campaigns.

However, the increasingly serious attention being paid to the new media by some of the large and small-scale political players was reflected in improvements in the design and image presented by the sites themselves in 2001. In particular, the parties' sites were noted to have developed a sleeker, more professional appearance (Auty and Cowen, 2001, p.343). Interactive features such as 'My Manifesto' appeared on the Conservative site, enabling voters to request a more customized document that matched their policy interests. Labour offered a mortgage calculator to prove the benefits of their tax policies, a designated question and answer page, and a text message service that fired off encouragement to friends' mobile phones to support the party. Some of the smaller parties also ran debate forums and bulletin boards for supporters to post their views. E-newsletters also rose in prominence during this period, with most parties offering some kind of email distribution list for voters to sign-up for that ensured they received regular updates from the campaign trail. The Conservatives and Labour even offered mobile access to their sites through WAP and PDA technology. Whilst parties were trying limited experiments with interactivity or message targeting—for example, Labour's widely derided 'RU UP 4IT' youth site in the 2001 campaign—they tended to remain cautious about such possibilities, fearing a fragmentation of key campaign themes and the risk of confusing voters with different messages to different groups (Jackson, 2001). Overall, however, sites were still seen to reflect a certain timidity on the part of the parties for the technology, with most focusing on representing and adding more detail to their offline material, rather than making use of the unique features of the web (Auty and Cowen, 2001). Indeed, parties were frequently accused of simply producing online propaganda for their activists (Dorling *et al*, 2002). By 2001, therefore, most parties now regarded the net as a useful supplementary campaign tool. It had become a necessary but not sufficient device for successful electioneering.

Party Competition Online

In relation to party competition online, the consensus is that prior to 2005 there was limited evidence of equalization. Certainly, in previous UK elections, there has been no indication that the Internet delivers votes for any particular party and, in any case, it would be difficult to demonstrate such a link (Gibson *et al*, 2003a). Studies do suggest, however, that the main parties, especially Labour, Conservative and Liberal Democrat, maintained an advantage in terms of the sophistication and visibility of their sites (Gibson and Ward, 1998, 2000a, 2000b; Gibson *et al*, 2003a; Margolis *et al*, 1999; Ward and Gibson, 1998). This is particularly pronounced at election time where mainstream parties have significantly more staff and financial resources (Gibson *et al*, 2003a). Nevertheless, any normalization process does not seem to be inevitable or inexorable. Smaller parties can close the gap between election times when their major counterparts tend to leave their sites to stagnate. Moreover, some smaller parties, notably the Greens and the BNP, have maintained reasonably sophisticated e-campaigns. Both have claimed that they derive useful benefits from the Internet and email in terms of organizing and recruitment (Gibson and Ward, 2000a; Gibson *et al*, 2003a; Voerman and Ward, 2000). The Greens and the far right have more incentives than most to use new media technologies, although for different reasons. For the Greens, their target audience tends to be amongst those groups that use the Internet heavily—the young, urban, middle class, students and environmental activists. For parties like the BNP, the semi-covert nature of their organization means that emails are a useful means of internal communication and organization. In terms of the public face of the party, a professional website can also convey the appearance of legitimacy and make the party seem larger than is actually the case (Copsey, 2003). Additionally, the far right are particularly enthusiastic about using the net as a means of circumnavigating the restrictions (as they see it) of the traditional 'liberal' media.

Audiences for Websites and Participation Online

From the beginning, parties have aimed at a relatively elite audience, which, whilst it has diversified, has at its core party members and activists, journalists, and those in higher/further education (students and researchers) as the primary groups. Initially, though, few took much trouble to monitor their online audience (Gibson and Ward, 1998). In terms of serious polling or server statistics, it was not until the late 1990s that major parties started to profile their web audiences and market test their web offerings and even now this still remains beyond many smaller parties.

From a wider, bottom-up perspective there has been very limited empirical evidence in the United Kingdom about political use of the web and involvement in online political campaigns. Recent surveys, however, suggest that the numbers accessing political organizational sites tend to be small. Around 5 to 8 percent of the British public have visited party sites according to most surveys whilst 2 or 3 percent have accessed local party websites or those of MPs (Lusoli et al, 2006). In the 2001 election, news sites were the most popular online destination, a pattern that has held firm throughout the past five years (Coleman, 2001). Similarly, another study at the last election found that the public, given the choice, did not want to visit parties directly and much preferred to visit traditional news media sites (Crabtree, 2001). A more recent survey indicated that around one quarter of the public gathered news online particularly from the BBC. Government sites, partly because of their service and information functions, were also significantly more popular than those of political parties or other political organizations (Lusoli et al, 2006). Yet Crabtree's focus group study found that, whilst the public might be reluctant to visit party sites, once exposed to candidate sites, they generally found some of the information to be useful and of a higher quality than they expected. Nevertheless, the problem that remains for parties and candidates is twofold: (1) creating significant awareness of their online presence, so voters can find them; (2) overcoming preconceived ideas that the sites will be dull and poorly designed and contain little useful information.

The profile of those engaged in political activity online has also remained fairly constant. The web tends, not surprisingly, to attract the middle-class, urban, well-educated population and, more particularly, those that are already politically active and engaged (Norris, 2003b), although some survey work has detected a small widening effect. Research conducted after the 2001 election, for example, indicated a possible small but intriguing mobilization effect amongst some younger people (Gibson *et al*, 2005b). Even if ICTs were not changing the profile of party supporters significantly, studies of party activists indicate that they are increasingly using the technologies to supplement and extend their off-line activities (Ward *et al*, 2002; Lusoli and Ward, 2004). In other words, for many activists the web was an increasingly useful day-to-day political tool.

Towards the 2005 Online Campaign: Watershed Expectations

If the 1997 election was about symbolic Internet use and 2001 about main-streaming the new media, the run up to 2005 election saw expectations rise, with techno-enthusiasts suggesting that the Internet could make a significant break-through. One leading commentator argued:

> Wherever we look it is clear that Internet tools like email, websites and chat are going to be central to this election. It will happen at every level and goes far beyond the national campaign run by the national parties (Bill Thompson, BBC News Online, 11 April 2005).

Several factors raised such expectations. By 2004, for the first time, a majority (between 52 and 60 percent in most surveys) of the British electorate had used the Internet and those regularly using the net had almost doubled since the last election. Furthermore, the rapid increase in broadband, with its enhanced online capabilities, and the massive increase in mobile phone technology suggested that there would be a greater demand for online activity around the election. More specifically, the previous couple of years had also seen the growth of the net as marketing tool. In particular, commentators highlighted the growing success of so-called virals (online films, games and cartoons) that spread rapidly via email, prompting suggestions that parties might usefully develop subtle viral campaigns so that the messages do not appear to come directly from the parties themselves.[3] The other major development in cyberspace, from a political campaign perspective, was the rapid development of blogs. By 2003–2004 a nascent and expanding blogsphere was in place in the United Kingdom, attracting the attention of some politicians, including seven blogging Westminster MPs.[4] Prior to the campaign, Iain Duncan-Smith, the former Conservative Party leader, not previously known for his technophile views, proclaimed the potential importance of blogs for the political right, suggesting that 'the Internet's level playing field gives Conservatives opportunities that the mainstream media has denied them'. Duncan-Smith even went on to claim:

> The Internet could do more to change the level of political engagement than all the breast beating of introspective politicians and commentators. A 21st century political revolution is now only a few mouse clicks away (*The Guardian*, 19 February 2005).

What arguably prompted most of this interest was online campaigning in the 2004 U.S. presidential campaign. As usual, the major UK parties sent staff to monitor the Bush and Kerry campaigns. However, it was Howard Dean's primary campaign that captured the imagination of net activists and journalists. His innovative use of blogs and online meet-up mechanisms to build supporter networks, along with his ability to raise funds from small-scale donors, renewed interest in the interactive possibilities of campaigning. Indeed, in the aftermath of the Dean campaign it was clear that some parties had been looking to learn lessons. For example, the Conservatives launched an online recruitment tool, 'Conservatives Direct', at their 2004 conference, aimed at recruiting online activists and volunteers, focusing initially on marginal seats.

Research Questions and Methods

In light of the discussion above, this study of the 2005 election campaign concentrated on the three main elements: (1) Party competition—How far did the nature of competition differ online and offline?' Did 2005 see an increase in gaps between large and small parties? (2) Professionalization—To what extent was the web facilitating new campaigning techniques and how far were local parties and candidates really developing localized web campaigning? (3) Participation—How far did parties use technologies to attract new voters or increase the depth of participation? Finally, in relation to all three areas, where possible we wanted to put 2005 in the context of previous elections by comparing back to data from our earlier studies.

In order to answer such questions we collected data on twenty parties.[5] These included all the parliamentary parties and a range of non-parliamentary parties. Specifically, the data we collected included:

- Presence and access data—The Google search engine was used to calculate the links into party websites. At local level we carried out a representative study of two hundred constituencies searching for candidate websites using party lists, search engines and the BBC site. We then assessed patterns of competition online to see whether factors such as marginality, incumbency and party made any difference to web presence. We also used the BBC news database to compare the level of online stories about parties during the election campaign.

- Website content surveys—Using the coding scheme developed in previous election studies we compared the content of national party websites for features such as information provision, interactivity, e-campaigning, resource generation and networking (see appendix for details). A similar, but more basic, feature analysis was used at the local level.

- Public opinion survey data—Public opinion data were gathered via an opinion survey of voters in the week following the election.[6] This asked about use of the net during the election campaign; whether people had gathered news/information from online sources; which websites they visited; whether they received email about the election; and voter attitudes towards online politics.

The 2005 National Party Online Campaigns: Party Websites—More of the Same?

Presence and Access

In relation to presence and access to party sites the evidence reveals a continuing picture of major party dominance (see Table 7.1). More traffic is clearly guided towards the sites of the major parties as in 2001. However, most of the parties have increased their links two or three fold since 2001, with Sinn Fein, the SDLP and the BNP seeing the biggest increases (although the latter was from a very small base). Nevertheless, links into the Conservative and Labour Party sites are still at least two or three times greater than those of the largest non-parliamentary party and generally at least twelve times greater than most of the other non-parliamentary parties. Again, the Greens are the only minor party to have a similar level of links to the parliamentary parties.

The BBC archives suggest that online news coverage is also distorted in favor of the three largest parties, particularly Conservative and Labour. With the exception of the Greens and Respect, Labour and the Conservatives generally have around ten times as many mentions in news stories as the other parties. Once more the broad trends are similar to our 2001 study. Hence, this factor, added to their predominance of the traditional media, means the online playing field is far from being level. It may allow presence, but access is still very much in favor of the three main parties.

Table 7.1 Links into Party Sites and Online News Coverage During the 2005 Election

Party Name	Links in	BBC News Online Stories
Labour	3990	347
Conservative	4820	345
Liberal Democrat	9000	217
Scottish National Party (SNP)	664	208
Plaid Cymru (PC)	460	40
Ulster Unionist Party (UUP)	874	29
Democratic Unionist Party (DUP)	684	27
Social and Democratic Labour Party (SDLP)	1620	33
Sinn Fein (SF)	1590	41
United Kingdom Independence Party (UKIP)	229	35
British National Party (BNP)	272	11
Green Party	1440	152
Veritas	47	22
Respect	313	132
English Democrats	47	N.A.
Pensioners Party	18	0
Socialist Labour Party (SLP)	69	N.A.
Liberal Party	102	N.A
Legalise Cannabis Alliance (LCA)	258	7
Your Party	N.A.	N.A.

Website Content

Primarily, party websites are about information provision and resource generation (Table 7.2). The vast majority of parties managed to score heavily in terms of information offered. The centerpiece to nearly all the sites was updated news and press releases, usually designed to focus on the issue/campaign theme of the day. Virtually all party sites followed the same standard set-up with sections on news, party organization, people, basic aims and objectives and a get-in-touch/involved feature. This basic format has barely altered from 1997 even if the content has become more extensive and the design more sophisticated. The area that seemed to have developed most on our measures was resource generation. Recruiting members and volunteers and gathering money online were increasingly becoming a central feature of many of the sites. Whilst resource generation has been a target from the start, parties are putting more effort into developing transactions purely online. The Labour Party was rumored to have raised some £50,000 in a few hours after an online appeal targeted at supporters by novelist John O'Farrell (O'Farrell, 2005).

By contrast, participation/interactivity measures reflected a more patchy performance and one that had changed little since the 2001 campaign. The inter-activity available tended to be with the website rather than with politicians or other voters. There were plenty of opportunities to send emails but these were not, it seems, designed to engage the electorate in debate or conversation. They lead not directly to politicians but more likely to anonymous party staff. Where one could interact and declare preferences on websites, the suspicion was that parties were simply trawling for email addresses or gathering information on visitors, rather than engaging in real dialogue. Thus, the process was more about marketing than about democratic discussion. Several parties did, however, make token gestures to respond to the blogging phenomenon, with six parties offering blogs or campaign diaries. Labour had two diaries in the name Prescott and Blair, both ghost written by party staffers. The SNP site contained a number of diaries from candidates. The Tories generated media coverage through the on-line diary of Sandra Howard (wife of the Conservative leader), although much of this coverage was about hairstyles rather than issues (*The Times*, 21 April 2005; *Daily Telegraph*, 3 May 2005). For the most part, the diaries were bland, anodyne accounts of campaign and in all but one case there was no direct com-ment facility available to visitors. The exception was the Liberal Democrats, whose interactive blog was designed to reinforce the party's desired image of openness as well as keeping the site fresh. The only other unique interactive feature was the online game introduced by the Conservatives halfway through the campaign: where visitors were invited to wipe the smile of Tony Blair's face. The purpose of the game, according to campaign staff, was to increase the 'stickiness' of the site, i.e. to keep people on the site and to try to make them return (authors' interview, London, 24 August 2005).

In part, the lack of interactive discussion reflects two factors: Firstly, there was the fear of abuse or opening up public space with little actual benefit for the party. This was confirmed by the experience of the English Democrats, whose comment facility was removed early in the campaign after persistent abuse. Sec-ondly, there was the belief that interaction and dialogue are best carried else-where, on neutral territory through more trusted media sites.

The development of other new e-campaign techniques was still viewed cau-tiously by parties. Only four out of twenty parties scored on more than half our measures. Over a third barely adopted any e-campaign techniques at all, scoring either 0 or 1. The viral phenomenon, first detected in 2001-2002, has begun to be more extensively incorporated into party sites, with seven offering the ability to forward a web page or, in the case of Liberal Democrats and the Greens, send e-postcards. Overall, the relatively low scores here tend to support the belief that parties are often offering more of the same rather than anything different online.

Table 7.2 Party Websites: Overall Functions 2001 and 2005 Elections

Parties	Information Provision		Resource Generation		Participation		e-campaigning		Networking
	2005	2001	2005	2001	2005	2001	2005	2001	2005
Parliamentary Parties									
Labour	11	13	12	13	6	15	3	7	6
Conservative	12	8	12	12	10	16	7	5	5
Liberal Democrats	11	11	12	12	9	11	5	4	7
SNP	12	12	12	8	7	10	2	4	1
PC	9	7	8	0	2	6	0	1	4
UUP	11	10	9	4	3	10	5	2	3
DUP	8	7	6	0	7	7	4	3	3
SDLP	8	9	6	2	7	5	1	0	3
SF	11	8	12	1	1	3	1	1	2
Mean Score	**10.2**	**9.4**	**9.9**	**5.8**	**5.8**	**9.2**	**2.8**	**3.0**	**3.8**
Range	**0-15**	**0-16**	**0-12**	**0-13**	**0-13**	**0-n**	**0-8**	**0-9**	**0-9**
Non Parl Parties									
UKIP	12	11	12	11	8	12	4	3	2
BNP	9	13	12	11	2	7	4	4	0
Green Party	11	11	9	13	7	21	5	4	3
Respect	7	N.A.	12	N.A.	3	N.A.	3	N.A.	3
Veritas	9	N.A.	9	N.A.	6	N.A.	2	N.A.	4
Pensioners Party	2	N.A.	3	N.A.	3	N.A.	1	N.A.	1
SLP	9	7	1	2	1	4	0	0	0
English Democrats	8	N.A.	6	N.A.	8	N.A.	3	N.A.	2
Liberal Party	9	N.A.	2	N.A.	3	N.A.	0	N.A.	2
LCA	10	N.A.	10	N.A.	9	N.A.	1	N.A.	1
Your Party	7	N.A.	9	N.A.	10	N.A.	1	N.A.	1
Mean Score	**8.5**	**9.5**	**7.7**	**7.2**	**5.6**	**9.0**	**2.2**	**2.6**	**1.6**
Range	**0-15**	**0-16**	**0-12**	**0-13**	**0-13**	**0-n**	**0-8**	**0-9**	**0-9**

Table 7.3 Party Websites: Delivery 2001 and 2005 Elections

Parties	Multi-media		Access		Navigation		Freshness	
	2005	2001	2005	2001	2005	2001	2005	2001
Parliamentary Parties								
Labour	2	6	2	4	3	4	6	6
Conservative	4	6	2	2	3	6	6	6
Liberal Democrats	3	5	1	1	2	5	6	6
SNP	2	2	2	1	2	0	6	5
PC	0	2	2	1	2	2	5	5
UUP	3	2	1	0	2	2	6	6
DUP	2	4	0	0	2	2	6	5
SDLP	0	1	2	0	2	3	5	4
SF	2	2	2	0	2		5	4
Mean Score	**2.0**	**3.6**	**1.4**	**1.0**	**2.2**	**2.8**	**5.7**	**5.2**
Non Parl Parties								
UKIP	0	5	3	0	2	4	5	5
BNP	2	4	1	0	2	1	5	6
Green Party	3	4	2	2	2	3	6	4
Respect	2	N.A.	1	N.A.	2	N.A.	5	N.A.
Veritas	2	N.A.	1	N.A.	1	N.A.	5	N.A.
Pensioners Party	0	N.A.	0	N.A.	1	N.A.	2	N.A.
SLP	0	2	0	0	1	2	2	4
English Democrats	2	N.A.	1	N.A.	1	N.A.	6	N.A.
Liberal Party	0	N.A.	0	N.A.	1	N.A.	3	N.A.
LCA	1	N.A.	1	N.A.	2	N.A.	5	N.A.
Your Party	0	N.A.	1	N.A.	1	N.A.	3	N.A.
Mean Score	**1.1**	**3.2**	**1.0**	**0.3**	**1.5**	**2.5**	**4.3**	**4.8**
Range	**0-5**	**0-6**	**0-4**	**0-5**	**0-4**	**0-n**	**0-6**	**0-6**

Finally, networking on websites was again limited. Few outside the main three tried to build links to a wide range of sites. Though most offered internal links to candidates (a notable exception being Labour) or other internal party sites, the ability to link outwards to other election sites was very limited. Surprisingly few parties (four) linked to news organizations such as the BBC.

Delivery and Sophistication

In terms of the way that messages were delivered online, use of extensive multimedia is still limited to a minority of parties (Table 7.3). Although around half our parties included some video footage, a clear distinction can be found between mainstream parties and outsiders. The major parties made considerable use of video/film clips of party broadcasts, speeches or events. Arguably, only the BNP, amongst the non-parliamentary parties had the same level of commitment. The BNP placed significant emphasis on their BNP TV feature claiming that this is proved to be one of the most popular features of their site. The party is now seeking to expand its multimedia use with the aim of creating its own fully-fledged alternative media platform (authors' interview, with BNP official, 10 August 2005). Two other more innovative features that came to prominence in the campaign (and were not included in our coding) were RSS feeds used by the Conservatives and Liberal Democrats producing their own new service and an experiment with podcasting by the Liberal Democrats. Both of these are likely to occur more prominently in the future.

It is not simply the sophistication of the site that might be important in attracting visitors but also ease of navigation. Results here were also patchy. Whilst over half the parties had search engines on their sites, significantly fewer offered navigation tips, only one offered a text-only version of the site and only three prominently offered options for those with visual impairments. Again, on these measures the larger parties and particularly the big three have the most advantages.

The updating of sites, whilst appearing similar to the 2001 campaign, showed an overall improvement. However, the minor party mean scores appeared to have fallen back, leading to a larger gap between parliamentary and non-parliamentary parties than before. This is largely due to the Pensioners Party and the SLP who seemed barely to update their site during the campaign. Of the remainder, sixteen of the twenty parties updated their sites at least every few days, with around third of the parties updating on a daily basis.

Summary

Overall, results from this content survey are mixed but reiterate the claim that straightforward normalization in relation to content is difficult to sustain. The basic patterns of functionality and delivery remained remarkably similar to the 2001 scores, especially in terms of information provision, e-campaigning and participation, although resource generation had clearly increased in prominence. Online donations and online joining/volunteering were now becoming the norm. However, there were divisions emerging between the parties both in the level of provision and the sophistication of delivery. Moreover, these gaps appeared slightly wider than in 2001. Yet, these were not straightforwardly between parliamentary and non-parliamentary parties. Nor were they uniformly large. The big three parties clearly outperformed the others on most of the measures coded here. Nevertheless, several of the non-parliamentary parties notably the Greens, BNP, UKIP and, to a lesser extent, Veritas, Respect and LCA all offered reasonably developed sites. Hence, the role of incentives (e.g. an online target audience and party culture), were just as important in explaining party online efforts as financial resources (Nixon *et al*, 2003). Hence, one explanation for the Pensioners Party and the SLP's low scores was that much of their target audience lay offline and, in the case of the SLP, their party culture was focused around traditional collective face-to-face recruitment, meetings and organization.

Local Campaigning Online in 2005: Just More?

If the national level showed continuity, local level e-campaigning appeared to demonstrate significant change. The 2005 election saw a large increase in the number of candidate and local party sites. In total, there were around 1,300 candidate websites, equating to 37 percent of the total number of candidates, although around 7 percent of these sites either lacked election content or were invalid URLs. There were, however, distinct differences between the parties. The Conservatives led the way, a reversal from the previous election, with 68 percent of constituencies covered by a local party or candidate site. They were followed by the Greens, although their sites focused on the local party or constituency rather than candidate. The Liberal Democrats and Labour had similar levels of local presence, with around 45 percent and 42 percent candidate coverage respectively (Table 7.4). This represented a large growth in local sites, with the Conservatives nearly tripling their web presence and Labour doubling theirs. The Conservatives e-campaigns team, in particular, made a conscious effort after the previous election to extend their web presence but also to integrate their national and local online campaigns.

Aside from the Greens, though, it was clear that few of the other smaller parties could compete online. Even parties running a large number of candidates, such as UKIP, had only a handful online. Others, such as the BNP, had no candidate websites whatsoever. In part, this is not simply a question of financial resources but more that many fringe parties simply lacked a local branch infrastructure. Moreover, the United Kingdom electoral system provides little incentive for smaller parties to create candidate sites or devote resources beyond a national site when they have virtually no chance of success.

The basic pattern of website presence was not unexpected. There was greater activity in marginal seats, particularly amongst the main contenders in those seats. Safe Labour constituencies were, by contrast, the least likely to have any web activity. This website electoral geography was also underpinned by the level of access to the net in certain constituencies—those where access to the Internet and broadband were low were unlikely to have seen much cyberspace activity. There was also an incumbency factor at work, with sitting MPs more likely to have developed a web presence than their challengers.

Table 7.4 Percentage of Local Parties/Candidates with 2005 Election Websites

Party	Total web-sites	Personal web-site	Local Party website
Conservatives	68%	36%	32%
Green Party	54%	5%	49%
Liberal Democrats	45%	24%	21%
Labour	42%	34%	8%
UUP	39%	33%	6%
SNP	34%	20%	14%
SDLP	28%	28%	0%
Independents/one-candidate parties	26%	22%	4%
Plaid Cymru	23%	20%	3%
DUP	22%	22%	0%
Other Minor Parties	15%	6%	9%
UKIP	12%	3%	9%
BNP	0%	0%	0%
Sinn Fein	0%	0%	0%

The patterns of web competition provide only a partial story. Although there was a clear development of the web locally this does not necessarily support a decentralization thesis. This was for two reasons. Firstly, there were still a large number of sites that were really no more than cyberbrochures or leaflets, that is, they were static sites with limited information—usually a biography, contact numbers and some key issue themes. They were in no way active campaign tools, since they were not updated during the course of the campaign. Secondly, there was a significant growth of party templates, especially in the Conservative and Liberal Democrat parties. These were sites with the same basic format and containing some of the same nationally determined content. For example, a large number of the main party sites carried a news feed direct from the national party site and a significant number of local Conservative Party websites carried identical information with very limited local content. By contrast, use of Labour's well-established 'web-in-a-box' template increased only marginally at this election. Nevertheless, even where templates were not used, websites tended to mirror the national party line.

As nationally, there was little in the way of interactivity, although blogs entered the local websphere. There were around sixty candidate blogs, but few of these had any developed dialogue between voters and candidates. Despite the prevalence of templates, there were the beginnings of candidates tentatively developing more individualized campaigns or targeting groups within their constituencies. Some Labour candidates and incumbents in marginal constituencies were keen to distance themselves from Blair and highlight their opposition to the war in Iraq or university tuition fees.[7] Students, perhaps because of their high levels of access to the net, were targeted online by Liberal Democrat candidates. Not only was there more web activity in seats with large student populations but Liberal Democrat candidates gave prominence to the top-up fees issue on their site and highlighted their links to student groups.

Overall, though, it is questionable whether websites in particular were any more than marginal campaign tools. Interviews with sitting MPs in the run up to the 2005 election highlighted three issue. Firstly, there was a continued belief in the traditional tools of local campaigns (canvassing, door-knocking, leafleting and generally pressing the flesh and being seen) were what voters wanted. As one Liberal Democrat MP stated:

> What's more important are: (1) leaflets—we drop thousands and they are designed to go from hand to bin in less than 10 seconds; (2) personal contact—it's not like the US where there are vast distances and a different style of politics. To be honest websites and email are just used as an excuse to avoid personal contact with electors ... We put half a million pieces of paper through people's doors and I visited 11,000 households personally. You couldn't do that electronically. Anyway, email pisses people off if you try and use it like leaflets. Email is time consuming and not as useful as face to face, door to door or telephone. It's just a little helpful extra. Face to face is by far the most effective means ... Electronic communication will make no difference to whether people will vote. The press and media and personal contact lead people to vote (authors' interview with Liberal Democrat MP, London, 15 June 2004).

Secondly, websites and email do not reach the voters you necessarily want to mobilize, such as the less politically interested. Thirdly, email and localized databases were more valued than websites as electoral tools. Hence, a small but growing number of MPs are starting to manage their postbags electronically and to develop email newsletters, allowing them to build more regular contact with constituents and send more personalized messages to them. Yet, as Richard Allan, former MP and techno-enthusiast, has argued, it is difficult to see what additional benefits are to be gained from local online campaigning in the United Kingdom other than organizational efficiency:

> The impact on the elector of a nicely printed letter landing on their doormat is far greater than that for any email the party might send. Direct contact on the

doorstep or via telephone is much more effective than any form of net interactivity. And glossy leaflets with photos of candidates that are pushed at the elector beat websites for putting a message across. In other words, we do not do much net campaigning because it is second best to the political campaign tools we have at our disposal.[8]

Public (Dis)connection? The Audience for Online Party Campaigns in 2005

So far we have dealt with the producer side of the election, i.e. what the parties were offering, but how far did they reach the voters and what impact did online campaigning have? The results reported below reflect a more bottom-up perspective on the online election.

Who Went Online? The Profile of Political Users

During the 2005 campaign, about 28 percent of British Internet users went online to get information about the election, corresponding to about 15 percent of the population. While the Internet compared unfavorably with established sources of electoral information, such as TV and newspapers (Table 7.5), it did represent an increasing proportion of the media diet of British Internet users at election time. Such consumption was, however, more occasional, but also more deliberate, than for traditional media sources: only about 6 percent of the public went online once a week or more often to gather information concerning the election.

Superficially, the profile of users mirrored that of previous surveys. It was mostly young, male, educated, and Internet literate citizens who went online for electoral information (Table 7.6). Respondents aged eighteen to twenty-four were twice as likely (33 percent) as the average to have used the Internet at least 'a little' in relation to the election; while twenty-five to thirty-four year olds were the age category who were most likely to have used the Internet 'a lot' (about 8 percent). Among young people, it is students who were the most regular Internet users. Around one in two students actually used the Internet to gather election information. Again, in line with previous studies, male (22 percent), educated (23 percent) respondents were also more likely to access information online. Perhaps not surprisingly, those with high levels of Internet skills, particularly those who were producers, rather than the just consumers, of digital content, were much more likely to have used the Internet as a source of election information (47 percent of Internet users).

Table 7.5 Sources of Information About the Election

	A lot	Some	A little	None	Don't Know
	%	%	%	%	%
TV	48.0	24.1	16.1	11.4	0.4
Newspapers	22.8	25.3	20.9	30.5	0.4
Party Literature	17.2	24.1	28.5	29.9	0.3
Radio	10.6	16.8	22.4	49.1	1.0
Friends/Family/ Colleagues	5.7	13.1	22.6	58.4	0.3
Internet	3.3	4.5	7.7	83.1	1.4
Magazines	1.5	5.3	9.8	82.5	0.9

Interestingly, the traditional predictors of political news consumption had less impact on the likelihood of accessing information online. Neither past voting behavior nor reported voting at the current election were significant predictors, while general political participation was only weakly related (phi = 0.07, $p <$ 0.05) to online information seeking. Nor did party support make a difference to one's likelihood to seek information though the web. As both participation and Internet use are usually based on the same range of socio-demographic predictors, except for age, this is an indication that the Internet is entering the social mainstream, and is accessible to a more diversified public.

Table 7.6 Profile of Citizens Using the Internet for Election News

	Percentage of category	Difference from Average
Male Gender	22	+7%
Young Age (18-24)	33	+18%
Young Age (25-34)	25	+10%
University Education	23	+8%
Student Status	47	+32%
B Social Grade	27	+12%
Skilled User*	47	+19%
Long-Term User*	37	+10%

Respondents who have gathered at least a little electoral information through the Internet n =301.
Differences are statistically significant at $p < 0.01$.
* Difference calculated on the average user.

Where and How? Online Destinations

We then asked how voters used the Internet once they were online. Specifically, we asked questions about whether users visited election websites, used search engines to locate information and came across electoral coverage by chance while navigating the net. In relation to websites, large news producers took the lion's share of the online information market. While about 17 percent of British users visited BBC News online, 9 percent reported visiting information portal websites (such as Yahoo and Tiscali) for election-related information. Newspapers only attracted 4 percent of all users, while party sites were visited by about 3 percent. Other purveyors of online information, most notably candidates and lobby groups, but also blogs and tactical voting sites, were virtually ignored. Such figures illustrate the difficulty for parties, candidates and other campaigns to break out beyond their traditional supporters.

We also asked users whether they had encountered election information unintentionally while online for other purposes. The results are intriguing, as 27 percent of users reported coming across such information. Of course, it is important to see whether it was active information seekers who were more likely to encounter this additional information. Although users getting 'a lot' of their electoral information from the Internet were indeed more likely to encounter it (or notice it), a significant group of users (8 percent) came across it unintentionally; this increased the number of British Internet users encountering some election information to around 36 percent.

In addition to the consumption side of online news, we were interested in potentially more 'active' forms of online electoral engagement, such as participating in the online campaigns of parties, online discussion fora and sending/receiving email messages about the election. With regard to email, a small minority of users had received electoral information (12 percent) and an even smaller proportion sent election related material (5 percent). While parties, candidates and friends contributed equally to voters email inboxes, voters' emails were mostly addressed to family and friends rather than parties or candidates (although the numbers here were small).

Finally, we looked at active engagement with the online campaign. Again, a small minority of users (8 percent) engaged in election-related online activities, including taking part in an online discussion (1.5 percent), signing an online petition (1 percent) or subscribing to election news (1.3 percent). Overall, citizens took very little part in the campaign by electronic means. Although, more than a fifth of the British public used the Internet, in one way or another, in relation to the election, only a very small fraction used new media to engage with party campaigns. It seems that where they have a choice, as with online communication, the public will avoid the offerings from parties. This lends some support to the contention that, whilst the public may be turned off by the parties, they were not necessarily turned off by politics or the election in general.

Why and Why Not? Motivations and Barriers

We then explored some of the reasons why citizens did or did not use the Internet during the election, and what benefits they derived from doing so. First, we asked the main group of information seekers identified above about their reasons for using the Internet to get election information. The most frequently reported reason was that information was available online all the time (46 percent of respondents) or was more up to date. Strikingly, a large number also indicated no specific reason for going online. Arguably, this may suggest that Internet information seeking is simply becoming part of people's day-to-day life (44 percent). Overall, the impression was that people went online because election information was more convenient to access, rather than to engage or play a more active role in the campaign.

We then asked specifically about what type of election information they sought online. Mostly, users were looking for information about issues (37 percent), followed by information about the parties (30 percent). Slightly less common was looking for more specific information about candidates (22 percent). Noticeably, about 25 percent also reported looking for the election results online.

Although it is difficult to assess the 'effects' of online information for citizens' election behavior, we asked respondents to identify whether, and if so how, the Internet affected their experience of the election. As younger people were more likely to be active online, we distinguished between eighteen to thirty-five year-olds and older citizens (Table 7.7). Overall, most users thought that the Internet was in some way important. Almost one in five responded that online information made for a more interesting election and helped them make a better voting choice. One in six also claimed that such information encouraged them to go out and vote. Much smaller numbers reported an effect on they way they voted, by either confirming or changing their vote decision, or encouraging them to vote tactically. Across the board, younger citizens reported much higher levels of Internet effects, especially, in terms of making a better choice and going to the polls.

If convenient access to issues was the main driver to seeking information online, which in turn led to an informed voting choice, what then discouraged other Internet users from using the medium for election information? Overwhelmingly, it seems that non-use stemmed from a lack of interest in the election and old media dynamics. About a third of users who did not gather information online reported lack of interest in the election as the main reason. This illustrates the point that access to technology alone will not produce a sudden interest in the political world. Additionally, 24 percent reported that they got enough information from the traditional media, or that access to traditional media was easier (another 11 percent).

Table 7.7 Self-reported Influence of the Internet by Different Age Groups

	Age		
	Below 35	35 and above	All
More interest in the election	22.3%	15.0%	18.4 %
Helped make a better informed choice *	24.2%	12.4%	17.8 %
Encouraged to vote *	12.9%	6.2%	16.2 %
Confirmed vote decision	18.2%	14.5%	9.3 %
Changed vote decision	4.0%	1.9%	3.5 %
Encouraged to vote tactically	4.0%	3.1%	2.9 %
Encouraged to take part in the campaign	2.1%	0.9%	1.5 %
Some effect *	62.7%	43.8%	52.5 %

Q12. Thinking about the information and news about the election you read or received online, do you think it ....
Internet users who looked for or came across information about the election, n = 401.
* = difference is statistically significant at $p < 0.05$.

The 2005 Online Election in Context

How does this compare with past elections? First, one needs to note that digital Britain changed dramatically between the 2001 and 2005 general elections. Just after the 2001 election, 33 percent of the British public enjoyed home Internet access and 33 percent said that they had access to email. In 2005, more than 33 percent had broadband connections in the home, while 56 percent accessed the Internet. More than 45 percent also used email. Also, digital inequality, as measured by home access to PCs, Internet and broadband, decreased between the two elections, albeit not dramatically.

On the one hand, the online political landscape did not seem to have changed that much. As the 2001 Hansard Society survey found (Coleman and Hall, 2001), Internet users and non-users had the same likelihood of voting. This largely depends on the social stratification of Internet access: both young people who are less likely to vote than average and older citizens who are more likely to vote than average are online, effectively averaging out the voting variance. In other words, enlarged access has not made the Internet either a more, or less, political place than before. On the other hand, however, actual online activity increased at least twofold between the two elections, as measured by a range of indicators. Out of all Internet users, about 13 percent sent or received emails about the election (5 percent in 2001); 17 percent used the Internet for election information on at least a few occasions (7 percent in 2001); 22 percent visited a media website (cf. 11 percent). Although the numbers for active online activities (online discussion, opinion polls, volunteered online, donated money) remains small in 2005 (see above), they are more than double the figures from 2001.

Finally, did such increased activity make a larger difference to citizens' voting choice than it did back in 2001? In 2005, 18 percent reported that the Internet helped them make a better informed choice, and 19 percent said that it helped them make their mind up, either by confirming their vote choice or by changing it. This figure was about 6 percent in 2001. Therefore, Internet users were as likely to vote in 2005 as they were four years previously, but the overall importance of the Internet for the election has greatly increased.

Summary and Conclusions

Trends in Online Campaigning

The 2005 election confirms many of the patterns that emerged in 2001 and in some cases 1997. New ICTs even appear to be accelerating some of the broader trends in political campaigning that pre-date the Internet.

- Pluralism and online party competition—The net is not a level-playing field. However, the concept of normalization is not nuanced enough to describe the current situation. There is a degree of equality in terms of presence and some aspects of content but less so in terms of site sophistication and much less when one looks at access to party sites. Clearly, some minor parties do punch above their weight online—the Greens, for example—but they are the exception. Essentially, the web allows some minor parties an enhanced presence and provides all with a platform but in reality the net widens, rather than levels, the campaign communication playing field. Consequently, the Internet might increase competition through supporting the current growth in the number of parties and candidates standing at elections but won't necessarily radically alter electoral competition in terms of seats or votes without changes to the electoral system.

- Postmodern elections—The professionalization of election campaigning continues apace and ICTs have created a new breed of campaign staff but the impact of new ICTs on parties and their campaigns is somewhat contradictory. Parties have developed some elements of interaction but this is mainly for marketing rather than democratic purposes. The way larger parties, in particular, are adopting new technologies is intended to increase effective voter targeting as well as mobilizing their core supporters. Hence, although email and websites are being used to mobilize and assist supporters, the technologies that are most valued by the big two parties are not so much websites, but the rather less sexy database technologies. Paradoxically, whilst much debate has focused on using technologies to engage more people in elections, one of the main consequences of the parties' adaptation of technologies has been to refine their campaign focus on ever-smaller groups of swing voters in marginal seats who determine the outcome of any election. Nor is it clear that use of new technologies will enhance the decentralization of campaigning. Databases tend to be centrally coordinated even if the actual follow-up is through traditional local campaigning. Moreover, whilst our study detected a significant growth in web campaigning locally, a lot of this was what one might call top-down localism or pseudo-localism, shaped directly and indirectly from above. Although one could see elements of candidates personalizing and developing localized campaigns the bigger picture was more nationalization of the local than localization of the national.

- Participation and voter engagement—Our survey data indicated that the net is becoming a more important source of information for the electorate but the online party campaigns barely penetrated the wider public consciousness. In fairness, the parties aimed less at the wider public and were more concerned with either converting the sympathetic or energizing and arming their own supporters and activists. It seems unlikely that, for mainstream parties, the net is going to reinvigorate them extensively. It may allow them to extract more from their existing activist base and temporarily draw on a looser group of supporters via more efficient campaigning and mobilization. However, it will not bring them significant numbers of new members or help them reach the relatively uninterested. If anything, the net may reinforce the participation gaps. However, in the longer term, parties and politicians may find themselves increasingly challenged by a new web-enabled activist class who are increasingly disenchanted with party politics and the UK political system.

The Shaping of Online Campaigns in UK elections

The introductory chapter of this book outlines some of the potential of Internet technologies but this study reinforces the idea that such potential is limited or shaped individually by the parties themselves and also by systemic factors such as the campaign environment. Parties have generally adapted ICTs to pursue their pre-existing goals. At one level, this means there are considerable similarities in the way parties have adopted ICTs—mainly for information provision and mobilizing core supporters. Clearly, financial resources do limit the level of sophistication of online campaigns but, as we have noted, party culture and incentives subtly shape online strategy and explain some of the finer differences between parties. Perhaps even more importantly though, our study underlines the importance of the systemic environment in limiting the potential of online campaigns in the United Kingdom. Despite the temptation to do so, we should not necessarily expect the U.S. experience to be replicated here. The United Kingdom's experience is always likely to be more low key. This is not because of lower levels of access to or, interest in, the Internet but rather because the British political system, the campaign and traditional media environments all erode some of the potency of the web as a campaign tool. There are fewer incentives here for both the parties and the public to use the web. In U.S. elections, especially primaries, candidates often have to build supporter networks almost from scratch, campaign over vast distances and, for challengers, develop a national profile, all of which lend themselves to online campaigning. In the United Kingdom, by contrast, well-entrenched party machines and the relatively localized nature of election campaigning mean that currently traditional communication tools work just as well. Why use email when direct mail and door knocking works better? Indeed, the Internet in Britain may be more suited to facilitating single-issue politics and flash campaigns outside elections where innovation, flexibility and networking are at a premium.

Notes

1. In 2005 Labour and the Conservatives had three broadcasts each and the Liberal Democrats two. The parties can choose three-, four- or five-minute broadcasts.
2. In 2005 the Greens, UKIP, the BNP and Veritas all qualified for broadcasts.
3. The Green Party was probably the first to try this in 2002 with a series of short films spread by email.
4. Prior to the 2005 election these were: Tom Watson, Clive Soley, Austin Mitchell and Sean Woodward (Labour); Sandra Gidley and Richard Allan (Liberal Democrat); and Boris Johnson (Conservative).
5. Parliamentary parties included: Labour, Conservative, Liberal Democrat, SNP, PC, UUP, DUP, SDLP and SF. The non-parliamentary parties were the Green Party (England and Wales), BNP, UKIP, Respect Coalition, Veritas, the Liberal Party, SLP, Pensioners Party, Legalise Cannabis Alliance, English Democrats and Your Party. The SNP only stood candidates in Scotland, PC in Wales and UUP, DUP, SDLP and SF in Northern Ireland constituencies.
6. The survey was based on a stratified representative sample of 1937 British adults (18+). Interviews were conducted face-to-face 12-17 May 2005.
7. See, for example, the site of Judith Blake (www.20six.co.uk/leedsnwblog), the defeated Labour candidate in Leeds North West.
8. www.voxpolitics.com/weblog/archives/2005-04.html. 29 April 2005.

Appendix: Scoring System: Party Web-Site Survey

Functions
Information Provision
Additive index—1 point assigned for each item present (0–5):
Organizational history

Structure
Values/ideology
Policies
Manifesto
Media releases
Speeches
People/Who's Who
Leader focus
Candidate profiles
Electoral Information 1 (statistics, information on past performance)
Electoral information 2 (postal voting info/voting registration)
Event Calendar (prospective or retrospective)
Frequently Asked Questions
Article Archive or Library

Resource Generation
Cumulative index (0–12) Three ordinal indices:
(i) Donation index 0–4
(ii) Merchandise index 0–4
(iii) Membership index 0–4
For each index: (1) reference made and postal address listed; (2) download and post form;
(3) Mixed email enquiry and/or download form; (4) fully online transaction.

Networking
Additive index—1 point assigned for each item present (0–9):
Internal
Candidates
Local parties
Other internal groups
External
Partisan links (associated orgs e.g. Trade Unions sister parties etc.)
Media links (news broadcasters, newspapers)
Election sites
Parliamentary/government sites
Commercial links are those promoting business services such as booksellers etc.
Opponents

Participation
Additive index (0–10):
Openness (0–4)
Email leader
Email other politicians/candidates
Email hq general
Email named officials/staff
Feedback (0–3)
(1) General feedback on the website etc. (2) feedback issues/policy general (3) solicited
email feedback on specific issue
Interactive debate/comment (0–4)

Discussion fora
Campaign diary/blog without comment facility
Blog with comments
Online q&a
Interaction with site (0–2)
Opinion polls
Games

Campaigning
Additive index—1 point assigned for each item present (0–8):
Negative campaigning (banner, pop-up ad etc. on home page)
Targeting ex-pat voters
Targeting marginal constituency/swing voter (explicit effort)
Join an email update list
Become online campaigner
Send a link/e-postcard
Download literature
Download screensavers/ banners

Delivery and Sophistication
Multimedia/Glitz Factor
Additive index—1 point for each item present (0–5):
Sound
Video
Live streaming
Flash
SMS

Access
Additive index—1 point for each item present (0–4):
Text only option (entire site)
Text only documents to download and print
Foreign language translation
Blind/visually impaired software

Navigability
Additive index—1 point for each item present (0–4):
Navigation tips
Search engines
Fixed menu bar on lower level pages
Site map/index

Freshness
Ordinal index (0–6):
Updated daily (6); 1–2 days (5); 3–7 days (4); every two weeks (3); monthly (2); 1–6 months (1); + 6 months (0)

Chapter Eight

Spain: Cyber-quake in a Soft Democracy? The Role of the Internet in the 2004 General Elections

José-Luis Dader

As the 2004 General Elections approached in Spain, the Internet's role in the campaign had been marginal. The Islamic bombing attacks on train stations in Madrid on the eve of the election stimulated massive Internet and cellular phone use by people searching for, and spreading, information about the events. The information provided through these channels was highly dissonant with that supplied by most of the conventional media and may have had an impact on public opinion, ultimately affecting the outcome of the election, including voter turnout.

New information and communication technologies (ICTs) and cyber political communication dramatically impacted the final days of the 2004 Spanish election campaign. Yet three years following this election, the audiences for political web pages are still small and the influence of cyber communication activities in the political arena remains negligible. The explanation for this apparent paradox will be the main subject of this chapter.

The Campaign and Media Environment in Spain

The structure of the political and electoral system of the Spanish democracy itself contributes to the low expectations about the impact of the Internet in election campaigns. Spain is a relatively new democracy. It was founded as a democratic state in 1977. Democratic political institutions are still in an adolescent stage. Since 1977, Spain has been a parliamentary monarchy with a bicameral system broadly inspired by the British model. The party system of the Spanish democracy can be described as an "asymmetrical" or "veiled" two-party system in which the two majority parties have obtained between 80 and 89 percent of the 350 seats of the Lower Chamber over the course of the nine elections that have taken place (Martínez Cuadrado, 1996; Linz, 1999; Román, 2001). The number of parties represented in Parliament has varied between a minimum of twelve and a maximum of fifteen. The "veiled" two-party system can be observed by the fact that many of the smaller parties have only a single representative. The majority of the remainder have less than six representatives. The two-party system is "asymmetrical" because only three or four groups present statewide lists of candidates, while the remainder are regional parties.

Party Structure

The dominance of the two main parties and the local hegemony of the main nationalist regional forces have led to a great stability in the electoral map. The two main parties alternate governing, with smaller parties participating through alliances with either the PSOE (Socialists) or the PP (Conservatives). Additionally, party structures are highly centralized. A single leader dominates the party, thus reducing internal competition or pluralism. Moreover, the election of the central leadership is determined by internal processes usually controlled by a small dominant group. Party leaderships control the lists of candidates that voters choose from in elections. In this centralized party structure, individual candidate names matter less than central party campaigning.

Political parties are financed primarily by state subsidies. How much each party gets is based on the party's previous electoral performance. In addition, parties receive large bank loans with very generous conditions. Consequently, the ordinary citizen customarily does not contribute money to a political party.

Media Structure

Campaigns are conducted through mass media rather than by personal candidate campaigning. Campaigns are centered on coverage by the traditional mass media, particularly the national radio and television networks. The Spanish media reflect the coexistence of state and private radio and television channels and a broad range of private newspapers. The newspaper market in Spain differs significantly from that in other European nations. There are over one hundred daily newspapers with only a handful reaching one hundred thousand readers, and coverage of local and regional events and politics is significant.

The Spanish news system is characterised by intense partisan polarization. State radio and television stations are supportive of national or regional governments, while privately owned media reflect the ideological biases of the corporations that own them. Politically polarized audiences gravitate to the news media reflecting their partisan views. Hallin and Mancini (2004) have described the Spanish media system as being dominated by a strong political parallelism, where commercial competitiveness and professional independence are conditioned by the ideological ties of each corporation and the loyalty of their equally polarized audiences. In this environment, campaigns become stark confrontations between competing media.

Campaign regulation aims for balance and fairness for news and other programming on state-owned broadcasting networks. Political advertising is unrestricted in private print and on radio, but it is forbidden on private television channels. On state-run television channels, advertising is restricted to a few "free presentation spaces" divided among parties according to a strict allocation of broadcasting time and based on past electoral success.

Prior to the official campaign, which lasts fifteen days, media coverage is less restricted, although explicit appeals to vote for a particular candidate or party are prohibited. On the day before the election, the so-called "Reflection Day," and on election-day itself, all campaigning is forbidden, and media coverage is restricted to information pertaining to the voting process.

These campaign regulations were written long before the emergence of the Internet. The lack of regulation of the Internet offers political parties and citizen groups the potential to use the Internet for campaigning. However, to date such usage has been limited in scope due to the small audiences for political websites.

The Spanish Internet Environment

Internet usage in Spain has grown slowly, lagging far behind that of more technologically advanced countries. In 2000, only 13.2 percent of the Spanish population (approximately 5.4 million people) was online. The percentage online grew to 32.5 percent of the population in 2004 (just over 14 million people), and reached 43.9 percent in 2006 (19.8 million people) according to Neilsen/Netratings (2006). The main reasons for low Internet penetration rates are connection costs, which are among the highest in Europe, and a poor connection infrastructure. Another problem is the lack of computer skills among the potential Internet audience. Broad sectors of the population have limited computer usage and skills, particularly people over sixty years of age, those in the lower and lower-middle classes, and rural populations.[1]

Given this context, it is not surprising that during the February-March 2004 General Elections the main source of media audience information (EGM/AIMC,

2005a) found that only 31 percent of the population aged over fourteen had used the Internet in the past month. This figure had risen slightly a year later. Another survey indicated that between 34 and 39 percent of the population aged over fourteen went online, depending upon whether Internet usage was measured in the past month or in the past three months.[2] It should also be noted that broadband connections were very rare until 2004, with normal connection speeds being lower than 51 kbps. A gradual reduction in fees has accelerated the adoption of connections with speeds of over 500 kbps during 2005, and over 1mb by the end of 2006.

Even fewer citizens use the Internet to access political information. In February 2005, a year after the General Elections, 28 percent of the population over fourteen years of age used the Internet to read about current events (EGM/AIMC, 2005a). However, even this percentage is inflated since it also includes other current events such as sports or the social lives of celebrities. While 96 percent of Internet users claimed to use it to "search for information," the percentage decreased to 46 percent when the question was limited to "reading news or newspapers," and only 30 percent claimed to "read newspapers regularly on the Internet" (BBVA, 2005).

It is not surprising that there are no specific statistics available from survey companies regarding web audiences for political parties or for other social or institutional groups related to politics. The limited data available reveal that only 2 percent of the adult Spanish population claimed to have participated in a political forum or newsgroup discussion on the Internet between May 2004 and the same month in 2005 (CIS, 2005b, Quest#19). And 16.1 percent of the population claimed to use Internet to get information about politics, at least from time to time, in January 2005 (CIS, 2005a, Quest#33). The BBVA Foundation survey (2005) found that 10 percent of the population claimed to have "searched for information provided by the Government or Public Administration" and only 6 percent had searched for "information about politics" in the months prior to June 2005. These figures mark the likely ceiling of the Spanish population that follows politics through the Internet. This ceiling has increased slightly two years later, according to another survey of the Centro de Investigaciones Sociológicas, which states that 22.7 percent of the population over the age of eighteen used the Internet to get information about politics or social matters, at least from time to time, in January 2007 (CIS, 2007, Quest#12).

In an attempt to identify the possible audience of political party websites, the author sent a questionnaire to the webmasters of the main parties represented in Parliament with an Internet presence in November 2005. Respondents were asked about the audiences for their respective websites. The lack of interest exhibited by the parties themselves in the effects of their online activities was reflected in the fact that of the nine parties consulted, only two—Convergència Democràtica de Catalunya (CDC) and Unió Democràtica de Catalunya (UDC) (two regional parties of Catalonia who together form a coalition—Convergència i Unió (CIU))—replied to the questionnaire. The CIU reported receiving an average of 809 daily visits in the month of March 2004 (at the time of the General

Elections) and a total of 12,298 visits in the fifteen days of the official campaign plus another 14,636 for the personal webpage of the main candidate of this coalition (CIU; www.duran.org). The party claimed to have received in October-November of 2005 an average of 885 daily visits plus another 969 to the new site of the coalition (www.ciu.info). The increase a year and a half later is relatively large, but not very significant in global terms. The UDC claimed not to keep statistics on web traffic to its sites. The webmaster of CDC reported an initial optimism in estimating that between 50 and 69 percent of the adult Spanish population visits a political website at some point during the year. But he noted that between 2 and 4 percent of the adult population visited his own website, which serves the region of Catalonia. The webmaster of the UDC estimated that only 2 percent of the Spanish population visited the website of any political party.

Given these circumstances, it is not surprising that personal websites of parliamentarians are very rare. Only fourteen representatives and one senator had a personal site or a blog on December 31 2005. These numbers climbed to thirty-one representatives and five senators in March 2007 (www.congreso.es and www.senado.es). This lack of a web presence by parliamentarians does not seem to be merely a question of technological backwardness or an underdeveloped Internet culture in general. The political system itself does little to encourage representatives to use the Internet as a tool for personal differentiation since it is heavily weighted towards strong, centralized party control.[3]

Cyberquake? The 2004 General Election

In light of the above, it is not surprising that online campaigning played a limited role during most of the campaign period of the 2004 Spanish national election. Political parties did launch websites that allowed their followers to read favourable news stories and statements by their candidates, including those that had previously appeared in the traditional news media. However, interactive features, such as forums and chats, were rare. In fact, just after the elections, some parties abandoned the websites they had created and others waited until just before the election to create a website.[4] There was even some retreat from the level of online engagement in the general election four years earlier. While the 2000 election in the United States had sparked widespread journalistic and public interest in the role of the Internet, by 2004 that initial curiosity had dissipated among the Spanish conventional mass media. Journalists dedicated much less space to information about political websites than they did during the 2000 Spanish elections.

The Bombings

All of that changed on Thursday, March 11, 2004. Only three days before the elections, a terrorist attack on the Madrid railway system killed 192 people and wounded over 1,700. The attack shocked the electorate and immediately led to government claims the bombings were the work of the ETA, a Basque terrorist group (Olmeda, 2005, p.19). However, evidence uncovered a few hours later pointed to al-Qaeda's involvement. While police and government officials frantically investigated leads, online rumors began to circulate among government opponents, particularly radical leftists, that the PP Government was "hiding the truth." These groups, through SMS messages and Internet communications, spread messages, such as "We want to know before we vote" and "The truth now, stop the manipulation, your war, our dead. Pass it on!" (Suarez, 2005). These actions triggered flash-mobs in front of the PP ruling-party headquarters and other public spaces which were supported by center-left party leaders and the socialist-aligned Grupo PRISA (the most powerful multimedia corporation). Between three thousand and four thousand people protested in front of the PP headquarters in Madrid and an additional three thousand gathered in Barcelona (Suarez, 2005). In addition, blogs spread information that countered the government's claims.

The election proceeded despite the attacks. The day before the attacks, the Conservatives were ahead by 5 percent in polls. On Voting Day, the Socialists (PSOE) won by a margin of 43 to 36 percent. The result was a remarkable shift of 12 percentage points in three days. Voter turnout was especially high in the election, as the PSOE received nearly three million more votes than in 2000. About half of these new PSOE voters tended to be younger, with six hundred thousand being newly eligible voters, and left-leaning. The others were former PP supporters who changed their vote and supporters of the former communists who voted for the Socialists for tactical reasons (Suarez, 2005).

The Role of the Internet

The role played by the Internet and new ICTs during the 2004 Spanish General Elections has been viewed differently by politicians, opinion leaders and scholars. One perspective holds that a conventional electoral process was at work. Opinion changes and the voter turnout reflected a cumulative trend of government discredit based coherently on images established by the conventional media and classical campaign activities. Another view is that a political and techno-media conspiracy was led by certain leaders of the main opposition parties and executives of the most important media corporation. This group consciously and successfully coordinated a disinformation campaign through traditional media and new ICTs that resulted in a PP electoral defeat. A third view assumes that the Internet's role was irrelevant, as it was superseded by the prominence of massive and uncoordinated SMS messages by ordinary citizens.[5] Another interpretation posits that the combination of SMS and an accelerated civic debate on the Internet represented a genuine expression of cyberdemocracy and pluralism. Ordinary citizens and small groups of politically-concerned activists spread information, deliberated about the orientations of the political parties and commented on coverage of events by the conventional mass media.

A better explanation may be that the electoral outcome can be attributed to the combination of traditional and new media, particularly the Internet, granting legitimacy to a public perception that countered the official frame of events that ETA was responsible and the government was stating the truth. The counter-frame that ETA was not the culprit and the government was hiding this information was fostered by some traditional media, as well as activists, and ordinary voters. The Internet became a forum for the dissemination of this counter-frame and its eventual emergence as the popular view held by voters. The changes in opinion and mobilization that occurred during the final days of the campaign would not have been successful without this combination.

The Internet's role was made possible by an increase in the size of the audience for news websites in the days preceding the election. Table 8.1 demonstrates that audiences for news websites increased dramatically after the bombings, particularly in comparison with increases in the size of the audience for traditional media. The audiences for these websites were still miniscule compared with those for television news, with the exception of the website for the newspaper *El Mundo*. Still, the crisis drove many more citizens to the Internet for news, thus allowing it to play an enhanced role as a source for information.

Exactly what site visitors saw and how it influenced their opinions is still unknown. Internet users could compare the official and mainstream Spanish media accounts attributing the bombings to ETA with Internet information, including news from foreign media sources, attributing the attacks to Islamic terrorists. They may have quickly concluded that government information was inaccurate, which eventually proved to be correct.

A crisis situation where the government's position is questioned by factual evidence can lead to confusion on the part of the electorate and a search for other sources of information. The Internet became that source for some citizens. Opposition forces benefited from this situation and utilized the Internet to take advantage of the confusion by distributing online information that disparaged the government.

Spanish political institutions and their electoral regulation were vulnerable on March 11, 2004. The fragility of the Spanish political system contributed to an atmosphere of political uncertainty and enhanced the Internet's role in exacerbating that uncertainty. The political transformation would not have been as extensive if the Spanish political framework had constituted a more consolidated democracy.

Table 8.1 Digital Audiences During the 2004 Spanish Election Campaign

Media	March 5-7	March 12-14	Absolute Variation	Percent Variation
TVE (TV Newsbulletin 1)	3,179,666	4,015,666	+836,000	+26.2
Antena 3 (TV. Newsb 1)	3,033,333	3,250,666	+217,333	+7.1
Tele5 (TV Newsb. 1)	2,359,333	2,962,333	+603,000	+25.5
ABC website	62,139	241,190	+179,051	+288.1
El Mundo website	833,471	2,165,552	+1,332,081	+159.8
El Periódico website	99,053	226,142	+127,089	+128.3
Libertad digital website	27,423	75,957	+48,534	+176.9
SER website	66,737	227,286	+160,549	+240.5
Messages to three current affairs forums*	2,928	18,761	+15,833	+540.7
Visits to eight major political blogs **	25,924	46,814	+20,890	+80.5
Visits to two radical left-wing pages ***	68,611	147,479	+76,868	+114.9

*Foros *Terra.es Nacional* /*Ya.com Elecciones*/*IBLNews*
**Ajopringue.com/Caspa *TV/E-Cuaderno.com/Escolar.net/Info-tk/Bitácora de las Indias/Libro de Notas/Pensamientos Radicalmente Eclécticos*
***Nodo50.org, Rebelión.org*
Source: Raw data from Sampedro and López-García (2005, pp.152-156), reanalysed by the author.

It is important to note that the websites of political parties and candidates were the most insignificant and marginal media during the crisis. This point has ramifications for general studies of the role of the Internet in political processes. A large proportion of existing studies have focused on the online activities of institutional actors (governments, political parties and candidates), but as the Spanish case illustrates, the most dramatic changes may be brought about by groups of activists, social movements and even individual bloggers who capture the attention of ordinary citizens. Research should explore whether the online initiatives of institutional actors turn out to be less relevant for cyberdemocracy than those promoted spontaneous or alternative groups. At the same time, scholars should consider whether, in the case of democracies that are not well established or whose political parties are poorly integrated among their constituencies, the intensification of emotional debates on the Internet and through new ICTs may actually contribute to distorting information through rumors and manipulation by hidden spin doctors. The quality of democracy could be diminished, and the leadership of traditional parties and politicians could be weakened under such circumstances.

The role of the Internet in Spanish political communication has had little lasting influence on the political and electoral processes. It flourished intensively only during an abnormal situation of political chaos. Spanish electoral campaigns have not taken advantage of new incentives for deliberative democracy, apart from a few small-scale experiences (such as the platforms "Candidato.net" and "Ciudadanos.net," organized by the news agency *Europa Press* in collaboration with several political institutions to provide direct consultation by citizens with national electoral candidates and local government politicians).[6]

However, the Internet and ICT usage figures cited earlier in this chapter indicate an acceleration that will perhaps lead to a very different scenario for the upcoming election in 2008. The proliferation of websites of institutions, parties and individual politicians may also lead to a transformation at the outset of this campaign. Changes in campaigning and in the role played by new political actors may turn out to be much more relevant.

Notes

1. According to a report by the AIMC (2005) in February-March 2004, only 27.9 percent of the Spanish population over fourteen years of age were frequent computer users. According to another study by the Fundación BBVA (2005), in June 2005 half of Spanish homes owned a computer, two-thirds of them having been acquired in the previous five years.
2. The Centro de Investigaciones Sociológicas (CIS, 2005a, Quest#4), which depends on the office of the Spanish Presidency, found that 34 percent of Spaniards had used the Internet at least once in the week before May 21, 2005. According the Fundación BBVA (2005), 37 percent had used it at least once in the past three months. A panel study, RED.es (2005) provided a more optimistic figure for the first quarter of the year of 44.4 percent of the population over fifteen years of age. The estimate of Nielsen/Netratings (2005), in January 2005, was around 39 percent of those sixteen years or older, and, in October 2005, the INE (2005) calculated the number of Internet users in the past three months as 41.1 percent of the population over fifteen years of age. However, EGM/AIMC

(2005b) still reported that 34.8 percent of the population aged over fourteen used the Internet in the past month (November 2005). The similar study (EGM/AIMC, 2006) established the figure of 38.4 percent for the population over fourteen who used the Internet in the past month in December 2006 (the last available rating).

3. More proof of the scarce interest shown by Spanish parliamentarians in online contact with citizens is provided by an experiment carried out by the author in May-June 2005. Only 17.4 percent of representatives and senators replied to a query by a simulated ordinary citizen sent to the official email address of each parliamentarian. This result was even lower than that obtained (21.7 percent) in another similar test carried out in 2001 (see Dader, 2003; Dader and Campos, 2006).

4. These details are based on unsystematic personal observations of the author during the campaign. A content analysis of Spanish political party websites during selected weeks of non-campaign periods throughout the second half of 2004 and 2005 (Dader and Diaz, 2007) revealed a small improvement in the Spanish parties' efforts to populate their official websites with more detailed and appealing information. Using complexity of information, interactivity, user friendliness and aesthetics as the main variables, these scholars applied a methodology based on previous measures developed for European political websites by De Landtsheer, *et al*, (2000). Despite the time lag, the average results obtained for the Spanish party websites in 2004-2005 were lower than those achieved for the political websites of the Netherlands, the United Kingdom and Germany in 1999. (Nevertheless, the lower Spanish scores in the above-mentioned analysis can be partly explained by the cultural differences of the coders and the progress made regarding the potential of Internet services.) Qualitative analysis augmenting this research revealed that the main flaws of the web pages of the Spanish political parties were, in this post-electoral period, the abuse of public-relations-oriented information and weak interactivity.

5. In 2003, 92 percent of the Spanish population had a cellular phone, and 20 percent used cellphones as their only method of telecommunication. On the Day of Reflection in 2004, SMS traffic increased by 20 percent (Suarez, 2005).

6. Public knowledge of these initiatives is limited, and the number of interactions among participating citizens and candidates or politicians is even more trivial. (See www.candidato2004.net and www.ciudadanos2005.net among other projects of deliberative democracy by this group.)

Chapter Nine

Belgium: Websites as Party Campaign Tools—Comparing the 2000 and 2006 Local Election Campaigns.

Marc Hooghe and Sara Vissers

In this chapter, we compare the Internet presence of Belgian political parties in 2000 and 2006, with special attention to three research questions. First, we try to ascertain to what extent political parties use new ICTs in a different way compared to the traditional communication channels. Second, we investigate whether all political parties use the Internet to the same extent. Is the gap between small and major political parties growing further or can we find some normalization? Finally, we compare the situation in 2006 with the data from an earlier study in 2000.

In order to answer these questions we draw principally on two types of data: (1) a detailed website content analysis of thirteen parties conducted during the 2006 local election campaign; (2) a series of semi-structured interviews with party webmasters.

Prior to discussing this empirical evidence, the chapter begins by setting out the Belgian campaign context and some of the important environmental factors, such as the fragmented party system, which potentially shape the use of the Internet for electoral purposes.

Results from our research underline the importance of campaign traditions, electoral geography and the state funding of parties as inhibitors to the use of the Internet for electioneering in the Belgian context. While access to the Internet grew significantly between 2000 and 2006, it developed only modestly in election campaigning terms. Nevertheless, the study does suggest that for some minor parties the Internet provides a much more level playing field than the traditional media.

The Campaign Environment

The Belgian party system can be considered one of the most fragmented in the Western world. Partly this extreme form of fragmentation is due to the presence of a very open and proportional electoral system. In 2003 a new electoral threshold of 5 percent at the provincial level was introduced, but thus far this threshold has not led to the actual disappearance of any of the small political parties (Hooghe *et al*, 2006). A second element to explain this extreme fragmentation is the linguistic segregation of the party system. From the 1970s, the former national parties split to fully autonomous Dutch and French political parties. Although there is still some informal coordination going on, e.g. the Dutch-speaking SP.A (Socialistische Partij) and the French-speaking PS (Parti Socialiste), in practice these parties function completely on their own. Given the fact that French-speaking parties do not compete in Dutch-speaking electoral districts, and vice versa, all parties run separate electoral campaigns. Only in the bilingual district of Brussels (ca. 10 percent of the total population), do both Dutch- and French-speaking parties compete with one another.

The overall result is that now thirteen political parties are represented in a federal or regional parliament in Belgium. For a population of a little more than ten million inhabitants, this amounts to a very fragmented party system. This build-up of the party system has a number of consequences for the way political parties conduct electoral campaigns. First of all, it has to be remembered that the two language groups remain completely segregated and do not compete with one another (Deschouwer, 2004). One could even argue that Belgium does not have a single party system, but rather two completely different party systems: one for the Flemish region (ca. six million inhabitants) and one for the French-speaking region of Wallonia (ca. four million inhabitants). Second, given the small scale of the country and the large number of political parties, most politicians in Belgium remain convinced of the fact that personal contacts with the electorate are still possible, and indeed have the strongest impact. The electoral system, with relatively small districts, also offers incentives to maintain these personal and local relations with one's constituency. For these reasons, politicians, particularly those from an older generation, initially were quite reluctant to adopt the Internet for electoral campaigns.

The campaign for the local elections of the year 2000 offered the first opportunity for Belgian political parties to use the Internet in an election campaign.

A study revealed, however, that Internet use remained very limited (Hooghe and Stouthuysen, 2001). A number of parties and candidates launched websites as they had the feeling that they could not remain completely absent from this new medium. Maintenance of the websites, however, was extremely limited, and most websites did not offer much more information than an html version of the leaflets and the brochures of the candidates and the parties.

The campaign for the local elections of 2006 offered us an excellent opportunity to ascertain the evolution of e-campaigning since 2000. We had every reason to assume that parties would increasingly rely on the Internet for campaigning. First of all, this was in line with an international trend (Lusoli *et al*, 2006). More specifically for Belgium, the percentage of the population with broadband access to the Internet increased substantially between 2000 and 2006. Second, political parties in Belgium became increasingly professionalized during this period. Following some corruption scandals in the 1990s, the Belgian parliament introduced a very generous system of financial allowances for political parties, allowing them to hire more professionals.

Internet Access in Belgium

Our expectation that parties would have intensified their use of the Internet as a campaign tool was based on the fact that the use of the Internet had risen substantially in Belgian society since 2000. Not only had the number of connections grown enormously but, maybe more importantly, the telephone line-based forms of access had almost completely disappeared in favor of broadband connections. This meant that consumers no longer pay per time unit, enabling them to spend longer on the web, and they could download more information more quickly. Partly because of aggressive marketing techniques by a number of large Internet providers, broadband access is affordable to most households (current prices ca. 40 euro/month for a full service package) (Ottens, 2006). An analysis of 2004 data also shows that Belgians were among the most active Internet users in the European Union (Lusoli, 2005).

This trend was confirmed when we look at data from the Belgian Association of Internet Providers (ISPA). In 2000 there were 736,000 private Internet connections in Belgium (one for every thirteen inhabitants), by 2005 this was up to 1,771,000 (one for every six inhabitants). While in 2000 a significant number of households still relied on free telephone line-based access (with costs for every minute online), this form of accessing the Internet had virtually disappeared by 2005 (Table 9.1).

As the number of private Internet connections does not inform us about the proportion of the population using the Internet we also included survey data on individual Internet use. Therefore we employed the European Social Survey data (2002, 2004), where we investigated the Belgian data. In the ESS the exact question was "How often do you use the Internet, the World Wide Web or email—whether at home or at work—for your personal use?"

Table 9.1 Internet Connections in Belgium, 2000-2005

	2000	2005	Change
Total private connection	736,483	1,771,016	+ 140.5 %
Free connection	394,766	209,649	-46.9 %
Paid connection	341,717	1,561,367	+ 356.9 %
No broadband connection	287,741	47,842	- 83.4 %
Broadband connection	53,976	1,513,525	+2704.1 %
Total connection companies	132,533	416,007	+213.9 %

Source: Internet Service Providers Association (ISPA 2005). Figures for July 2000 and 4th quarter 2005.
Note: The data cover 97 percent of all the Belgian Internet-providers.

Comparing the data from the 2002 and the 2004, the ESS confirms the trend that the use of the Internet is spreading very rapidly in Belgian society (Table 9.2). In 2002 34.7 percent of the Belgian respondents could be considered as frequent Internet users (at least once a month), whereas in 2004 this percentage increased to 51.7 percent. As we already indicated, the Dutch and the French political parties can be seen as completely segregated party systems, and therefore it makes sense to make a distinction between the Internet in the Dutch and the French communities of Belgium. While we could see a small difference, for all practical purposes we observed that both communities have adopted the Internet to the same extent. In this regard, both party systems were confronted with the same situation.

Table 9.2 Private Internet Use in Belgium (2002-2004)

	2002	n	2004	n
Dutch	44.3%	1,200	52.5%	992
French	41.8%	643	50.2%	711
Total Belgium	43.7%	1,896	51.7%	1,776

Source: European Social Survey 2002, 2004.
The Internet use is measured as frequency of Internet use for personal purposes. This variable is categorized between frequent users (at least once a month) and infrequent users (less than once a month). Distinction based on the language used most often at the home of the respondent.

Research Methodology

Within the international literature, various methods have been proposed to analyze political website content in a systematic manner. In this chapter, we will mainly use the method developed by Gibson and Ward (2000). In this method, the focus is on two central aspects of political party websites, namely their purpose and function on the one hand; and their effectiveness in delivering these functions on the other hand. Initially this method was conceived of as a very elaborate coding instrument, involving fifty different criteria. The analysis of the party websites' functioning was based on five primary goals of party websites: information, resource generation, networking, participation and campaigning. As various authors pointed out, the use of quantitative indicators in some cases posed serious problems concerning comparisons with other parties (Gibson and Ward, 2000c; Hooghe and Stouthuysen, 2001). In a later version, (see Ward *et al*, this volume), they simplified their method by relying on a simple dichotomous coding scheme (present=0 vs. not present=1). Moreover, they adapted the model to new developments in the ICT sector. In this chapter we use the later version of the method, but we also added some new features, like the possibility of RSS feeds and the presence of podcasting.

In coding the website content we followed the Gibson and Ward scheme quite closely, resulting in five main categories:

First, the website can be used for the simple provision of information, which amounts to a top-down process of distributing information from the party to individual users. This form of institutional communication is measured by coding the presence of information on organizational history, party structure, party program, party statutes, media releases, speeches, who's who, etc. We also coded the presence of information about the party leader, personal profiles (or curriculum vitae) of the candidates, information about the previous elections, an event calendar, frequently asked questions and an article archive or library.

Secondly, parties can use their websites to generate resources. This can include seeking donations, selling merchandise and mobilizing users for party membership. Following Gibson and Ward we used an ordinal index for measuring this function, ranging from a simple listing of the postal address of the party (1), through the possibility to download a file to be posted (2) and other mixed download/postal combinations (3) to a fully online transaction (4). Self-evidently, the higher a party scores on this ordinal index, the more innovative its use of new ICTs.

Thirdly, political parties can use their websites as networking tools. Networking can extend both to internal links (local candidates, local chapters, ideologically related parties) and to external links (to other parties or to non-political actors).

Fourthly, websites can be used to allow or even to invite participation by citizens. Here we coded openness (presence of email address of the party leader, other politicians, party offices in general, named staff), feedback opportunity (presence of (general) standardized message forms, possibility to give feedback directly to the webmaster), interactive debate or comment opportunities (presence of discussion forum, campaign/diary blog without comments, blog with an opportunity to give a comment, online questions and answers) and lastly the interaction with the site (presence of opinion polls, games, petitions).

Lastly, we coded how parties used their websites for specific campaigning purposes, including targeting specific groups, allowing the downloading of campaign materials, etc.

Separate from these main dimensions we also included a number of technical aspects of the websites (multimedia use, navigation tools, etc.). We limited our investigation to all political parties that are present in one of the parliamentary assemblies in Belgium (national or regional parliaments), i.e. eight Flemish parties, and five French-speaking parties (Table 9.3).

Table 9.3 Belgian Political Parties

Name	Lan-guage	Website	Ideology	% Vote 2003
SP.A	NL	s-p-a.be	Socialist	14.9
Spirit	NL	spirit.be	Progressive-Nationalist	14.9
CD&V	NL	cdenv.be	Christian-Democrat	13.3
N-VA	NL	n-va.be	Conservative National-ists	3.1
VLD	NL	vld.be	Liberal	15.4
Vivant	NL/FR	vivant.org	Liberal	1.3
Vlaams Belang	NL	vlaamsbe-lang.org/be	Extreme Right	11.6
Groen!	NL	groen.be	Greens	2.5
PS	FR	Ps.be	Socialist	13.0
MR	FR	Mr.be	Liberal	11.4
CdH	FR	lecdh.be	Christian Democrat	5.5
Ecolo	FR	ecolo.be	Greens	3.1
Front National	FR	frontna-tional.be	Extreme Right	2.0

Parties included in this chapter. Name, language (Dutch= NL; French = FR), URL and ideology. Percentage of the vote in the 2003 federal elections. SP.A and Spirit formed a joint cartel for these elections. Election results: Ministry of the Interior.

In this research project we analyzed different layers of websites belonging to these parties, using MetaProducts Offline Explorer to download the content of the websites. To supplement the content analysis, we interviewed the webmasters of different political parties, namely: Veerle De Gryse (SP.A), Pieter Verstraelen (Vivant), Steven Cryelman (Vlaams Belang), Piet De Zaeger (N-VA), Lieven Vanhollemeersch (Groen!), Patricia Van Overstraeten (CD&V), Pieter Montsaert (VLD), Angelo Callant (Spirit), Raphaël Thièmard (Ecolo), Nancy Vilbago (PS), Arnaud Vervoir (CDH), and Joanna Delaunoy (MR). The interviews were based on a semi-structured questionnaire and were carried out by telephone. The questions concerned practical issues of the activities of the webmaster and were focused on the following aspects: the budget spent on the website, the number of persons responsible for updating the site (full-time vs. part-time), the use of a content management system, cooperation with ICT companies, forms of cooperation at the national and local level, the average number of unique visitors per day, the time and localization specification of the website visitors, directories to a website (direct via URL of the website, via search engine, etc.) and the characteristics of the decision-making process on the content and design of the website. In comparison with the research conducted in 2000 (Hooghe and Stouthuysen, 2001), the webmasters were much more willing and/or able to indicate the number of visitors in a more reliable manner. On the other hand, we found it difficult to obtain information on the cost of website management, as the parties often did not know themselves the exact amount spent on it, or did not include this as a separate line in their budgets.

In order to address the first research question on how parties use ICT, website content was analyzed and it was ascertained to what extent political parties actually used the new communication opportunities being created by the Internet. We can distinguish three forms of communication via Internet (Hooghe and Stouthuysen, 2001). First, the "pure-interactive communication" is based on a dialogue between non-institutionalized actors, without any interference from institutionalized actors. A political chatroom would be a typical example of such interaction. The second form is "institutional communication." Here, an institutional actor (e.g. a political party) provides top-down information to other actors (individual or institutionalized), without any possibility for feedback or interaction. A political party or the government offering information on a website can be seen as a clear example of this communication form. The third form can be seen as a mixture of the two former types and is called an "institutional-interactive communication." Again, the initiative comes from the institutionalized actor, but at the same time non-institutionalized visitors have the possibility to interact with the institutionalized actor. The opportunity to comment on website content would be a typical example of this communication form. In this third setting there is no possibility for a simultaneous interaction between two non-institutional users of the website. Mostly, they do not even know from each other how they reacted. In this case we can speak of a sequential interaction. Our basic assumption for this analysis was that the more the parties used the interactive opportunities being created by new ICTs, the more democratic potential these new technologies have.

Content Analysis of Political Parties Websites

Information Provision

Almost all political parties use their websites to provide information about their party to potential voters, explaining their point of view on various policy issues (Foot and Xenos, 2005). Only Vivant and Front National, two minor parliamentary parties, obtained low scores on the information provision function (Table 9.4). Vivant presented only the party program, the event calendar, the media releases and the related archive on its website, whilst on the website of the Front National one only found media releases. The party program was removed from the Front National site following the decision of the Brussels Court of Appeal (April 2006) that the party leader was guilty of inciting racism, an illegal act according to Belgian law. All parties presented an overview of the most recent media releases on their websites. Moreover, they gave access to article archives or to a library, enabling users to find older press releases or articles. With the exception of Vivant and FN, all parties had an event calendar and a kind of "who's who" about their party leaders and representatives. It is striking here that the Groen! website offered very little information on individual members of parliament. It only listed their names and contact details, but no additional information on activities or other individual actions was provided.

Larger parties more often provided information about the history of the party, the structure and statutes, and detailed profiles of their representatives. Frequently asked questions and information about the previous elections appeared on only a few websites. Almost all parties tried to avoid giving too much attention to the party leader and often one even had to look to find relevant information on the party president. There were only two exceptions to this pattern: PS and MR sites both contained highly visible index links to the websites of their party presidents. This was no coincidence; while, in general, party presidents cannot be a minister in a government, the PS president was the Prime Minister of the Walloon regional government, and the MR president was the Vice Prime Minister of the Belgian federal government.

Table 9.4 Website Information Provision and Resource Generation by Belgian Political Parties

	SP.A	CD&V	VLD	VB	Vivant	Spirit	GRN	N-VA	PS	MR	CdH	ECOL	FN
Information provision													
Organizational history	X	X	X			X	X		X	X	X		
Party structure	X	X	X	X		X		X	X	X	X		
Party program	X	X	X	X	X	X	X	X			X	X	X*
Party statutes		X	X			X		X	X		X		
Media releases	X	X	X	X	X	X	X	X	X	X	X	X	X
Speeches		X	X	X		X		X	X	X			
Who's who	X	X	X	X		X	X	X	X	X	X	X	
Leader focus									X	X			
Candidate profiles	X	X		X				X	X	X	X	X	
Electoral information	X		X	X				X					
Event calendar	X	X	X	X	X	X	X	X	X	X	X	X	
Frequently asked questions				X				X					
Article archive or library	X	X	X	X	X	X	X	X	X	X	X	X	
Total	9	10	10	10	4	9	6	11	10	9	9	6	2
Resource generation													
Donation index							3						3
Merchandise index		1	4	3			1	4	4	4			
Membership index	4	4	4	4	3	2	4	4	4	4	4	3	3
Total	4	5	8	7	3	2	8	8	8	8	4	3	6

X = feature present on site * Party program removed from website during campaign following a court ruling

Comparing the results from the analyses, conducted in 2006 and 2000 (Hooghe and Stouthuysen, 2001) showed that little had changed with regard to the provision of information. We did see, however, that parties are slowly finding more imaginative ways to provide information on their websites. While in 2000 it was still customary to reproduce the entire speeches of party presidents, this practice seemed to have been abandoned by 2006.

The results from both years showed that parties saw their websites as an important medium for the quick dissemination of large amounts of information. In general, it is safe to argue that information provision remains by far the most important function of party websites in Belgium. It seems clear that parties remain much more interested in websites as tools for institutional communication rather than in using the interactive possibilities created by the new technology.

Resource Generation

Websites can also be used to generate material resources, by explicitly asking for donations, offering articles for sale or soliciting membership dues. While all parties used the opportunity to reach out to (potential) members online, we saw strong differences with regard to this function. All the parties, with the exception of three minor parties (Vivant, Ecolo and Front National), provided an enquiry form on their websites. While all parties made some attempts to attract members online, only three of them offered the possibility to buy merchandise and only two parties explicitly solicited donations online. Only the two liberal parties (VLD and MR) actively used their website to sell merchandise online. Again, maybe it is not a coincidence that these are liberal parties that in general are quite supportive of private enterprise. Vlaams Belang was the only other party selling merchandise online, but without providing for online transactions (payment by bank transfer). The Flemish Christian-Democratic Party CD&V provided a list of books, but for more information they referred to the websites of the publisher or local division or the personal website of a politician. The Flemish Green Party website enabled visitors to subscribe to their monthly review by providing a bank account number.

The two parties that explicitly solicited donations—Groen! and Front National are quite small and because of their scale they are largely excluded from the Belgian system of party financing. Consequently, they are more dependent on donations than any of the larger parties.

A comparison with our observations from 2000 does not reveal any remarkable differences. In comparison with other countries, Belgian political parties remain quite modest in soliciting donations or other forms of financial support. Largely this is the result of the official system of party financing, so that political parties are not dependent on financial support from the public. The effort to generate resources usually remains limited to offering an online membership form.

Networking

To measure the networking function of the party websites, we coded internal and external links (Table 9.5). The coding revealed that all parties devoted a lot of attention to networking. All parties, with the exception of the small Vivant and Front National parties, placed links to the personal websites of their politicians, local parties and other internal groups on their websites. Table 9.6 lists the number of links to local party and candidate websites for every party. The figures showed that the practice of linking to other party-related websites was much more widespread among the Dutch language parties than among the French language parties. Also, larger parties (obviously with more elected officials) provided many more links than the smaller parties. Moreover the number of links to local chapters and candidate websites also informs us about the nature of the party structure. A striking example is the SP.A, which had lots of links to websites by local chapters and relatively few to more informal personal websites. This conveyed the message that the SP.A was a rather strictly organized party where the local chapters were encouraged to adopt a nationally developed format. On the other hand, local politicians received little leeway in the party to develop their own personal campaigns and ideological profiles.

In relation to external links, all the parties except Vlaams Belang provided links to ideologically related organizations, like sister parties in other EU countries, affiliated organizations, etc. Furthermore, all parties except CD&V and Vlaams Belang provided links to politically neutral websites such as news broadcasters, newspapers, government sites and national libraries. CD&V and Vlaams Belang were the only parties that provided a link to a commercial publisher.

We can observe a distinct pattern with regard to providing a link to other, competing parties. In Flanders, this was clearly not a common practice and we found these links only on the N-VA website. In Wallonia, on the other hand, all parties did so with the exception of the Front National. The interviews with the party webmasters, however, revealed that this is largely a symbolical linkage. Very few visitors actually entered the websites from a link provided by a different political party. There seem to be very few people interested in surfing from one party website to another.

Table 9.5 Networking by Belgian Political Parties

	SP.A	C&V	VLD	VB	Vivant	Spirit	GRN	NVA	PS	MR	CdH	ECOL	FN
Internal													
Candidate links	X	X	X	X		X	X	X	X	X	X	X	X
Local party links	X	X	X	X		X	X	X	X	X		X	
Other internal groups	X	X	X	X	X	X	X	X	X	X	X	X	
External													
Partisan links	X	X	X		X	X	X	X	X	X	X	X	X
Reference links	X		X		X	X	X	X	X	X	X	X	X
Commercial links				X									
Opponents								X	X	X	X	X	
Total scores	5	4	5	4	3	5	5	6	6	6	5	6	3

X = feature present on site

Table 9.6 Number of Links to Local Party Chapter and Candidate Websites

	Local party chapter websites	Personal candidate websites
SP.A	312	48
CD&V	158	133
VLD	158	97
Vlaams Belang	102	24
Spirit	51	14
N-VA	105	14
Groen!	108	1
Vivant	-	1
PS	46	64
MR	91	67
CdH	-	16
Ecolo	(83)	5
FN	-	3

Note: Belgian has 589 local councils: 308 in Flanders, 262 in Wallonia and 19 in Brussels. Theoretically, Flemish parties could have 327 local chapters; French parties 281.

Interaction

If we look at the overall scores on the participation index (Table 9.7), we notice that all the political parties performed rather weakly. Parties did not pay much attention to providing discussion fora, blogs or online dialogues. Again, as in 2000, allowing for interactive communication clearly was not a priority for political parties. Only six parties (three from each language group) provided some platform for allowing interactive debate and comment. In order to get a better insight into the character of these virtual discussions, we examined one (recent) discussion on each of these six websites in more depth (Van Selm *et al*, 2002). What is striking is that discussions were usually well managed (Table 9.8). The discussion was initiated by a statement from a member of parliament or another politician, and most parties succeeded in managing the discussion quite efficiently, ensuring that most contributors remained on topic.

The PS provided the opportunity to post some "humorous" comments. However, this platform was not a real discussion forum, but gave the opportunity to state a private opinion, criticize or praise something. The MR organized a chat session (via webcam) with a special guest (politician) on a regular basis. Citizens were also encouraged to send questions in advance. This communication forum was more an online question and answer (Q&A) session than a real debate between citizens and politicians. In Flanders, too, online discussion was not the major function of the party websites. Two smaller parties (Vivant and N-VA) were the most active in this regard by offering discussion fora on different issues. Moreover, both parties provided a platform for online Q&A. Pieter Verstraelen, the webmaster of Vivant, admitted that at first party officials feared that the forum would be used by opponents for all-out attacks on the party (Foot and Xenos, 2005), but in practice this seldom occurred. In Flanders, SP.A was the only major party that enabled online debates and comments via a large variety of blogs on different issues. Here any party member was allowed to start a new blog by posting a new statement.

The figures in Table 9.8 suggest that women are practically absent from these online discussions. In the Flemish online discussions all contributions were posted by men, and on the French sites we counted only a few contributions by users with a female name. By itself this is a troubling finding: if party elites in some way or another get the impression that the online discussions are in any way representative of the opinion of their voters or their constituency members, this in practice means that only the male party members or voters are being heard, while women do not have any voice at all.

CD&V provided a weekly diary without allowing visitors to react. The CD&V webmaster told us that the party used to have a discussion forum for the last three years but they decided to remove this from the website. The reason was that too many people used the forum for undesirable goals and it was too difficult and time-consuming to control what happened on the forum. Vlaams Belang indicated the same reason for the removal of its forum.

It is striking that parties apparently invested more in maintaining chat forums or other interactive discussions in 2000 than they did more recently. (Hooghe and Stouthuysen, 2001). Even then, however, several webmasters voiced complaints that these discussions easily led to offensive behavior and damaging actions by opponents of the party. Since 2000 it appears that parties have changed their tactics. In 2006 we saw less emphasis on a public dialogue than existed in 2000, and users had fewer opportunities to post comments that could be read by other visitors.

However, parties did keep up the effort to create some kind of interactive communication, although less so in public. Users received the email address of the party leader and other politicians, as well as the personal (named) email addresses of the party officials. This asynchronous communication form was already popular in 2000 and remained the most popular form on the 2006 websites. From the perspective of the party, it had the advantage that it allowed for interaction and communication while at the same time the party itself controlled the flow of communication, avoiding possibly embarrassing web content. If political parties exploited the interactive possibilities of the Internet, they tended to opt for what Hooghe and Stouthuysen (2001) have called an "institutional-interactive" form of communication, where they still control the flow of information.

Table 9.7 Website Participation and Interactivity by Belgian Parties

	SP.A	C&V	VLD	VB	Virant	Spirit	GRN	NVA	PS	MR	CdH	ECOL	FN
Openness													
E-mail leader	X	X		X		X	X	X	X	X	X		
E-mail other politicians	X	X	X	X		X	X	X	X	X	X		
E-mail party office													
E-mail named officials/staff	X	X	X	X		X	X	X	X	X	X		
Feedback													
General feedback		X	X		X		X		X			X	
Standardized message form	X	X	X		X	X		X	X	X	X	X	
Interactive debate/comment													
Discussion fora					X			X	X	X			
Diary/blog without comments		X											
Blog with comments	X							X				X	
Online Q&A					X			X					
Interaction with site													
Opinion polls		X	X		X			X					
Games				X									
Petition									X		X		
Total scores	5	7	5	4	5	4	4	8	6	5	5	3	

X = feature present on site

Table 9.8 Political Party Web-Based Discussions

	SP.A	Vivant	N-VA	MR	Ecolo
Subject	Monopolistic behavior of brewery multinational	Dependency on oil supplies	Railways to become regional competence	Ethics & politics	Democracy in the Dem Rep Congo
No of contributions	18	106	28	19	14
posted by:					
MP	-	6	-	-	-
citizens	18	100	28	19	14
men	1̄6	101	27	17	10
women	0	0	0	2	3
gender not known	2	5	0	0	1
Formula	Citizens discussing a statement posted by a politician	Citizens discussing a statement posted by a citizen	Citizens discussing a statement posted by a politician	Guest (politician) answers questions by users	Blog (politician) with comments (citizens)
Participants					
MP	-	1	-	-	-
citizens	11	17	14	15	8
Quality	comments restricted to statement; well composed contributions	comments restricted to statement; well composed contributions	comments sometimes off-topic; emotional	a broad variety of topics/questions	comments restricted to topic blog
Tone of speech	informal	informal	informal	informal	informal

In addition to the e-mail addresses, most of the parties, except Vlaams Belang, PS and Front National, also offered a standardized message form. Half of the parties made it possible to send a message directly to the webmaster. Some of the websites used features that did not fit into our coding scheme, e.g. they encouraged visitors to react by telling them that their opinion is important for the party ("send us your idea," "time for action," "contact us"). The aim was to convey to users the idea that the party cared about the opinions of ordinary citizens.

Campaigning

All the parties undertook some form of online campaigning, though in general Belgian parties score rather low on these features in comparison with other countries (Bimber and Davis, 2003) (Table 9.9). This is in line with the general observation that election campaigns in Belgium are conducted in a rather low-key, non-aggressive manner. Negative advertising is completely absent in Belgian electoral campaigns, for the simple reason that the fragmentation of the party system inevitably leads to coalition governments and local level coalitions. Parties, therefore, are discouraged from creating hostile feelings toward their competitors or potential coalition partners.

All parties except Front National provided the chance to join an email update list and to download text. Five Flemish parties and two Walloon parties gave the opportunity to download promotional material, such as television clips, posters, cartoons, desktop wallpaper and the party logos. Some parties provided the html code for placing advertisements and the party logo on other websites. On the websites of Groen!, Vlaams Belang, PS and MR, one could send e-cards to other Internet users.

Parties did not take full advantage of the new possibilities that multimedia create for online campaigning. In practice, "old-fashioned" forms of campaigning (bulletin boards, leaflets, personal visits, public meetings, etc.) still play an important role in Belgian electoral campaigns, partly because of the small scale of the country. Most politicians still find it possible to reach out face-to-face to voters during election campaigns, and, therefore, they do not emphasize the role of modern and more mediated forms of communication. Even the Prime Minister, Mr. Guy Verhofstadt, took time to visit voters' houses during the September 2006 campaign for the local elections.

Table 9.9 Website Campaigning and Multimedia Use by Belgian Political Parties

	SP.A	CD&V	VLD	VB	Vivant	Spirit	GRN	NVA	PS	MR	CdH	ECOL	FN
Campaigning													
Negative campaigning													
Targeting expatriates													
Targeting marginal constituency													
Join an e-mail list	X	X	X	X	X	X	X	X	X	X	X	X	
Become online volunteer	X											X	
Send a link/ e-postcard				X			X		X	X			
Download literature	X	X	X	X	X	X	X	X	X	X	X	X	
Download screensavers/ banners		X										X	
Download promotion materials	X	X		X				X	X	X			
Total scores	4	4	2	4	2	2	3	3	4	4	2	4	0
Multimedia													
Audio content				X									
Video	X			X						X	X	X	X
Live streaming													
Flash						X							
SMS													
RSS	X			X			X					X	
Total scores	2	0	0	3	0	1	1	0	0	1	1	2	1
Accessibility													
Text only option (whole website)													
Text only documents to download/ print	X	X	X	X	X	X	X	X	X	X	X	X	
Foreign lan-													

guage transla- tion			X	X	X	X	X	X	X			
Blind/visually impaired soft- ware		X									X	
Total scores	1	2	2	2	2	2	2	2	2	1	2	1
Navigation												
Navigation tips											X	
Search engines	X	X	X			X	X	X	X	X	X	X
Fixed menu bar on lower level pages	X										X	
Site map/index	X					X		X	X	X	X	
Total scores	3	1	1	0	0	1	2	1	2	2	3	3	0
Freshness												
Update daily	1	1	1	1	1	1	1	1				1

X = feature present on site

Table 9.10 Summary Codings for Website Content

	SP.A	CD&V	VLD	VB	Vivant	Spirit	GRN	NVA	PS	MR	CdH	ECOL	FN
Information provision	9	10	10	10	4	9	6	11	10	9	9	6	2
Resource generation	4	5	8	7	3	4	8	4	4	8	4	3	6
Networking	5	4	5	4	3	5	5	6	6	6	5	6	3
Participation	5	7	5	4	5	4	4	8	6	5	5	3	0
Campaigning	4	4	2	4	2	2	3	3	4	4	2	4	0
Multimedia	2	0	0	3	0	1	1	0	0	1	1	2	1
Accessibility	1	2	2	2	2	2	2	2	2	1	2	1	0
Navigation	3	1	1	0	0	1	2	1	2	2	3	3	0
Freshness	1	1	1	1	1	1	1	1	0	0	0	0	1
Total score	34	34	34	35	20	29	32	36	34	36	31	28	13

Multimedia

While nearly all the parties presented pictures on their websites (photo galleries), only six out of thirteen provided video clips, generally these covered events and speeches. Here we could see a clear division between the Flemish and Walloon parties. Four out of five French-speaking parties had video clips on their websites, whereas on the Flemish side only SP.A and Vlaams Belang did the same. Other websites limited their multimedia use to moving icons.

Not a single party provided live streaming or used of SMS. In our coding scheme we added the relatively new Really Simple Syndication (RSS) technique. The RSS feeds provided web content or summaries of web content together with links to the full versions of the content as an XML file. The feeds facilitated a website's frequent readers to track updates on the site by using an aggregator. In the event, only four parties gave users the opportunity to use this new method.

Accessibility

The option to have a text-only version of the entire website, that was available in 2000, had completely disappeared by 2006. Additionally, the Flemish and French Christian-Democrats were the only parties who offered special software for blind and visually impaired users in 2006, which was in line with their ideology on social inclusion.

In terms of website navigation the results of our analysis were mixed. Small websites like those of Vivant or Front National hardly needed any navigation tips. But even on the major party sites there was not always a website map available and the presence of search engines seemed to be fairly random across the party sites.

Summary of Content Analysis

When combining all the codings into a summary table (Table 9.10), we do not find all that much variation between political parties. All the major parties received a total score in the range of 32 to 36. It has to be remembered that all of these were major parties, receiving a substantial amount of state funding. This allowed them to maintain an online website presence. It is just as clear that these major parties shared the same priorities: they devoted a lot of attention to providing information, while they scored lower on offering various interactive possibilities. Pure forms of interactive use were sometimes completely absent.

The smaller political parties, however, have but a few members of parliament and as a consequence they receive less state funding. Their online presence clearly was more limited. However, only the Front National experienced difficulties in maintaining a visible web presence, but this, in part, was due to the dubious legal status of this extreme right party.

Information from Interviews

We used the interviews with the webmasters to obtain more information on the actual development and maintenance of the websites. Almost all parties left the development and technical management of the website to an outsourced company. Cooperation between the party headquarters and the outsourced company was based on a content management system. Within this system the party was only responsible for the content and the updating of the website. The Flemish Green Party had to terminate the contract with their outsourced company due to financial problems, as in 2003 it lost most of its state funding following a severe electoral defeat. Four parties (CD&V, Vivant, Vlaams Belang, CDH) developed their websites themselves and they were also responsible for maintenance and updating. Two French-speaking parties, PS and Ecolo, developed their websites internally but relied for the more advanced technical and graphical elements on an external company. The webmasters of CDH and PS mentioned that for the creation of the future national website the party would rely on an outsourced company. Moreover, PS would employ two outsourced companies with one specifically taking care of the interactive part of the site.

We also asked how many people were professionally involved with the websites, but the answers to this question were rather vague. It does seem clear, however, that within the larger and well-funded parties at least one full-time staff member was responsible for the website (webmaster). The smaller parties in general did not have a full-time author. Most of the time this was solved by making the authors of the various texts and messages responsible for posting content on the website. Smaller parties like Vivant, Groen! and Ecolo also used volunteers to take care of website content and updating. It seems clear that money was a dividing line here. Major parties could manage their website presence in a very professional manner, but this was not necessarily the case for the smaller parties.

Internet campaigning is a special challenge in local elections, since local candidates and party chapters do not always have the resources available to use all the new ICTs (Strachan, 2003). Examining the cooperation between the national and local level within parties, some differences in autonomy and responsibility could be seen. Major parties like SP.A, CD&V, VLD, CDH and MR used a system of content management for the local chapters and these chapters were encouraged to use the same format. One of the webmasters, Patricia Van Overstraeten of CD&V, explained that the national party headquarters offered a package with layout, banners and national information. The local chapters only had to add their own local information. By the local electoral campaign of September-October 2006, this form of offering a centrally organized content management system to the local party chapters had become widespread.

As we have already mentioned, the interviews did not provide a clear estimate of the costs involved in maintaining an Internet presence. Nevertheless, we did see clear differences between the main political parties and the smaller ones. SP.A indicated that (in 2006) they spent 4,200 euros a month on their website: 3,500 euros for maintenance of the website and 200 euros on hosting costs. CD&V, on the other hand, used its own server and therefore did not receive a monthly invoice from an ICT company. The party, however, employed a full-time webmaster and here too the total personnel cost was estimated at 4,000 euros every month.

The smaller parties had less money to spend on a website presence. Ecolo spent on average 1000 euros per month on their online presence. Spirit estimated that they spent no more than 4,000 euros a year on the maintenance of the website. Vivant was a special case because the founder and president of the party actually owned a major ICT company, and there was not a clear financial division between those two. Groen! indicated that after the severe financial cuts the party suffered following the 2003 electoral defeat, the party has had to limit itself to a simple update of the website, without any money for additions or restructuring. All webmasters indicated that the party websites were updated daily, especially with regard to the press releases. The major parties estimated that website content was being refreshed up to six times a day.

Table 9.11 Unique Visitors Per Day (2006)

	May 2006	September 2006
SP-A	2,822	4,604
CD&V	1,600	3,089
VLD	n.a.	n.a.
VL BL	7,456	12,488
Vivant	350	n.a.
Spirit	800	1,060
Groen!	473	993
N-VA	2,272	2,003
PS	3,800	6,000
MR	560	n.a.
CDH	262	n.a.
Ecolo	557	810
FN	1000*	n.a.

Source: Webmasters of these parties, interviews April/May 2006 and September 2006 (election campaign). Unique visitors are counted only once no matter how many times they visit the site (per day). Unique visitors are identified with their IP number.
*webmaster could not tell whether or not unique visitors. n.a. = data not available

In 2000, there was not a common standard for counting the success of a website. At that time, some webmasters counted the number of "hits," sometimes even the numbers of pages visited, and others counted the number of unique visitors. In 2006, however, this problem seemed to have been solved as most webmasters provided us with information on unique visitors. In 2000 Vi-

vant attracted on average thirty visitors a day; in 2006 this was up to 350. For
CD&V the increase was from two hundred to one thousand six hundred visitors
per day. VLD measured three hundred visitors per day in 2000, but the webmaster could not inform us about the number of visitors in 2006. SP-A had in March
2006 an average of 2,822 visitors per day. Looking at the percentage of the vote
in the 2003 federal elections, it remains clear that the number of (unique) visitors does not stand in a linear proportion to the presence in parliament. These
findings suggest that while looking at the party websites and the number of visitors is important, it is also important to take the broader political party culture
and the background of the traditional electorate into consideration. As the figures in Table 9.11 make clear, the extreme-right Vlaams Belang claimed to have
by far the most-visited website of all political parties in Belgium. Vlaams Belang is also by far the most outspoken and the most controversial party in Belgium and it tends to polarize public opinion. So theoretically it might be possible
that more people visit its website compared to those of the more "mainstream"
political parties. On the French speaking side, however, it seemed that the PS
was the only party able to attract visitors to their website, more or less in relation
to its parliamentary representation. Table 9.11 suggests that, despite the quite
equal Internet penetration in Flanders and Wallonia, Walloons were less enthusiastic in visiting the (national) party websites.

   If we compare the number of unique visitors from May 2006 (pre-electoral)
to September 2006 (local elections campaign), it seems that the number of daily
visitors increased significantly for almost all parliamentary parties.

Conclusion

In this chapter we wanted to document the way Belgian political parties use the
Internet as part of their communication and campaigning strategy. It seems clear
that Belgian political parties rely on a mix of various media. Given the fact that
2006 was a year of local elections, and given the small scale of the country, parties still believe in small-scale contacts with their constituency, using traditional
media. The Internet is an addition to this campaign mix, especially for political
parties catering for a relatively young audience, but clearly it does not replace
any of the older campaign tools.

   If we consider the functions of the websites, it turns out that little has
changed since the 2000 elections. Political parties use their websites primarily
for fast distribution of information, in a one-way and top-down communication
process. Opportunities for interaction and dialogue are relatively scarce, and
most often they are conducted in such a way that the party controls the flow of
information. It is clear that for political parties the institutional flow of information remains more important than any of the interactive forms of communication
that are offered by the Internet. In general, the extent of the campaigning function of the websites remained limited to updating e-mail lists and downloading

information and promotion materials. This is line with the general observation that election campaigns in Belgium might be professionalized, but in general they are still quite traditional compared to the United States or the United Kingdom (Gibson and Römmele, 2001). Multimedia use is very limited, and this is related to the fact that political parties are not allowed to buy commercial television spots. While in other countries video clips can also by distributed on the Internet, this is not the case in Belgium. Resource generation is very limited, given the fact that parties can rely on a generous system of state funding.

While parties tend to offer the same kind of information on their websites, we also see some clear differences, revealing distinct party features. Just from the structure of the party website, for example, it is already clear that the presidents of the PS and MR enjoy a very strong power position, which is not the case for other party presidents. The SP.A reveals itself to be a well-organized but rather centralized structure, which is not the case for VLD or CD&V. The Christian-Democrats on the other hand, practise their inclusive ideology by offering information to visually impaired Internet users.

One of the major concerns about Internet campaigns is that major political parties will be able to monopolize campaigning because they have more resources available to develop and maintain attractive websites. Smaller parties, on the other hand, risk being marginalized since they do not have the means to use all the new communication techniques that have become possible in the Internet era. The Belgian results, however, do not really confirm this negative hypothesis. Only for two of the smallest parties, Vivant and Front National, is it obvious from the website that they have few resources and that they find it difficult to maintain an attractive website.

For all the other parties, however, it seems as if they can actually manage a real website presence. We can observe that the updates are much more regular on the website of the large parties than on those of the small parties, but there is certainly not a linear relation between size of the party and attractiveness of the website. Here much seems to depend on the personality and the enthusiasm of the webmasters and their technical staff. It is also clear that the parties reach out to different audiences. The Christian-Democrats, for example, traditionally attract older voters, and their use of the website is fairly mainstream and modest. Spirit, Groen! or SP.A, on the other hand, attract a younger electorate, and apparently they are more willing to take a risk with regard to the layout of their websites, which would appeal a younger electorate.

Our Belgian findings, therefore, suggest a "threshold" model with regard to the relation between party size and website presence: once a party has crossed a certain threshold with regard to resources, it can maintain a viable website presence. The answers from the webmasters suggest that a 40,000 euros per year budget seems an absolute minimum amount required to make daily updates on a website. Parties falling below the threshold have a hard time producing a viable and up-to-date website. For parties above that threshold this task is easier, and we certainly do not have an indication that the more you spend on a website, the more attractive it becomes. In Belgium, eleven of the thirteen parties studied clearly have sufficient money to spend, because they are included in the system of state funding. Systems of party funding might not solve all the problems, but they can make it easier for even relatively small political parties to join the era of online-campaigning.

Chapter Ten

The Netherlands: Digital Campaigning in the 2002 and 2003 Parliamentary Elections

Gerrit Voerman and Marcel Boogers

The parliamentary elections of 15 May 2002 were the first in the history of Dutch politics in which the Internet played a key role. A substantial group of voters used this comparatively new medium to obtain political information. The online Voting Guide (*StemWijzer*), based on answers to a number of policy questions, attracted hundreds of thousands of visitors. The various political party sites were also popular—particularly in the aftermath of the murder of Pim Fortuyn on 6 May, when all parties suspended their campaigns. The parliamentary elections of January 2003 made it clear that this increased interest was not a one-off event, as voters continued to access the *StemWijzer* and the party websites in large numbers. It would appear, that at the start of the twenty-first century, the Internet has become an integral part of Dutch politics, and of party election campaigns in particular.

This chapter focuses on the campaign function of websites for both parties and voters. We begin by describing, in general terms, the campaign environment and the development of online campaigning in the Netherlands. In the second section we move on in more detail to the Internet campaigns of 2002 and 2003.

Here we look at both the national party websites and leader and candidate sites. The latter reveals a growing trend towards the personalization of politics online.[1] In terms of the demand side of election campaigning (the voters), we report the number of visits to party websites and to the *StemWijzer*. We also compare visitors to party websites with the electorate as a whole in relation to age, sex and education. The question we are seeking to answer here is whether it is the average voter who accesses these sites, or whether they attract a diverse audience in socio-demographic terms. The data is derived, in particular, from two surveys conducted during the 2002 and 2003 parliamentary election campaigns.[2] Data from these studies was also able to answer the question as to why voters visit particular sites. Are they primarily interested in political information, or do they mainly want to voice their opinion? In the third section, we examine the questions of whether and how parties used their websites as a campaign tool. Were the websites first and foremost a means of holding on to their core support or were they also part of an offensive to win over undecided voters and to sow doubt amongst supporters of other parties?

The Campaign Environment

The political system in the Netherlands is based on a pure system of proportional representation, with a very low electoral threshold (0.66 percent of the vote). Since the Second World War, on average ten parties have been represented in parliament after each election. Nevertheless, Dutch politics was stable for a very long time. Parties with a religious background had a majority until 1967; the liberals and the social democrats attracted about 10 percent and 25 to 30 percent of the votes respectively. This stability was linked to the "pillarization" of Dutch society. Protestants, Catholics, socialists and, to a lesser extent, liberals operated within separate networks of like-minded organizations and institutions. Instead of being founded on a horizontal, class-related division, society was primarily divided into vertically-oriented socio-political pillars. There was a tradition of consultation between the elites that resulted in social consensus. However, in the 1960s the pillarized system began to break down as a result of increasing affluence, individualization and secularization. These developments drove the political system towards greater electoral volatility. Voting behaviour became less determined by religion and social class, whereas inter-party competition increased. Parties with a religious background lost their traditional majority. In a defensive front they closed ranks to merge into the CDA (*Christen Democratisch Appèl*—Christian Democratic Party). Although the conservative liberal VVD (*Volkspartij voor Vrijheid en Democratie*—People's Party for Freedom and Democracy) and the social democrats (*Partij van de Arbeid*—Labour Party) were challenged by a new progressive liberal party, D66 (*Democraten 66*—Democrats 66), they still managed to gain votes.

After a period of relative tranquillity during the 1980s, Dutch politics entered a further period of volatility. In the 1994 elections, the two governing parties (CDA and Labour) both experienced historic setbacks. The increasingly strong electoral volatility and inter-party competition was also apparent in the 2002 and 2003 elections. In 2002 the losers were the governing parties: Labour (minus twenty-two seats), VVD (minus fourteen seats) and D66 (minus seven seats); the winners were the opposition party CDA (plus fourteen seats) and especially a new party LPF (*Lijst Pim Fortuyn*—List Pim Fortuyn), led by the neo-populist Pim Fortuyn, which gained twenty-six seats. Fortuyn challenged the consensus-seeking Dutch political culture (the famous 'poldermodel'). With his new personalized political style and populist issues, notably an anti-immigration stance, he brought about a new politicization, but his murder nine days before the parliamentary elections of 15 May 2002 led to further instability. The subsequent coalition government, consisting of CDA, VVD and LPF, collapsed just eight months later, leading to new elections at which LPF lost sixteen of their seats whilst the traditional Labour Party regained nineteen seats.

This electoral volatility at the end of the twentieth century was also a result of growing indifference about, and a weakening ability to discriminate between, the position of the different parties. Just as in other established liberal democracies, the Dutch political parties are facing a diminishing appeal. The decreasing number of party members (reduced from 10 percent of the electorate in 1960 to less than 3 percent in 2005) is the most obvious aspect of the changing significance of political parties. Parties are also heavily criticised for their detachment from civil society, their inability to organise and integrate political debates and their strong orientation toward governmental decision-making. They are searching for new roles and practices to legitimize their position as an intermediary institution between citizens and government. In this search ICTs are gaining more and more attention as one possible solution (Tops *et al*, 2000, p.88).

Campaign Style and Regulation

In general, negative campaigning by the largest parties is rather unusual within Dutch political culture. In the multi-party system, parties have to work together after the elections. As no party has ever gained a majority, coalitions were always needed; therefore the parties are not interested in blackening each other or attacking political opponents personally during the campaign.

Within the parties, it is the party leadership that is in control, assisted by a limited number of hired professionals. For a long time, parties prohibited their candidates from conducting personal campaigns, but this has changed as television and increasingly the Internet, especially websites, facilitated personalized campaigns by candidates. Television is, of course, still the primary means by which people obtain political information during the election campaign and parties are increasingly competing against each other to gain media coverage. However, in the era of twenty-four-hour news and the Internet they are no longer able to determine the content of the message as they once did; the 'party logic' has been replaced by the 'media logic' (Brants and van Praag, 2005).

In terms of campaign regulation there are few special rules governing campaign activity, except that parties, until 2005, were not allowed to use state subsidies for campaigning activities. Parties that want to participate in the national elections have to register at the Election Board, gather 570 signatures and pay 12,000 euros (if they want to run in all the administrative electoral districts). In return, during the election campaign they get several allocated broadcasting slots on the public broadcasting network (television and radio).

The Development of Online Campaigning in the Netherlands

Over the past decade, the Internet has become more important as a news medium within the election campaign, in part due to its rapid diffusion through Dutch society. In 1997, only 6.4 percent of the Dutch population had access to the Internet. Just four years later, in 2001, this share had risen to 57.7 percent, giving the Netherlands a leading position within the European Union (Information Society Statistics, 2001, p.38). By 2004, nearly two-thirds of all Dutch households were online and 31 percent had a broadband connection (Demunter, 2005).

Despite low levels of access, Dutch political parties could be found on the web at a fairly early stage. In January 1994 *GroenLinks* (GreenLeft), an environmentalist party, was the first party represented in parliament to start a website (Voerman, 1998). Then, more or less in a movement from left to right across the political spectrum, the other parties followed suit: the Labour Party in November 1994, the left-liberal D66 and the centre-oriented Christian Democrats in the middle of 1995, and the right-liberal VVD in the spring of 1997. The digital début of the SP (*Socialistische Partij*—Socialist Party) does not entirely fit this picture: its first appearance on the Internet was not until autumn 1997. The last party represented in parliament to move online was the Orthodox-Protestant SGP (*Staatkundig-Gereformeerde Partij*—Political Reformed Party), in the autumn of 2000. Thus by the eve of the general election of May 1998, all parties, with the exception of the SGP, had a website. However, the Internet campaigns were not a central part of the parties' electoral strategies, largely because the sites attracted few visitors. At most, an estimated 100,000 visited a party website during the month preceding election day (Voerman, 2000, p.206). The parties were also not exploiting the potential of such websites. Nearly all of them offered large quantities of information on their websites: information concerning the party's candidates, manifesto and campaign. However, narrowcasting— attuning the political message of the party to special groups like younger or female voters—was rare. Furthermore, the parties were also reluctant to use their sites for interactive, bottom-up communication, fearing them to be open to possible abuse from opponants.

The 2002-2003 Online Election Campaigns

In order to understand the evolution of online election campaigning we present four types of data concerning the 2002 and 2003 parliamentary elections. Firstly, an analysis of the national party websites: their content, the differences between parties and their major functions. Secondly, an assessment of web campaigning at the individual level (leaders and candidate sites), which appears to support a growing trend towards personalization in Dutch politics. Thirdly, general survey data on those who gathered information online during the campaign and, in particular, trends in visiting patterns to party websites and also the significant growth of online voter guides. Finally, we report details of large-scale online surveys of visitors to Dutch party sites in terms of their characteristics, voting behaviour and reasons for using party websites.

National Party Websites During the Election Campaigns

As in 1998, the main objective of all the sites in the 2002 and 2003 campaigns was to transmit information.[3] The election programme, which, of course, never received the full attention of other media, was the primary focus. Visitors were usually able to download the text in its entirety, an opportunity which parties claim visitors often took advantage of. According to most parties, the total number of election programmes issued in digital and printed form was higher than in previous parliamentary elections. In most instances, election programme content was readily accessible on the websites, with many parties listing subjects alphabetically. The CDA offered voters a personalized election programme. After entering personal details about age, marital status, children, residence, work and the like, visitors were presented with points relevant to them. In addition, some parties offered information for special target groups, young people in particular. Although most of the site was taken up with policy statements, two coalition partners—Labour and D66—also looked back to the lead-up to the 2002 elections. Labour presented a summary of their achievements during eight years of coalition government, arranged in part by target group (parents of young children, teachers, those on the minimum wage and motorists). In addition to the election programmes, all sites offered an agenda of election activities and considerable information—biographical and otherwise—about the parliamentary candidates. Press reports were often included as well, and occasionally articles from party newspapers or summarized reports and media commentaries about a particular party. Some sites also outlined the procedures for proxy voting and voting from abroad.

During the 2002 and 2003 election campaigns, most party websites were also used to mobilize personal and financial support. In general, parties had already been employing their sites to attract new members, and in recent years most had proceeded to the online recruitment of financial contributors. In addition, D66, the SP, GreenLeft, Labour, and also the LPF explicitly requested financial support during the electoral campaign. Visitors to the sites were also called upon to come forward as campaign workers. When the LPF was founded in February 2002, the party had to draw up its list of candidates very quickly. When submitting the lists to the administrative-electoral districts two months later, they were required to present thirty declarations of support from voters in each of the nineteen districts. Visitors to the party site were asked to come to the chief polling stations with proof of identification in order to sign the declarations required by the Election Act.

All the party websites were deployed to some degree in the campaign. Almost all sites allowed visitors to subscribe to the electronic newsletters with which parties kept their supporters and sympathizers informed. In addition, visitors could download promotional material, such as photos of politicians, posters, logos (for websites or printed matter) and screensavers. Some parties offered visitors the chance to persuade others to vote for them. The SP and D66 websites, for example, had e-cards (digital postcards featuring a portrait of the party leader) for emailing to friends and acquaintances. Along with these 'cyberfolders', visitors to the SP site who had submitted the mobile phone numbers of potential recipients could arrange for a free SMS message to be sent as a reminder on election day.

By and large, the Dutch party websites offered few opportunities for interaction on matters of substance. Of course, each site gave visitors the chance to contact party headquarters by email. Most personalized websites of party leaders and other candidates offered visitors the opportunity to contact them by email. Labour and D66 used a special email address in an attempt to separate responses on matters of substance from requests for information and campaign material.

The party websites of the CDA and the ChristenUnie (but not their election sites) and those of the LPF, GreenLeft and the SP offered opportunities for discussion during the 2002 and 2003 campaigns. Participants in the debate on the ChristenUnie site had to register, while the CDA and the SP moderated contributions before they were posted. Participants in the GreenLeft discussion forum were not required to supply their names. After the murder of Fortuyn, the GreenLeft site had to contend with an avalanche of hate mail, with its party leader being blamed since the animal rights activist who assassinated Fortuyn was perceived as a GreenLeftist. As a result, the discussion forum was 'temporarily' shut down, and it was not reintroduced for the 2003 campaign. GreenLeft also closed its visitors' book for the course of the campaign but reopened it the day after the elections.

Almost all sites offered voters the opportunity to express their views on party-political statements. The parties were of course aware that the outcome was unlikely to be representative, especially as individual visitors could vote as often as they liked. Presenting statements to which visitors can respond is a rather primitive tool for gauging voter opinion. The CDA adopted a smarter approach in late 2001, when they used their site to generate ideas for the 2002 election programme. Thousands of visitors (party members and non-party members) participated. The actual number of useful ideas was not very high, but of far greater importance was the fact that the CDA was able to gain an impression of what mattered to its supporters. The growing discontent and alienation among large groups of citizens that partly led to the rise of Fortuyn became evident in these online reactions.

Altogether, the content of the political party websites ties in well with the wishes of the average visitor (see below). The emphasis is on information rather than participation. This is not particularly unusual, of course, given that party webmasters are fully aware of what motivates visitors to their sites. However, this may be a vicious circle: people who prefer debate may avoid party websites and join mailing lists, Usenet news groups or take part in blogging.

Beyond the National Party Sites: Leaders, Candidates and the Personalization of Politics Online

Whereas television campaigns place great emphasis on a politician's image, the virtual campaign can, at least in theory, highlight a party's policies by providing information (party platform, press releases, etc.). That was certainly the case during the 1998 elections.

> If there was a single aspect in which the virtual election campaign differed markedly from the real one, that was in the area of the personalization of politics. The figure of the party leader was accentuated far less on websites than in the "real", TV-dominated electoral contest (Voerman, 2000, p.208).

In the run-up to the 2002 elections, however, there was little evidence on party websites of this relative lack of attention to party leaders. In addition to their own party sites, most political parties had set up a special party leader's website. In 2003 too, the majority of party leaders had their own sites.

The party leaders' sites focused entirely on the figure of the party leader, whose name made up the URL; the abbreviation of the party name was not included. The format of these sites had much in common. Visitors could read all about the party leaders: their publications, media reports about them, speeches they had given and their campaign agendas. They could also view and listen to TV and radio commercials in which the leaders featured. However, arguably the greatest appeal of the party leaders' sites was their personal character. Most of the photos depicted leaders on the campaign trail; private snapshots were less common. The party leaders' sites also provided considerable biographical detail. In addition to career summaries, information of a more personal nature was divulged: hobbies, the sports they played, their cultural, musical or literary tastes, and their favourite holiday destinations. Most leaders also tried to add a personal touch: the leader of the Labour Party (PvdA) had a 'recipe of the month' feature, and the leader of the conservative liberal VVD could be seen jumping up and down behind a pinball machine in his 'game zone'. He claimed: 'It is a very accessible way of showing people something more of yourself and the party' (Braam, 2003, p.29). The site is said to have attracted one hundred thousand visitors over a two-week period, a rate that continued during the campaign period. According to the VVD webmaster, more people visited the party leader's site than that of the party itself.

Apart from giving an opportunity for political identification, leaders' sites also seek to win voter sympathy by allowing them to share a little in the personal life of the party's leading man or woman. The weblog, a digital diary that might contain personal disclosures, is an excellent tool for this purpose. The VVD leader maintained a weblog from autumn 2002, writing the pieces himself. He reported on domestic matters like his children's after-school jobs or the films he had just watched on TV. He also responded to political rivals, where necessary correcting media reports about his party or himself (Joosten, 2003).

In addition to party leaders, an increasing number of lower placed candidates launched their own websites. In 2002, of the first fifty candidates on each party list, nine (18 percent) had their own site in the Labour Party, fifteen (30 percent) in the Christian–Democratic CDA, twenty-five (50 percent) in the left-liberal D66 and forty-two (84 percent) in the VVD. The VVD scored so highly because the party offered its candidates a standard site, using their first and last names as the URL. The fortieth candidate on the VVD list placed ads in national newspapers referring to his own site, but he gained too few votes to win a seat. None of the radical socialist SP and only two of the ecological GreenLeft (*GroenLinks*) candidates had their own site.

This development does, of course, entail risks for parties. Individual parliamentary candidates who conduct their own campaign for election by preferential votes can in principle reach a wider audience through a website than was previously the case. By profiling themselves in this way, they make it more difficult for the party leadership to control the composition of the parliamentary party. The Internet thus offers candidates an opportunity to withdraw a little from centralized control by the party leadership.

It was not just the introduction of party leaders' and candidates' websites that personalized the digital election battle—the rise of Fortuyn had the same effect. Fortuyn's selection as leader of the political party called 'Livable Netherlands' (*Leefbaar Nederland*) in autumn 2001 spawned a host of sites, both sympathetic and opposed to Fortuyn, where fierce discussions raged. Supporters and critics of the man who challenged the established political order also gave full vent to their feelings in Usenet newsgroups. The Lijst Pim Fortuyn (LPF) was established following a rift between Leefbaar Nederland and Fortuyn in early February 2002. On 19 February, his birthday, Fortuyn's campaign team presented him with his own website. When Fortuyn was murdered on 6 May 2002, the Internet became an outlet for the collective outpouring of grief. That evening, the official LPF site was immediately transformed into a condolence register for the public. Within the space of a few hours, about fifteen thousand messages of sympathy were posted against a black background and under a white cross (Chorus and de Galan, 2002, p.10). Four days later, the number of messages from shocked and angry visitors had risen to one hundred and sixty thousand. In addition, dozens of 'in memoriam' sites specially devoted to Fortuyn were set up. These often highly personal sites featured burning candles and mourning music (Klaver, 2002).

Online Campaign Audiences

Given the rapid increase in Internet access, it is hardly surprising that more and more people have started using the Internet to find political information. According to data from the Dutch Parliamentary Election Studies (PES), about 6 percent of the electorate made occasional use of the Internet during the 1998 election campaign to seek political information (e.g. on sites of the broadcasting channels, the *StemWijzer*, the Lower House of Parliament or political parties). By May 2002, this figure had risen to 30.6 percent of voters, reflecting the extraordinary events surrounding the murder of Fortuyn, but then declined back to 20.7 percent by January 2003, corresponding to 3.7 and 2.5 million people respectively.

The visits to party websites and other political sites in the period before the 2002 parliamentary elections undoubtedly reflect the special circumstances following the murder of Fortuyn on 6 May. That evening, the number of visits to party websites increased dramatically and, not surprisingly, the LPF site was especially popular. Party websites continued to attract large numbers of visitors in the days that followed. Because the election campaign and political debate had been suspended, the traditional media carried few reports on party policies (Kleinnijenhuis *et al*, 2003, p.44). As a result, the websites had become a rather important means of broadcasting party messages. Most sites featured a statement from the party expressing abhorrence of the murder of the LPF party leader, while at the same time communicating the usual campaign information, albeit in a more restrained form.

Despite the extraordinary circumstances, there were fewer visits to party websites in the final three weeks (25 April–15 May) of the 2002 election campaign than in the equivalent period (2–22 January) for the 2003 elections (Table 10.1). A true comparison of the total visitor numbers cannot be made because precise figures for 2002 are not available for D66 and only partially available for the LPF. An estimate suggests over one and half million visitors in 2002 and one and three-quarter million in 2003, though the exceptional visitor numbers to the LPF site may have pushed figures for 2002 higher than would otherwise have been the case.[4] We should also bear in mind that these totals do not involve 'unique' visits but rather the number of visits (user sessions) made to a site. It is very likely that some voters will have visited several party websites, or the same site more than once. The figure of 1.5 to 2 million visitors in 2002 and 2003 therefore indicates the absolute upper limit.[5] This does not detract from the fact that numbers were massively higher than the one hundred thousand that visited in the five-week period of the 1998 campaign (Voerman, 2000, 206).

Table 10.1 Number of Visitors to Party Websites in the 2002 and 2003 Election Campaigns

Party and Year	Week 3	Week 2	Week 1	Total
CDA				
2003	n.a.	n.a.	n.a.	245,901
2002	23,931	43,185	105,418	172,534
CU				
2003	14,199	18,741	29,145	62,085
2002	8,978	17,062	24,802	50,842
D66				
2003	20,397	34,000	72,016	126,413
2002	n.a.	n.a.	n.a.	n.a.
GL				
2003	34,222	51,355	79,494	165,071
2002	28,684	46,129	79,124	153,937
LPF				
2003	28,379	37,513	58,092	123,984
2002	-	319,825	237,864	557,689
Labour				
2003	118,928	172,045	193,242	484,215
2002	19,294	40,870	60,382	120,546
SP				
2003	78,697	88,616	137,883	305,196
2002	28,525	57,214	89,673	175,412
VVD				
2003	59,100	74,600	140,000	273,700
2002	16,461	27,457	65,005	108,923

N.B.: no information available regarding D66 in 2002 and the LPF in week 3 in 2002.

This increase must be attributed to the continuing integration of the new medium into society. Whilst we have already noted the rapid rise in Internet access, another factor is that politicians increasingly refer, in newspapers and TV commercials, to their own website or that of their party. The traditional media also make considerable use of cyberspace to report on the campaign activities of parties and politicians, or they refer to them in their columns and broadcasts. Party website URLs have become integrated into all aspects of the campaign material produced by the parties.

NKO data also provides an insight into the profile of online information seekers. Those who claim to have visited a party site during the election campaign can be distinguished from other voters in several respects. They tend to be younger, more highly educated and male, and have an above-average interest in politics. This is true of both the 2002 and 2003 campaigns (Table 10.2). For the rest, party websites only succeed to a limited extent in reaching an audience that cannot be reached via traditional media such as magazines, newspapers, radio and television (Boogers and Voerman, 2004, p.274). With the exception of young people, who are generally somewhat less politically involved, party websites attract first and foremost a politically committed elite.

Table 10.2. Percentage of Visitors to Party Websites During the 2002 and 2003 Electoral Campaigns (by age, gender, educational level and political interest)

Characteristic	Visited party website 2002	Visited party website 2003
18-34 year	32.9	31.7
34 and older	12.3	11.1
difference	**20.6**	**20.6**
male	18.5	21.3
female	13.7	13.7
difference	**4.8**	**7.6**
higher educated	17.3	23.6
lower educated	11.1	16.0
difference	**6.2**	**7.6**
very much interested in politics	20.1	26.4
not/moderately interested in politics	14.8	14.6
difference	**5.3**	**11.8**
Total population (visiting party websites)	16.0	17.3

* all figures in percentages

Opinions vary as to whether this should be viewed as a problem. In the light of initial promises that the Internet would make it easier for people to become politically informed and involved, the unrepresentative nature of such involvement in party websites could be described as disappointing, despite increased Internet use. Party websites only partially succeed in reaching new social groups. The selective visits to party websites can also be viewed positively, however. Assuming a two-step flow of communication, whereby public opinion is influenced through opinion leaders rather than directly (Lazarsfeld *et al*, 1955), the sites offer parties an excellent opportunity for retaining the loyalty of these opinion leaders through targeted information and opportunities for interaction.

StemWijzer

Some voters who surfed the Internet for information also visited the *Stem-Wijzer* site, where voters could test their political preferences on the basis of policy statements and quotes from the parties' election programmes (De Graaf *et al*, 2003). In the sixty-five days that it was online in 2002, the vote guide made over two million recommendations—a huge increase compared with the figure of 6,500 in 1998. By the 2003 elections, the number of recommendations had risen to almost 2.3 million, despite the fact that the *StemWijzer* was online for two weeks less. On 22 January, election day itself, the *StemWijzer* provided over two hundred thousand recommendations.[6]

Studies have shown that 18 percent of voters used the *StemWijzer* during the 2002 campaign. The site was particularly popular among younger voters: 30 percent of those aged eighteen to thirty-four completed the online *StemWijzer* (as opposed to 18 percent of thirty-five to fifty-four year-olds, and 6 percent of those fifty-five and older). It also emerged that three quarters of users rated the *StemWijzer* a fairly useful or very useful tool. More than a third indicated that the voting recommendation coincided exactly with their political preference, while 45 percent felt that there was a considerable degree of correspondence. Almost 19 percent stated that the recommendation did not on the whole match their own political views. The suggestions offered by the *StemWijzer* were certainly of some influence. Although only 4 percent of users said that they had altered their voting preference on the basis of a recommendation, and 17 percent attached no value to the recommendation, at least one quarter of those polled reported that the voting recommendation had set them thinking or had influenced their decision.[7]

Party Website Visitors: Online Survey Evidence

An online survey was conducted during the 2002 and 2003 election campaigns to learn more about visitors to political party websites (for the 2002 survey, see Boogers and Voerman, 2004). In the weeks leading up to the elections, the webmasters of almost all parties introduced a button on their website which visitors could use to access the online survey.[8] Each of the two surveys was completed by more than ten thousand visitors to political websites (see Appendix). It appeared that, although party websites add a new dimension to the election campaign, they supplement rather than replace the traditional media as a means of obtaining political information. As already reported, party websites were not very good at reaching voters who cannot be reached via radio, television, newspapers or magazines. Almost threequarters of visitors to party websites kept up with politics on an almost daily basis through newspapers, radio and television.

The surveys also revealed that people visit party websites primarily in search of information about political parties, party policy and the election campaign (Table 10.3). Reasons mentioned far less frequently are participation in political discussion and seeking email contact with a party or politician. Those who do wish to interact tend to be more highly educated, somewhat older males—in other words, the usual 'participatory elite'.

Table 10.3 Most Important Reason for Visiting Party Websites (2002 and 2003)

Most important reason	2002 (%)	2003 (%)
Information about party policy	45	46
Information about political party	9	14
Information about election campaign	10	12
Information about candidates	16	6
Participating in political debate	4	3
Email contact with party	4	6
Email contact with politician	3	3
Other reasons	9	10
Total	100	100

Visitors to the different party websites sometimes display a marked divergence in their reasons for accessing the sites. Most notably, those visiting the websites of parties that did not take part in the major televised election debates were generally more interested in information about party policy. This was the case for those who viewed the site of the SP, which was excluded from the national televised debates in 2002. In 2003, when the SP party leader did participate, interest in party policy among visitors to the site dropped. The reverse was true of the D66 site. In 2003, when the party was unable to join the televised debates for the first time in a long while, the number of visitors interested in party policy rose in comparison to 2002. Inasmuch as a causal link exists, it suggests that the Internet campaign can offer voters a substantial addition to the traditional media campaign.

The Party Site as a Campaign Tool

The fact that more and more people are accessing party websites does not automatically make these sites effective campaign tools. A targeted Internet campaign must also ensure that different political messages are communicated to visitors in accordance with their political inclinations. Party supporters have to be mobilized to go out and vote, those who support other parties must be encouraged to reconsider their choice, and undecided voters must be persuaded. To assess the effectiveness of the party site as a campaign tool, we need to know to what extent these different categories of voters visit a party website. Are visits confined to party supporters, or do websites also attract supporters of other parties and undecided voters? In contrast to the experiences of party and candidate websites in the United States (Kamarck, 2002; King, 2002), Dutch party websites are not visited exclusively by those already intending to vote for the party in question (Table 10.4). In the 2002 and 2003 campaigns, about one third of the visitors were considering voting for another party, or were still undecided. A party site is, therefore, more than simply 'preaching to the converted'. The fact that floating and undecided voters also find their way to party websites makes these sites a potentially effective campaign tool.

Table 10.4 Party Website Visitors and Intended Voting Behaviour

Intended voting behaviour	2002 (%)	2003 (%)
For the party of the website visited	62	69
For another party	27	21
Does not yet know	11	10
Total	100	100

Different Categories of Visitors

An in-depth comparison of the various groups visiting party websites reveals that party supporters are motivated differently from those who intend to vote for another party or who are still undecided. The different categories can also be distinguished in terms of political interest, age, sex and education.

- Party supporters primarily seek information about the election campaign and the party organization. They tend to be male and more interested in politics, and are also slightly more inclined to take part in discussions. They visit their own party website comparatively more often and other party websites comparatively less often, as one could expect. Presumably, they visit the site to affirm or re-affirm their choice, or to find arguments with which to defend their choice to others.
- Visitors who intend voting for another party are comparatively more interested in party policy and information about candidates. They are also somewhat keener to

join in online debates. In general, they pay a single visit to the party site in question, surfing many different party websites during the campaign. This group is characterized by a high interest in politics, and contains comparatively more men, and young and well-educated people.

- The undecided voters primarily seek information about party policies. Their web surfing behaviour is the reverse of that of loyal party supporters who have already made up their minds, more closely resembling that of the second category above. Most undecided voters visit a party website just once, although they may look at several party sites during the course of the campaign. Compared with the other groups, undecided voters are less interested in politics and more likely to be female, less educated and younger.

There are almost no differences between the 2002 and 2003 election campaigns in terms of reasons for visiting a site and the backgrounds of people in the different categories. The only respect in which the 2002 campaign differs is the greater interest in information about, and contact with, candidates among those who did not intend to vote for the party in question. This appears paradoxical: why are people interested in candidates of a party that they do not support? One possible explanation could be that they visit the site in order to be able to clarify their reasons for not supporting it, focusing above all on individual politicians they dislike. Events during the 2002 election campaign will certainly have played a role here: in the wake of Fortuyn's murder, there was a doubling in the percentage of visits from 'non-party voters' who accessed a party site so that they could send an email to a politician. Thus the above survey reveals that, in addition to Labour supporters, the Labour leader's site attracted mainly LPF sympathizers. The fact that politicians, particularly Labour politicians, received hate mail (and even viruses) from angry or disappointed voters at the end of the campaign seems to tie in with the survey data.[9]

Impact on Voting Behaviour

The significance of party websites as a campaign tool is once again confirmed by the percentage of voters claiming that their visit to a website influenced their decision about who to vote for during the 2003 elections.[10] As Table 10.5 shows, undecided voters attribute the greatest influence to such visits. More than half of this relatively small group claims that the visit influenced their political preference. Although we do not know whether these visits left the voters more or less attracted to the party in question, this information shows that party websites apparently play a fairly substantial role in voters' choices. In particular, undecided voters visiting the sites of the VVD, GreenLeft or D66 found that this had a major impact on their decision. Party supporters also attribute some influence to visits to 'their' party website, especially adherents of Leefbaar Nederland, D66 and the SP. As expected, visits to party sites had the least impact on voters intending to vote for another party.

Table 10.5 Percentage of Visitors per Category Indicating that the Party Web-
site Had Some or Substantial Influence on Their Vote, 2003

Visitors to party sites	Party support-ers	Supporters of other parties	Undecided voters
CDA	30	29	52
Labour	32	28	50
VVD	27	15	62
SP	42	34	52
GreenLeft	40	32	62
D66	46	29	62
Christenunie	32	25	53
SGP	23	23	46
Leefbaar Nederland	71	3	59
Total	34	27	52

Targeting Specific Groups

The analysis of the content of the various party websites in the run-up to the 2002 and 2003 elections reveals that different categories of visitors, such as activists as opposed to the undecided, were barely catered for. As we have seen, most websites confined themselves to a rather matter-of-fact presentation of party policies and campaign news, although, there were the occasional glimpses of other initiatives. The Labour site featured a 'question and answer' column, where voters could ask questions about social problems of concern to them. Loyal Labour supporters could then use the answers to defend themselves against criticism from family and friends.

Another example of an approach targeting the various categories (outlined above) is that of GreenLeft, which compared its policies with those of other parties. This self-assured, offensive approach may well have persuaded undecided voters to vote for GreenLeft, but whether it was enough to persuade those who had already decided to cast their vote elsewhere is another matter. Perhaps negative campaigning would be more effective here, but running down one's political opponents is not really an acceptable form of campaigning in Dutch political culture. Moreover, the parties generally tended to refer to each other in a fairly unpolemical manner. The LPF website, for example, showed little trace of Fortuyn's aversion to the ruling coalition, with criticism of Labour, D66 or the VVD not a feature on the home page in either 2002 or 2003. Nor did the SP focus specifically on Labour, even when the latter succeeded in eliminating the

SP's 'virtual' increase in seats in the opinion polls in the weeks leading up to 22 January 2003.

Conclusion

In quantitative terms, the Internet campaigns of 2002 and 2003 were not comparable to those of 1998. Visitor numbers to party websites and the *StemWijzer* rose enormously in the intervening four to five years, with the sites beginning to play a key role in communications between parties and politicians on the one hand and the electorate on the other. Qualitatively speaking, however, it was a different matter. The surveys reveal that some of the high expectations associated with the rise of the Internet have not been fulfilled. Political party websites were only partly able to engage those who had thus far remained aloof from politics. Visits to party websites tended to be confined to politically active groups. These websites did suceed, however, in reaching young people—a category that tends to be less politically active but that makes more frequent use of the Internet. Another expectation of the Internet was that it would lead to direct contacts between voters, parties and politicians. However, Dutch political parties are at the moment even less willing to exploit these interactive possibilities than in the past. Like most party sites, their primary focus is to communicate information about party policy and politicians, with some sites offering a better visual presentation than others. The surveys discussed above do show, though, that this content ties in well with the needs of those visiting the party websites: they want to be informed, and to a much lesser extent to participate.

The information requested was usually also available in printed form. The online election campaigns of 2002 and 2003 did little to generate new information. For instance, party leaders' websites featured little or no debate between leaders, and party websites contained few attacks on political rivals. Inasmuch as there was an alternative 'digital' public domain during the Internet election campaign, this lay outside the sphere of the established parties. The rise of Fortuyn led to pro- and anti-Fortuyn sites, with heated discussions about him as an individual. The murder of the LPF leader ushered in a form of collective online condolence never before seen in the Netherlands. But party websites did prove their usefulness during this period: while the 'real' campaign was suspended and the media remained to a greater or lesser degree silent on the subject, parties were able to serve the information-seeking voter through their websites.

The emphasis that the sites place on party policy seems to counterbalance to a degree the focus on the party leader's image that is so prevalent in modern election campaigns. The fact that party websites have a comparatively wide reach further underlines this. At the same time, Internet campaigning is becoming increasingly personalized. Party leaders and other candidates have their own websites, where to varying degrees they offer visitors a glimpse of their private lives. However, this personal approach goes hand in hand with the communication of information on the views of the politician and his or her party. Whereas the personalization of the TV campaign often comes at the expense of the political message, these aspects appear more balanced on the websites.

There is considerable voter interest in the quantity of information offered on party and candidate websites. They are visited not only by the party faithful, but also by confirmed supporters of other parties and by undecided voters. Websites have the potential to become an effective campaign tool; it is up to the parties to take full advantage of them.

Notes

1. Here we used the versions of the party and party leaders' websites archived by the Documentation Centre for Dutch Political Parties (DNPP); see www.archipol.nl.
2. This study was made possible by two grants from the Netherlands Organisation for Scientific Research (NWO) (project numbers 014-43-608 and 458-02-016).
3. In addition to the party site, the CDA, ChristenUnie and VVD also set up special election sites for the 2002 and 2003 elections.
4. This estimate assumes about one hundred thousand visitors to the LPF site in the third campaign week in 2002, and an equivalent number to the D66 site over a three-week period. This would bring total visitor numbers to 1,539,883 in 2002 and 1,870,664 in 2003, excluding the number of visitors to the Leefbaar Nederland and SGP websites.
5. Interestingly, NKO data points to higher visitor numbers for the party websites. 16 percent of respondents in 2002 indicated that they had visited a party site, and 17.3 percent in 2003. Expressed in terms of the voting population, this amounts to 1.9 million and 2.1 million visitors respectively.
6. Press release from the Dutch Centre for Political Participation (IPP), 23 January 2003.
7. IPP press release, 31 July 2002; data from a NIPO study commissioned by the IPP.
8. The survey button also featured on a number of political websites without party affiliations, including the *StemWijzer*. GroenLinks did not take part in the 2002 survey, and the LPF was absent from the 2003 survey. For a summary of the responses for each party site, see Appendix.
9. Statement by the PvdA webmaster at a webmasters' meeting, dated 9 October 2002.
10. The question about the perceived impact of visits to party websites was not asked in 2002.

Appendix: Number of Responses for Each Party Website in the 2002 and 2003 Election Surveys

Political party	Website	Response 2002	Response 2003
CDA	*cda.nl*	425	2424
	j.p.balkenende.nl	20	
LPF	*lijst-pimfortuyn.nl*	2468	NA
VVD	*vvd.nl*	80	225
PvdA	*pvda.nl*	1133	4145
	admelkert.nl	502	
	wouterbos.nl		1584
	klaasdevries.nl		112
D66	*d66.nl*	220	568
	thomdegraaf.nl	60	
SP	*sp.nl*	1264	2344
	janmarijnissen.nl	181	
GroenLinks	*Groenlinks.nl*	NA	956
ChristenUnie	*christenunie.nl*	325	772
	andrerouvoet.nl		
SGP	*sgp.nl*	12	888
Leefbaar Nederland	*LN.nl*	457	195
TOTAL		10180	16979

Chapter Eleven

Italy: The Evolution of E-Campaigning 1996-2006

Sara Bentivegna

The Internet campaign has been emerging slowly in Italy. While general Internet use has been spreading rapidly in recent years, online electoral opportunities have only partially been realized. In 1992, when the Clinton-Gore ticket used email as a tool for contacting American voters, connecting to the Internet for campaign purposes had not even been considered in Italy. Internet use was completely absent in the 1994 Italian election, as television was the dominant campaign medium. The situation was largely repeated during the 1996 campaign, although a small number of campaign websites were established. Since 2000, political parties and candidates have established a modest presence online. However, voters' participation in the online campaign has remained limited.

This chapter explores the evolution of electronic campaigning in Italy in its nascent phases. It begins by examining the Italian campaign context and media environment to provide a background for investigating the Internet's role in elections. The development of the Internet campaign from its very limited introduction in the 1996 election through to its presence in the 2006 campaign is examined. The chapter concludes by speculating about the future of Italian e-campaigning.

The Campaign Environment in Italy

In order to understand the reasons for the adoption of a particular campaign style it is useful to look at factors such as the electoral system, the structure of the party system, citizens' identification with a party, electoral participation, and the regulation of election campaigns. In general, conditions in Italy are analogous to those that have led to innovative uses of the Internet in other countries within the context of political institutions.

The Italian electoral system has undergone changes in recent years. The electoral system that was in place until December 2005 may be defined as a mixed-member or segmented system that combined features associated with a plurality-majority system with elements of a proportional representation system. Reforms of Italian electoral law were enacted in 1993 that maintained, but weakened, proportional representation (Katz, 2001; Gibson *et al*, 2000). Under these reforms, the majority of seats in both the Chamber of Deputies (the lower house) and the Senate are allocated under a majoritarian system. Within the proportional system a minimum qualifying threshold of 4 percent means parties that do not reach this threshold at the national level are not allocated seats.

The coexistence of majoritarian and proportional systems lends itself to a mixed style of campaigning, in part candidate-based and in part party-based. This type of electoral system 'stimulates both individual and candidate-centered campaign practices in competitive districts, while simultaneously activating a party-based campaign style addressing the national electorate' (Plasser and Plasser, 2002, p.109). Candidates who compete in the majoritarian system use a style of campaigning characterised by practices that highlight their personal experiences and abilities, their capacity to listen and their willingness to interact with constituents. Direct competition with other candidates produces ruthless confrontations. Conversely, candidates competing within the proportional system use a style of campaigning focused on the party to which they belong, rather than on candidates' personal characteristics or links with voters within a specific constituency. In this case, competition is primarily between political parties.

Despite widespread awareness of the difficulties of building alliances and the periodic crises surrounding government coalitions, attempts at transforming the Italian multi-party system into a two-party system have failed. Paradoxically, these failures have opened the way for a return to proportional rule, as demonstrated by a legislative proposal presented to Parliament by the center-right coalition in September 2005 and approved in December 2005. The proposal established a system of proportional representation with qualifying thresholds that vary according to the different types of party coalitions. This reform changed the style of Italian campaigns once again to favor predominantly party-driven practices. No matter the number of parties present, the electoral campaign focuses on the party rather than the candidate.

Media-focused campaigns and the professionalization of politics have emerged in Italy as a result of the need to replace the work of volunteers to reach the electorate (Mair and van Biezen, 2001), the increase in electoral volatility (ITANES, 2001) and the availability of funds for campaigning (Della Porta, 2001). Although these trends date back to the 1980s, citizens expressed concerns about these developments in the early 1990s when Silvio Berlusconi made his entry into the political arena. Berlusconi was an entrepreneur with a strong presence in the multimedia sector (television, dailies and weeklies) but without an organised party behind him. Berlusconi and his party's use of political marketing techniques illustrated the inadequacy of previous communication and electoral strategies. His candidacy also revealed the problems that result when access to the media is largely controlled by a single candidate. This imbalance gave rise to the approval in 2000 of a law designed to regulate electoral campaigning. The so-called 'par condicio' (28/2000) or 'equal treatment' law guarantees that all majority and opposition political parties have equal access to radio and television time. It also prohibits radio and television commercials outside of those aired via transmissions dedicated to the campaign (Gibson et al, 2000).

The failure of Italian political actors to take advantage of the opportunities offered by the Internet is not the result of institutional factors. Rather, candidates' and parties' lack of experience with new technologies coupled with the country's fairly rudimentary Internet culture have contributed to the slow adoption of online election campaign tools.

The Development of Online Campaigning in Italy

To understand the development of online campaigning, it is necessary to consider the diffusion of the Internet in Italy. While technology alone cannot explain the styles of Italian campaigning or forms of political action, it is equally true that technology plays a significant role in creating the correct conditions for their development. In fact, the Internet can be considered as both an agent of change, shaping contexts for use, and an object of change, as users redesign familiar campaign offerings (van Dijk, 2005).

Data on users in the early years provide some insights into the reasons behind the lack of interest in the Internet. Data first became available in 1996, and indicates that there were around six hundred thousand Internet users (Bentivegna, 1999). This low level of online diffusion justifies the lack of interest in the new communication technologies shown by political actors. Soon after this modest beginning, however, the Internet rapidly took root. In 1997, a year usually considered to be a benchmark for measuring progress in the spread of the Internet, the estimated number of users stood at around two million. In 2005, it is estimated that the number of Italians online was between fourteen and sixteen million, or 39 percent of the population.

In the space of ten years, users had not only increased in number, their profile had also changed profoundly. A gender gap favoring male users has closed significantly. The difference in the online presence of young people (aged fourteen to twenty-four) and adults (aged twenty-five to fifty-four) has decreased, as this older segment of the population has become more engaged online, now constituting 56 percent of users. Users are still, though, concentrated at the higher educational levels (high school/college degree) and higher income brackets. Even with these remaining imbalances, the Internet is slowly reaching those individuals who were initially uninterested and detached from the new online opportunities. By the end of 2005, 9.8 million Italians were using a broadband connection.

The number of individuals online says little or nothing about the reasons people navigate the Internet and use new online opportunities. Other data offer information useful for understanding the quality of the presence of political actors online. A 2004 survey (Censis, 2005a) gives a snapshot of the reasons for Internet use by Italians. These data indicate that use of the Internet is predominantly individual rather than social. The impetus for navigating the Internet for most Italians is, broadly speaking, information gathering rather than connecting with others (see Table 11.1).

Table 11.1 Reasons for Going Online in 2004

Italian people go online in order to*:	%
Obtain information on any subject	39.9
Obtain real-time updates on current events	23.4
Find things only found on the Internet	23.1
Navigate the most unexpected sites	21.3
Make contact with other people	12.8

* Multiple answers were accepted.
Source: Censis, (2005a).

Political institutions at all levels of government have invested primarily in online technologies aimed at providing information and services. They have been less concerned with developing interactive online features. A study conducted by Censis (2005b) demonstrated that only three out of twenty regional governments had active citizens' online forums, and four out of twenty had created online forums involving administrators. The situation was similar at the provincial and municipal levels. Citizens' forums were present in 22.5 percent of the provinces and 15.7 percent of the municipalities, while those involving administrators were present in just 1 percent of the provinces and were completely absent in municipalities. Furthermore, forums hosting debates on specific issues within the context of decision-making processes were almost completely absent.

A similar picture emerges with regard to the online presence of political parties. Italian political parties on the Internet have gone through two phases (Bentivegna, 1999, 2001; Bartali, 2000; Newell, 2001). The first, running from the initiation of party websites in the late 1990s until the early 2000s, is characterised by the prevalence of information and networking at the expense of online discussion and political action. During this phase, Italian political parties were 'making tentative steps rather than great strides into cyberspace; they [were] mainly attempting to do old things in new ways rather than completely new things' (Gibson *et al*, 2000; Newell, 2001, p.85). In brief, parties exported real-world structures and trends into cyberspace, and did not provide substantially new online offerings. Thus, the second, current, phase is characterized by the need to update the Internet presence and broaden opportunities for interactions with citizens. Political parties are attempting to move in new directions, as well as to respond to pressure from civil society. Citizens have requested opportunities for interaction and participation, which have provided an incentive for parties to adopt interactive formats, such as blogs, that facilitate the involvement of Internet users in initiatives aimed at supporting party positions on matters of public significance.

While the political system as a whole has been delayed in its use of the new opportunities offered by the Internet, this can be attributed largely to the nature of Italian political parties. As Bartali notes, 'in spite of the many upheavals of the 1990s, there are lingering political cultures whose apparatus makes it difficult to use the new communication technologies in a dynamic and innovative way' (Bartali, 2000, p.35). In sum, Italy has been late to adopt the Internet, even though it has rapidly made up for lost ground. This delay explains why Internet culture in Italy remains elementary, and political uses are focused on broadening opportunities for the dissemination of information, rather than on facilitating interactions with citizens.

Phase I of the Internet Campaign: The Election of 1996

The 1996 electoral campaign marked the first phase of e-campaigning in Italy. This phase continued until 2000 and was characterized by minimal and superficial use of the Internet. The Internet user base during this period was around six hundred thousand—too few, perhaps, to justify heavy investment in the technology. Phase I of the Italian Internet campaign is also characterized by a widespread lack of interest in interactivity or user involvement by both parties and the public. The creation of 'showcase' sites, or rudimentary sites that only exist to introduce the candidate or party to voters while allowing them to claim that they have an Internet presence, was prevalent. Other common mistakes made by parties and candidates included setting up sites very late in the campaign and the development of sections of sites that were never activated.

In 1996, all of the Italian parties and the main center-left and center-right coalitions[1] had created websites a month before election-day. For a few parties, such as the Rifondazione Comunista, Lega Nord and the l'Ulivo coalition, the production of the site coincided with the opening of the official campaign. This illustrates political organizations' ignorance about the characteristics of the Internet during that period, as well as the difficulty of integrating the online and offline campaigns. Despite this common naivety, the three sites clearly differed. The Rifondazione Comunista site represented a slightly more elaborate version of the classic 'showcase' site. It focused on the party symbol and presented the basic points of the party programme. The showcase form of the site was the result of hasty production and the lack of day-to-day website management. As the site manager declared in an interview (Cappucci and Cappucci, 1996), there were no full-time staff and the party leaders did not show much interest in the initiative. However, party leaders expressed greater interest in the l'Ulivo website. Although it was created for the electoral campaign and abandoned at its completion, the site was characterized by rich content designed to perform both information and networking functions. The information component of the site was created by a press office that continuously produced bulletins and news items about the coalition. The networking function created direct channels of communication between the committees 'for the Italy we want', publicizing their initiatives. There was space on the l'Ulivo site enabling direct contact with citizens who could vote electronically on amendments to the party programme. Users also were invited to participate in discussion forums. Finally, the Lega Nord site included an 'Election Special' section, a 'Calendar' of party and candidate initiatives, and allowed users to print the electoral manifesto for the campaign.

The websites of the major political parties, which had been online for a longer period of time, offered a more traditional printable product, although not all included election-related material. An 'Election Special' was available on the Democratici di Sinistra site, alongside pages that communicated party initiatives and provided information on party offices, joining the party and making contributions. The Alleanza Nazionale provided space for the 'Political Election Special', where pages were dedicated to the party programme. Pages for 'Meetings' and 'Candidates' were created, but never activated. The Forza Italia site did not have any pages dedicated to the election. The only reference to the campaign was a link to the site of a research company offering a kit to create a personalized electoral campaign.

Phase II of the Internet Campaign:
The General Election of 2001

Conditions were more favorable for establishing an online presence during the 2001 Italian Parliament elections. The number of Italians connected to the Internet now exceeded ten million. Moreover, the competing political parties' online campaigns were strengthened by several years' experience in Internet communication. However, their websites were still primarily oriented towards information provision and only occasionally included features related to mobilization, such as downloadable manifestos and promotional material. Nor did many of the official sites of the political parties publish lists of candidates or their website addresses. In their attempts to reach the electorate, the political parties largely invested their resources elsewhere.

Individual candidates began to establish a presence on the net during the 2001 campaign.[3] Of the 2,018 Senate candidates and 2,002 House candidates, 552 candidates established websites. In percentage terms, 13 percent of the candidates had an online presence (17 percent of House candidates and 10 percent of Senate candidates). The presence of candidate sites on the net was limited to the official duration of the campaign (thirty days prior to the vote); sites often disappeared at the end of this period. Candidates' Internet presence consisted primarily of displays of electoral manifestos by means of posters and billboards that disappeared the moment the polls closed.

A first glance at a content analysis of campaign websites indicates that the cyberworld reflected real world campaign dynamics. The polarizing conflict between the two major coalitions, the center-left Ulivo and the center-right Casa delle Libertà, that marked the entire campaign was carried out on their websites. The two opposing coalitions predominated on the Internet, as 45.5 percent of campaign websites were affiliated with the center-left and 44.2 percent with the center-right. The data on individual parties forming the two major coalitions revealed that Forza Italia was the party that contributed the most to the campaign on the Internet with 18.7 percent of the total online election content, followed by the Democratici di Sinistra (15.6 percent), Alleanza Nazionale (13.4 percent) and 'Margherita' (12 percent).

Candidates used their presence online to introduce themselves to voters, as 86.8 percent of the candidates presented their biographical profile and 86.1 percent featured their career background on their websites. Professional profiles were presented on 58 percent of the registered sites. Photo galleries with pictures of the candidates, their family and friends (26.3 percent), information about their hobbies (15.8 percent) and campaign pictures (13.2 percent) were provided. Incumbent candidates, who constituted 57.1 percent of the field, provided summaries of their most important activities during their time in political office, such as bills they had drafted. The information component of the site occasionally included an outline of the candidate's program (27.7 percent), although sometimes viewers were simply referred back to the coalition program (22.1 percent). Interestingly, about half of the websites did not reference any electoral program. Instead, candidates offered netizens a selection of news from the traditional media. The principal criteria for the selection of news items were that they showed direct support for the candidate (21.6 percent), support for the coalition (12.9 percent), or attacked his/her opponent (8.7 percent) or the opposing coalition (12.9 percent). Websites also included direct messages from the candidates (46.9 percent).

Candidates encountered greater difficulties in populating the areas of the sites concerned with networking and mobilization. For example, only a small number of websites contained information about the office and staff (29.9 percent). Even when present on the website, the reference was limited to indicating the postal address and phone number of staff headquarters (23 percent). No information was given about staff activities or organization, nor were any upcoming meetings announced. The distance between the online and offline campaign is confirmed by looking at the call-up among netizens for offline volunteers. Only a small percentage of websites were used to enlist people in campaign activities, such as joining the electoral committee (10.3 percent), attending an electoral rally (11.1 percent), sending an electronic postcard (2.9 percent), or encouraging online participation (3.3 percent). The data also confirm that even those candidates who launched a campaign website relied mostly on TV advertising or on door-to-door canvassing. The possibility of joining an e-list (9.8 percent) or downloading posters or other campaign material (11.6 percent) was extremely limited.

To complete the picture of the first e-campaigning experience in Italy, it is necessary to focus on the audience for online communication—the voters. The data available (ITANES, 2001) are not very encouraging for those who have invested in the Internet. 93.8 percent of respondents, when asked to indicate the activities in which they engaged throughout the electoral campaign, declared that they 'had never consulted websites regarding the elections'. A further 2.8 percent stated that they had viewed websites 'without interest' and only 3.5 percent maintained that they had had any interest in the material present online. Only 0.1 percent of respondents indicated that the Internet was their primary source of information about the electoral campaign, while 0.4 percent listed it as their second source. This lack of interest would appear to justify candidates' limited investment in the online campaign. However, it may be the case that the limited nature of the available material online failed to provide an incentive to voters. Italian candidates mainly established a web presence devoid of any meaningful message other than to announce their existence in cyberspace. They missed a good opportunity to create an ongoing dialogue with voters and to stimulate new forms of involvement.

Italy's First Primary Elections

Italy's first primary elections, held in 2005, illustrate the most recent tendencies in online campaigning. National primary elections had never before been held, and they were preceded by lively discussions about the usefulness, abolition or postponement of the primaries. Seven candidates competed for the role of leader of the center-left coalition. For the first time in Italy, all of the major candidates running in an election had a personal website.

A content analysis of seven primary candidate websites was conducted (see Appendix for methodology). All of the candidate sites offered some common features. They provided some autonomously produced information and some material drawn from the traditional media (see Table 11.2). They invited citizens to participate, with the first phase designed to gather the signatures necessary for candidacy and a second phase aimed at increasing the visibility of the candidate by offering downloads of propaganda and encouraging the distribution of this material. They created incentives for offline activities, including attempts to build an informed and cohesive community through the use of newsletters. They also provided opportunities for interaction with netizens through discussion forums and blogs, and they gave voters the chance to make donations. From this brief list, a profile of a rich and well-articulated online product based on the lessons learned from the experience of the 2004 American presidential campaign emerges.

Table 11.2 Raw Content Scores for Features of Candidate Websites in the 2005 Primary Election

Candidate	Information	Net-working	Participation/ Interactivity	Campaigning	Multimedia/ Navigability	Total
Prodi	7	2	3	4	4	20
Bertinotti	6	0	4	6	3	19
Scalfarotto	6	2	4	5	2	19
Pecoraio	6	4	3	2	0	13
Di Pietro	7	3	2	1	3	16
Mastella	4	2	4	2	2	14
Panzino	5	1	2	1	2	11
Range	(0-8)	(0-5)	(0-8)	(0-7)	(0-6)	(0-34)
Mean Score	5	2	3	3	2	16

See Appendix for details about the source of these scores.

However, a more in-depth analysis reveals that the innovative aspect of the Italian online campaign is less impressive. The limited amount of website innovation is illustrated by the fact that while five of the candidates offered a subscription to a newsletter, only one newsletter was produced in a period of two weeks. In the same vein, candidate Romano Prodi's blog was forced to close as he did not have the time to dedicate to it. Further, the effect of the Internet on the overall coverage of the campaign by the traditional media was marginal. For the most part, coverage was limited to presenting the URL of candidates' sites within the profile dedicated to candidates in each contest.

The marginality of the online campaign merely reflects the attitudes of the candidates toward the Internet election. These cases are examples of what happens when communication strategies imported from other contexts are adopted without candidates making any real investment in personal or economic terms. Candidates' awareness of the Internet as a potential resource was widespread, but was not accompanied by an equal acceptance of its role in their overall campaign strategy. Nevertheless, significant steps had been taken: more interactivity for site visitors and greater professionalism in website design emerged. However, the 2005 primary election campaign online cannot be considered a success, especially if one considers the Internet as an important space in which voters can make their voices heard.[3] This e-campaign was another in a long line of examples of the Italian tendency to introduce innovations originating in other countries without making real investments in them or reinterpreting new methods within the Italian context.

The 2006 Campaign

The electoral law approved in December 2005 reintroduced the proportional representation system in Italy. As a consequence, political parties proliferated and reached the astonishing number of 174. By April 2006, over fifty of these parties had an active web presence.

The existence of such a large number of political parties with an online presence may, at first glance, seem to be an indicator of modernity and of the transformation of electoral campaigns bringing Italy in line with other countries. However, the availability of cyberspace does not automatically translate into use. Instead, the new medium hosts old content (Bimber and Davis, 2003).

A content analysis was performed to assess the overall quality of the online campaign conducted in Italy in 2006 (see Appendix for the methodology). Websites were coded to indicate the presence of site content within the conventional dimensions of information, networking, interaction, mobilization and technological sophistication (Gibson and Ward, 2000c). Starting with the official presentation of the party lists at the beginning of March 2006, a weekly analysis was undertaken of all sites representing parties belonging to the two coalitions as well as those outside the coalitions. Overall, four content analyses were conducted, on March 14, 21 and 28 and April 4. The sites analyzed were those representing:

- Ulivo (the Olive Tree coalition)—Democratici di Sinistra, Margherita, Rifondazione Comunista, Federazione dei Verdi, Italia dei Valori, Comunisti Italiani, Udeur, I Socialisti con Bobo Craxi, Partito dei Pensionati, Lista Consumatori, Rosa nel Pugno, SVP, Liga Fronte Vento, PSDI, Consumatori Uniti, Democratici Cristiani Uniti, Repubblicani Europei Sbarbati;

- The Casa delle Libertà coalition—Forza Italia, Alleanza Nazionale, Unione dei Democratici Cristiani e di Centro (UDC), Lega Nord, DC-Partito Socialista, Pli, Alternativa Sociale, Movimento Sociale, Verdi Verdi, Movimento Pensionati, Patto Cristiano Esteso, No Euro, Unione Nord Est, Italia di Nuovo Scelli, Pri, Riformatori Liberali, Nuova Sicilia, Patto per la Sicilia;

- Parties not belonging to either of the two coalitions—Partito Umanista, Partito del Popolo Siciliano, Terzo Polo, Democratici Europei Centro, Partito Internettiano, Partito Democratico Cristiano, Movimento Altra Moneta, Democrazia Attiva, Unione Cattolica Italiana, Alleanza Monarchica, Democrazia Cristiana-Scudo Crociato, Progetto Nord Est, IRS, Partito Solidarietà, Dimensione Cristiana, Unione Federalista Meridionale, MIS Lista Rauti, Destra Nazionale, Movimento Sociale Cristiano.

The sites were coded for features within five general categories of content—information, networking, interactivity, mobilization and technology. Additive indices were constructed which summed the total number of features within each content category for all the sites in the sample. Mean scores were computed to indicate the average number of features per site within the five content categories. Table 11.3 allows us to identify aggregated areas of strength and weakness on the websites.

Table 11.3 Range of Raw Scores and Mean Scores on Additive Indices of Party and Candidate Website Features for the 2006 Election

Dimension	Range	Mean Score
Information	0-33	11
Networking	0-16	3
Interactivity	0-14	3
Mobilization	0-14	3
Technology	0-17	4
General Index	0-94	23

See Appendix for details about the source of these scores.

As the findings indicate, political actors, both candidates and parties, are primarily disposed towards producing information on their sites rather than featuring interactive or mobilization components. The center-left candidates' sites for the primary elections scored highest in the information category. Websites are used predominantly as an opportunity for disseminating information such as news, declarations and speeches made elsewhere. Conversely, networking, interactivity and mobilization are marginal aspects of the sites.

Looking at the individual parties (Table 11.4), the most sophisticated and multi-dimensional websites are those of the parties that participated in the previous government (Alleanza Nazionale, Forza Italia, Lega Nord, UDC) or those that formed the current government (Democratici Sinistra, Comunisti Italiani, Italia dei Valori, Margherita, Udeur, Rosa nel Pugno). These established parties all rank in the top ten in the study in terms of the features that their websites offered, confirming that minor parties, or those occupying a marginal position within the Italian political spectrum, face difficulties in creating interesting websites. The websites offered by the traditional parties are decidedly different from the typical American election site. Howard Dean's blogs and organized online groups of supporters remain a largely theoretical point of reference for Italian parties and candidates. The proportional election law has played a significant role in fostering this minimalist interpretation of the online campaign, as it has had the effect of marginalizing candidates in favour of parties. Parties, as the central protagonists of the political scene, are intent on 'keeping under strict control all mechanisms of communication and electoral involvement' (Bentivegna, 2006, p.39). In sum, the 2006 election experience has not advanced e-campaigning among traditional political actors.

Table 11.4 The Main Political Parties on the Net During the 2006 Election

Political Party	Information	Networking	Interactivity	Mobilization	Technology	General Index
Margherita	22	10	8	7	8	55
Democratici Sinistra	21	4	5	12	7	49
Alleanza Nazionale	18	5	5	5	11	44
Forza Italia	18	6	3	6	10	43
Italia dei Valori	20	8	6	4	5	43
Comunisti Italiani	15	5	5	6	9	40
Rosa nel Pugno	19	3	4	6	7	39
Lega Nord	21	4	2	3	5	35
Udeur	15	4	5	3	6	33

Scores based on additive indices for presence of features (see Appendix).

Italian Internet users are aware of the limited importance of electronic campaigning. A questionnaire on the website of Italy's most widely read daily newspaper, *La Repubblica*, provides some empirical validation of this point. The questionnaire, was posted for an entire day during the electoral campaign, (March 14, 2006), and was completed by 1,048 respondents. (See Table 11.5 for results.) Although the survey employed a convenience sample and was not statistically representative, the results provide an indication of current trends. The findings demonstrate respondents' profound and widespread lack of interest in the political parties' websites despite the fact that they acquire daily political information via the Internet (92.6 percent), television (49.8 percent) and newspapers (42.5 percent). Sites associated with parties of the center-right and center-left are rarely of interest to respondents, as 50.6 percent of respondents had never visited the center-left sites and 77.7 percent had never visited those of the center-right. Aside from the higher interest in center-left sites, which may derive from the greater affinity this group shares with *La Repubblica*, it is surprising to note the level of indifference of users to the websites of any party.

Table 11.5 Political Party Website Visitors During the 2006 Election

Frequency	During the last week, have you visited:				
	Sites for centre-left parties	Sites for centre-right parties	Humorous sites	Other politics-related sites	Blogs
Never	50.5	77.7	61.3	37.8	48.8
Once or twice a week	27.6	15.8	23.7	26.3	22.6
3 or 4 times a week	13.4	3.0	9.5	17.7	12.2
Every day	8.5	3.5	5.5	18.2	16.4
Total %	100.0	100.0	100.0	100.0	100.0
n	(1048)	(1048)	(1048)	(1048)	(1048)

All figures are percentages.
Source: *La Repubblica* March 14, 2006.

The lack of interest shown by users towards the political party sites cannot, however, be extended to all online products offered throughout the course of the electoral campaign. Users search for information, details, curiosities and comments on sites associated with the traditional media or those taking an alternative approach to politics. The fact that the party sites are judged as unattractive and uninteresting does not amount to a hasty dismissal of all campaign websites. As Table 11.6 shows, blogs and nonpartisan sites receive frequent visits.

La Repubblica's questionnaire also indicates some of the audience's motivations for using the Internet during the campaign. First, users went online to exchange emails with friends and acquaintances regarding the campaign and to participate in online surveys, discussion groups and blogs. The intense exchange of emails and widespread use of online surveys may be one of the defining characteristics of this campaign. The percentage of respondents who participated in a survey in the week before the election (78.8 percent) gives us an idea of the extent of the phenomenon. Similarly, the percentage of interviewees who participated in email exchanges (61.8 percent) indicates the volume of communication produced. The success of these activities among Internet users does not, however, constitute a specifically Italian tendency; indeed, U.S. and British citizens consider these aspects to be the most significant features of the online electoral campaign (Lusoli and Ward, 2005; Pew Internet & American Life Project, 2005).

Table 11.6 Surfing the Internet and Political Engagement During the 2006 Election

In searching for information on the Internet during the last week, have you:	Yes	No
Looked for information about a coalition's position on a specific issue	63.1	36.9
Looked for information about a candidate	44.0	56.0
Looked for information about voting methods	22.2	77.6
Looked for declarations of support	23.7	76.3
Received/sent humorous emails about the campaign	61.8	38.2
Participated in surveys	78.8	21.2
Written in blogs	33.3	67.7

All figures are percentages.
Source: *La Repubblica* March 14, 2006.

An analysis of the overall volume of emails in circulation throughout the 2006 campaign, based on *La Repubblica*'s survey, reveals some interesting findings. Political parties, as opposed to Internet users, initiated the email exchanges during the campaign. According to the survey respondents, the center-left coalition sent emails to 30.2 percent of Internet users and the center-right to just 8.7 percent; conversely, the respondents stated that they had sent emails to political figures and parties belonging to the center-left coalition in 13.2 percent of cases, and to those of the center-right in 3.1 percent of cases. The limited tendency of Internet users to initiate email contact provides yet another confirmation of their profound lack of interest in political parties in cyberspace.

A completely different situation emerges with regard to the sending of emails to friends, family, colleagues, participants in discussion groups and mailing list members (Table 11.7). In this informal type of political exchange, respondents sent emails to solicit votes for a candidate or specific party. Within a network of informal relationships, or in terms of activities aimed at political-electoral support without centralized control, email is an extremely versatile tool adapted to the satisfaction of Internet users' needs.

In conclusion, this 2006 data indicates that Internet users tend to stay away from the official electoral campaign conducted on parties' and candidates' websites. However, they follow the events of the campaign through alternative rather than official channels. Internet users also discuss the campaign in electronic mail, in posts sent to blogs and by participation in discussion groups. Alongside the official electoral campaign carried out on the Internet, users conduct a shadow campaign through the exchange of opinions, jokes and cartoons.

The extent to which this alternative campaign influences the election result is not known, but it certainly contributes to the background noise that accompanies voters right up to the moment they cast their ballots.

Table 11.7 The Use of Email in Informal Politics

Throughout the campaign, have you:	Yes	No	Total
Exchanged emails with friends/family/ colleagues	40.5	59.5	100.0
Sent emails to canvass for votes	15.3	84.7	100.0
Sent emails to members of discussion groups, or mailing lists	15.4	84.6	100.0

All figures are percentages.
Source: *La Repubblica* March 14, 2006.

Conclusion: The Future of E-Campaigning in Italy

The data on e-campaigning presented here provide an overall picture of where Italy has been and where the country is heading. The Italian style of e-campaigning clearly inclines towards tradition rather than innovation. In this respect, tradition refers to an online political presence characterized by reproduction of old content using new means, thus relegating online campaigning to a marginal position.

Generally speaking, the Italian experience echoes what Margolis and Resnick (2000, pp.2-3) contend: 'political life on the Net is therefore mostly an extension of political life off the Net'. The empirical confirmation of the normalization of cyberspace does not, however, provide the only reason for locating the Italian case on the side of tradition. Parties' and candidates' approaches to the electoral campaign were based substantially on traditional models and strategies developed for an older media environment that featured television, and in which the interactive element was practically nonexistent. As in the pre-Internet era, the real arena for political communication remains television. The website, therefore, becomes a surrogate for the television screen from which messages may be broadcast, but to which citizens may not always have access. It follows that candidates' sites are characterized predominantly by the distribution of information, according to a top-down model. This also gives rise to the limited attention paid to interaction, which is alien to television culture but central to the Internet.

For its part, television, alongside newspapers and radio, has covered the Internet-based campaign only tangentially when searching for 'colorful' elements. The only exception to this widespread indifference was the use of the Internet by netizens who initiated a competition to distort Silvio Berlusconi's election posters in the 2001 campaign. Berlusconi covered the walls of all towns with giant posters depicting his face along with simple messages summarising some of the main issues of his party. The netizens reacted to this invasion in a spontaneous and unorganised way, spreading false pictures of the leader on the web together with spoof messages (Bernardini, 2000).

Italians are profoundly unfamiliar with Internet culture. Thus, relative inexperience in the use of the new technologies may have played a significant role in the low level of citizen involvement online. Low levels of Internet use are exacerbated by the marginality of the interactive dimension and the difficulties of offering opportunities for citizen participation in campaigns.

Innovations on the Internet come from the bottom, or from citizens' needs, rather than from the top, or organized by political actors. However, even interesting experiences based in the United States, such as MoveOn and Meetup, emerged within civil society and then went on to engage the party political system at the time of the election campaigns.[4] The increased capacity for mobilization shown by these actors during the 2004 American presidential campaign would support the interpretation that real innovation can be introduced by independent political websites developed by national and local advocacy groups and civic organizations (Foot and Schneider, 2002) rather than by traditional political actors who are 'simply consumed with the immediate business of getting candidates elected in the next election cycle' (Kippen and Jenkins, 2004, p.258).

The recognition that citizens' associations have the greatest chances for successful innovation in the use of the Internet in the politico-electoral field does not, however, mean that these groups have acquired a stable role within the Italian electoral campaign. Indeed, to date they have not gone beyond the production of satirical messages (in 2001) and the exchange of emails (in 2006). While they may not have influenced the general campaign climate, their experiences have demonstrated Internet users' interest and willingness to participate in various ways in the online electoral campaign. Such trends will place Internet users at the centre of the process of constructing political discourse.

Notes

1. The center-left coalition was the Ulivo (Olive Tree) consisting of the PDS, the Popolari, the Federation of Greens, the Italian Renewal list and the Sardinian Action Party. The right-of-center coalition Polo per le Libertà (Alliance for Freedom) comprised Forza Italia, Alleanza Nazionale, the CCD and the CDU.
2. A content analysis was performed using a coding scheme consisting of fifty items referring to the functions typically recognised by researchers in the study of Internet sites in electoral campaigns (Davis, 1999, 2001; Gibson and Ward, 2000c). These general functions include providing information, volunteer recruitment, mobilization, participation and interactivity
3. The primary elections are not regulated at national level. They are therefore treated as the initiatives of specific actors and thus are not subject to the regulations regarding access to the media. This means that, other than in the case of events judged as 'newsworthy' according to journalists, no space is guaranteed for campaign coverage.

4. There is an extensive literature on the history and role played by MoveOn and Meetup in the 2004 U.S. campaign. Cornfield (2004a) and Kerbel (2005) present an overview, while an insider's account is offered by Trippi (2004).

Appendix

The information in Table 11.2 comes from a content analysis of the websites of seven candidates contesting the primary election. The presence of particular features within five content categories was recorded (see Davis, 2001; Gibson and Ward, 2000c). Eight features relate to information, five relate to networking, eight relate to participation and activity, seven relate to campaigning, and six relate to multimedia and navigability. If a particular feature was present on the website, it received a score of one point. A total of thirty-four features were coded. The maximum number of features found on a single site was 20.

Table 11.3 is based on a content analysis of fifty-four party and candidate websites during the 2006 general election. Websites were accessed and coded at four time points during the campaign (March 14, 21, 28 and April 4). The sites were coded for features within five general categories of content— information, networking, interactivity, mobilization, and technology. Thirty-three features related to information (press releases, position papers, campaign speeches), sixteen related to networking (link to parties allied at the national level, link to associations and/or pressure groups), fourteen related to interactivity (presence of blog, discussion forum, email campaign), and fourteen related to technology (downloading programmes, search engines). At the end of the campaign, mean scores were computed to indicate the average number of features per site within the five content categories.

After analyzing the performance of all political parties in the aggregate (Table 11.3), attention was focused on the specific performance of individual parties. Table 11.4 shows the best ten performances (out of the total of fifty-four websites), according the score computed for each content category achieved by single parties. Mean scores were computed on the basis on the average number of features per site during the campaign.

Chapter Twelve

Germany: Online Campaign Professionalism in the 2002 and 2005 National Elections

Eva Johanna Schweitzer

"www.election-chance-missed.de,"[1] wrote the national newspaper *Die Welt* on election day 2005 (Beckermann, 2005). "Under Construction", commented the German edition of the *Financial Times* (Virtel, 2005). And the *Frankfurter Allgemeine Sonntagszeitung* spoke of a "campaign like that of thirty years ago" (Niggemeier, 2005). The conclusions of journalistic observers on the 2005 online activities could hardly have been formulated in a more unanimous manner. While the 2004 U.S. presidential election set new standards in interactive and decentralized campaigning, German parties demonstrated a startling "faintheartedness" in their web strategies (Wenzel, 2005). The home pages were "colorful, banal, and occasionally even polemic" (Hannemann and Lehmkuhl, 2005). They were "highly unimaginative" (Virtel, 2005) and hardly more than "a continuation of customary campaigns" (Schemel, 2005). "Interactivity, metacommunication, and thinking 'from the net'" were lacking (Schemel, 2005), and there seemed to be no squad of "visionaries" to exploit the potentials of online mobilization in the Federal Republic (Wenzel, 2005).

"Welcome (then) to the Internet campaign, lowest rung on the totem pole" (Virtel, 2005) in the "digital developing country" (Beckermann, 2005).

This journalistic thesis on the lack of innovativeness on German party websites is, in fact, as old as national e-campaigning. Ever since the first political uses of the Internet in the 1998 general elections, journalists have complained about the quality of federal online activities. In most instances, though, this criticism is based on a rather questionable line of argument. First, journalists have become used to comparing German e-campaigns with the American role model of election communication. In this way, they ignore the differences in the political culture, the media, and the election system that also shape the way political advertising is conducted on the Internet. Second, German journalists tend to refer in their news articles primarily to anecdotal evidence, i.e. to single examples of very successful or unsuccessful e-campaigns, while leaving out the total spectrum of candidate and party websites in both countries. Finally, these news reports often miss a long-term perspective that is essential to describe adequately the development of e-campaigning over time. In general, these journalistic observations therefore do not provide a valid basis to assess the quality of German online campaigns in a rigorous way.

From a scientific point of view, such an analysis requires instead an empirical inner-state examination of federal web presences, based on a systematic longitudinal survey. Up to now, however, German research has lacked an appropriate procedure for this short history of national Internet practices and the transitoriness of the medium set natural boundaries for retrospective comparisons. In addition, there has only recently been a strengthened effort in this country to establish an empirical-quantitative research tradition on forms of computer-mediated political communication (Römmele et al, 2003; Schweitzer, 2005).

In light of this research deficit, it is therefore the main objective of this chapter to provide a first temporal assessment of national online campaigns in order to draw conclusions about the evolution of party-oriented e-campaigning in Germany. Based on a comparative content and structure analysis of national party websites in the 2002 and 2005 general elections, which extends an earlier study by the author, significant developments of respective Internet presences shall be detected and these illuminated against the country-specific background of electoral politics (Schweitzer, 2005).

For this purpose, the longitudinal analysis starts with contextual information about the campaign environment, including the political and electoral system in Germany, the structure of the national media market, and traditional media and Internet usage in the German population. The chapter then provides a historical development of online campaigning in the Federal Republic and an empirical comparison of the 2002 and 2005 German elections.

The Campaign Environment

Germany's Political and Party System

Germany's political system is built up of sixteen individual states, the so-called *Länder*. Due to the principle of federalism, these Länder exert an independent legislative authority in the fields of culture (including the mass media), education (schools and universities), and the police. Moreover, each state is represented according to its size of population in the *Bundesrat* (Federal Council), which is one of two chambers at the federal level.

The other chamber, the national parliament (*Bundestag*), currently comprises 614 members. These represent the five leading parties in the country: the Social Democratic Party (SPD), which is Germany's oldest political organization; the conservative Christian Democratic Union (CDU), which forms a permanent association with its regional sister party, the Bavarian Christian Social Union (CSU); the liberal Free Democratic Party (FDP), which is situated at the center of the political spectrum; the Green Party, which entered parliament first in 1983 as an ecologically-oriented group; and the Leftist Party (Die Linke), which has its roots in the Socialist Unity Party (SED) which governed the Eastern part of Germany (the German Democratic Republic) before reunification.

The most important figure in the German political system is the Chancellor. Elected by the members of the national parliament by majority vote, he or she determines the direction of federal policy and appoints the members of the government, i.e. the ministers.

As absolute majorities in the national parliament are virtually unknown, establishing and maintaining a government in Germany means building political power coalitions among those parties represented in the Bundestag. The Chancellor has always come from one of the two major parties—CDU/CSU or the SPD. In the past, these groups have formed a government coalition usually with a minor partner: The CDU/CSU with the liberal FDP and the SPD with the Green Party (first in 1998). The power of the two major factions is enhanced by a threshold clause that requires a party to obtain a certain percentage of the vote to be represented in the German Bundestag.

Some scholars therefore speak of Germany as a multi-party nation ruled by a two-bloc system. In fact, only twice has a grand coalition of both major organizations been formed. Such a coalition has been in place since the 2005 election, where the CDU/CSU and SPD have established a common government coalition with Angela Merkel (CDU) as the first woman Chancellor in German history.

Germany's Electoral System

Parties play a central role in the German political landscape. Their function is codified in the German constitution, which states that they are responsible for "participating in the formation of public opinion and political will."

The power of parties is enhanced by electoral laws that encourage party-based voting. For example, German federal elections operate under a mixed proportional and majority representation system, which has become known as the "German Model" (Holtz-Bacha, 2004a). In practice, the German population has two votes in national elections: one for the candidate in the constituency, and one for the party. The overall number of seats obtained by a party in parliament is based on the second vote. Moreover, past electoral studies have shown that candidates in the constituencies suffer from low name recognition so that citizens, even in their first choice, most of all concentrate on the respective party label of these politicians to help determine their own voting decision (Holtz-Bacha, 2004b, p.85).

In addition, it is a further peculiarity of the mixed-member proportional system that the number of direct mandates won in the constituencies can possibly exceed the number of seats attributed to a party based on its total share in the second vote. In this case, surplus mandates are established in parliament in order to enlarge its total size beyond the official proportion of at least 598 seats.

As a result, the German electoral model fosters split-voting which means voters have the option of supporting a candidate from one party in the first vote and deciding for another party in the second choice. This mode has become increasingly popular in the last twenty years, especially among the younger and more educated citizens, as they are losing the traditional affective bonds connecting them to specific parties. This general process of dealignment and political disaffection, which has become influential in most Western democracies, has led to shrinking voter turnout, decreasing party membership (especially among the major parties SPD and CDU/CSU), and widespread political distrust (Scarrow, 2004).

Campaign Regulation

In Germany, national elections have to be held no earlier than forty-six months and no later than forty-eight months after the beginning of a legislative period. Election day is thus usually scheduled in the middle of September. The only exception to this rule is a vote of no-confidence in parliament against the Chancellor, which opens the way for early elections. This has only happened three times (in 1972, 1982, and 2005) in German history.

When national elections are scheduled, the active phase of the campaign typically encompasses the last four weeks before election day. During this period, parties set up billboards, publish ads, and are allowed political spots on radio and television. These campaign activities are regulated by the German

Party Law, which first passed in 1967, and supplements the legal framework as defined by the electoral system.

The guiding principle here is "equal opportunity", which means that all public institutions have to provide the same prospects of publicity to all competing parties with regard to their use of public spaces for assemblies (e.g., rooms, streets, places), party financing, and the allocation of billboards and free advertising time on public broadcasting. In terms of funding, for example, this means that all registered parties receive public money provided they obtain more than 0.5 percent of the vote.

The exact amount of state financing granted to an individual party is calculated in accordance with its success in earlier elections, its total membership fees, and the volume of its past donations. These quantities have to be disclosed each year in parties' annual statements of account. Based on the verified reports, the political organizations receive 70 euro cents for each valid vote in recent elections and 38 euro cents for every additional euro gained through financial contributions such as membership fees or donations. In total, there is an annual maximum of 133 million euro to be spent by the state on party financing ("absolute limit"). Moreover, the public subsidy for each party should not exceed the total sum of its respective external revenues ("relative limit"). With regard to campaigning, however, there is no upper limit on the entire donations or expenditures allowed to candidates and their political organizations.

Due to this comprehensive system of public financing, fundraising has always played a minor role in German elections. With the rise of the Internet as a new channel of mass-mediated political communication this has not changed. In fact, past efforts on national online fundraising have been rather unsuccessful among both the major and the minor parties: after the Greens, for example, first initiated a system of web donations in 2001, the Liberals took over this model for their large-scale campaign in the 2002 national elections. Following the American model, they established a separate website for online fundraising, hoping to obtain an additional amount of about eighteen million euro. At the end of the campaign, however, only about one thousand Internet users had visited this particular site and had spent a total of 21,000 euro, with an average contribution of 92 euro. In conjunction with their regular offline activities this added up to a total fund of 2.32 million euro for the FDP, i.e. 12.9 percent of the original revenue they had hoped for (Lamatsch and Bilgeri, 2001, p.233; Beerfeltz and Heuser, 2004, pp.302-303). Later efforts on online donations were no more successful.

Apart from party financing and fundraising, Germany's basic principle of "equal opportunity" also influences the conduct of political advertising on radio and television. Here, the rule is transferred in practice in a graded allocation system (Holtz-Bacha, 2006, p.166). This means that the number of spots permitted to individual parties in public broadcasting is calculated on the basis of their success in earlier ballots and their expected strength in the upcoming election. In this way, minor parties not represented in parliament each receive two slots per public broadcasting channel, minor parliamentary parties four slots, and major parties eight slots. The maximum spot length for all parties in public broadcasting is ninety seconds. Although the exact time of broadcasting is determined by the public stations themselves, they are obliged to secure a wide audience share for political advertising. For this reason, party spots typically air in the evening, i.e. from 6:00 p.m. to 11:00 p.m. The exact placement and sequence of the spots is determined at random. The spots are introduced by an official announcement and are purposely separated from other broadcast content. This practice undermines their persuasive effect. The major parties therefore have begun to lose interest in political spots on public television or radio channels and instead are turning to other campaign media such as billboards or the Internet (Holtz-Bacha, 2005). The use of the latter, for example, is not restricted by any electoral law.

In addition, commercial broadcasters are not bound by presentational constraints or regulations. Here, all parties are allowed to purchase additional advertising time and to decide themselves about the placement and sequence of their spots. They only pay the costs of production, which means in practice about half of the usual spot prices. This mode of buying extra time on commercial channels has undermined the principle of equal opportunity in German election campaigning as experience has shown that it is mainly the major parties that can afford these additional payments.

The Media System

The German media system is based on the constitution, which guarantees freedom of expression and the freedom of the press. Its legal regulation is specified in several additional laws at the federal state level to ensure free and democratic journalism.

Since the deregulation of broadcasting in the mid-1980s, the media market has become highly differentiated and particularly competitive: on average, there are forty-seven television and about thirty radio channels available in German households. Radio is primarily organized at the regional level, while television is dominated by national stations. In both outlets, public and commercial broadcasters coexist.

Apart from radio and television, Germany's media landscape is also characterized by a strong newspaper market. Nearly all of the 138 independent daily newspapers are regional, but eight are distributed nationally. Among them are the elite newspapers *Die Welt* (average circulation about 220,000), *Frankfurter Allgemeine Zeitung* (about 380,000), *Süddeutsche Zeitung* (about 430,000), and *Frankfurter Rundschau* (about 180,000). These dailies are ideologically-based.

Across all media, political coverage has dramatically changed in recent elections (Schulz and Zeh, 2005; Wilke and Reinemann, 2001): television and the newspapers have expanded their electoral coverage with greater emphasis on the respective candidates. Stories concentrate more on the candidates' appearance, behavior, and images. This trend towards personalization was intensified following the 2002 national elections, when Germany experienced its first television debates between the respective Chancellor candidates. Moreover, the national news media have become more adversarial in their approach to politicians. Like U.S. media, German news outlets have increasingly become journalistic commentaries with shrinking sound bites and quotations as a result. This development has reduced the opportunities for political actors to advertise themselves in the traditional mass media.

Media Usage in Germany

Since the 1970s, media usage in Germany has doubled. In 2006, the average citizen spends a gross total of ten hours a day with different media outlets, primarily television and radio. Surfing on the web, however, accounts only for forty-four minutes a day (van Eimeren and Ridder, 2005). In recent years, this Internet usage has grown from 6.5 percent in 1997 to 59.5 percent by 2006 (van Eimeren and Frees, 2006). In comparison with the other twenty-five member states of the European Union, Germany ranks fifth in Internet penetration behind the Netherlands, Denmark, Sweden, and Luxembourg (Eurostat, 2006). Moreover, 48 percent of the national population use broadband. In the past decade, the earlier differences in Internet usage between men and women, the young and the old, and people with higher and lower educational attainment have slowly begun to disappear (van Eimeren and Frees, 2006, p.404).

In terms of political information, however, Internet usage is still of minor importance: most citizens turn to the World Wide Web primarily to send and receive emails (78 percent), to search for data of personal interest (75 percent), or to visit specific websites (50 percent) (van Eimeren and Frees, 2006, p.406). This widespread use of ICT, however, has not translated into electoral purposes. Only 6 percent of the population relied on the Internet as a primary information source in the 2005 national elections, compared to 56 percent and 24 percent who used television and newspapers respectively. These are still the most important media outlets among German voters for election-related matters (Geese et al, 2005, p.614).

Moreover, only 30 percent of Germany's Internet users (i.e., about 14 percent of the total population) have ever visited a specific party or candidate home page. Past analyses have shown that German campaign websites seem to be preaching predominantly to the already converted and affluent opinion leaders (Emmer et al, 2006; Merz, 2006a, 2006b). For the main part, their audience consists of men (70 percent), aged sixteen to forty-five (78 percent), with high educational attainments (41 percent graduated at least from high school), and an above average household income of more than 2,500 euro per month (51 percent). These voters are particularly interested in politics (48 percent) and share a strong believe in their political efficacy (78 percent). Moreover, they are already bound to a specific party (65 percent), are more likely to volunteer in campaigns (35 percent), and donate online (9 percent) (Merz, 2006a, pp.26-30; Merz, 2006b, p.42). Finally, those Internet users are characterized by an intensive traditional news media consumption, including specifically newspapers and magazines, and are in fact more likely to get out to vote on election day (Wagner, 2004, p.130, p.136). Yet, even among this elite group, most people (71 percent) spent less than 5 percent of their total time online with political information on the web (Merz, 2006a, p.29).

The Development and Characteristics of German On-line Campaigning

Despite the low interest in electoral information on the Internet, national parties in Germany have established online presences since the mid-1990s. Germany's first e-campaign occurred in 1998 when twenty-seven out of thirty-three competing parties offered home pages during the elections (Kaiser, 1999, p.176).

With this initial movement to the web, parties had hoped to demonstrate modernity and to raise additional attention among journalists covering elections. Often, though, these early sites resembled more or less electronic brochures, rather than models of online communication featuring multimedia or interactivity. This cautious approach to the new medium was attributable to parties' concerns about maintaining control in external communication. Political organizations were, in fact, reluctant to allow interactivity that would facilitate a democratic bottom-up discussion.

With the spread of the Internet and the growing experience in global web campaigning, however, politicians started to recognize this technical underutilization: on preparation for the 2002 national elections and in response to trends in e-campaigning in the United States, several parties relaunched their websites to take advantage of previously neglected Internet features (Schweitzer, 2005). Websites were enlarged and supplemented with multimedia elements, live streams, and participatory features to capture the audience's attention. The focus of the sites shifted to campaign involvement. Users were encouraged to identify themselves in order to help the party build a web-based network of grassroots activists. In comparison to the beginning of German e-campaigning in 1998, parties now understood the Internet not only as a means of symbolic politics, but also as an effective logistical tool to strengthen the traditional campaign. Consequently, the 2002 national elections, in which twenty-seven out of twenty-eight competing parties maintained web presences, became known as Germany's first professional online campaign.

Today, e-campaigning has acquired a niche in German electoral politics. Parties spend 1 to 5 percent of their whole campaign budget on their Internet provision (among the parliamentary parties this means about 100,000 to 250,000 euro) (Schweitzer, 2003, pp.196-197). Major campaign events, like party conventions or television debates, are accompanied by extensive web coverage to synchronize online and offline activities and to offer additional background information specifically for journalists. Also, parties have established blogs, although this innovation is primarily symbolic in order to keep up with the American role model and to give an image of political authenticity and responsiveness.

Overall, web campaigning has not dramatically changed the traditional style of German electioneering. Due to the Internet's limited audience share, campaign managers still rely on it mostly as a supplemental tool while the main tasks of campaigning (image-building, voter mobilization, or conversion), take place first of all in the classical offline channels (television, press, and billboards).

The 2002 and 2005 National Elections: A Longitudinal Analysis of Parties' Website Professionalism

Although empirical analyses of candidate and party websites are becoming increasingly common, only a few studies have dealt so far with e-campaigning in a longitudinal perspective (Greer and LaPointe, 2004; Kamarck, 2002; Sadow and James, 2000; Schneider and Foot, 2006; Williams and Gulati, 2006). This chapter thus undertakes a time comparison of parties' website professionalism over two German national elections.

In general, past longitudinal analyses have operationalized the process of professionalization in e-campaigning by focusing on two aspects of online communication: content and structure. With regard to content, scholars have concentrated on traditional indicators of professionalization as applied to offline campaigning (e.g., Swanson and Mancini, 1996), i.e. the amount of *personalization* (candidate orientation vs. party orientation), *negative campaigning* (criticism on political opponents vs. positive self-promotion), and *de-ideologization* (campaigning as a central theme vs. policy issues as dominant features). In terms of structure, past research has included aspects of website configuration. More specifically, this encompasses *informational* and *interactive elements* as well as the degree of *sophistication* as measured by the presence of integrated multimedia or navigation options. This type of technical expansion of the professionalization concept corresponds to methodological considerations that advocate a multidimensional analysis of dynamic online content to capture facets of website usability. Moreover, this procedure bears a resemblance to already established approaches for studying other campaign media, which also suggest a differentiation between technical and content-based features to be analyzed in election studies (Kaid and Johnston, 2001).

According to this operationalization, greater professionalization in e-campaigning occurs if, over time, the quantitative share of each online characteristic mentioned increases. This augmentation indicates in detail either (a) a growing convergence between the online and offline style of election communication in terms of content, or (b) a structural reorganization of the web presence in support of a stronger user orientation. In total, this means that there should be a greater emphasis on the campaign itself rather than policy substance (de-ideologization), an increased concentration on the top candidates as the main subjects of the site content (personalization), more criticism of political competitors (negative campaigning) as well as an extension of the informational, interactive, and service-related elements of the website.

By applying this measure, the past longitudinal analyses confirm, in part, the assumed professionalization process in computer-mediated political communication: candidate websites studied from the U.S. presidential, senatorial, and gubernatorial elections in the years 1996, 1998, 2000, and 2004 showed a significant growth in interactive options over time as well as an increase in informational background material on the candidates and their political positions. In addition, there was a more varied inclusion of graphics and service elements ("sophistication") and a partially higher ratio of negative campaigning, which speaks of a further development of the respective websites. Greer and LaPointe (2004, p.130) therefore conclude that:

> new technologies are producing a bifurcation in campaign strategy. Campaign websites are becoming both more informative and interactive, but are also using more sophisticated graphics and taking a more negative stance towards opponents.

Contrary, though, to the original expectations, these studies showed neither a trend towards a stronger personalization nor an intensified reference to the campaign as the main subject of the website. Instead, serious policy issues were more often discussed thus leading to the impression of a partial professionalization process in e-campaigning. This takes place especially at the formal level of the website, while the content dimension seems to change only slightly over time.

As a consequence, the question arises of whether similar results can also be obtained for the development of German party websites in the 2002 and 2005 national elections. This notion can be specified by six research hypotheses:

H 1:   The party websites in 2005 exhibit more informational elements than in 2002.
H 2:   Over time, the home pages show a growth of interactive options.
H 3:   The number of service elements rises within the time frame of the study.
H 4:   Between the 2002 and 2005 national elections, home pages deal more with campaigning than with policy issues.
H 5:   The degree of personalization on the party websites increases.
H 6:   In 2005, there is a larger proportion of statements that can be considered negative campaigning.

If these hypotheses are correct, a comprehensive professionalization of German online campaigning has taken place, which is reflected both in the structure and in the content of those party websites. In order to test these hypotheses, a two-tiered method is necessary that includes both these dimensions of political online communication and thus enables a reliable longitudinal comparison of e-campaigning in the 2002 and 2005 national elections.

Method

In the 2002 national elections, a pilot study of party websites was conducted (Schweitzer, 2003, 2005). This study examined the question of normalization in German online campaigns with regard to the home pages of the leading national parties, i.e. the Social Democrats (SPD), the Conservatives (CDU), the Green Party (Greens), and the Liberals (FDP). In the 2005 national elections, that study became the baseline for a second analysis which was expanded to include all thirty-two competing parties with an Internet presence.

The individual party websites were downloaded and saved in the last four weeks before election day and coded for their formal configuration (structure analysis) and their online content (content analysis). The structure analysis coded for absence or presence of sixty-nine website elements, categorized into three functional groups, i.e. information, interactivity, and sophistication (see Appendix). To allow for quantitative comparisons, a party-related index quotient was calculated for each home page function based on the total number of website options given in one class divided by the total number of elements found per category on the home page. This procedure resulted in an index value ranging from 0 (no presence of the website elements in the respective group) to 1 (complete presence of all website elements in the category). If the index values for the Internet presences in the 2005 election outnumber the index quotients of the previous online campaigns in 2002, then the party websites can be considered as having become more professionalized.

The study also included a quantitative content analysis of the online news articles published every day on the home pages of the parliamentary parties (SPD, CDU, CSU, Green Party/Greens, Liberals/FDP, Leftist Party/Left). In the last four weeks before the election, these were printed out daily, archived, and manually coded.[2] The content analysis considered the issues discussed in those news articles, their political statements, and the sources of these statements. Other variables included text length, author, and the period of time these items remained on the home page.

Results of the Structure Analysis

The structure analysis dealt with the question of whether a technical advancement can be observed on the party websites during the online campaigns for the 2002 and 2005 national elections. The assumed process of professionalization should be indicated over time by an increase of the political informational elements (H 1), by a rise of interactive options (H 2), and finally by a growing website sophistication (H 3).

At first sight, though, the respective results reveal a similar picture for the party home pages in 2005 as in 2002 (see Figure 12.1).

Figure 12.1 Website Structure in Party Comparison in the 2005 National Elections

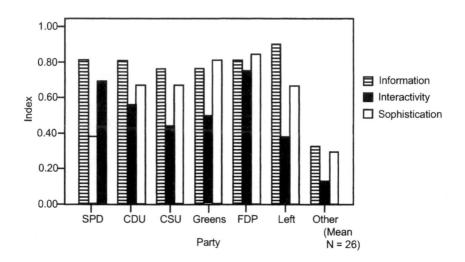

Once again the information-oriented options were the dominant features on parties' websites in 2005. These included, for example, items on the election program, the party history, its internal organization, the candidates, the political events of the party, or the broadcast times of the television spots. Likewise service elements were usually present. In particular, these encompassed article archives, downloads, photos, and graphics.

Interactive functions, however, proved to be less frequent. All party websites displayed email contacts, and most provided a means for joining online (twenty-six of thirty-two). Half used the site for fundraising. But other interactive options were less common. Only twelve home pages offered the opportunity to express personal views in discussion forums, only five had weblogs, and merely three included online opinion polls. Two possible explanations for the lack of interactive elements are: 1) the cost of integrating such online functions and 2) concern for the loss of centralized control over communication. Only the Liberals (FDP) appeared to be an exception to this rule, as their interactive home page options were developed to an above average standard in both the 2002 and the 2005 national elections.

Another important finding was the significant gap in website professionalism between parliamentary and non-parliamentary parties. While the SPD, CDU/CSU, the Greens, the FDP, and the Leftist Party included most of the structural elements on their home pages, the web presences of those parties not represented in the Bundestag were noticeably lacking in information density, degree of interactivity, and user-friendliness. Irrespective of their ideological orientation, these non-parliamentary sites featured newsletters, campaign information, and the description of internal party projects, but were deficient in the interactive and service-related aspects such as printing, email, and feedback options for text articles; site maps; information tours; search engines; multimedia offerings; picture archives; and gimmicks.

This discrepancy between major and minor parties confirms the convergence or normalization thesis regarding political online communication: according to the given paradigm, typical offline features of politics (e.g. power or resource relations) are transferred to the Internet. In this way, the less influential political actors abstain from having a sophisticated self-presentation on the web as they fear additional and unnecessary burdens on their limited personnel and financial resources through the continual support of an expensive online offering. By the same token, though, this means a lost chance of effective self-promotion for the minor parties, which becomes all the more apparent when taking into account the growing website professionalism of the parliamentary parties (see Table 12.1).

While the Internet presences of the non-parliamentary groups in 2005 were characterized throughout by low index values in information, interactivity, and sophistication, the already advanced home pages of the parliamentary parties became even more effective in these dimensions between 2002 and 2005: over time, the respective index values increased both in total and in most cases of individual party comparison. These enhancements are due in part to the growing online experiences of political organizations as well as to technological innovations that were first introduced in the strategic website relaunches before the 2005 national election. In this way, campaign-related information was added, navigation and text elements improved, and interactive options expanded. These developments correspond to the previously formulated structure-related hypotheses (H 1-3) and thus suggest a partial technical professionalization in German e-campaigning.

Table 12.1 Website Structure in Time Comparison

Index	SPD		CDU		Greens		FDP		Total	
	2002	2005	2002	2005	2002	2005	2002	2005	2002	2005
Inform-ation	0.81	0.81	0.76	0.81	0.57	0.76	0.57	0.81	0.68	0.80
Inter-activity	0.53	0.38	0.40	0.56	0.40	0.50	0.80	0.75	0.53	0.55
Sophis-tication	0.68	0.69	0.74	0.67	0.71	0.81	0.74	0.84	0.72	0.75

NB. Due to a hypothesis-related reorganization of the functional groups used in the 2002 pilot study, different index values might arise for these categories in comparison with an earlier publication of the author.

This finding, though, is subject to two basic limitations when compared to the results of the American longitudinal analyses. First, a technological professionalization in German online campaigns is true—at present—only for parliamentary parties, but not for minor groups. Second, even for the parliamentary parties, change was not uniform across the political organizations. The home pages of the SPD, CDU, and FDP occasionally expanded their service options in some areas while simultaneously weakening others. For example, the CDU site abandoned individual navigation aids while the SPD site replaced chats and discussion forums with weblogs. Those adjustments can be attributed to the short duration of the election period and its planning phase and the replacement of previous options with technical alternatives, which contribute to the impression of a non-uniform state of e-campaigning. For this reason, the findings put forth so far by the structure analysis point only to a partial professionalization process in German online campaigns.

Results of the Content Analysis

While the structural coding concentrated on the technical configuration of the websites, the content analysis addressed the text-based communication strategies underlying the respective Internet presences. The daily online news articles published on the home pages of the parliamentary parties (SPD, CDU, CSU, Greens, FDP, Leftist Party) were analyzed with regard to their main issues, their political statements, and the sources of those statements.

In total, the content analysis included 451 articles. These were distributed evenly over the active phase of the election campaign and stayed online for a similar period of time as in the 2002 national elections (about three days). In addition, the majority of those online items (66.7 percent) were presented in a matter-of-fact news style and, just as in the previous election, the authors were listed as the Internet editors of the respective parties (72.2 percent). Only the Leftist home page appeared to be an exception from this rule as it pushed statements of individual party members into the foreground and thus relied less on a journalistic news style and more on commentaries (65.6 percent).

By comparison to the 2002 national elections, the 2005 online news articles were also longer (an average of 349 words vs. 286 words in 2002) and were more often accompanied by photos (66.3 percent), graphics (22.2 percent), additional hyperlinks (53.3 percent), or background material (23.9 percent). The SPD home page proved to be particularly prominent in this context. This underscores the greater technical professionalization of German Internet campaigns in 2005, in content as well as structure.

Moreover, on their websites parties concentrated primarily on the election campaign as the dominant political theme (see Figure 12.2).

While the discussion of serious policy issues slightly prevailed in the 2002 elections, campaigning became the most important subject in 2005 across all parties and over the whole period of time. More than half of all articles were dedicated to the campaign activities of the parties. Strong emphasis was given to the national canvassing tours (19.7 percent of all campaign-related articles) and the television debate (7.4 percent). By contrast, other areas of politics, such as foreign, economic, or tax policy, were mainly moved to the sidelines.

On the whole, the intensified campaign orientation on the party home pages confirmed the first text-based research hypothesis (H 4). This implies a corresponding partial professionalization on the content level. But does this also hold true for the assumed degree of personalization on parties' web presences (H 5)? In order to answer this question, the statement and source levels have to be considered in addition to the thematic orientation of the articles.

With regard to the latter indicator, there was not a significant concentration on the leading politicians as the main issue of the articles. Similar to the 2002 national elections, only about 3 percent of all news reports dealt predominantly with the outward appearances, behaviors, and images of the respective candidates. In addition, these leading political personalities were not at the center of the statements analyzed in the news items (see Figure 12.3).

In the last four weeks before election day 2005, altogether 1,289 statements were coded. These appeared primarily in the last week of the campaign period and stemmed for the main part from the SPD home page. Contrary to the original research assumption, the quotations were particularly concerned with the respective parliamentary parties. Three quarters of all political statements dealt with the competing organizations and their positions, mostly involving mutual criticism by the SPD and the CDU/CSU. The Conservatives blamed the governing coalition of the SPD and the Green Party for being responsible for the economic misery in Germany and for having misused people's trust, while the Social Democrats accused the opposition of a lack of social empathy, of being insincere, and reactionary. By contrast, the top candidates were named only in 18.9 percent of all announcements. This closely represents the statement distribution as it had been observed in the 2002 national elections, when the majority of all comments were party-oriented while a quarter dealt specifically with the individual leaders. Hence, even in this aspect of online content, no increase in personalization could be observed for 2005.

Figure 12.2 Campaign Issues on German Party Websites

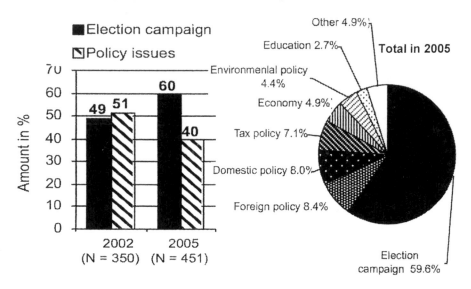

Figure 12.3 Statements on German Party Websites in the 2005 National Elections

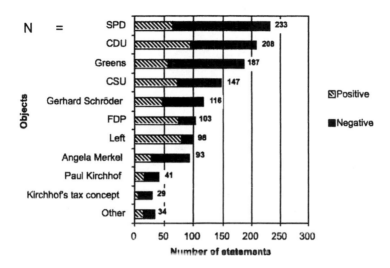

This also applies to the sources of these statements. In the 2002 and 2005 national elections the majority of the quotations originated not from the respective candidates (28.3 percent), but from other representatives of the parties (64.1 percent). This was true for all weeks of the active campaign phase and for all but one of the websites. Only the SPD site proved to be an exception in 2002, when there was greater coverage of former Chancellor Gerhard Schröder (SPD) compared with his other colleagues. In 2005, however, he lost this advantage in a dramatic manner: While he was identifiable as a source in more than one third (37.1 percent) of all SPD accounts in 2002, this number dropped to 17 percent of all party claims in 2005. By contrast, his challenger, Angela Merkel (CDU), became more visible in the 2005 election: compared to the incumbent, she was named more often in the respective news articles (36.8 percent vs. 35.3 percent), was seen in twice as many photos (12.2 percent vs. 6.2 percent), and was finally more extensively quoted than Schröder in the online reports (9 percent vs. 4.7 percent). Even other minor politicians like Guido Westerwelle (FDP) (6.7 percent) or Edmund Stoiber (CSU) (5.4 percent) were cited more frequently than the former Chancellor, so that in the 2005 Internet campaign one can without doubt speak of Schröder's communicative disempowerment. In addition, Angela Merkel also became more popular by comparison to her predecessor, Edmund Stoiber. Compared with Stoiber's appearance as a candidate for the Chancellorship in 2002, Angela Merkel was represented more regularly on the CDU home page in her own words (42.3 percent vs. 17.8 percent) and in addition she received more explicit acknowledgements from her party colleagues (8.7 percent vs. 6.4 percent of all CDU statements). Despite Merkel's frequent presence in 2005, though, there was in total no significant increase in the number of candidate-based statements. Instead, general comments by other party members prevailed. In view of the corresponding results of the issue, statement, and source level, the fifth research assumption for rising personalization in German online campaigns cannot therefore be confirmed.

This is also true for the last hypothesis of the present study, which dealt with the amount of negative campaigning in the online news items analyzed. Comparing the 2002 and 2005 national elections, an increase in the use of negativism on the respective party websites was expected. This assumption, however, proved to be wrong (see Figure 12.4).

Although the tone of parties' online statements was predominantly negative, in both 2002 and 2005, there was no significant increase in the number of attacks. Instead, the parties differed in their approach to negative campaigning, depending on the electoral environment: while the Greens and the FDP almost maintained their argumentative stance, the SPD and CDU changed their respective communication strategies over time. In the 2002 election, the SPD, as the incumbents, concentrated on positive self-promotion, emphasizing their power for reform and their fight for social justice as well as the expertise and charisma of their Chancellor. In 2005, however, the Social Democrats took on a more negative campaign strategy against the CDU/CSU, while the Conservatives responded overall with a more positive attitude as the party underlined the need for political reform, the team spirit and solidarity of the party, and their commitment to honesty. Three years earlier, the CDU/CSU had taken a predominantly negative stance, attacking the governing coalition for political failures in the economy and social security. This change of the communication strategies displayed by both parties illustrates the situational variability of campaigning and in this way contradicts the assumption of a general trend towards more negativism on German party home pages.

Figure 12.4 Percentage Balances Between Positive and Negative Party Statements

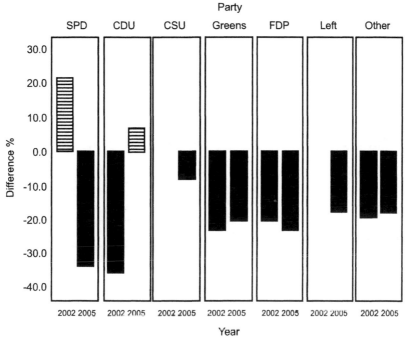

Consequently, the hypothesis of a rise in negative campaigning (H 6) has to be rejected. This is also true for the presumed increase in personalization on those party websites (H 5), while the postulated de-ideologization of e-campaigning could be sustained (H 4).

In sum, these findings about website content lead to the conclusion of a partial professionalization process taking place in national online campaigns, which corresponds to the results of the structure analysis. Changes in the content-related dimensions of e-campaigning appear to be much weaker than those encountered on the structural level as only one out of three content-specific research hypotheses could be empirically validated in the analysis, while the structure coding of the home pages rendered confirmation of all three of the configuration-related hypotheses. In addition, this observation supports the findings of similar American longitudinal studies, which also demonstrated a primarily technically driven professionalization process in national online campaigns.

Conclusion

The original question was whether there has been a greater professionalization process in German online campaigning in national elections. The answer is mixed. In accordance with the research hypotheses formulated, the home pages of the parliamentary parties did in fact display a larger total amount of information, interactivity, and sophistication in 2005 than in the previous 2002 election. In addition, they exhibited a more distinct marketing orientation, which was reflected in the growing thematic focus on the campaign and in a repression of factual political debates. A reinforced personalization of online communication or an increased amount of negative campaigning, however, could not be universally observed.

Moreover, several divergences in the individual party developments were detected, both for the structural and for the content-based dimensions of the study. These differences cast doubt on the basic assumption of a uniform process of political adaptation to the modern conditions of campaigning. Instead, the present findings suggest a *partial professionalization process* taking place on German party home pages which—in accordance with comparable American results—is expressed primarily in the technical structure of the websites rather than in their content.

Notes

1. www.wahlkampfchance-verpasst.de
2. In order to determine the intracoder reliability, 5 percent of the material was recoded. Using Holsti's formula, the intracoder reliability was assessed at .89.

Appendix

Categorization of Website Elements Coded in the Structure Analysis

Category	Website elements	
Information (N=21)	Items on the political system	Items on campaign organization/strategy
	Items on the election system	
	Items on the party history	Download of party documents
	Items on the party organization	Current party news
	Items on party members	Dossiers on background topics
	Items on the election program	
	Items on party conventions	Newsletter
	Items on junior party organizations	Event calendar
		Press releases
	Items on party projects/foundations	Local candidates
		Campaign coverage

	Items on canvassing tour	Party members in the media Times of party broadcast slots
Interactivity (N=16)	Online fundraising/donations Online membership Online friendraising E-volunteers Intra-/Extranet Feedback option on text articles Online petitions/protest mails E-cards	Online opinion polls Discussion forums/ news- groups Weblogs Chat rooms for non-party members Computer games/quizzes/ gimmicks Lotteries Tax calculator Bulletin board/guestbook
Sophistication (N=32)	Press accrediting News archive Photo archive Imprint Offers of post Hotline Email contact SMS service E-shop English version Text-only version of articles Print option for text articles Email option for text articles Download option for text arti- cles Offers of additional software Site map/index Information tour	Search engine Home page icon on lower levels of the website Toolbar Back button Upward button Photos Graphics Animated icons/banner Audio/video streams Online subscription/use of party publications Download of party parapher- nalia Internet packages Download of party broadcasts Download of party billboards Web radio/podcasting

Conclusion

Richard Davis, Diana Owen, David Taras
and Stephen Ward

As the Internet developed as a mass medium, it seemed tailor-made to have a political role in an electoral system that was candidate-centered, decentralized, and featured a single-district, winner-take-all electoral system, i.e. an American-style electoral system (Bimber and Davis, 2003; Davis, 1999; Davis and Owen, 1998; Selnow, 1998; Rash, 1997; Corrado and Firestone, 1996). The Internet potentially would reinforce and magnify the individualistic, decentralizing forces in a candidate-centered electoral system (Menefee-Libey, 2000; Wattenberg, 1991 and 1998). The Dean phenomenon reinforced the sense that American-style campaigns can become breeding grounds for candidate reliance on the Internet to reshape electoral politics (Kerbel and Bloom, 2005; Cornfield, 2004a, 2004b).

But across the globe, the American model is the exception rather than the rule. Previous studies of the Internet's electoral role have suggested that the Internet's impact is hardly uniform across varying national systems (Kluver, 2004; Gibson *et al*, 2003a, 2003b; Ward and Gibson, 2003; Zittel, 2003; Boogers and Voerman, 2003; Tkach, 2003; Gibson and Ward, 2002; Newell, 2001; Carlson and Djupsund, 2001).

What might cause these discrepancies in a medium that was initially viewed as revolutionary in altering politics across the globe? We argue it is context. Most electoral systems are dissimilar to the U.S. system in their preference for a party-centered, parliamentary system incorporating varying forms of proportional representation rather than a candidate-oriented, presidential system with a winner-take-all model.

Nor is it just electoral structure. Across liberal democracies, party systems are dissimilar to that in the United States. Parties as organizations in liberal and emerging democracies typically are stronger, more coherent, and more ideological than their counterparts in the United States. Moreover, other factors of political culture, media structure, and extent of Internet access vary across the globe, and often significantly from the United States.

The purpose of this book was to examine the role of such contextual factors in the shaping of the Internet's importance in each electoral campaign. It is important to note that the list of factors was wide ranging to cover an array of systems and contexts. Not all of these factors are meaningful in every country. Therefore, the case studies have focused on some factors that play the most significant roles and have minimized or omitted discussion of others that are less important. The chapters engage in a prioritization of factors based on the specific case. Nevertheless, we can see a broad portrait of similarities and contrasts based on this array of diverse cases. Before we start contrasting these cases, perhaps we should begin by noting the commonalities we found.

Common Trends

Growth of the Internet

One commonality is the growing reach of the Internet. From Indonesia to the United Kingdom, Internet access has increased. In all cases, either current usage constitutes a majority of the population—as in Australia, Belgium, Canada, the United States, the United Kingdom, Germany, and Singapore—or growth rates are dramatic such as in Spain, Indonesia, Chile, and Italy. However, rates of growth are slowing where the Internet already has reached near saturation, such as in the United States and Canada.

Growth percentages can mask the difficulty in expanding Internet access in poor nations. For example, while Internet access in Indonesia has doubled, the percentage of Indonesians online is still in single digits. Access in developed nations has increased due to the rapid expansion of broadband, especially in Europe. And as noted in the Singapore chapter, already 40 percent of Internet users go online via broadband. Not only does broadband allow for more extensive usage of the multimedia features of the Internet, it also means users no longer face time unit charges that limit their time online.

As Internet access spreads across a society, the audience expands beyond the affluent and well-educated. We see a vast disparity between the reach of the Internet in Indonesia (where one-half of 1 percent were online by the time of the 2004 election) and Australia (where the same year 66 percent of the public went online to retrieve election information). While the Indonesians were primarily academics and other elites, the Australians clearly included a broad middle class.

But the same expansion may not be true for the audience for campaign websites. As several chapters noted, those who are most likely to use campaign-related websites are males, the better educated, and the highly politically interested. Not only are they demographically different from the general public, they also have media habits and political interests that vary from others who are online. As Owen and Davis argued, U.S. campaign website visitors were already politically interested. Similarly, Voerman and Boogers found that in the Netherlands, three-quarters of party website visitors were already strong news consumers, keeping up with politics through traditional media. Schweitzer concluded that German party websites are preaching to the converted, not only in the sense that sites' visitors are partisans but also in that they possess strong feelings of political efficacy and are more likely to be politically engaged.

Obviously, this contradicts the thesis that the Internet provides the opportunity to reinvigorate and even expand political participation (Selnow, 1998; Hauben and Hauben, 1997; Grossman, 1995; Burstein and Kline, 1995). As some chapter authors noted, this is one of the missed opportunities of the Internet. Yet, the active effort required to access campaign information (in addition to the easy avoidance of online political information online for the less politically interested) makes preaching to the converted much more likely than reinvigoration.

New and Old Media

In all cases, new information technologies are being incorporated into campaigns, albeit at varying levels. Parties and candidates are adopting websites, email, blogs, etc., as new forms of communication with select groups of voters. These new information technologies join traditional means such as television, newspapers, and radio in reaching certain audiences of voters.

But as the Internet becomes a widely used form of mass communication, traditional media are not disappearing. Instead, Internet campaigns are add-ons to traditional modes of campaigning. Again, in some states such as Indonesia, where Internet access is limited, the supplement is minor. Even in advanced industrialized democracies where Internet access is more widespread, television still dominates media-based communication.

Yet, in some Internet-developed nations, the web campaign has acquired a significant role in campaigns through functions such as supporter identification, reinforcement and targeted voter mobilization. These functions have not gravitated wholly online, but they have acquired a niche.

Interactivity

Another commonality is the cautious approach to interactivity. Interactivity was once viewed as one of the virtues of the Internet since average voters would have the opportunity to express opinions to the powerful (Davis, 2005, pp.20-21; Coleman, 2001, p.685; Hauben and Hauben, 1997, p.4; Corrado and Firestone, 1996, p.117). Various forms of online interaction—email, chat, and bulletin boards—are available to campaigns today (Davis, 2005). The newest form is the blog, which appeared in several cases including the United Kingdom, the United States, and Chile.

But approaches to interactive blogs varied across systems. While interactive blogs were common in Chile and Canada, their usage in other nations was less adventurous. In the United States, the Bush campaign website in 2004 included a blog, but it was not interactive. Posts were made only by designated Bush campaign staff or supporters. In the United Kingdom, neither of the two major party's blogs was interactive. Only the Liberal Democrats' blog allowed interactivity. Similarly, only a small minority of German party sites included blogs.

Blogs, like other forms of interactivity, run the risk of allowing opponents, extremists, or even over-zealous supporters to dictate the agenda of the online discussion and wreak havoc on the public's perception of the campaign (Bimber and Davis, 2003, pp.86-87; Coleman, 2001, p.681).

Overall, interactivity is less common than we would have thought given the features of the Internet. Our cases show that the emphasis remains on unidirectional communication. Even when earlier efforts included interactivity, party and candidate webmasters have steered away from it more recently. And perhaps users want it that way? The reality of interactivity points to that preference. Voerman and Boogers note that party website users go to these sites primarily to get information, not so much to participate. As Bentivegna pointed out, Internet users in Italy are far more likely to be recipients of campaign email than to be senders even though they possess the ability to do both.

Even when interactivity was featured, it seemed more an illusion than a reality. For example, in Chile, both major candidate websites used web surveys to gauge public opinion, at least ostensibly. However, framing of choices and emphasis on non-controversial questions through most of the campaign made site visitor input nearly meaningless.

The problem with parties' and candidates' approaches to interactivity may lie less with what they do than with what scholars expect they will do. Why do we expect interactivity? Admittedly, two-way communication is natural to the medium. Indeed, the original uses of the Internet were to facilitate multidirectional communication among researchers and/or the U.S. military. But such an expectation is not natural in a viable electoral campaign. It is as if one expected a candidate giving a speech to repeatedly give part of their allotted time to the opposition or someone in the crowd who wants to have their say as well.

In nearly all cases, the emphasis of the party or candidate is to use the medium to reach voters with a designated message (Bimber and Davis, 2003).

The Competitive Edge?

Another shared trait is the failure to level the playing field of competition among parties. One of the early predictions about the Internet's role in the United States was that minor parties would be able to compete more effectively because the Internet offered broad access to the electorate at a much lower cost than traditional advertising. In fact, some predicted that with the Internet the party system as Americans knew it might disappear (Friedenberg, 1997, p.205; Corrado and Firestone, 1996, p.12).

However, that has not happened. Both major and minor parties have gone online. Our only real exception was Indonesia where only half the parties posted websites, although in Belgium Hooghe and Vissers posit that small parties must pass a certain threshold of financial viability before they can acquire a web presence.

While an online presence may encourage smaller parties because of the perception that such a presence offers a platform for parties to compete with larger parties, it does not equate to greater influence in electoral politics. Moreover, as several cases show, small parties and minor party candidates can suffer disadvantages because they tend to lack the resources that would duplicate the characteristics of larger, more resource-rich parties and candidates. Hence, overall, in our case studies, a web presence has not resulted in significant electoral gain to upset the existing balance of power between major and minor parties

One partial exception—and one significantly present in a candidate-centered system—is the case of the Dean campaign in the 2004 U.S. elections. Dean's Internet use did have two significant effects for the little-known, initially resource-poor candidate. One was the creation of a base drawn largely from the online community. That base helped Dean raise $52 million (much of it online). The other was the traditional media attention that Dean garnered for his untraditional media campaign. For a brief period at the end of 2003 and early 2004, news coverage of Dean outpaced that of the other candidates as he vaulted into the frontrunner position in the Democratic nomination.

The Dean case may point to the power of the Internet to take a candidate to a certain point—to identify and mobilize a base of core supporters. But it also may show that the Internet effort only goes so far. Moreover, it is unlikely any future U.S. presidential candidate will receive such mainstream publicity for their use of the Internet since the medium is no longer novel.

The Role of Context

Yet, there are differences across these cases in how the Internet has impacted the electoral system. Our cases refute the argument that "technological change in telecommunications ... will drive different systems of political representation towards a single model" (Zittel, 2003, p.49). Instead, contextual factors become highly relevant in explaining how the Internet has become incorporated into varying electoral systems. In drawing out the role of context we focus on organizational and systemic factors: the former include the role of resources and the culture of campaigning, while the latter consists of the electoral system, the regulatory environment and the traditional media structure.

Organizational Factors

Culture of Campaigning

Candidate-centered and party-centered systems approach Internet use differently. The two clear candidate-centered systems in our sample of case studies were the United States and Chile. In these systems, the individual presidential candidates had websites and used them extensively to communicate with voters. Party websites were not the focus of attention online, which was a reflection of their public role in campaigns in these systems. In both cases, the tools of blogs, email, and online volunteer solicitation were common. Donor solicitation was prominent in the United States, but is still in its infancy in Chile. It is likely that online donations will become more common in future Chilean elections as well, particularly since there is no public funding of campaigns. Also, in the United States, the Internet itself became the object of intense media coverage of candidate campaigning, particularly in relation to the Dean campaign.

By contrast, in party-based systems, candidate sites were less common. Only a minority of candidates in the United Kingdom, Italy and Australian elections even created websites. While over 60 percent did so in Canada, one major party's candidates (Bloc Quebecois) essentially ignored the web. Nevertheless, the growth of candidate sites over time suggests that they eventually may be the norm, even in party-based systems. However, even then, a significant number are likely to contain standardized party content rather than be individually-designed, independent creations as was the case in candidate-centered systems.

Yet, the increasing personalization of campaigns (i.e. the American model) in party-based systems may be furthered by the Internet. The party sites in some party based systems were designed to promote candidates. In Canada, for example, when the user gave a postal code, the local candidate's photo appeared with a link to that candidate's site.

Even more personalization may be occurring when online communication emphasizes party leaders over the organizational party. In Italy and the Netherlands, party leaders created their own separate sites. In Italy, the primary campaign encouraged independent party leader use of the Internet for voter communication. As a result, these leader sites have eclipsed party sites as a source of information and campaign contact for voters in both the Netherlands and Italy.

By contrast, this personalization has not occurred in Belgium. Discussion of individual party leaders is buried in website content rather than highlighted on party pages or even in separate leader sites. Nor was it the case in Germany. The attention to party leaders did not increase over time as would be expected by the personalization model.

The question to be raised is whether candidates will distance themselves from the party and loosen central party control over their campaigns. This phenomenon could have occurred prior to this point with the introduction of the personalized medium of television. Yet, media regulations (as we will discuss later) made that change more difficult for individual candidates. That prospect may be brighter for the Internet since it lacks those regulations on party/candidate advertising and it is relatively inexpensive for an individual candidate to maintain. But what incentive is there for candidates to effect this distancing? Moreover, since those who frequent the candidate sites are likely to be party supporters, will we see a candidate use an Internet site to send a distinctive message rather than one that conforms to the party's message?

One distinction between systems (again based on candidate versus party emphases) is the use of the Internet for information dissemination. While candidate sites offer snippets of information about candidate positions—typically brief discussion on a variety of issues—the party sites are more likely to be dense with party platforms and substantive issue information. In the Netherlands, party leader sites looked more like candidate sites as they featured personal information about the individuals rather than discussion of their party platforms.

Another aspect of the culture of campaigning has to do with candidate and public expectations of candidate interaction with voters. In the United States, congressional districts include several hundred thousand constituents. Personal campaigning by candidates becomes impossible. However, such interaction is expected in systems where constituencies are smaller geographically and in terms of population. In the United Kingdom, Belgium, and Canada, for example, candidates expect that they can rely on personal campaigning. They can and do spend their time talking directly to voters rather than relying on mediated communication.

Campaign Resources

Resources matter. Online communication tools such as email lists, websites, blogs, podcasts, and the like carry the potential of generating resources for parties and candidates. In a few of our cases, that potential was fulfilled or was at least in its embryonic stage. Yet, the source of campaign funds helps determine the extent of Internet use for resource generation. Where government funding is the primary or exclusive source of campaign revenue, the Internet cannot or need not play the role of financial resource generator. Where all or nearly all parties receive government funding, there is no need for online donation solicitation. In other systems where government funding is partial and private donations become the main source of campaign income (as the United States), the Internet becomes a critical tool for fundraising. And we would expect that in other nations, such as Australia or Chile, where conditions are similar in terms of government funding, online giving will become more common.

Electoral systems vary in the amount of resources parties and candidates are allowed to spend on electoral campaigns. Where legal limitations force parties (and particularly candidates) to make choices over spending on traditional campaign methods or new ones, the latter can suffer. In Chile, candidates and parties face spending limits that may inhibit Internet communication development as traditional campaign methods continue to receive the lion's share of candidate/party attention and funding. Another variant is when candidates are more limited than parties by campaign limits, as is the case in the United Kingdom and Canada. The result is a funneling of resources to party organizations rather than campaign organizations, and the strengthening of party Internet activities rather than candidate online communication.

By contrast, in the United States, where candidates or parties are essentially limited by their own ability to raise money, candidate or party websites flourish not only in quantity but also in quality. The U.S. campaign finance system does offer funds to parties in order to run national conventions and to presidential candidates (via matching funds in the primaries and a grant in the general election) in order to finance their campaigns. Yet, growth in Internet use as a fundraising tool in the United States may be fueled as future presidential candidates abandon government funding and raise their own campaign funds (with the help of the Internet). The Dean and Kerry examples of eschewing federal funds in the primaries and relying on the Internet may become the model for future viable presidential campaigns.

Systemic Factors

Internet Access

Our country studies lay on a continuum in terms of Internet access levels. However, there are three broad categories. At the one end are states with access levels well beyond a majority of the population (United Kingdom, Germany, Netherlands, Belgium, United States, Canada, Australia, Singapore). In the middle are nations with growing access rates that suggest levels of access between one third and one-half the population, such as Spain, Italy, and Chile. And at the other end is one state with a miniscule Internet presence (Indonesia).

Where there is greatest accessibility to the Internet, there is a more significant and sustained role in electoral campaigning. The logic is clear: parties and candidates are reluctant to invest in a medium that has limited reach. However, even for states with similar access levels, the nature of the system is important. Chile, with its candidate-centered system, saw more expansive uses of the Internet than Italy with a party-based system with candidate-oriented features such as a primary campaign. And Italy's parties engaged the Internet much more than did their counterparts in Spain.

The Electoral System

The electoral systems of our cases varied significantly. Some fit the model of presidential, candidate-centered systems with weak parties. The United States, Indonesia, and Chile are examples, although even they vary significantly from each other. Others are parliamentary, party-based systems typically featuring varying levels of centralized party control. Yet, even in many of these systems, candidate-centered politics have become more important at both the national and sub-national levels. For example, the personalization of campaigns has been an increasingly prominent trait in the Netherlands, the United Kingdom, Italy, and Canada.

If the presidential, candidate-centered model is the most adaptable to Internet use, then we would expect that the Internet's intrusion into the electoral system's operation would be more visible in these systems. That is indeed what we see. Two examples are the U.S. and Chilean models. In the United States, a little-known governor of a small state promoted the Internet as a campaign tool for identifying and mobilizing potential supporters. Moreover, Internet fundraising became a major source of funds and other Internet-related developments such as blogs and online-driven meet-ups became important mechanisms for mobilizing the grassroots.

In Chile, the strong presidential (and therefore strong presidential candidate) system led to active integration of the Internet as a tool for enhancing the personal politics of the system.

Parties nominate candidates, but the candidate is the center of attention, not the party. The fact that the candidate heads a coalition of parties and even distances himself or herself from the party magnifies candidate orientation. The online campaign was one between candidates. Candidates in Chile were more likely than those in party-based systems to employ the Internet to distinguish themselves from other candidates, recruit volunteers, and mobilize the electorate.

That is not to say that the Internet does not have impacts on party-based systems. The Internet is part of the campaign mix of the vast majority of political parties in the cases we examined. Parties are employing the Internet to communicate the party's platform, solicit donations, mobilize voters, etc.

One impact is the further personalization or "Americanization" of campaigns. Parties are facilitating (or allowing) individual leader and candidate website creation. This is true across party-based systems such as the United

Kingdom, Canada, the Netherlands, and Italy. As Voerman and Boogers suggest, this development could have the impact of loosening party control over candidate communication. However, centralized control may be more easily retained if parties offer template sites that follow party guidelines and are hosted by a server run by the party and require candidates to use those sites exclusively.

One of the novel uses of the Internet in a multi-party system that has not appeared in candidate-centered systems is the online guide that matches voters' stated preferences to the party with policy proposals closest to their own. In Belgium in the 2004 elections, over 150,000 people used this system (Hooghe and Teepe, 2005). In the Netherlands, the guide made 2.3 million recommendations in the 2003 elections. Whether such a system really assists voters in sorting out the multitude of party options is still undetermined. However, voters self-reported that it made a difference.

The Regulatory Environment

Another contextual factor is election law or regulation, which can impact how the Internet is utilized in a political system. The Australian compulsory voting laws are one good of this. While in some systems the Internet is used as a tool to mobilize voters, this becomes unnecessary where voters already are present at the polls.

Another important example is regulation of media use by parties and candidates. In some nations, media regulations prohibit the broadcast of election information during certain time periods (such as immediately prior to an election) or limit the type of content available (such as release of polling data). Regulation of the Internet, however, is in an embryonic stage throughout the world, although Singapore (with its extensive restrictions on free speech online) maybe considered an exception. As a result, until and unless the Internet is accorded similar regulatory treatment as traditional news media outlets, the new medium can become a vehicle for bypassing the traditional news media. Where the traditional news media are extensively regulated and the Internet is not, information reporting and retrieval may gravitate to the most open medium. For example, the official "Reflection Day" in Spain created a vacuum that Internet messages could have filled, although they did not. The terrorist attack in the last days of the 2004 campaign provided an opportunity for alternative media as traditional media were blocked from disseminating campaign messages but the Internet and other new technologies were not. However, the lack of citizen usage of the Internet, particularly for electoral purposes, diminished their potential impact. On the other hand, Singapore's limits on visual material about candidates and a requirement that any entity disseminating political information (including websites) be licensed by the government have depressed animated Internet content about campaigns.

Another contextual difference related to electoral law is in the amount of free traditional media exposure provided for parties. Where free media exposure is available (such as in Australia, Chile and most European democracies), parties and candidates spend a small fraction of their budget on broadcast media to convey their messages. Similarly, the Internet becomes less essential as a tool for reaching undecided voters when parties can rely on free traditional broadcast media time to do so. In the United States, broadcast media are required to be evenhanded in the offer to sell time, but there is no requirement to give time to candidates. As a result, candidates seek methods to reach voters that will reduce the financial cost; hence, the attractiveness of the Internet as such an alternative. (Televised debates may be viewed as an equivalent to the free media time offered in other nations, but in another sense they are not because of the lack of candidate control of the debate agenda or even whether an opponent agrees to a participate in the debate in the first place.)

Along with traditional media regulations campaign finance is arguably the other key contextual regulatory factor. Where electoral regulations limit campaign revenue generation to state-provided funds, the Internet plays little role in fundraising. Similarly, in those cases where private money fuels campaigns, caps placed on spending force parties and candidates to choose between traditional and new modes of campaigning in the allocation of resources. For example, when a candidate in the United Kingdom or Australia has a limit on total spending, the Internet ranks relatively low in the priority list. Most of our case studies fit in these categories. On the other hand, where such caps do not exist (such as in the United States outside of the presidential general election campaign finance system), Internet-based fundraising is viewed by campaigns as a potential supplement to traditional fundraising methods (and at much lower cost). In fact, fundraising in the U.S. electoral context may well be the medium's primary electoral function (Jamieson, 2006, p.36; Bimber and Davis, 2003).

Media Structure

The media structures within our cases also vary widely. Although all feature a relatively free press (Singapore may be at the edge of the spectrum) and at least some private ownership and control of mass media, the commonalities stop there. In the political systems where media are almost exclusively private and commercial, media outlets are motivated primarily by audience ratings and economic competition. The result may be a lessened emphasis on politics and government as audience surveys direct the nature of news media content toward less political, more sensational stories. Or, to the extent politics is covered, it becomes newsworthy because of the presence of the salacious (scandal) or conflict. Moreover, the presence of journalistic professionalism and autonomy from political organizations results in the employment of news values that consider candidate statements to be newsworthy only to the extent that they fit values of conflict, drama, timeliness, etc. In Chile and the United States, a soundbite culture has emerged where traditional media limit candidate access to the voters and candidates reciprocate by finding alternative methods of communicating to the electorate. One such alternative is the Internet. However, there are two other cases where the need for alternative communication fora is less acute. One is where a public broadcast medium (such as the BBC in the United Kingdom or the CBC in Canada) devotes large blocks of time to parties and candidates— either by law or through its public service remit. The other is where a partisan press offers parties, and to a lesser extent candidates, access in order to communicate with partisans. In some cases, such as the United Kingdom, both of these conditions exist.

In the former systems, we see a more rapid adoption of the Internet as a new medium to reach voters. However, as was noted in the Netherlands and the United States, the primary audience for candidate/party online communication is the existing base of support. Hence, the online audience for candidate communication is unlike the traditional news media audience and the lack of strong overlap means that candidates and parties cannot treat their online message as a substitute for the traditional media one. The Internet's greatest influence may well occur in systems where media ownership is private, fragmented, driven by commercial concerns and where there is a considerable degree of distrust in the traditional media.

Summary

In the U.S. case we see the ingredients for Internet impact—high rates of Internet access, a media structure that is private and commercial and is populated by journalists who consider most candidate statements (particularly those related to policy issues) to be non-newsworthy, extensive candidate resources due to limited campaign finance regulation, a porous electoral system that allows interest groups heavily to influence the nomination and election process, a presidential system, a weak party system both organizationally and culturally, and a resulting candidate-centered process that rewards entrepreneurial candidates who find their own means for campaign communication.

Some of these features are also present in other systems. And they may become more characteristic of other systems (such as Italy, the Netherlands, the United Kingdom and Canada) undergoing a greater personalization of politics that weakens political parties.

Yet, the argument for increasing Internet influence typically rests on only a few universal factors: increase in the rates of Internet access, growth in usage of the Internet as a source for campaign communication, and an online presence by parties and candidates. Our study has shown that approach to be simplistic. Factors of context weigh heavily in the role the Internet plays in electoral systems. A strong party system where centralized leadership dominates resources and decision-making and national partisan appeals override local candidates or issues is one where Internet campaign use will be less widespread among candidates because they lack the resources, the motivation or the autonomy to communicate with voters individually. And usage by party organizations occurs within the context of party electoral and organizational goals rather than abstract standards established by the presence of a new technology.

Bibliography

Abernathy, J. 1992. "New Constituency of Computer Users; Electronic Communities Gain Clout in Political Campaigns." *Houston Chronicle*. 3 May. p.A18.

Agre, P. E. 2002 "Real-Time Politics: The Internet and the Political Process." *The Information Society*, 18, pp.311-331.

Ahyani, M. M .I. 1999. "Internet fails to woo most political parties." *The Jakarta Post*, 29 May, on www.TheJakartaPost.com, sighted 21 August 1999.

AIMC. 2005. *Navegantes en la Red. 7ª Encuesta a usuarios de Internet*. Febrero. www.aimc.es/aimc.php.

Ananta, A., E. N. Arifin and L. Suryadinata. 2004. *Indonesian Electoral Behaviour: A Statistical Perspective*. Singapore: Institute for Southeast Asian Studies.

———. 2005. *Emerging Democracy in Indonesia*. Singapore: Institute for Southeast Asian Studies.

Aninat, C., J. Landregan, P. Navia, and J. Vial. 2006. "Political Institutions, Policymaking Processes and Policy Outcomes in Chile." Research Network Working Paper R-521, Inter-American Development Bank. http://www.iadb.org/res/publications/ pubfiles/ pubr-521.pdf.

Antlöv, H. and S. Cederroth. 2004. *Elections in Indonesia: The New Order and Beyond*. London: Routledge Curzon.

Arriagada, G. 2000. "La estrategia comunicacional: Marketing vs. contenido?" In Larenas, F. *et al.* (eds.), *Como ganar una elección? Un nuevo paradigma en la comunicación política*. Santiago, Chile: Konrad Adenauer Stiftung.

Australian Election Commission. 2005. *Funding and Disclosure Report Election 2004*. Canberra: Australian Election Commission, available at www.aec.gov.au/_content /How/political_disclosures/2004_report/index.htm.

Auty, C. and A. Cowen. 2001. "Political Parties on the Net: 4 Years Closer to Cyber Utopia." *Aslib Proceedings*, 53 (9), pp.341-352.

Auty, C. and D. Nicholas. 1998 "British Political Parties and their Web Pages." *Aslib Proceedings*, 50 (10), pp.283-296.

Baldez, L. and J. M. Carey. 1999. "Presidential Agenda Control and Spending Policy: Lessons from General Pinochet's Constitution." *American Journal of Political Science*, 43 (1), pp.29-55.

Banerjee, I. and B. Yeo. 2003. "Internet and Democracy in Singapore: A critical appraisal." In Banerjee, I. (ed.). *Rhetoric and Reality: the Internet challenge for democracy in Asia*. Singapore: Eastern Universities Press.

Barber, B. 2004. "Which technology and which democracy?" In Jenkins, H. and D. Thorburn (eds.), *Democracy and New Media*. Cambridge, MA: MIT Press. pp. 33-48..

Barber, B., K. Mattson and J. Peterson. 1997. *The State of Electronically Enhanced Democracy: A Survey of the Internet*. New Brunswick, NJ: Walt Whitman Center for Culture and Politics of Democracy.

Bartali, R. 2000. *La Nuova Comunicazione Politica: Il Partito Telematico. Una Ricerca Empirica Sui Partiti Italiani*. Working Paper, Università degli Studi di Siena.

Baskoro, S. E. 1998. "Peranan Internet dalam Reformasi Indonesia." *Info Komputer Online*, June, at http://www.infokomputer.com/100798-1.shtml, sighted 19 December.

BBVA (Fundación). 2005. *Estudio sobre Internet en España*. Octubre. http://w3.grupobbva.com/TLFB/dat/presentacioni_internet2.pdf. Benedanto, P. (ed.). 1999. *Pemilihan Umum 1999: Demokrasi atau Rebutan Kursi?* Jakarta: Lembaga Studi Pers dan Pembangunan.

Becker, T. L. and C. D. Slaton. 2000. *The Future of Teledemocracy*. Westport CT : Praeger.

Beckermann, A. 2005. "www.wahlkampfchance-verpasst.de: Noch ist die Wahl offen, doch eines ist schon sicher: Die Parteien haben die Möglichkeiten des Internets nicht genutzt,"*Welt am Sonntag*, 18 September, p. 9.

Beerfeltz, H.-J. and K.-H. Heuser. 2004. "Der Bürgerfond der FDP: Aufbruch zu einer neuen politischen Spendenkultur." In Kreyher, V. J. (ed.), *Handbuch Politisches Marketing: Impulse und Strategien für Politik, Wirtschaft und Gesellschaft*. Baden-Baden: Nomos, pp. 295-305.

Bennie, L. 2002. "Towards Moderate Pluralism: Scotland's Post Devolution Party System 1999-2002." *British Parties and Elections Review*, 13, pp.134-155.

Bentivegna, S. 1999. *La Politica in Rete*. Roma: Meltemi.

———. 2001. "La Prova Generale del 2001: Candidati ed Elettori Nel Mare di Internet." *Comunicazione Politica*, 2 (2).

———. 2006. *Campagne Elettorali in Rete*. Roma Bari: Laterza.

Berger, A. A. 1991. *Media Research Techniques*, Newbury Park, CA.: Sage.

Berke, R. L. 2003. "A New Movement Logs on to the Democracy Party and May Reshape It." *New York Times*, 28 December, p.A5.

Bernardini, M. 2000. www.cavalieremiconsenta. Milano: Gruppo Ugo Mrusia Editore: Mursia.

Bimber, B. 2001 "Information and Political Engagement in America: The Search for Effects of Information Technology at the Individual Level." *Political Research Quarterly*, 54 (March), pp.53-67

———. 1998. "The Internet and Political Transformation: Populism, Community and Accelerated Pluralism." *Polity*, 31 (1), pp.133-160.

Bimber, B. and R. Davis. 2003. *Campaigning Online: The Internet in US Elections*. New York: Oxford University Press.

Bishop, P. and L. Anderson. 2004. "E-government to E-democracy: High-tech 'solutions' to 'no-tech' problems?" Proceedings of the Australian Electronic Governance Conference 2004, 14-15 April, University of Melbourne. Chen, P. and W. Roberts (eds.), CD-ROM.

Blackburn, S. (ed.). 1999. *Pemilu: the 1999 Indonesian Election*. Clayton: Monash Asia Institute.

Blog Timeline.Sg. No date. Available online at blogtimelinesg.blogspot.com. Last Accessed 22 September, 2005.

Blumler, J., and M. Gurevitch. 2001. "Americanization' reconsidered: U.K.-U.S. campaign communication comparisons across time." In Bennett, W. L. and R. Entman (eds.), *Mediated Politics: Communication in the Future of Democracy*. Cambridge: Cambridge University Press.

Blumler, J. and D. Kavanagh. 1999. "The Third Age of Political Communication: Influences and Features." *Political Communication*, 16 (3), pp.209-230.

Boas, T. C. 2005. "Television and Neopopulism in Latin America: Media Effects in Brazil and Peru." *Latin American Research Review*, 40 (2), pp.27-49.

Boogers, M. and G. Voerman. 2003. "Surfing Citizens and Floating Voters: Results of an Online Survey of Visitors to Political Web Sites During the Dutch 2002 General Elections." *Information Polity*, 8 (1-2), pp.17-27.

———. 2004. "De betekenis van partijsites tijdens de campagne voor de Tweede-Kamerverkiezingen van 2002. Een onderzoeksverslag." In Voerman, G. (ed.), *Jaarboek 2002 Documentatiecentrum Nederlandse Politieke Partijen*. Groningen: University of Groningen, pp. 267-280.

Bowers-Brown, J. 2003. "A Marriage made in Cyberspace? Political Marketing and British Party Websites." In Gibson, R. K., P. G. Nixon and S. J. Ward (eds.), *Political Parties and the Internet: Net Gain?* London: Routledge, pp.98–119.

Bowman, J. 2006. "2006: Year of the Blog." *Policy Options*, 27 (3), pp.88-90.

Braam, G. 2003. "Surfen met Gerrit Zalm." *Politiek*, 4 (1), pp.26-29.

Brants K. and P. van Praag (eds.). 2005. *Politiek en media in verwarring: de verkiezingscampagnes in het lange jaar 2002*. Amsterdam: Het Spinhuis.

Budge, I. 1996. *The New Challenge of Direct Democracy*. Cambridge: Polity Press.

Burstein, D. and D. Kline. 1995. *Road Warriors: Dreams and Nightmares Along the Information Highway*. New York: Dutton.

Cappucci, M. and P. Cappucci. 1996. *Analisi Dei Siti Tematici Dei Partiti Politici Italiani Durante la Campagna Elettorale 1996*. Roma: Magnet–Pubblicazione Elettronica di Cultura della Contemporaneità.

Carlson, T. 2007. "It's a Man's World? Male and Female Election Campaigning on the Internet." *Journal of Political Marketing*, 6 (1), pp.41-67.

Carlson, T. and G. Djupsund. 2001. "Old Wine in New Bottles? The 1999 Finnish Election Campaign on the Internet." *Harvard International Journal of Press Politics*, 6 (4), pp.68-88.

Carney, T. F. 1972. *Content Analysis: A Technique for Systematic Inference from Communications*. Winnipeg: University of Manitoba Press.

Caron, A. H. 2005. "The Americas and Internet (North and South America): A Comparison." Presentation at the meeting of the World Internet Project, Santiago, Chile, 26-28 July. Available at http://www.wipchile.cl/wipbit/private/presentaciones/andre_caron_eng.ppt.

CastleAsia. 2002. "SMEs and E-Commerce." A Report prepared for The Asia Foundation, January, downloadable from http://www.asiafoundation.org/pdf/ID-SME-ecommerce-study-6-02.pdf, sighted 30 September 2002.

Censis. 2005a. *Rapporto Sulla Situazione Sociale del Paese 2004*. Milano: Franco Angeli.

———. 2005b. *I Media Che Vorrei. Quarto Rapporto Sulla Comunicazione in Italia*. Milano: Franco Angeli.

Cerf, V. 2005. "A Brief History of the Internet and Related Networks." The Internet Society. Available at http://www.isoc.org/internet/history/cerf.shtml. Accessed 19 August.

Chaples, E. A. 1994. "Developments in Australian Election Finance." In Alexander, H. E. and R. Shiratori (eds.), *Comparative Political Finance Among the Democracies*. Boulder, CO: Westview, pp.76-94.

Chase, S. and G. Galloway. 2004. "Broadbent video goes 'viral' as NDP launches new ad push." *The Globe and Mail*, 10 June.

Chen, P. 2001. "Political Big Brother Site Masks Curious Agenda." Australian.Internet.com, 10 October. Available at <http://eprints.unimelb.edu.au/ archive/00000313/01/PoliticalBigBrother.pdf> Accessed 26 June 2006. Original listing http://au.Internet.com/r/article/jsp/sid/11132.

———. 2002a. "Australian Elected Representatives Use of New Media Technologies 2002" Research Report. 17 June. Canberra, Australia: Australian Computer Society. Available at <http://eprints.unimelb.edu.au/archive/00000180/01/electedrepsonline.pdf.pdf>. Accessed 26 June 2006.

———. 2002b. "Virtual Representation: Australian Elected Representatives and the Impact of the Internet." *Journal of Information, Law and Technology*, 3 <http://elj.warwick.ac.uk/jilt/02-3/chen.html>.

————. 2005. "e-lection 2004? New Media and the Campaign?" Paper Presented at the Australian Federal Election 2004 Symposium, University House, Australian National University, January.

————. 2006. "The New Media: E-lection 2004?" In Simms, M. and J. Warhurst (eds.), *Mortgage Nation: The 2004 Australian Election.* Curtin, Australia: Bentley, API Network, pp.117-130.

Chorus, J. and M. de Galan. 2002. *In de ban van Fortuyn. Reconstructie van een politieke aardschok.* Amsterdam: Mets & Schilt.

Chua, H. H. and S. Luo. 2005. "Cyberspace may be next front in fight against racism." *Straits Times* (Singapore). 15 September, p.H4.

CIS. 2005a. *Representación y participación política en España.* ESTUDIO 2.588. Del 12 al 18 de enero de 2005. www.cis.es/cis/opencms/-Archivos/Marginales /2580_2599/e258800.html.

————. 2005b. *Globalización y relaciones internacionales.* ESTUDIO 2606: Del 21 al 29 de mayo de 2005. www.cis.es/File/ViewFile.aspx?FileId=2925.

————. 2007. *Barómetro Enero 2007.* ESTUDIO 2672. Del 22 al 31 de enero de 2007. www.cis.es/cis/opencms/-Archivos/Marginales/2660_2679/2672/e267200.html.

Clarkson, S. 2001. "The Liberal Threepeat: The Multi-System Party in the Multi-Party System." In Pammett J. and C. Dornan (eds.), *The Canadian General Election of 2000.* Toronto: Dundurn. pp. 13-57.

————. 2005. *The Big Red Machine.* Vancouver: University of British Columbia Press.

Clift, S. 2002. "E-Governance to E-Democracy: Progress in Australia and New Zealand toward Information-Age Democracy." Available at http://www.publicus.net /articles/aunzedem.html.

CNN.com. 2004. "Election Night Traffic Eclipses Site's Record." Time Warner press release. November 3. Available at http://www.timewarner.com/corp/newsroom/pr/ 0,20812,750712,00.html.

Coleman, S. 2001. "Online Campaigning." *Parliamentary Affairs,* 54 (3), pp.679-688.

Coleman, S. and N. Hall. 2001. "Spinning on the web." In Coleman, S. (ed.), *2001 Cyber Space Odyssey.* Hansard Society: London, pp.19-21.

Conway, M and D. Dornan. 2004. "An Evaluation of New Zealand Political Party Websites." *Information Research,* 9 (4). Available at http://informationr.net/ir/9-4/infres94.html.

Copsey, N. 2003. "Extremism on the net: the far right and the value of the Internet." In Gibson, R. K, P. G. Nixon and S. J. Ward (eds.), *Net Gain? Political Parties and the Internet.* London: Routledge, pp.218–233.

Cornfield, M. 2004a. *Politics Moves Online: Campaigning and the Internet.* New York: The Century Foundation Press.

————. 2004b. "The Internet and Campaign 2004: A Look Back at the Campaigners." Washington, D.C.: Pew Internet and American Life Project. Available at http://www.pewinternet.org/pdfs/Cornfield_commentary.pdf. Accessed 2 October, 2005.

Cornfield, M., L. Rainie and J. Horrigan. 2003. "Untuned Keyboards: Online campaigners, citizens, and portals in the 2002 elections." 20 March. Pew Internet and American Life Project. Available at http://www.pewInternet.org /pdfs/PIP_IPDI_Politics_ Report.pdf. Accessed 20 June 2006.

Corrado, A. and C. Firestone. 1996. *Elections in Cyberspace: Toward a New Era in American Politics.* Washington D.C.: Aspen Institute.

Crabtree, J. 2001. *Whatever happened to the e-lection?* London: Industrial Society.

Crewe, I. and D. Denver. 1985. "Great Britain." In Crewe, I. and D. Denver (eds.), *Electoral Change in Western Democracies*. London: Croom Helm.

Crewe, I. and K. Thomson. 1999. "Party Loyalties: Dealignment or Realignment?" In Norris, P. and G. Evans (eds.), *Critical Elections*. London: Sage.

Cross, W. 2004. *Political Parties*. Vancouver: University of British Columbia Press.

Cunha, C., I. Martin, J. Newell, and L. Ramiro. 2003. "Southern European Parties and Party Systems and New ICTs." In Gibson, R. K., P. G. Nixon and S. J. Ward (eds.), *Political Parties and the Internet: Net Gain?* London: Routledge, pp.70-97.

Curtin, J. 2001-2002. "A Digital Divide in Rural Regional Australia?" Parliamentary Library Current Issues Brief, 1, 2001-2002 (7 August 2001). Canberra, Australia. Available at http://www.aph.gov.au/library/pubs/cib/2001-2/02cib01.htm>. Accessed 22 June 2006.

Dader, J-L. 2003. "Ciberdemocracia y comunicación política virtual: El futuro de la ciudadanía electrónica tras la era de la television." In Berrocal, S. (ed.), *Comunicación política en televisión y nuevos medios*. Barcelona: Ariel.

Dader, J-L and E. Campos. 2006. "Internet parlamentario en España (1999-2005): Los recursos para el contacto ciudadano y su uso, con una comparación europea." *ZER, Revista de Estudios de Comunicación*, Bilbao, Universidad del País Vasco, n° 18, mayo.

Dader, J-L. and I. Díaz. 2007. "Las webs de partidos españoles 2004-05: Una investigación preliminar y de comparación europea, con una propuesta metodológica." *II Congreso de Comunicación Política*. Facultad de Ciencias de la Información, Universidad Complutense, Madrid, 8-9 March, http://www.ucm.es/info/compolit/articuloscongresoincopo/dader.pdf

D'Alessio, D. 1997. "Use of the World Wide Web in the 1996 U.S. Election." *Electoral Studies*, 16, pp. 489-500.

Dalton, R. J., I. McAllister and M. P. Wattenberg. 2002. "Political Parties and their Publics." In Luther, K. R. and F. Muller-Rommel (eds.), *Political Parties in the New Europe: Political and Analytical Changes*. Oxford: Oxford University Press, pp.19-42.

Dalton, R. and M. Wattenberg. 2000. "Partisan Change and the Democratic Process." In Dalton, R. and M. Wattenberg (eds.), *Parties Without Partisans*. Oxford: Oxford University Press, pp.261-285.

Davis, R. 1999. *The Web of Politics: The Internet's Impact on the American Political System*. New York: Oxford University Press.

———. 2001. "Internet Nelle Elezioni Presidenziali Americane Del 2000." *Comunicazione Politica*, 2 (2).

———. 2004. "Mobilizing Voters Online." Paper presented at the annual meeting of the American Political Science Association. Chicago, IL. September 2-5.

———. 2005. *Politics Online: Blogs, Chatrooms, and Discussion Groups in American Democracy*. New York: Routledge.

Davis, R. and D. Owen. 1998. *New Media and American Politics*. Oxford: Oxford University Press.

De Graaf, J., P. Lucardie and P. Schuszler. 2003. "Zin en onzin over de StemWijzer 2002: een reactie." *Beleid en maatschappij: tijdschrift voor beleid, politiek en maatschappij*, 30 (3), pp.194-200.

Della Porta, D. 2001. *I Partiti Politici*. Bologna: Il Mulino.

De Landtsheer, C., Krasnoboka, N., and C. Neuner. 2000. "La facilidad de utilización de los 'websites' de partidos políticos. Estudio de algunos países de Europa del Este y

Occidental (1999)." *Cuadernos de Información y Comunicación-CIC*, 6, Madrid. Universidad Complutense, pp.107-140

Demunter, C. 2005. *The digital divide in Europe*. Brussels: Eurostat.

Denver, D and G. Hands. 2002. "Postfordism in the Constituencies? The Continuing Development of Constituency Campaigning in Britain." In Farrell, D. and R. Schmitt-Beck (eds.), *Do Campaigns Matter?* London: Routledge, pp.108-126.

Denver, D., G. Hands and I. MacAllister. 2004. "The Electoral Impact of Constituency Campaigning in Britain 1992-2001." *Political Studies*, 52 (2), pp.289-306.

Deschouwer, K. 2004. "Political Parties and Their Reactions to the Erosion of Voter Loyalty in Belgium." In Mair, P., W. Muller and F. Plasser (eds.), *Political Parties and Electoral Change*. London: Sage, pp.179-206.

Dickert, S. 2005. Chief Technology Officer, Kerry for President. Telephone Interview. 26 July.

Donahue, H. C., S. Schneider, and K. Foot. 2000. "While TV Blundered on Election, the Internet Gained Users." *Nieman Reports* (Winter), pp.21-22.

Donny B. U. 2003. "Rakyat, awasi pembangunan TI Pemilu 2004." http://free.vlsm.org/v17/com/ictwatch/paper/paper050.htm, sighted 13 March 2006, published originally in *Bisnis Komputer*, November 2003.

Dorling, D., H. Eyre, R. Johnston and C. Pattie. 2002. "A Good Place to Bury Bad News? Hiding the Detail in the Geography on the Labour Party's Website." *Political Quarterly*, 73 (4), pp. 476–492.

Dulio, D. A. and E. O'Brien. 2004. "Campaigning with the Internet: The View from Below." In Thurber, J. A. and C. J. Nelson (eds.), *Campaigns and Elections American Style*. Boulder, CO: Westview Press, pp.173-184.

Dunleavy, P. 2005. "Facing up to Multi Party Politics: How Partisan Dealignment and PR Voting have Fundamentally Changed Britain's Party Systems." *Parliamentary Affairs*, 58 (2), pp.503-532.

Dunleavy, P., H. Margetts, S. Bastow, and J. Tinkler. 2003. "E-Government and Policy Innovation in Seven Liberal Democracies." Paper presented at the annual conference of the UK Political Studies Association, Leicester, 15-17 April.

Drezmer, D. and H. Farrell. 2004. "Web of Influence." *Foreign Policy*, 145, Nov/Dec, pp.32-41.

Edwards, D. 2005. *The Use of Internet Communication Technologies by Global Social Movements in Australia*. Unpublished PhD Thesis, Canberra: Australian National University.

EGM/AIMC. 2005a. *Audiencia de Internet.* 2ª Ola 2005, abril-mayo. www.aimc.es/aimc.php.

———. 2005b. *Audiencia de Internet.* 3ª Ola 2005, octubre-noviembre.

———. 2006. *Audiencia de Internet.* 3ª Ola 2006, octubre-noviembre

Electoral Commission. 2002. *Voter Engagement and Young People*. London: Electoral Commission.

———. 2003. *Online Election Campaigns*. London: Electoral Commission

Emmer, M., M. Seifert and G. Vowe. 2006. "Internet und politische Kommunikation: Die Mobilisierungsthese auf dem Prüfstand—Ergebnisse einer repräsentativen Panelstudie in Deutschland." In Filzmaier, P., M. Karmasin and C. Klepp (eds.), *Politik und Medien: Medien und Politik*. Wien: WUV, pp. 170-187.

Endres, D. and B. Warnick. 2004. "Text-based Interactivity in Candidate Campaign Websites: A Case Study from the 2002 Elections." *Western Journal of Communication*, 68 (Summer), pp.322-342.

Eurostat. 2006, "Nearly Half of Individuals in the EU25 Used the Internet at Least Once a Week in 2006." Press release, retrieved from http://epp.eurostat.ec.europa.eu, 20 November.

Farnsworth, S. J. and Diana Owen. 2004. "Internet Use and the 2000 Presidential Election." *Electoral Studies*, 23 (September), pp. 415-429.

Farrell, D., and I. McAllister. 2005. *The Australian Electoral System: Origins, Variations and Consequences*. Sydney: University of NSW Press.

Farrell, D., and P. Webb. 2000. "Political Parties as Campaign Organizations." In Dalton, R. and M. Wattenberg (eds.), *Parties Without Partisans*. Oxford: Oxford University Press, pp.102-128.

Feith, H. 1957. *Indonesian Elections of 1955*. Ithaca, NY: Cornell University Modern Indonesia Project.

———. 1962. *The Decline of Constitutional Democracy*. Ithaca, NY: Cornell University Press.

Fernández, F. J. and S. Goldenberg. 2004. "WIP Chile: Scanning the Reality of the Internet in Chile." Paper presented at the meeting of the World Internet Project, Tokyo, Japan, 13-15 July. Available at http://www.wipchile.cl/estudios/japan/WIP_article_2_RU_for_Japan_jul04.pdf.

Films Act (Chapter 107). Singapore Statutes Online: http://statutes.agc.gov.sg/non_version/html/homepage.html. Last accessed 22 September 2005.

Firmansyah, Notosusanto, S. and Y Sipahutar (eds.). 2004. *Radio dan Pemilu 2004*. Jakarta: Friedrich-Naumann-Stiftung.

Fisher, J. 2005. "Campaign Finance." In Geddes, A. and J. Tonge (eds.), *Britain Decides: The UK General Election 2005*. Basingstoke: Palgrave, pp.170-186.

Fisher, J., D. Denver, E. Fieldhouse, D. Cutts and A. Russell. 2005. "Constituency Campaigning in the 2005 British General Election." Paper presented to the Annual Conference of the PSA specialist group on Elections, Opinion Polls and Parties, University of Essex, September, 2005.

Flew, T. and G. Young. 2004. "If they come they will build it: Managing and Building e-Democracy from the Ground Up." Proceedings of the Australian Electronic Governance Conference 2004, 14-15 April, University of Melbourne, Chen, P. and W. Roberts (eds.), CD-ROM.

Foot, K. A., S. M. Schneider, M. Dougherty, M. Xenos, and E. Larsen. 2003. "Analyzing Linking Practices: Candidate Sites in the 2002 US Electoral Web Sphere." *Journal of Computer-Mediated Communication*, 8 (July), at http://jcmc.indiana.edu/vol8/issue4/foot.html.

Foot, K. A. and S. M. Schneider. 2002. "Online Action in Campaign 2000: An Exploratory Analysis of the US Political Web Sphere." *Journal of Broadcasting and Electronic Media*, 46 (2), pp.222-244.

Foot, K. and M. Xenos. 2005. "Politics as Usual, or Politics Unusual? Position Taking and Dialogue on Campaign Websites in the 2002 U.S. Elections." *Journal of Communication*, 55(1), pp.169-185.

Friedenberg, R. V. 1997. *Communication Consultants in Political Campaigns : Ballot Box Warriors*. Westport, CT: Praeger.

Friedman, T. 1999. "Foreign affairs: Are you ready?" *New York Times*, 1 June.

Frye, N. 1982. *"Sharing the Continent."* Divisions on a Ground: Essays on Canadian Culture. Toronto: Anansi Press.

Fuentes, C. 2004. *El Costo de la Democracia*. Santiago, Chile: FLACSO.

Fuenzalida, V. 2002. "The Reform of National Television in Chile." In Fox, E. and S. Waisbord (eds.), *Latin Politics, Global Media.* Austin: University of Texas Press, pp.69-88.

Geese, S., C. Zubayr and H. Gerhard. (2005) "Berichterstattung zur Bundestagswahl 2005 aus Sicht der Zuschauer: Ergebnisse einer Repräsentativbefragung und der GfK-Fernsehforschung." *Media Perspektiven*, No. 12, pp. 613-626.

George, C. 2005. *Calibrated coercion and the maintenance of hegemony in Singapore.* Asia Research Institute Working Paper Series, # 48. Available online at http://www.ari.nus.edu.sg/docs/wps/wps05_048.pdf. Last accessed 22 September 2005.

Gibson, R. K., Newell, J. L. and S. J. Ward. 2000. "New Parties, New Media: Italian Parties and the WWW." *Southern European Society and Politics*, 5 (1), pp.123-142.

Gibson, R. K., I. McAllister and T. Swenson. 2002. "The Politics of Race and Immigration in Australia: One Nation Voting in the 1998 Election." *Ethnic and Racial Studies* 25, pp.823-844.

Gibson, R. K., M. Margolis, D. Resnick and S. J. Ward. 2003a. "Election Campaigning on the WWW in the US and UK: a comparative analysis." *Party Politics*, 9 (1), pp.47–76.

Gibson, R. K., A. Rommele, and S. J. Ward. 2003b. "German Parties and Internet Campaigning in the 2002 Federal Election." *German Politics,* 12 (2), pp.79-108.

Gibson, R. K., D. Gow, C. Bean and I. McAllister. 2005a. *Australian Candidate Study, 2004* [computer file]. Canberra: Australian Social Science Data Archive, The Australian National University.

Gibson, R. K., W. Lusoli and S. J. Ward. 2005b. "Online Participation in the UK: Testing a Contextualised Model of Internet Effects." *British Journal of Politics and International Relations*, 7 (4), pp.561-583.

Gibson, R. K. and A. Römmele. 2001. "Changing Campaign Communications. A Party-Centered Theory of Professionalized Campaigning." *Harvard International Journal of Press/Politics*, 6(4), pp.31-43.

Gibson, R. K. and I. McAllister. 2006. "Does Cybercampaigning Win Votes? Online Political Communication in the 2004 Australian Election." *Journal of Elections, Public Opinion and Parties*, 16 (3), pp.243-263.

Gibson, R. K. and S. J. Ward. 1998. "UK Political Parties and the Internet: Politics as Usual in the New Media." *Harvard International Journal of Press Politics*, 3 (3), pp.14-38.

———. 2000a. "New Media, Same Impact? British Party Activity in Cyberspace." In Gibson, R. K. and S. J. Ward (eds.), *Reinvigorating Government? British Politics and the Internet.* Aldershot: Ashgate, pp.106-129.

———. 2000b. "An Outsider's Medium? The EU Elections and UK Party Competition on the Internet." In Cowley, P. (ed.), *British Parties and Elections Review Vol.10.* London: Frank Cass, pp.173-191.

———. 2000c. "A Proposed Methodology for Studying the Function and Effectiveness of Party and Candidate Websites." *Social Science Computer Review*, 18 (3), pp.301-319.

———. 2002. "Virtual Campaigning: Australian Parties and the Impact of the Internet." *Australian Journal of Political Science*, 37 (1), pp. 99-130.

———. 2003. "Letting the Daylight in? Australian State Parties and the WWW." In Gibson, R. K., P. G. Nixon and S. J. Ward (eds.), *Net Gain? Political Parties and the Internet*, London: Routledge, pp.139-161.

Goot, M. 1985. "Electoral Systems." In Aitkin, D. (ed.), *Surveys of Australian Political Science*. Sydney: Allen and Unwin.

Gomez, J. 2002. *Internet Politics: Surveillance and Intimidation in Singapore*. Singapore: Think Centre.

———. 2005. "Free Speech and opposition parties in Singapore." Available online at http://www.jamesgomeznews.com/articles/Free_Speech-Oppn_Parties_In_Spore_29 0705.pdf. Last accessed 12 September 2005.

Government Children and Young People's Unit. 2002. *Young People and Politics: A Report Yvote? Ynot?* London: DfES.

Grass, G. 2003. *Crabwalk*. New York: Harcourt.

Greer, J. D. and M. E. LaPointe. 2004. "Cyber-Campaigning Grows Up: A Comparative Content Analysis of Websites for US Senate and Gubernatorial Races, 1998-2000." In R. K. Gibson, A. Römmele and S. J. Ward (eds.), *Electronic Democracy: Mobilisation, Organisation and Participation via new ICTs*. London: Routledge, pp. 116-132.

Grossman, L. 1995. *The Electronic Republic: Reshaping Democracy in the Information Age*. New York: Penguin, 1995.

Guha, A. 2004. "Of Websites and Windmills." cbc.ca http://www.cbc.ca/canadavotes/thecampaign/aguha210604.html, 30 May.

Gulati, G. J. 2003. "Campaigning for Congress on the World Wide Web and the Implications for Strong Democracy." Paper presented at the annual meeting of the American Political Science Association, Philadelphia, PA, 28 31 August

Hallin, D. and P. Mancini. 2004. *Comparing Media Systems. Three Models of Media and Politics*. New York: Cambridge University Press.

Hannemann, U. and F. Lehmkuhl. 2005. "Sag mir, wo du stehst: Bunt, banal und bisweilen auch polemisch kämpfen die Parteien im Web um Stimmen: Jungwähler suchen fundierte Informationen." *Focus*, 29 August, p. 88.

Hastuti, E. F. 2001. "I don't like people being dishonest." (Interview with Alvin Lie) *The Jakarta Post*, 4 February 2001, at http://www.library.ohiou.edu/indopubs/2001/02/03/0032.html, sighted on 29 September 2003.

Hauben, M. and R. Hauben. 1997. *Netizens*. Los Alamitos, CA: IEEE Computer Society Press.

Hill, D. T. 1996. *The Press in New Order Indonesia*. Perth: University of Western Australia Press.

Hill, D. T. and Sen, K. 2005. *The Internet in Indonesia's New Democracy*. London and New York: Routledge.

Hill, J. and K. Hughes. 1998. *Cyberpolitics: Citizen Activism in the Age of the Internet*. Lanham, MD: Rowman & Littlefield.

Hillwatch e-services. 2006. "Still virtually lawn signs." January, p.3.

Holsti, Ole R. 1969. *Content Analysis for the Social Sciences and Humanities*. Reading, MA: Addison-Wesley.

Holtz-Bacha, C. 2004a. "Germany: The 'German Model' and Its Intricacies." In Roper, J., C. Holtz-Bacha and G. Mazzoleni (eds.), *The Politics of Representation: Election Campaigning and Proportional Representation*. New York: Peter Lang, pp. 9-27.

———. 2004b. "Germany: From Modern to Postmodern Campaign." In Roper, J., C. Holtz-Bacha and G. Mazzoleni (eds), *The Politics of Representation: Election Campaigning and Proportional Representation*, New York: Peter Lang, pp. 77-97.

———. 2005. "To the Advantage of the Big Parties but They Seem to Lose Interest—TV Advertising During the 2002 German National Election Campaign." *Journal of Political Marketing*, 4 (4), pp. 75-84.

————. 2006. "Political Advertising in Germany." In Kaid, L. L. and C. Holtz-Bacha (eds.), *The Sage Handbook of Political Advertising*. Sage, CA: Thousand Oaks, pp. 163-180.

Hooghe, M., B. Maddens and J. Noppe. 2006. "Why Parties Adapt. Electoral Reform, Party Finance and Party Strategy in Belgium." *Electoral Studies*, 25(2), pp.351-368.

Hooghe, M. and P. Stouthuysen. 2001. "Het politiek gebruik van Internet naar aanleiding van de gemeenteraadsverkiezingen van 8 oktober 2000." *Res Publica*, 43 (4), pp.507-528.

Hooghe, M. and W. Teepe. 2005. "Party Profiles on the Web: An Analysis of the Log Files of Nonpartisan Interactive Political Internet Sites in the 2003 and 2004 Election Campaigns in Belgium." Paper presented at the annual meeting of the American Political Science Association, Washington, D.C.

Howland, L. and M. Bethell. 2002. *Logged Off? How ICT can Connect Young People and Politics*. London: Demos.

"How Many Online." 2005. NUA Survey. Available at http://www.nua.ie/surveys/how_many_online/index.html. Accessed 18 August.

Hull, C. 2004. "e-Organization: The Role of Online Organization in the 2004 Iowa Caucus." Paper presented at the annual meeting of the Midwest Political Science Association, Chicago, IL, 15 April.

INE (Instituto Nacional de Estadística). 2005. *Encuesta sobre Equipamiento y uso de tecnologías de la información y comunicación en hogares*. Octubre. http://www.ine.es/inebase/cgi/um?M=percent2Ft25percent2Fp450&O=inebase&N= &L=0.

IFES (International Foundation for Election Systems). 1999. "Public Opinion in Indonesia Following the June 1999 Elections." Unpublished preliminary report, Washington: International Foundation for Election Systems.

————. 2005. *Public Opinion Survey Indonesia 2005*. Jakarta: International Foundation for Election Systems.

Information Society Statistics. 2003. *Pocketbook 2003*. Brussels: Eurostat.

ISPA. 2005. *Statistics on Internet Access in Belgium*. Brussels: Internet Service Providers Association.

ITANES. 2001. *Perché Ha Vinto Iil Centro-destra*. Bologna: Il Mulino.

ITU (International Telecommunication Union). 2002. http://www.itu.int/ITU-D/ict/ statistics/at_glance/Internet02.pdf, sighted 6 August 2003.

Jackman, C. 2004. "Websites putting angst in their pants." *The Australian*, 7 September, p.6

Jackson, J. 2001. "View from the parties: the Conservatives." In Coleman, S. (ed.), *2001: Cyber Space Odyssey*. London: Hansard Society.

————. 2001. "E-campaigning: Active and Interactive." In Painter, A. and B. Wardle (eds.), *Viral Politics: Communication in the new media era*. London: Politicos, pp.142-153.

Jackson, N. 2004. "Party E-Newsletters in the UK: A Return to Direct Political Communication?" *Journal of E-Government*, 1 (4), pp.39-62.

Jacob, P. 2005. "Singaporeans did it with a mouse." *Straits Times* (Singapore), 23 July.

Jamieson, K Hall (ed). 2006. *Electing the President 2004: The Insiders' View*. Philadelphia: University of Pennsylvania Press.

"Jayce." 2005. Blog: Dreamer in an Unreal world. Blog entry: We have an effective government. Available online at http://jyaisu.blogspot.com/2005/09/we-have-effective-government.html. 6 September. Last accessed 9 September 2005.

Jennings, M. K. and V. Zeitner. 2003. "Internet use and Civic Engagement: A Longitudinal Analysis." *Public Opinion Quarterly*, 67 (Fall), pp.311-334.

Johnson, T. J. and B. K. Kaye. 2003. "A Boost or Bust for Democracy? How the Web Influenced Political Attitudes and Behaviors in the 1996 and 2000 Presidential Elections." *Harvard International Journal of Press/Politics*, 8 (Summer), pp.9-34.

Johnson, W. 2005. *Stephen Harper and the Future of Canada.* Toronto: McClelland and Stewart.

Joosten, C. 2003. "Een klein mirakel." *Elsevier*, 30 August, pp.16-17.

Kaid, L. L. and A. Johnston. 2001. *Videostyle in Presidential Campaigns: Style and Content of Televised Political Advertising.* Westport, CT: Praeger.

Kaiser, R. 1999. "Online-Informationsangebote der Politik: Parteien und Verbände im World Wide Web." In Kamps, K. (ed.), *Elektronische Demokratie.* Opladen: Westdeutscher Verlag, pp. 175-190.

Kamarck, E. C. 1999. "Campaigning on the Internet in the Elections of 1998." In Kamarck, E. C. and J. S. Nye, Jr. (eds.), *Democracy.com?Governance in a Networked World.* Hollis, N.H.: Hollis Publishing, pp.99-123.

———. 2002. "Political Campaigning on the Internet: Business as Usual?" In .Kamarck, E. C. and J. S. Nye, Jr. (eds.), *Governance.com: Democracy in the Information Age.* Washington, DC: Brookings Institution Press, pp. 81-103.

Katz, R. 2001. "Reforming the Italian Electoral Law 1993." In Shugart, M. S. and M. P. Wattenberg (eds.), *Mixed-Member Electoral Systems: The Best of Both Worlds?* New York: Oxford University Press, pp.96-122.

Kavanagh, D. 1995. *Election Campaigning: The New Marketing of Politics.* Oxford: Blackwell.

Kerbel, M. R. 2005. "The Media: The Challenge and Promise of Internet Politics." In Nelson, M. (ed.), *The Election of 2004.* Washington, D.C.: Congressional Quarterly Press.

Kerbel, M. R. and J. D. Bloom. 2005. "'Blog for America' and Civic Involvement." Paper presented at the annual meeting of the Midwest Political Science Association, Chicago, IL. 1 April.

King, D. Y. 2000. "The 1999 Electoral Reforms in Indonesia: Debate, Design and Implementation." *Southeast Asian Journal of Social Science*, 28 (2), pp.89-110.

———. 2002. "Catching Voters in the Web." In Kamarck, E. C. and J. S. Nye. (eds.), *Governance.com: Democracy in the Information Age.* Washington D.C.: Bookings Institution Press, pp.104-116.

Kippen, G. and G. Jenkins. 2004. "The Challenge of E-Democracy for Political Parties." In Shane, P. M. (ed.), *Democracy Online. The Prospect for Political Renewal Through the Internet.* London: Routledge, pp.253-266.

Klaver, M. J. 2002. "Verwerking op het web." *NRC Handelsblad*, 11 May.

Kleinnijenhuis, J., D. Oegema, J. de Ridder, A., van Hoof and Rens Vliegenthart. 2003. *De puinhopen in het nieuws. De rol van de media bij de Tweede-Kamerverkiezingen van 2002.* Alphen aan den Rijn—Mechelen.

Kluver, R. 2004. "Political Culture and Information Technology in the 2001 Singapore General Election." *Political Communication*, 21, pp.435-458.

———. 2005. "Political culture in online politics." In Consalvo, M. and M. Allen (eds.), *Internet Research Annual, volume 2.* Newbury Park, CA: Sage Publications, pp.75-84.

Kluver, R. and Ang P. H. 2004. "Media Law and Information Technology in Singapore." *Journal of Media Law, Ethics, and Policy*, 3 (2), pp.15-26.

Kluver, R, and I. Banerjee. 2005. "Political Culture, Regulation, and Democratization: The Internet in Nine Asian Nations." *Information, Communication, and Society*, 8 (1), pp.1-17.

Kompas. 1999. "Terjamin, Pengamanan Data pada Sistem Jaringan Komputer Pemilu." 21 June, p.29.

———. 2004. "Penghitungan Peroleh Suara Pemilu Legislatif Terus Dikritik," from www.kompas.co.id/kompas-cetak/0404/10/utama/961137.htm, but cached at http://groups.or.id/pipermail/genetika/2004-April/001924.html, sighted 13 March 2006.

KPU. (Komisi Pemilihan Umum). 1999. "Laporan: Tim Verifikasi System Komputer KPU (Tim 4)." Unpublished report, 25 July, Jakarta: KPU.

———. 2004. "TNP Pemilu Presiden dan Wakil President buka sampai 15 Juli." http://www.kpu.go.id/pemilu_president/pemilupresident_list8.php, sighted 13 March 2006.

Krippendorff, K. 1980. *Content Analysis: An Introduction to its Methodology.* Beverly Hills, CA: Sage.

Krueger, B. 2002. "Assessing the Potential of Internet Political Participation in the United States: A Resource Approach." *American Politics Research*, 30 (5), pp.476-498.

Kuo, E., A. Choi, A. Mahizhnan, W. P. Lee and C. Soh. 2002. *Internet in Singapore: a study on usage and impact.* Singapore: Times Academic Press.

Kuo, E., D. Holaday, and E. Peck. 1993. *Mirror on the Wall: media in a Singapore election.* Singapore: Asian Mass Communication Research and Information Centre.

Lamatsch, D. and A. Bilgeri. 2001. "Online-Fundraising—Der Weg zu neuen Spende(r)n." In Joos, K., A. Bilgeri and D. Lamatsch (eds.), *Mit Mouse und Tastatur: Wie das Internet die Politik verändert.* München: Olzog, pp. 230-243.

Lazarsfeld, P., B. Berelson and H. Gaudet. 1955. *The people's choice; how the voter makes up his mind in a presidential campaign.* Columbia: Columbia University Press.

Lee, B. 2005. "'What's sedition?' debate goes online." *Today Singapore.* 14 September, p.26.

Lee, T. 2005. "Internet control and auto-regulation in Singapore." *Surveillance and Society*, 3 (1), 74-95. Available online at http://www.surveillance-and-society.org/Articles3(1)/singapore.pdf. Last accessed 23 September 2005.

Lim, L. 2003. "The Internet: the new political ward?" *Straits Times* (Singapore), 29 November.

Linz, J. 1999. *The Party Systems of Spain: Old Cleavages and New Challenges.* Madrid: Juan March.

Lloyd, R. and A. Bill. 2004. *Australia Online: How Australians are using Computers and the Internet 2001.* Canberra: Australian Bureau of Statistics.

Lofgren, K. and C. Smith. 2003. "Political Parties and Democracy in the Information Age." In Gibson, R. K., P. G. Nixon and S. J. Ward (eds.), *Political Parties and the Internet: Net Gain?* London: Routledge, pp.39-52.

Lopez, M. H., E. Kirby, and J. Sagoff. 2005. "The Youth Vote 2004." College Park, MD: Center for Information and Research on Civic Learning and Engagement, July.

Loveday, P. 1977. "The Federal Parties." In Loveday, P., A. W. Martin and R. S. Parker. (eds.), *The Emergence of the Australian Party System.* Sydney: Hale and Iremonger, pp. 383-452.

Low, A. 2005. "Online or off, if it fans hatred, Govt will act." *Straits Times* (Singapore), 18 September, p.1.

Low, P. No date. Penny Low—My NDP. Blog. Available online: http://www.moblog.com.sg/blogger/home.asp?uid=FBBC06CB-D8AA-42D9-B2EB -5D8D8B9C30BA. Last accessed 22 September, 2005.

Lupia, A. and T. S. Philpot. 2002. "More Than Kids Stuff: Can News and Information Websites Mobilize Young Adults?" Paper presented at the annual meeting of the American Political Science Association, Boston, MA, 29 August - 1 September.

Lusoli, W. 2005. "A Second-Order Medium? The Internet as a Source of Electoral Information in 25 European Countries." *Information Polity*, 10, pp.247-265.

Lusoli, W. and S. J. Ward. 2004. "Digital rank and file: activists perceptions and use of the Internet." *British Journal of Politics and International Relations*, 6 (4), pp.453–470.

———. 2005. "Logging on or Switching Off? The Public and the Internet in the 2005 General Election." In Coleman, S. and S. J. Ward (eds.), *Spinning the Web*. London: Hansard Society, pp.13-21.

Lusoli, W., S. J. Ward and R. K. Gibson. 2006. "Reconnecting Politics? Parliament, the Public and the Internet." *Parliamentary Affairs*, 59 (1), pp.24-42.

Mack, A. M. 2004. "How the Internet is Changing Politics." *Adweek*, 26 January.

Mackerras, M. and I. McAllister. 1999. "Compulsory Voting, Party Stability and Electoral Advantage in Australia." *Electoral Studies*, 1, pp.217-233.

Magarey, K. 1999. "The Internet and Australian Parliamentary Democracy." *Parliamentary Affairs*, 52 (3), pp.404-428.

Mair, P. and I. van Biezen. 2001. "Party Membership in Europe." *Party Politics*, 7 (5), pp.5-21.

March, L. 2005. "Virtual Parties in a Virtual World: Russian Parties and the Political Internet." In Oates, S., D. Owen and R. K. Gibson (eds.), *The Internet and Politics: Citizens, Activists and Voters*. London: Routledge.

Margolis, M., D. Resnick and J. Wolfe. 1999. "Party Competition on the Internet: Minor Versus Major Parties in the UK and the USA." *Harvard International Journal of Press Politics*, 4 (4), pp.24-47.

Margolis, M., and D. Resnick. 2000. *Politics as Usual: The Cyberspace Revolution*. Thousand Oaks, CA: Sage.

Martínez Cuadrado, M. 1996. *La democracia en la España de los años noventa*. Barcelona. Ariel.

Marzolini, M. 2004. "Public Opinion Polling and the 2004 Election." In Pammett, J. and C. Dornan (eds.), *The Canadian General Election of 2004*. Toronto: Dundurn.

McAllister, I. 2002. "Calculating or Capricious? The New Politics of Late Deciding Voters." In Farrell, D. and R. Schmitt-Beck (eds.), *Do Political Campaigns Matter? Campaign Effects in Elections and Referendums*. London: Routledge, pp.22-40

McBeth, J., D. Murphy and M. Cohen. 1999. "Free at last." *Far Eastern Economic Review*, 17 June. Reprinted in Indonesian General Election Commission. 2001. *Analyzing Indonesian Election 1999* [sic]. Jakarta: KPU, pp.161-169.

McCarthy, T. 1999. "Count 'em all." *Asiaweek*, 14 June, reprinted in Indonesian General Election Commission. 2001. *Analyzing Indonesian Election 1999* [sic]. Jakarta: KPU, pp.155-160.

McCormick, R. P. 1966. *The Second American Party System*. New York: Norton.

McMullin, R. 1995. *The Light on the Hill: the Australian Labor Party, 1891-1991*. Melbourne: Oxford University Press.

Media Development Authority, Government of Singapore. No Date. *Registration of Internet Class Licensees.* Available online: http://www.mda.gov.sg/wms.www/ devnpolicies.aspx?sid=161#5. Last accessed 23 September 2005.

Media Development Authority, Government of Singapore. No Date. *Newspaper permit.* Available online at http://www.mda.gov.sg/wms.www/devnpolicies.aspx?sid=223. Last accessed 23 September 2005.

Medvic, S. 2001. *Political Consultants in U.S. Congressional Elections.* Columbus, OH: Ohio State University Press.

Menefee-Libey, D. 2000. *The Triumph of Campaign-Centered Politics.* New York: Chatham House.

Merz, M. 2006a. "Nutzer von Politikerhomepages: Die im Onlinewahlkampf praktisch erreichbare Bevölkerungsgruppe." In Merz, M., S. Rhein and J. Vetter (eds.), *Wahlkampf im Internet: Handbuch für die politische Online-Kampagne.* Münster: Lit Verlag, pp. 25-32.

———. 2006b. "Zielgruppen des Online-Wahlkampfes: Helfer, Spender, Meinungsführer und andere Zielgruppen im Detail." In Merz, M., S. Rhein and J. Vetter (eds.), *Wahlkampf im Internet: Handbuch für die politische Online-Kampagne.* Münster: Lit Verlag, pp. 33-42.

Meyer, T. and L. Hinchman. 2002. *Media Democracy: how the media colonize politics.* Cambridge: Polity Press.

Miskin, S. 2005. "Campaigning in the 2004 Federal Election: innovations and traditions." Research Note no.30 2004-2005. Politics and Public Administration Section, Parliamentary Library of Australia. Available at <http:www.aph.gov.au /library/pubs/m2004-05/05rn30.htm>. Accessed 25 April 2006.

Miskin, S. and R. Grant. 2004. "Political Advertising in Australia." Parliamentary library Research Brief 5, 2004-2005. Canberra, Australia. Available at http://parlinfoweb .aph.gov.au/piweb/view_document.aspx?id=2487&table=PRSPUB.

Morris, D. 2000. *Vote.com.* Los Angeles: Renaissance.

Mosco, V. 2004. *The Digital Sublime: Myth, Power and Cyberspace.* Cambridge, MA: The MIT Press.

"Mr Wang says so." Blog: But why did Mr. Wang say so? Entry: political website? 5 July 2005. Available online at http://commentarysingapore.blogspot.com/2005/07/ political-website.html. Last accessed 23 September 2005.

Mutz, D. C. and P. S. Martin. 2001. "Facilitating Communication Across Lines of Political Difference: The Role of Mass Media." *American Political Science Review,* 95(1) pp.97-114.

Nadarajan, B. 2003. "Is it over for Steve Chia?" *Straits Times* (Singapore), 21 December.

National Democratic Institute for International Affairs (NDI). 1999. *Prospects for Democratic Elections in Indonesia: Pre Election Report,* Jakarta: NDI.

———. 2004. *Advancing Democracy in Indonesia: The Second Democratic Legislative Elections since the Transition.* Jakarta: National Democratic Institute for International Affairs, June. Available at <www.accessdemodracy.org/library/ 1728_id_legeletions_063004.pdf >. Accessed 8 March 2006.

Negrine, R. 1996. *The Communication of Politics.* London: Sage.

Newell, J. L. 2001. "New Parties, New Media: Italian Political Parties and the Web." *Harvard International Journal of Press Politics,* 6 (4), pp.60-87.

Nielsen/Netratings. 2005. "Los internautas desde el hogar crecen un 9.3 percent en enero." 10-Marzo. http://www.netratings.com/pr/pr_050310_sp2.pdf.

Niggemeier, S. 2005. "Die Blogfreiheit der deutschen Politik: Statt das Internet als politisches Medium zu nutzen, führen die Parteien lieber Wahlkampf wie vor dreißig Jahren." *Frankfurter Allgemeine Sonntagszeitung*, 19 June, p. 33.

Nie, N. H. and L. Ebring. 2000. "Internet and Society: A Preliminary Report." Stanford: Stanford Institute for the Study of Quantative Society.

Nixon, P. and H. Johansson. 1999. "Transparency through technology: the Internet and political parties." In Hague, B. and B. Loader (eds.), *Digital Democracy*. London: Routledge, pp.135-153.

Nixon, P. G., R. K. Gibson and S. J. Ward. 2003. "Conclusions: The Net Change." In Gibson, R. K, P. G. Nixon and S. J. Ward (eds.), *Net Gain? Political Parties and the Internet*. London: Routledge, pp.234-243.

Norris, P. 2000. *A Virtuous Circle: political communications in postindustrial societies*. Cambridge: Cambridge University Press.

———. 2001. *Digital Divide*. Cambridge: Cambridge University Press.

———. 2003a. "Will New Technology Boost Turnout? Evaluating Experiments in E-Voting v. All-Postal Voting Facilities in UK Local Elections." Kennedy School of Government Working Papers Series No. RWP03-034. Available at SSRN: http://ssrn.com/abstract=437140.

———. 2003b. "Preaching to the Converted? Pluralism, Participation and Party Websites." *Party Politics*, 9 (1), pp.21-46.

Notodlpiuju, R.E. 2004 "Quick Count, TI-KPU, dan Perhitungan Manual." http://cdc.eng.ui.ac.id/index.php/article/articleprint/2216/-1/2/, sighted on 13 March 2006.

Nugroho, H. 2004. "Workshop: Pemanfaatan Teknologi Informasi untuk Pemilu," dated 12 April, cached at http://groups.or.id/pipermail/genetika/2004-April/001972.html. Retrieved on 9 November 2004, and sighted on 13 March 2006.

O'Farrell, J. 2005. "Laugh—I nearly voted Conservative." *The Guardian*, 6 May.

Olmeda, J. A. 2005. "Amidst the fear or against the cheat: Framing 3/11 terrorist attacks in Madrid and electoral accountability." Paper presented to ECPR Joint Sessions, Granada, Spain, 14-19 April.

Open Net Initiative. 2005. *Internet Filtering in Singapore in 2004-2005: A Country Study*. Available online at http://www.opennetinitiative.net/studies/singapore/. Last accessed 23 September 2005.

Ottens, M. 2006. *Use of the Internet among individuals and enterprises*. Brussels: Eurostat.

Owen, D. 2005. "The Internet and youth civic engagement in the United States." In Oates, S., D. Owen and R. K. Gibson (eds.), *The Internet and Politics: Citizens, voters and activists*. Abingdon, Oxon: Routledge.

P3TIE (Pusat Pengkajian dan Penerapan Teknologi Informasi dan Elektronika). 2002. *Indikator Teknologi Informasi dan Komunikasi Tahun 2002*. Jakarta: Badan Pengkajian dan Penerapan Teknologi, Pusat Pengkajian dan Penerapan Teknologi Informasi dan Elektronika (P3TIE), downloaded from http://www.apjii.or.id/ dokumentasi/arsip/indikator/siti2002.pdf, sighted 28 July 2003.

Palser, B. 2003. "Virtual Campaigning." *American Journalism Review* (October/November). Available at http://www.ajr.org/Article.asp?id=3419.

Pareanom, Y. A., I. Setiawan, and D. Arjanto. 1999. "Menjual Partai di Dunia Maya." *Tempo*, 22 March, p.54.

Pavlik, J. V. 1996. *New Media Technology: Cultural and Commercial Perspectives*. Boston: Allyn and Bacon.

Peh, S. H. and T. R. Rajan. 2005. "No contest, no surprise." *Straits Times* (Singapore). 14 August, p.3.

Pew Research Center for the People & the Press. 1996. "News Attracts Most Internet Users: One-in-Ten Voters Online for Campaign 96." 16 December. Available at http://people-press.org/reports/display.php3?ReportID=117.

———. 2000. "Internet News Election Seeks Convenience, Familiar Names," 3 December 2000. Available at http://people-press.org/reports/display.php3?ReportID=21.

———. 2005. "Public More Critical of Press, But Goodwill Persists," 26 June. Available at http://people-press.org

Pew Internet & American Life Project. 2005. *The Internet and Campaign 2004* (Lee Rainie, John Horrigan, and Michael Cornfield), 6 March, Washington, D. C.

Pikiran Rakyat. 2005. "Penyimpangan TI KPU Besa." Pikiran Rakyat, 30 April, at http://www.pikiran-rakyat.com/cetak/2005/0405/30/0105.htm, sighted 13 March 2006.

Pilot and Jo Show. 2005. Blog Entry: Imagine: http://pjshow.blogspot.com/2005/08/imagine_112462795073393621.html. 21 August.

Plasser, F. and Plasser, G. 2002. *Global Political Campaigning. A Worldwide Analysis of Campaign Professionals and Their Practices.* Westport, CT: Praeger.

Powers, W. F. 1994. "Virtual Politics: Campaigning in Cyberspace." *Washington Post*, 8 November, p.E1.

Rainie, L., M. Cornfield and J. Horrigan, 2005. "The Internet and Campaign 2004." 6 March. Pew Internet and American Life Project. Available at www.pewInternet.org/pdfs/PIP_2004_Campaign.pdf. Accessed on 26 June 2006.

Rash, W. 1997. *Politics on the Internets: Wiring the Political Process.* New York: Freeman.

RED.es. 2005. *Uso y perfil de usuarios de Internet en España.* Octubre http://observatorio.red.es/estudios/documentos/presentacion_uso_perfil.pdf.

Reeve, D. 1985. *Golkar of Indonesia: an alternative to the party system.* Singapore: Oxford University Press.

Resnick, D. 1999. "The Normalization of Cyberspace." In Toulouse, C. and T. Luke (eds.), *The Politics of Cyberspace.* London: Routledge, pp.48-68.

Rheingold, H. 1995. *The Virtual Community: Finding Connection in a Computerised World.* London: Minerva.

Roberts, K. M. 2002. *Deepening Democracy? The Modern Left and Social Movements in Chile and Peru.* Stanford, CA: Stanford University Press.

———. Forthcoming. *Changing Course: Parties, Populism, and Political Representation in Latin America's Neoliberal Era.* New York: Cambridge University Press.

Rodan, G. 1998. "The Internet and Political Control in Singapore." *Political Science Quarterly*, 113 (1), pp.63-89.

———. 2004. *Transparency and Authoritarian Rule in Southeast Asia: Singapore and Malaysia.* London: Routledge.

Román, P. (ed). 2001. *Sistema político español.* Madrid: McGraw-Hill.

Römmele, A. 2003. "Political Parties, Party Communication and New Information Communication Technologies." *Party Politics*, 9 (1), pp.7-20.

Römmele, A., R. Gibson and S. Ward. 2003. "German Parties and Internet Campaigning in the 2002 Federal Election." *German Politics*, 12 (1), pp. 79-104.

Rosyid, I. 2004. "Sistem TI PKU Solo Macet." *Tempointeraktif*, 7 April, http://www.tempointeraktif.com/hg/nusa/jawamadura/2004/04/07/brk,20040407-05, id, sighted 13 March 2006.

Sadow, J. D. and K. James. 1999. "Virtual Billboards? Candidate Websites and Campaigning in 1998." Paper delivered at the annual meeting of the American Political Science Association, Atlanta, GA, 2-5 September.

———. 2000. *A Theory of Internet Political Campaigning: A Revolution That Isn't, Yet*, Paper presented at the Annual Meeting of the Southwestern Political Science Association, Galveston, TX.

Sampedro, V. and G. López-Garcia. 2005. "Deliberación celérica desde la periferia." In Sampedro, V. (ed.), *13-M, Multitudes on line.* Madrid: Los Libros de la Catarata, pp.119-158.

Samydorai, S. 2005. "Singapore: Restriction on Freedom of Expression. Think Centre." Available online at http://www.thinkcentre.org/article.cfm?ArticleID=2623. 5 August. Last accessed 21 September 2005.

Sawer, M. (ed.). 2001. *Elections Full, Free and Fair.* Sydney, NSW: The Federation Press.

Scammel, M. 2001. *Designer Politics: How Elections are Won.* Basingstoke: Palgrave.

Scarrow, S. E. 2004. "Embracing Dealignment, Combating Realignment: German Parties Respond." In Mair, P., W. C. Müller and F. Plasser (eds.), *Political Parties and the Electoral Change: Party Responses to Electoral Markets.* London: Sage, pp. 86-110.

Schemel, B. 2005. "Politische Kommunikation im Internet 2005: Quo vadis?" *Politik & Kommunikation,* Wahlkampf Special 2, p. 15.

Schneider, S. M. and K. A. Foot 2006. "Web Campaigning by U.S. Presidential Primary Candidates in 2000 and 2004." In Williams, A. P. and J. C. Tedesco (eds.), *The Internet Election: Perspectives on the Web in Campaign 2004.* Lanham, MD: Rowman & Littlefield, pp. 21-36.

Schulz, W. and R. Zeh. 2005. "The Changing Election Coverage of German Television: A Content Analysis, 1990-2002." *Communications* 30 (4), pp. 385-407.

Schweitzer, E. 2003. "Wahlkampf im Internet: Eine Analyse der Internetauftritte von SPD, CDU, Bündnis '90/Die Grünen und FDP zur Bundestagswahl 2002." In Holtz-Bacha, C. (ed.), *Die Massenmedien im Wahlkampf: Die Bundestagswahl 2002*, Wiesbaden: Westdeutscher Verlag, pp. 194-215.

———. 2005 "Election Campaigning Online: German Party Websites in the 2002 National Elections." *European Journal of Communication* 20 (3), pp. 327-351.

Scully, T. R. 1995. "Reconstituting Party Politics in Chile." In Scully, T. R. and S. Mainwaring (eds.), *Building Democratic Institutions: Party Systems in Latin America.* Stanford, CA: Stanford University Press, pp.100-137.

Secombe, M. 2004. "PM pays his son to dish up spam." *Sydney Morning Herald*, 27 August, p.1.

Sedition Act, Government of Singapore. 2005. Available online at http://statutes.agc.gov.sg/non_version/cgi-bin/cgi_getdata.pl?&actno=1964REVED-290&date=latest&method=whole. Last accessed 23 September 2005.

See, M. 2005. Blog: "No political films, please, we're Singaporeans." 6 September. Available online at http://singaporerebel.blogspot.com/2005/09/activist-files-complaint-against.html. Last accessed 23 September 2005.

Selnow, G. 1998. *Electronic Whistle Stops: The Impact of the Internet on American Politics.* Westport, CT: Praegar.

Sen, K. and D. T. Hill. 2000. *Media, Culture and Politics in Indonesia.* Melbourne: Oxford University Press.

Seyd, P. and P. Whiteley. 2004. "British Party Members: An Overview." *Party Politics*, 10 (4), pp.355-366.

Shea, D. M. 2001. *Campaign Craft: The Strategies, Tactics, and Art of Political Campaign Management*. Westport, CT: Praeger.

Siavelis, P. 2002. "Exaggerated Presidentialism and Moderate Presidents: Executive/ Legislative Relations in Chile." In Morgenstern, S. and B. Nacif (eds.), *Legislative Politics in Latin America*. New York: Cambridge University Press, pp.79-113.

Sinclair, L. 2004. "Campaign websites go the way of Jeff after costly 99 debacle." *Weekend Australian*, 2 October, p.10.

Smith, C. 1998. "Political Parties in the Information Age: From Mass Party to Leadership Organization." In Snellen, I. and W. van de Donk (eds.), *Public Administration in the Information Age: A Handbook*. Amsterdam: IoS Press.

———. 2000. "British Political Parties: Continuity and Change in the Information Age." In Hoff, J., I. Horrocks, and P. Tops (eds.), *Democratic Governance and New Technology*. London: Routledge, pp.57-70.

Stevensen, M. and A-B. Albrectsen (eds). 1999. *Transition to Democracy: Report on the UNDP Technical Assistance Programme for the 1999 Indonesian General Elections*. Jakarta: United National Development Programme, available from http://www.un.or.id/ge/report.htm, sighted 27 August 2002.

Strachan, C. J. 2003. *High-Tech Grass Roots: The Professionalization of Local Elections*. Lanham, MD: Rowman & Littlefield.

Strandberg, K. 2006. *Parties, Candidates and Citizens Online*. Abo: Abo Akademi University Press.

Street, J. 1997. "Citizenship and Mass Communication." *Contemporary Political Studies, Vol.1*. Belfast: Political Studies Association, pp.502–510.

Stromer-Galley, J. 2000. "On-line Interaction and Why Candidates Avoid It." *Journal of Communication*, 50 (Autumn), pp.111-132

Suarez, S. L. 2005. "Mobile Democracy: Text Messages, Voter Turnout, and the 2004 Spanish General Election." Paper presented at the Annual Meeting of the American Political Science Association, 1-4 September.

Sunstein, C. 2001. *Republic.com*. Princeton, NJ: Princeton University Press.

Suryadinata, L. 2002. *Elections and Politics in Indonesia*. Singapore: Institute of Southeast Asian Studies.

Swaddle, K. 1988. "Hi-tech Elections: Technology and the Development of Electioneering Since 1945." *Contemporary Record*, Spring, pp.32-35.

Swanson, D. and P. Mancini (eds.). 1996. *Politics, Media and Modern Democracy: An International Study in Electoral Campaigning and their Consequences*. Lanham, MD: Rowman & Littlefield.

———. 1996. "Patterns of Modern Electoral Campaigning and Their Consequences." In Swanson, D. and P. Mancini (eds.), *Politics, Media, and Modern Democracy: An International Study of Innovations in Electoral Campaigning and their Consequences*. Westport, CT: Praeger, pp. 247-276.

Tabor, C. and M. Lodge. 1999. "Motivated Skepticism in the Evaluation of Political Beliefs." Paper delivered at the annual meeting of the American Political Science Association, Atlanta, GA, 2-5 September.

Tan, T. H. 2001. "Sintercom founder fades out of cyberspace." *Straits Times* (Singapore). 22 August, p. H4.

Taylor, C. 1993. *Reconciling the Solitudes: Essays on Canadian Federalism and Nationalism*. Montreal and Kingston: McGill-Queen's University Press.

Thompson, K. 2006. "The Impact of the Internet on the Modern Campaign—'Now Bloggier'." Paper submitted to Communication Studies 627, University of Calgary, Winter.

Tkach, L. 2003. "Politics@Japan: Party Competition on the Internet in Japan." *Party Politics*, 9 (1), pp.105-123.

Tironi, E. and G. Sunkel. 2000. "The Modernization of Communications: The Media in the Transition to Democracy in Chile." In Gunther, R. and A. Mughan (eds.), *Democracy and the Media: A Comparative Perspective*. New York: Cambridge University Press, pp.165-194.

Tolbert, C. J. and R. S. McNeal. 2003. "Unraveling the Effects of the Internet on Political Participation?" *Political Research Quarterly*, 56 (2), pp. 175-185

Tops, P., G. Voerman and M. Boogers. 2000. "Political websites during the 1998 Parliamentary Elections in the Netherlands." In Hoff, J., I. Horrocks and P. Tops (eds.), *Democratic Governance and New Technology: Technologically mediated innovations in political practice in Western Europe*. London/New York: Routledge, pp.87-99.

Toulouse, C. and J. Gross. 1998. "The British Diaspora: Using the Internet as a Tool for Organizing UK Citizens Living Abroad." Paper presented to the American Political Science Association Annual Meetings, Boston, MA, 1 September, .

Trippi, J. 2004. *The Revolution Will Not Be Televised: Democracy, The Internet, and the Overthrow of Everything*. New York: HarperCollins.

Van Dijk, J. A. G. M. 2005. *The Deepening Divide. Inequality in the Information Society*. London: Sage.

Van Eimeren, B. and B. Frees. 2006. "Schnelle Zugänge, neue Anwendungen, neue Nutzer? ARD/ZDF-Online-Studie 2006," *Media Perspektiven*, No. 8, pp. 402-415.

Van Eimeren, B. and C-M. Ridder. 2005. "Trends in der Nutzung und Bewertung der Medien 1970 bis 2005: Ergebnisse der ARD/ZDF-Langzeitstudie Massenkommunikation." *Media Perspektiven*, No. 10, pp. 490-504.

Van Praet, N. 2000. "American election websites have bite: Canadian parties' lack pizzazz, though." *The Gazette* (Montreal), 7 November, p.A15.

Van Selm, M., N. Jankowski and L. Tsaliki. 2002. "Political Parties Online: Digital Democracy as Reflected in Three Dutch Political Party Websites." *Communications*, 27, pp.189-209.

Van Onselen, P. and W. Errington. 2004. "Electoral Databases: Big Brother or Democracy Unbound?" *Australian Journal of Political Science*, 39 (2), pp.349-366.

"Virgin undergraduate." 2005. "The good news and the bad news for the Singapore blogosphere. Blog: Catharsis of a virgin undergraduate." 13 September. Available online at http://tantive-iv.blogspot.com/2005/09/good-news-and-bad-news-for-singapore.html. Last accessed 23 September 2005.

Virtel, M. 2005. "Under Construction: Der Internet-Wahlkampf in Deutschland bleibt weit hinter seinen Möglichkeiten zurück: Was alles geht, zeigen die USA." *Financial Times Deutschland*, 15 August, p. 25.

Voerman, G. 1998. "Dutch Political Parties on the Internet." *ECPR-News*, 10 (1), pp.8-9.

———. 2000. "Elektronisch folderen: de digitale campagne." In van Praag, Ph and K. Brants (eds.), *Tussen beeld en inhoud. Politiek en media in de verkiezingen van 1998*. Amsterdam: Het Spinhuis, pp.193-213.

Voerman, G. and S. J. Ward. 2000. "New Media and New Politics: Green Parties, Intra-party Democracy and the Internet." In Voerman, G. and P. Lucardie (eds.), *Jaerbook documentatiecentrum Nederlandse Politieke Partijen 1999*. Groningen: University of Groningen, pp.192-215.

Wagner, S. 2004. "Die Nutzung des Internet als Medium für die politische Kommunikation: Reinforcement oder Mobilisierung?" In Brettschneider, F., J. van Deth and E. Roller (eds.), *Die Bundestagswahl 2002: Analysen der Wahlergebnisse und des Wahlkampfes*. Wiesbaden: VS Verlag für Sozialwissenschaften, pp. 119-140.

Ward, K. 1974. *The 1971 election in Indonesia: An East Java case study*. Clayton, Victoria: Centre of Southeast Asian Studies, Monash University.

Ward, I. 2003. "Localizing the National? The Rediscovery and Reshaping of Local Campaigning in Australia." *Party Politics*, 9 (5), pp.583-600.

Ward, S. J. and R. K. Gibson. 1998. "The First Internet Election? UK Political Parties and Campaigning in Cyberspace." In Crewe, I., B. Gosschalk and J. Bartle (eds.), *Political Communications: Why Labour Won the General Election of 1997*. London: Frank Cass, pp.93–112.

————. 2003. "Online and On Message? Candidate Websites in the 2001 UK General Election." *British Journal of Politics and International Relations*, 5 (2), pp.188-205

Ward, S. J., Lusoli, W. and R. Gibson. 2002. "Virtually Participating: A Survey of Online Party Members." *Information Polity*, 7 (4), pp.199-216.

Ward, S. J. Gibson, R. K. and W. Lusoli. 2003a. "Online Participation and Mobilization in Britain: Hype, Hope and Reality." *Parliamentary Affairs*, 56 (4), pp.652-658.

Ward, S. J., R. K. Gibson, and P. G. Nixon. 2003b. "Political Parties and the Internet: An Overview." In Gibson, R. K, P. G. Nixon and S. J. Ward (eds.), *Net Gain? Political Parties and the Internet*. London: Routledge, pp.11–38.

Ward, S. J. and W. Lusoli. 2005. "From Weird to Wired? MPs, the Internet and Representative Politics in the UK." *Journal of Legislative Studies*, 11 (1), pp.57-81.

Warhurst, J. (ed.). 1997. *Keeping the Bastards Honest: The Australian Democrats' First Twenty Years*. Sydney: Allen and Unwin.

Warta Ekonomi. 2001. 22, XII.

Webb, P. 2002. "Political Parties in Britain: Secular Decline or Adaptive Resilience?" In Webb, P., D. Farrell and I. Holliday (eds.), *Political Parties in Advanced Industrial Democracies*. Oxford: OUP, pp.16-45.

Wenzel, S. 2005. "Vertane Chancen: Ein Kommentar zum Internetwahlkampf 2005." *politik-digital.de*, 4 August. Retrieved from http://www.politik-digital.de/text /edemocracy /wahlkampf/bundestagswahl05/vertanechancen050804.shtml

Widyatmoko, T. 2004. "Yayan Sopyan: Tanpa Audit, Sistem TI Pemilu Bikin Resah Publik." *detikcom* 12 April, located at http://www.yayan.com/index.php? option=content&task=view&id=93&Itemid=, sighted 13 March 2006.

Wilke, J. and C. Reinemann. 2001. "Do the Candidates Matter? Long-Term Trends of Campaign Coverage: A Study of the German Press Since 1949." *European Journal of Communication* 16 (3), pp. 291-314.

Williams, C. B. and J. Gulati. (2006) *The Evolutionary Development of Campaign Websites: The U.S. Senate, 2000-2004*. Paper presented at the annual meeting of the American Political Science Association, Philadelphia, PA.

Williams, C. B., Weinberg, B. D. and J. A. Gordon. 2004. "When Online and Offline Politics 'Meetup': An Examination of the Phenomenon, Presidential Campaign and its Citizen Activists." Paper presented at the annual meeting of the American Political Science Association, Chicago, IL, 2-5 September.

Willis, S. and B. Tranter. 2006. "Beyond the "Digital Divide: Internet diffusion and inequality in Australia." *Journal of Sociology*, 42 (1), pp.43-59.

World Bank. 2006. *World Development Indicators*. Available at http://devdata.worldbank.org /dataonline/.

Wring, D. and I. Horrocks. 2001. "The Transformation of Political Parties?" In Axford, B. and R. Huggins (eds.), *New Media and Politics*. London: Sage, pp.191-209.

Zittel, T. 2003. "Political Representation in the Networked Society." *Journal of Legislative Studies*, 9 (3), pp.32-53.

About the Contributors

Sara Bentivegna is professor of theories of mass communication and political communication in the faculty of communication sciences, University of Rome "La Sapienza." She is the author of "Politics and New Media" in *The Handbook of New Media* edited by L. Lievrouw and S. Livingstone (London, Sage, 2002), as well as *Politics of the Net* (Roma, Meltemi, 1999), *Politics and New Communication Technologies* (Roma-Bari, Laterza, 2002), and *Theories of Mass Communications* (Roma-Bari, Laterza, 2003).

Taylor C. Boas is a Ph.D. candidate in political science at the University of California, Berkeley. His dissertation examines the professionalization of presidential election campaigns in Chile, Peru, and Brazil. He has also done extensive research on the role of the Internet in authoritarian regimes and is coauthor of *Open Networks, Closed Regimes: The Impact of the Internet on Authoritarian Rule* (Carnegie Endowment for International Peace, 2003). His publications have appeared in *Latin American Research Review*, *Studies, Comparative International Development*, and *The Washington Quarterly*.

Marcel Boogers is senior lecturer at the Tilburg School of Politics and Public Administration at Tilburg University, The Netherlands. His research interests include the modernization of democratic intermediaries through the use of ICTs. He has published articles about party websites in the Netherlands and about the political attitudes and online behaviour of the visitors of these websites.

José-Luis Dader is a full professor in the Department of Journalism at Universidad Complutense of Madrid. He is the author of "Cyberdemocracy and Virtual Political Communication: The Future of Electronic Citizenship after the Television Age," in *Comunicación política en Televisión y Nuevos medios* (Barcelona: Ariel, 2003) edited by S. Berrocal; and "Cyberdemocracy and Cyberparliament: The Use of Email Correspondence of a Common Citizen with the Spanish Parliamentarians (1999-2001)," *TELOS. Cuadernos de comunicación, tecnología y sociedad*, 2003. He is also a member of the editorial board of Political Communication.

Richard Davis is a professor of political science at Brigham Young University. He is the author or co-author of several books on the Internet and American politics including *Politics Online: Blogs, Chatrooms, and Discussion Groups in American Democracy* (Routledge, 2005); *Campaigning Online* (Oxford, 2003); *The Web of Politics* (Oxford, 1999); and *New Media and American Politics* (Oxford, 1998).

Rachel Gibson has held academic posts in a number of countries including Australia, the United Kingdom and Germany. She is currently professor of new media at the University of Leicester in the United Kingdom. Her work in the area of Internet and politics has focused on parties use of new media in election camapaigning as well as new methodologies for study the performance of political actors on the Web. Recent publications on these topics include *The Internet and Politics: Citizens, Voters and Activists* (London: Routledge, 2005), co-edited with Sarah Oates and Diana Owen, and *Electronic Democracy: Political Organisations, Mobilisation and Participation Online*, co-edited with Stephen Ward and Andrea Roemmele (London: Routledge. 2004).

David T. Hill is professor of southeast Asian studies and fellow of the Asia Research Centre at Murdoch University, Western Australia, where he teaches Indonesian studies. His research interests cover Indonesian media, literature, culture and politics, and he publishes in both English and Indonesian. His recent books, co-authored with Krishna Sen, include *The Internet in Indonesia's New Democracy* (Routledge: London, 2005) and *Media, Culture and Politics in Indonesia* (Oxford University Press: Melbourne, 2000), which appeared in Indonesian as *Media, Budaya dan Politik di Indonesia* (ISAI & Media Lintas Inti Nusantara: Jakarta, 2001). Earlier works include *The Press in New Order Indonesia* (University of Western Australia Press: Perth, 1994); Pustaka Sinar Harapan: Jakarta, 1995) and *Beyond the Horizon: Short Stories from Contemporary Indonesia* (Monash Asia Institute: Clayton, 1998).

Marc Hooghe is associate professor of political science at the University of Leuven (Belgium). He holds Ph.Ds in political science (Brussels) and sociology (Rotterdam). Recently, his articles have appeared in *British Journal of Political Science, Electoral Politics, Party Politics, Political Behavior* and *Harvard International Journal of Press and Politics*. He is co-editor, with Dietlind Stolle, of *Generating Social Capital* (Basingstoke: Palgrave, 2003). He is editor of *Acta Politica: International Journal of Political Science*.

Randolph Kluver is executive director of the Singapore Internet Research Centre and an associate professor in the School of Communication and Information at Nanyang Technological University. His current research interests include the role of the Internet in Asian societies, Asian political communication, globalization, and the political impact of information technologies. His most recent book, *Asia.com: Asia Encounters the Internet*, was published in 2003 by RoutledgeCurzon. He is the author of *Legitimating the Chinese Economic Reforms: A Rhetoric of Myth and Orthodoxy* (SUNY Press, 1996). His co-edited book, *Civic Discourse, Civil Society, and Chinese Communities*, received the Outstanding Book Award from the International and Intercultural Division of the National Communication Association in 1999. His article, "The Logic of New Media in International Relations," received the 2003 Walter Benjamin Award for outstanding article in media ecology.

Wainer Lusoli is a lecturer in political communication at the University of Chester in the United Kingdom and has written widely on the topic of e-democracy.

Ian McAllister was director of the Research School of Social Sciences at the Australian National University from 1997 until 2004, and is now professor of political science there. He is the co-author of *How Russia Votes* (Chatham House, 1998) and *The Australian Electoral System* (UNSW Press, 2006), and co-editor of *The Cambridge Handbook of the Social Sciences in Australia* (Cambridge University Press, 2003). He is currently completing a book on the Northern Ireland conflict. He is chair of the 50-nation Comparative Study of Electoral Systems group.

Diana Owen is associate professor of political science at Georgetown University. Her areas of specialization include political communication, public opinion, political socialization, political culture, mass behavior, and elections and voting. She is the author, with Richard Davis, of *New Media and American Politics* (Oxford University Press: Oxford, 1998) and *Media Messages in American Presidential Elections* (Greenwood, 1991). She has written articles on campaign media, talk radio, political implications of the Internet, and media and transnational security. She also has published work on preadult political learning, civic education, and adult political orientations. Currently, she is completing *Mass Communication and the Making of Citizens* (Columbia University Press), which focuses on the role played by mass media in the process of political socialization over the past half century. She is engaged in a major writing project entitled *American Politics: Realities and the Media* with Timothy Cook and David Paletz.

Eva Johanna Schweitzer is a Ph.D. candidate in the Department of Journalism and Mass Communication at the University of Mainz, Germany. As a lecturer and research associate, she is particularly interested in political communication and online communication. Her work on German e-campaigns in federal and European parliamentary elections has been presented at international conferences and published in national election volumes as well as in the *European Journal of Communication*.

Tamara A. Small is a PhD candidate in the Department of Political Studies at Queen's University, Kingston. She has recently contributed a chapter to *The Canadian General Election of 2004*. Her graduate work focuses on the use of the Internet by Canadian political parties and candidates during the 2004 federal election.

David Taras is university professor and professor in the faculty of communication & culture at the University of Calgary. He has a doctorate in political science from the University of Toronto and is a graduate of the Ontario Legislative

Internship Program at Queen's Park. He was a visiting professor at the University of Amsterdam in the Netherlands and has served as an advisor to the Alberta government and to the House of Commons Standing Committee on Canadian Heritage. Professor Taras has written extensively on the Canadian mass media and on Canadian politics. He is the author of *The Newsmakers: The Media's Influence on Canadian Politics, Power & Betrayal in the Canadian Media* and co-author of *The Last Word: Media Coverage of the Supreme Court of Canada.* He is also co-editor of *How Canadians Communicate and A Passion for Identity: Canadian Studies for the 21st Century* among other works. David Taras was president of the Canadian Communication Association and has been on the Board of Governors of the University of Calgary.

Gerrit Voerman is director of the Documentation Centre on Dutch Political Parties of the University of Groningen, The Netherlands. He is editor of the Yearbook of the Documentation Centre and has published frequently on Dutch political parties in general and the use of ICTs by parties. He analyzed the first Internet campaign of the Dutch national elections of 1998 and he conducted with Marcel Boogers (University of Tilburg) research projects regarding political participation on the Internet during the campaign for the national elections in the Netherlands in May 2002 and January 2003.

Stephen Ward is a senior lecturer at the European Studies Research Institute at the University of Salford, United Kingdom. He is the co-editor of *Political Parties and the Internet* and *Electronic Democracy,* both published by Routledge. He has also co-edited a number of journal special issues on e-politics including *Party Politics* 9 (1), (2003) and *Parliamentary Affairs* 56 (2), (2006).

Sara Vissers is a PhD candidate at the Department of Political Science of the Catholic University of Leuven. She obtained a master's degree in sociology, and her main research interests are political participation, ICT, and the information society.

Index

advertising:
    Internet's effect on, 5
    media, 20, 22, 40, 95, 136, 163,
      224, 239-241
    negative, 95, 187
    paid, 40
    regulations of, 20, 40, 263
    spending on, 40, 95, 135, 261
    transition to the web, 20-22, 25
    of websites, 96, 121
    on websites, 187
Allan, Richard, 150
Alliance for Chile, 19
Arriagada, Genaro, 15, 16, 31, 32
Australia.
    Australian Broadcasting
      Commission (ABC), 39
    Bureau of Statistics (ABS), 43, 50,
      54
    Candidate and Election Studies, 43
    political parties:
      Australian Democrats, 37, 44
      Australian Labor Party (ALP):
        candidate websites, 44
        party website, 35, 40, 41,
          45
        power of, 36, 37
        supporter characteristics,
          53
      Country Party, 37
      Free Traders, 37
      Greens, 38, 41, 44, 51, 53
      Liberal Party:
        coalitions of, 37
        voter database, 41
        websites of, 40, 44, 45,
          46
      National Party, 37, 44, 45, 51
      One Nation Party, 38, 41
      Protectionists, 37
      United Australia Party, 37
Americans Coming Together (ACT),
    104-105
audience:

characteristics of, 139
    demographics of, 151, 241,
      259
    polarity of, 163
    political involvement of, 21-
      22, 268
effect of Internet on, 4-5, 99-100
growth of, 43, 96, 104
identification of, 164
reasons for visiting websites, 229
size of, 21, 96, 139, 163, 167, 205,
    224
target audience, 11, 138, 148, 195
use of campaign websites, 104

Bachelet, Michelle:
    campaign strategy, 19-20
    website features, 25
      blog, 26
      contributions, 30
      email, 27-28
      mobilization, 28
      question of the week, 26
Bartlett, Andrew, 44
Becerra, Maria José, 30
Belgium:
    electoral system:
      linguistic segregation, 172,
        174
      state funding to parties:
        effect on resource
          generation, 195
        funding websites, 191,
          196
        loss of, 192
        major vs. minor parties,
          191
      Walloon regional government,
        178
        parties of, 187, 191
    political parties:
      Christian-Democratic Party,
        180, 191, 195
      Ecolo, 180, 192, 193